THE OFFICIAL INVESTORS GUIDE™

BUYING · SELLING

SILVER DOLLARS

BY
MARC HUDGEONS, N.L.G.

CW01390628

SECOND EDITION
THE HOUSE OF COLLECTIBLES
NEW YORK, NEW YORK 10022

Important Notice. The format of *The Official Price Guide Series,* published by *The House of Collectibles,* is based on the following proprietary features: *All facts and prices are compiled through a nationwide sampling of information* obtained from noteworthy experts, auction houses, and specialized dealers. *Detailed "indexed" format* enables quick retrieval of information for positive identification. *Encapsulated histories* precede each category to acquaint the collector with the specific traits that are peculiar to that area of collecting. *Valuable collecting information* is provided for both the novice as well as the seasoned collector: How to begin a collection; how to buy, sell, and trade; care and storage techniques; tips on restoration; grading guidelines; lists of periodicals, clubs, museums, auction houses, dealers, etc. *An average price range* takes geographic location and condition into consideration when reporting collector value. *An inventory checklist system* is provided for cataloging a collection.

All of the information, including valuations, in this book has been compiled from the most reliable sources, and every effort has been made to eliminate errors and questionable data. Nevertheless the possibility of error, in a work of such immense scope, always exists. The publisher will not be held responsible for losses which may occur in the purchase, sale, or other transaction of items because of information contained herein. Readers who feel they have discovered errors are invited to *write* and inform us, so they may be corrected in subsequent editions. Those seeking further information on the topics covered in this book are advised to refer to the complete line of Official Price Guides published by The House of Collectibles.

Published by: The House of Collectibles
201 East 50th Street
New York, New York 10022

Distributed by Ballantine Books, a division of Random House, Inc., New York and simultaneously in Canada by Random House of Canada Limited, Toronto.

Manufactured in the United States of America

Library of Congress Catalog Card Number: 81-83403

ISBN: 0-87637-537-9

10   9   8   7   6   5   4   3   2

TABLE OF CONTENTS

AUTHOR'S NOTE

We're going to show you how to make money by investing in silver dollars. The opportunities to do this are so favorable that *thousands* of people have already made financial profits with silver dollars *without even trying to.* These are the coin hobbyists who have bought uncirculated silver dollars for their collections, without having the slightest intention of being "investors." The passage of just a few years, and rising prices in both the coin and silver bullion markets, has brought them solid cash profits. In some instances they have doubled or even tripled their money. By approaching silver dollars as a financial investment, and buying along the proven lines of success we outline in this book, the returns can be much greater.

Silver dollar investing has become so popular that it has led to numerous books, articles, courses, "investment packages" and advertising campaigns. Much of the advice being circulated is erroneous, and much of the merchandise is overpriced. This book has been designed to remove the confusion from silver dollar investing. It presents the only known sound strategy for selecting the dates and mint marks to buy. It shows you how to buy, where to buy and how to recognize offerings that should be avoided. Then, it guides you through the holding period, and finally to selling.

Exclusive price comparison charts are presented, showing the actual retail prices of every U.S. silver dollar from 1955 to 1985, along with a great deal of other valuable information. You can use this data to make your own investment selections. Or you can purchase the coins that we have *specifically recommended* as having the brightest growth potential within the next five to ten years. Along with our recommendations of coins to buy, you will also find advice on silver dollars that are *unfavorable* for investment purchase in our opinion.

One of the great advantages of silver dollar investment is that you can start with just about any sum. There are many Morgan and Peace dollars available under $100 in uncirculated condition, and some of them have excellent investment qualities. For those with more flexible capital, investment grade rarities can be had for amounts of four and five figures. *All* are detailed in this book.

Whether you are an expert on coins or investments, or know nothing about either subject, we think you will enjoy, and profit from, this book.

Good reading and good luck!

MARC HUDGEONS, N.L.G.

INTRODUCTION

There are two ways to make a profit. One is to be lucky and find a rare coin which you can then sell. The other is to learn, and learn, and learn, until you can turn your knowledge into a profit. All of us "get lucky" at one time or another. A few of us have spent the time to learn all we possibly can about the area in which we would like to profit. We are turning our knowledge into money in the bank and you can too. To earn a living, you learn a skill, or a trade, or practice. To make a profit investing in or collecting silver dollars, you need to learn — a lot! — and *The Official Investors Guide to Buying and Selling U.S. Silver Dollars* is intended to help, in as many ways as possible.

There are a number of excellent books on the market relating to both collecting and investing in the various U.S. silver dollar coins. However, in most cases this available literature dwells on one specific area or form of accumulating the coins. Nowhere have we been able to find a comprehensive guide that the average collector or investor can turn to and at a glance be able to determine what might be available. This book is intended to fill that need, both by assembling necessary data and by pointing out some of the little known, yet potentially highly profitable, ways that you can invest in silver dollars and expect a high rate of return on your investment.

Everyone would like to buy at wholesale and sell at retail, the principle of the free enterprise system. The individual investor rarely has the chance to do this, much more frequently finding himself buying at retail and selling at wholesale. We have assembled some tips and suggestions to help you get around this barrier to private profit.

In this book we have described some of the ways in which you can use your know-how to assemble a variety of coins at normal retail prices which actually may be worth far more than what you pay for them — instantly! If you aren't content with putting your silver dollar coins in a vault and letting them slowly appreciate over the years, learning to "cherry pick" the varieties can help you make genuine, and often surprising immediate profits.

Few investors, dealers, or collectors think of these coins as just "dollars." They are described as "Silver" dollars, even though the last circulating dollar with any silver in it was minted in 1935, and none of the circulating Eisenhower or Anthony dollars have any silver at all. In the pages that follow we will show you how the fluctuating silver and gold bullion prices are likely to affect your dollar investments.

We have devoted a chapter to each of the major "types" or series of U.S. silver dollars. In each series, we have put together the specific information, including the highly specialized minting variety information. The chapter on Minting Varieties will provide you with a general idea of what to look for and a good idea of values, so that you can buy the right coins at the right price — and, just as importantly, sell them at the right price.

Undoubtedly, if you have been involved with coins for any period of time, you have noted an increasing number of minting varieties cropping up in major auction catalogs. This is a trend that you should be riding to profit; if you are willing to learn, we are happy to help you. *The Official Investors Guide to Buying and Selling U.S. Silver Dollars* should be one of your best learning tools.

HISTORY OF THE DOLLAR

One is almost tempted to start with "Once upon a time," since our U.S. dollar traces back into the history of central Europe where the Germanic Thaler was one of the distinct forerunners of our dollar, both in size and general appearance.

Even earlier, in 1486, Archduke Sigismund of Tyrol, Austria, introduced the first large size silver coin, to which our dollar traces its roots. It was called a guldengroschen. This particular coin was in a precarious position because there were few sources of any significant amount of silver in Europe at that time. It would be over 100 years (1624) before the huge Kongsberg silver mines were discovered in Norway which provided silver for many of the Scandinavian coins of that era.

In 1515, the Thaler came upon the scene, the product of Bohemia, minted from the silver found in St. Joachim's Valley, or as it is called in German, St. Joachimsthal. Logically, the coins were called Joachimsthalers and within months they were one of the accepted coins of commerce; no small feat when one considers the suspicion and distrust that merchants of the era had for the variety of coins that turned up.

The merchants shortened the term to thaler and soon every coiner on the Continent was turning out silver coins of the same general size, all called thalers, or talers, regardless of their actual denomination. The "H" is silent, so it was dropped, and as the term spread to England it was quickly corrupted to "dollar." The term was not used by the British for their coins until 1895 when they began striking Trade Dollars, but their first "Crown" was dated 1551. The five shilling piece was also the forerunner of the general class which are frequently described as "Crowns."

The American colonies were in a similar situation to that of many European countries today, that is, a wide variety of coins of many lands were to be found in commerce. Back in the 17th century, however, business was conducted with whatever coins or tokens happened to be at hand, while today the trading at least is based on the values of local currency.

Coins of the Netherlands, especially the Rijksdaalder which was better known on this side of the Atlantic as the "Lion Dollar," were one of the favorites for large trades. But as time went on, after the British ousted the Dutch from New York, the Spanish 8 Reale gradually replaced it. This was known as the Spanish dollar and millions of them were minted from the fabulously rich silver mines of Peru and Mexico.

This mass production of relatively high quality coins of standard weight had a major impact on the Colonies through most of the 1700s; so much so that contracts were written in terms of Spanish dollars, and most other coins, other than fractional Spanish pieces, were driven out of circulation. It is reported that the first U.S. Mint in Philadelphia in the 1790s leased land on a contract payable in Spanish dollars. Despite the fact that the first U.S. dollars would be minted in 1794, the Spanish dollar or 8 Reale piece continued to be the prime coin of American commerce well into the 1800s.

The 1700s were noted perhaps for the attempt to run American commerce on paper. The many dubious notes, often counterfeited, never worth full value, tended to reinforce the demand for the stable dollar, even if it bore the image of a Spanish Monarch. The British attitude of extreme reluctance to provide a solid currency, combined with taxation that roused the ire of the colonists, were the major points that turned the Yankees against the British King. Thus was sparked the cry for independence. It was a telling argument when a Yank pointed out that the face of King George was a rare visitor to American shores.

This demand stepped up during the War of Independence, and most silver and gold coins went into hiding as a result of hoarding. The Continental Congress tried futilely in 1776 to create an American silver dollar. But as silver had already disappeared, most were struck in pewter and a few in brass. These are considered by some authorities to be patterns only, although it's believed that the silver coins actually did circulate.

Thomas Jefferson proposed that a new silver dollar be coined in 1783, as part of a plan that would have included both gold and silver. His efforts were sidetracked by an egoist of the day, Robert Morris, who happened to be the Minister of Finance of the young Confederation. Morris, to the dismay of all but his compatriots in Congress, proposed an extremely complicated, unreliable and confusing system of denominations based on the oddball paper currency of the day issued by the various states.

It was not until January, 1790, when President Washington finally took notice of the problem and proposed that a uniform system be applied to coining, that we were on the way to an American dollar. Later that year, a proposal was submitted to Congress offering to mint coins in Europe, but the idea was dropped after the then Secretary of State, Thomas Jefferson, indicated he was strongly opposed to the idea because of the problem of accurately judging the weight and fineness of the coins, and the likelihood of interruptions in delivery in the event of another war. Remember, at this time Spanish coins, and those of several other nations, were freely circulating but creating serious difficulties because of the wear, clipping and other damage they were subject to which often reduced their silver content .

Jefferson became involved in our coins a third time when he proposed that the American dollar contain 376 grains of pure silver, about the same amount as the universal Spanish dollar. However, Treasury Secretary Alexander Hamilton decided, after weighing and assaying a number of the circulating Spanish coins, that they had been debased and that the circulating and thus worn coins contained an average of only 371 grains. The Spanish had secretly started reducing the amount of silver in the 8 Reale piece starting about 1740, according to one report, and by 1790 the coin was down to 375 grains, or about 24.3 grams of silver. Prior to the debasing, the coin contained 27.07 grams of silver. Hamilton then proposed that the new dollar weigh 405 grains, with 371.25 grains of silver.

Robert Morris got a second chance at history by chairing a Senate Committee charged with drafting a coinage law, a committee that ultimately overruled Hamilton and set the gross weight of the U.S. Dollar at 416 grains, the same total weight as the Spanish dollar it was intended to replace. The amount of silver (a compromise?) was left at 371.25 grains, giving the dollar an awkward fineness of .892 which it was to retain through 1803. Hamilton's 412 grain choice was not to be until the Coinage Act of 1837 reduced the weight to 412½ grains. In deference to the problems for the Mint, it raised the fineness to an even .900.

Jefferson's final act of note in connection with the dollar coin was to halt its production in early 1804. Thanks to Hamilton's calculations, the U.S. dollar contained slightly more silver than the Spanish dollar, making traders rich by shipping them out of the country in exchange for the 8 Reales which were then sold at a profit to the Mint.

The first American dollar came within a very close margin of appearing with the portrait of George Washington on it. A provision calling for the depiction of the current President was actually passed by the Senate, but the House refused to go along with the idea, and it was eventually stricken from the Coinage Act of 1792 before finally passed and sent to the President for signature.

One interesting note in passing is that when the U.S. Mint was built it was under control of the Secretary of State (Jefferson) rather than the Secretary of the Treasury, undoubtedly due to Jefferson's influence on the whole concept of minting coins. It was a number of years before control was finally transferred to the Treasury Department. Construction of the first mint began in 1792, but a provision in the Coinage Act requiring both the Assayer and the Chief Coiner to post $10,000 bonds if they handled precious metals was the key factor in delaying the striking of any silver dollars until 1794.

R. W. Julian, in his articles on the history of American coinage, indicates that despite specifications laid down by Congress, the Director of the Mint, David Rittenhouse, ordered that the 1794 dollars be minted of .900 fine silver. The weight was left at 416 grains but the amount of silver was increased. This led to a number of documented cases where depositors of silver bullion were underpaid by the Mint. Records were altered to hide the use of the additional silver in the coins. While most sources list the official fineness, none of the coins were actually struck to specification.

Julian also believes, with good reason, that not all of the recorded 1,758 struck coins were ever actually released to the public, since problems with the coin press, large enough only to strike half dollar size coins, left the new dollars with weak areas in their design. Rittenhouse was anxious for the first examples of the young nation's largest silver coin to be as perfect as possible since the world was watching closely, so he directed that several hundred of the defective strikes be stored for use as planchets for later coins.

The special new press, large enough to strike dollars and medals, was put into service in 1795. Much of the Mint production of that year was limited to the dollars, explaining why there are so many more of that year.

The latter design was continued through 1803 and early 1804, when a quantity of 1803 dated dollars were struck before production was halted. The 1804 dated coins would not be struck until the 1830s.

In 1836, patterns were struck for a new, Seated Liberty Dollar and later in the year, 1000 of the coins, according to Mint records, were struck for circulation. Julian says that the Mint struck these coins for circulation in 1836 and 1839, with patterns stuck in 1838, but the grand total for the four years was only 1900 coins. This point has led many past researchers to the mistaken belief that all of the strikes were patterns.

The coins were noted for Gobrecht's artistic design of the flying eagle, later to be used on the cent. When full scale production of the Seated Liberty dollars began in 1840, the John Reich eagle, which was used on the lesser silver coins, was placed on the dollar reverse as well.

Congress, as we have noted, had "legalized" Rittenhouse's covert upgrading of the fineness. The Seated Liberty dollars were .900 fine and weighed 412.5 grains, a weight that continued for the dollars through 1964, except for Trade Dollars.

Even then the dollar was not what could be called a popular coin. It was primarily intended as a convenient means for banks to store their reserves, but the production of $5 gold pieces was large enough to amply supply banks with an even more compact form of bullion. Commercial demand was light, from a public that hadn't seen a dollar coin in nearly four decades, and production proceeded at a fitful pace, evidenced by the widely fluctuating mintage figures. Speculators were already at work by the early 1850s, melting down all the silver coins for profit. This was one of several periods when large quantities of coins were melted down, either privately or by the Mint, resulting in unreliability of the mintage figures to reflect current availability.

This period was also noted for some skullduggery at the Mint with the forced resignation of Chief Coiner Franklin Peale in 1853. It is believed that both he and Director James Snowdon were involved in the frequent restriking of many earlier coins of that era, in some instances at the request of what few collectors there were, and in a couple of instances to trade for coins needed to complete the Mint's own collection. Up until then, used dies were stored. Those for many of the earlier issues were still available or were reproduced.

The Coinage Act of 1853 left the dollar high and dry, the only silver coin worth more than its face value. That year only 46,110 were struck, compared to very high mintages for all the subsidiary silver coins. The dollar limped along until it was eliminated by the Act of 1873 and replaced by the 420 grain Trade Dollar, intended to compete with other trade coins, especially in the Orient. It has the unique position of being the only U.S. coin to be demonetized; in 1876 Congress removed its legal tender status and designated it only for trade outside our borders.

In 1878, the Morgan dollar was authorized, ending production of the Trade Dollar at the same time, except for proofs, which were continued until 1885. In 1887, the Trade dollar was withdrawn and about 7.7 million of the coins were redeemed, melted down and recoined into Morgan dollars and the subsidiary silver coins. In this fashion almost one fifth of the Trade dollars were removed from circulation. Thus, they are somewhat scarcer than mintage figures suggest.

The "Silver Senators" literally forced the Morgan down Uncle Sam's throat. After the lapse in production from 1873 to 1878, the silver forces returned in strength, armed with a law which forced the Treasury to accept large quantities of silver and mint it into dollars in numbers far exceeding the relatively small demand.

One of the curious parts of the Morgan story is that despite the lengthy experience that the U.S. Mint had in striking the Seated Liberty Dollars, and the five years of continuing experience with the Trade Dollars, production of the first Morgans in 1878 yielded some of the same problems that would confront the Mint when it began striking Ike dollars in 1971 after a gap of more than 35 years. The 1878 Morgans have literally hundreds of die varieties resulting from some often serious problems with the dies and some equally serious bickering over the actual designs, the more familiar being the change from eight to seven tail feathers.

Based on the volumes of correspondence still in Government files, there actually was a substantial, and mostly behind the scenes, competition between Chief Engraver William Barber and the "young upstart" from England, George T. Morgan as to who would design this series. Morgan's work won out over Barber's, but it is rather obvious (from various complaints voiced by Morgan, in the correspondence) that Barber and his son, Charles, were undoubtedly responsible for many of the problems and delays surrounding introduction of the Morgan dollar. The Mint Director, Dr. Henry Linderman, who was in the middle of the conflict, undoubtedly thus laid the groundwork for Charles Barber's eventual prominence as designer of the "Barber" series of dimes, quarters and halves beginning in 1892. This series presented a departure from the past concept of similar designs on the various denominations.

With gaps, the Morgans were minted from 1878 to 1921, a 43 year period which makes them the longest lived series for the dollars although relatively "young" compared to the already 73 year old Lincoln cent. The coins, at the time they were issued, were known as "Bland" dollars in recognition of the Bland Act which authorized them. It was not until some time later, as numismatists recognized the labors of the designer, that they became known as Morgans.

By 1904, the Government had run out of silver and production was halted, not to resume until 1921. The Pittman Act of 1918 resulted in the melting of more than 270 million Morgans, undoubtedly also including a quantity of the earlier dollars as well. The Morgan went out in style, with the Denver Mint striking its first dollars since it was opened in 1906, two years after the Morgan was suspended. Denver struck more than 20 million, Philadelphia nearly 45 million and San Francisco nearly 22 million before the Peace dollar dies were introduced late in the year at Philadelphia.

Just over one million 1921 Peace dollars were struck and again the mint encountered problems with a new series. The design had too high a relief and the dies had to be modified before production of the 1922 coins began. The Peace dollar was proposed by noted numismatist Farren Zerbe, Historian of the American Numismatic Association at their 1920 convention. The idea was for a coin to commemorate the peace after the "world war to end all wars." Although Congress failed to pass a resolution because of the continued resistance to a silver dollar, the Secretary of the Treasury approved the design change by invoking provisions of the Pittman Act and the Coinage Act of 1890. This permitted design changes after a 25 year life span of a coin.

After the initial spurt, which saw 51 million 1922 dollars struck at Philadelphia and 32 million more at the branch mints, total production dropped below 38 million for the three mints in 1923, below 14 million in 1924 and below 12 million in 1925, with Denver not even striking any in the latter two years. Mintage held below 12 million again in 1926, dropped sharply to about three million in 1927, two million in 1928 and then production was halted until 1934 and 1935 when 3.5 million were struck in each of the two years before the series came to an end. But did it?

In 1964, 30 trial pieces were struck at Philadelphia for a renewal of the Peace Dollar. These were sent to the Mint Lab in Washington where all but two were destroyed. Orders and dies were sent to Denver to strike the coin, and 316,076 1964-D Peace dollars were struck in May of 1965, just days before the authorizing legislation was due to expire. Amid considerable confusion, generated in part by a severe subsidiary coin shortage and some strong opposition in Congress, plus conflicting testimony and news releases from the Treasury, President Johnson ordered a halt to production.

To avoid legal problems with Congress, the Treasury changed the status of the coins — on paper — to "trial strikes" and proceeded to melt them down. The two examples of the 1964-P were finally destroyed in 1970, so that not a single example of this coin is known to exist, legally.

The Treasury Department's contention that this was a "not legally issued" coin has resulted in a lot of work for the Secret Service. Rumors abound that the relatively lax security in effect at the time at Denver, plus the fact that the coins were destroyed by weight rather than individual count and date verification, resulted in a number of the coins escaping by the back door. It would have been a relatively simple matter to substitute old silver dollars for the new ones and come up with the correct weight. There were also unsubstantiated rumors that Mint employees were given the opportunity to purchase samples of the coins during production and that the employees were later questioned by the Secret Service.

The current status of the coins is still cloudy. The Treasury Department has never officially said it will seek out and confiscate the coins, only that they are "subject to seizure." For that matter, so are the 1913 "V" nickels and the Government has never made a serious attempt to recover those. During a period of several years in the early and mid 70s, we spent a considerable time attempting to trace down some of the rumors. We talked with at least one person who claimed to have seen one of the coins and we suspect that as many as 100 to 200 actually got out of the Mint, some of which undoubtedly still survive.

Our interest was aroused by veteran dollar dealer, Bob Cohen, who ran an ad in the ANA club publication in April 1973 offering $3000 for an example. A similar ad was run in the same magazine in August 1978, with a "name your price" offer from Carson City Associates, Inc. Cohen has since raised his offer, and is continuing to search for one of the coins. We presume that the other offers, including several more that we have heard of, still stand. We suspect that one of the coins will not surface, unless by accident, before the turn of the Century. The Government feels it has right on its side, in the form of a court decision on confiscation of some 1933 $20 gold pieces which were also "not legally issued."

1964 marked the last date for a 90% silver dollar. In 1971, production of dollars was resumed, with the same size and specifications except that the coins were struck on copper-nickel clad planchets with a copper core. Special Uncirculated and Proof coins were however struck on 40% silver planchets of a similar composition to the half dollars struck between 1965 and 1970.

The new dollars, bowing in part to demand from the Nevada casinos, bore a likeness of President Eisenhower and were immediately nicknamed "Ikes," the name by which thousands of World War II GI's knew their Commanding General. The likeness is one of the less lovely depictions on a U.S. coin, accenting the baldness Ike was noted for. By 1971 there was no one left in any of the U.S. Mints who knew anything about the problems of striking a dollar size coin. The new coin had plenty of problems, including a series of dies which had been modified, probably by the Chief Engraver. One result was a "Peg Leg" R in LIBERTY on some of the coins. The official explanation at the time was that the serifs had been "polished off the die in producing the proof surface." However, a reliable source in the Mint has since revealed that this was not the true story.

Later it was found necessary to modify the design to improve striking qualities of the coin. The new design was but one of as many as 20 reported changes made in this coin in its short seven year life, including the Bicentennial design used in 1975-76.

Aside from the casinos and foreign visitors, there was little demand for the big dollars, especially since they no longer even contained any silver. Yet, hundreds of thousands of people continue to hold Ike dollars, thinking they are really silver coins. Many thousands were brought out and offered to dealers during the bullion boom in early 1980, the first time that many non-collectors woke up to the fact that they were not silver.

In an effort to make the dollar a circulating coin, the Treasury Department added one more to its long line of miscalculations and mistakes and decided that if the dollar was too big, it would reduce the size to between that of a half dollar and a quarter. The half literally dropped out of circulation in 1964 as millions hoarded the new Kennedys. Despite the reduction to 40% in 1965 and the dropping of all silver from the coin in 1971, the half has never fully regained a circulating status.

Despite this, the Treasury Department felt that a small size dollar coin would work. A Liberty head similar to that on the 1794 dollar was proposed, but supporters of a portrait of Susan B. Anthony won out and the new economy size dollar became a reality in 1979. The public immediately expressed its disapproval, supported by both the lay press and the numismatic press, the most common complaint being that despite the 12 sided interior edge of the rim, the coin was easily mistaken for the only slightly smaller quarter. In a desperate effort to "sell" the coin, which was intended by officials to replace the dollar note, the Treasury launched an expensive publicity campaign. Post offices were ordered to pass the coins out at every opportunity. At one point, the Treasury even compelled the Armed Forces serving overseas to accept the coin instead of paper dollars. This move caused serious problems in countries where foreign coins were unacceptable for exchange, and in most cases resulted in a drastically discounted exchange rate, often reaching as low as 50% of that of a comparable paper dollar. Serious consideration was given to withdrawing the paper dollar in this country as well but officials finally realized that the public simply would not stand for the change.

Tremendous quantities of the coins were struck in 1979, the bulk of which remained in Federal Reserve vaults, as those in circulation were immediately returned to local banks by merchants as fast as they were received from customers. Merchants refused in some cases to even accept them as legal tender. Despite reserves of some 750 million coins, the Mint continued to strike the coins in 1980, although on a reduced scale, and announced in late 1980 that the coins would appear only in the 1981 Proof and Mint sets, with none struck for circulation. Early in 1981, the Treasury announced that funds to strike the coin had been dropped from the 1982 budget, in effect pronouncing the demise of an expensive experiment.

A quirk of fate destined the '79 proof SBA dollars for fame, since there were less than 500,000 of the coins struck which bear a new, modified mint mark, used because the old letter punch broke in mid-summer. The actual delivered mintage is probably closer to 300,000 since mint records show that about 350,000 proof sets were shipped in a period of slightly over two weeks in December, the only sets in which all six of the coins could have had the "Type II" mint mark. Since not all of the sets shipped during this period had the Type II SBA dollar, the last of the six coins to be struck with the new mint mark, we believe from this and other evidence that a quantity of the 500,000 officially reported mintage was destroyed and never shipped.

Mint officials tried to keep the SBA dollar going. An alloy with silicon added, which would have given the coin a distinctive brassy color was proposed, and efforts were made to replace the eagle reverse with a large numeral 1 but these proposals died when budget cuts were made in early 1981. Mint officials and officials of the Federal Reserve complained that the press had stampeded the public into refusing to accept the coin (and the $2 note which suffered a similar fate). But attempts to shift the blame cannot eclipse the fact that the public never has seriously accepted the dollar coin. For a variety of reasons, the SBA dollar had several strikes against it that no amount of favorable publicity could have overcome. Some sources even tried to claim that the public was "anti-feminist" in refusing to use the coin, or unimaginative in thinking that a dollar coin should be big and heavy.

Have we seen the last of the dollar coin? Probably not. Printing paper money is expensive, and the average life of a one dollar note is less than two years while a coin is projected to have a minimum life of 15 years. It is a potent argument in favor of minting the less expensive, and longer lived, coin and eventually it may be forced upon us. By the time that happens, the coin is likely to be plastic or ceramic, since other more practical uses, will undoubtedly be found for our remaining stocks of metals. As long as the printing presses don't outrun the government's ability to back its currency, the paper money will be more readily acceptable.

MINTAGES

The number of coins struck at a specific mint during a given year is described as the "Mintage" for that mint. The mints may be identified by either a letter, or, in the case of Philadelphia, the lack of a letter. The following list of mintages is the number believed to have been struck, according to the best available data, based on mint records that are in some cases incomplete, conflicting, or missing entirely. The numbers do not always reflect the relative rarity of a given coin, since many of the dollars over the years have been melted down or lost. They are usually used as a basis for estimating the potential rarity of a particular date and mint.

Most potential collectors and investors assume that the old axiom "The older the better" always applies. However, there are a number of other factors and very often a recent date coin may be worth far more than one a hundred years older. So, never depend on age as a pricing factor by itself.

To make it easier to refer to the mintages, we have eliminated all variety listings, which you will find in the chapter devoted to the particular series, and added together all production by year. We have also separated each year by spaces where more than one mine was operating so that the mint by mint comparison can be seen at a glance.

Another fallacy that you can dispel by comparing the figures below is that the branch mints, especially Carson City and San Francisco, always had lower output than Philadelphia or Denver.

Mint Mark Letters:

No Letter - Philadelphia
P - Philadelphia beginning in 1979
CC - Carson City, NV
D - Denver
O - New Orleans, LA
S - San Francisco, CA

Flowing Hair Silver Dollars

DATE	MINTAGE
1794	1,758
1795	**203,033**

Draped Bust - Small Eagle

DATE	MINTAGE
1795	Included Above
1796	72,920
1797	7,776
1798	327,536

Draped Bust - Heraldic Eagle

DATE	MINTAGE
1798	Included Above
1799	423,515
1800	220,920
1801	54,454
1802	41,650
1803	85,634
1804	15

Gobrecht "Patterns"

DATE	MINTAGE
1836	1,000
1838	25
1839	300

Liberty Seated Dollars

DATE	MINTAGE
1840	61,005
1841	173,000
1842	184,618
1843	165,100
1844	20,000
1845	24,500
1846	110,600
1846-O	59,000
1847	140,750
1848	15,000
1849	62,600
1850	7,500
1850-O	40,000
1851	1,300
1852	1,100
1853	46,110
1854	33,140
1855	26,000
1856	63,500
1857	94,000
1858	80
1859	256,500
1859-O	360,000
1859-S	20,000
1860	218,930

Liberty Seated Dollars

DATE	MINTAGE
1860-O	515,000
1861	78,500
1862	12,090
1863	27,660
1864	31,170
1865	47,000
1866	4
(Motto Added on Reverse)	
1866	49,625
1867	47,525
1868	162,700
1869	424,300
1870	416,000
1870-CC	12,462
1870-S	Unknown
1871	1,074,760
1871-CC	1,376
1872	1,106,450
1872-CC	3,150
1872-S	9,000
1873	293,600
1873-CC	2,300
1873-S	700

Trade Dollars

DATE	MINTAGE
1873	397,500
1873-CC	124,500
1873-S	703,000
1874	987,800
1874-CC	1,373,200
1874-S	2,549,000
1875	218,900
1875-CC	1,573,700
1875-S	4,487,000
1876	456,150
1876-CC	509,000
1876-S	5,227,000
1877	3,039,710
1877-CC	534,000
1877-S	9,519,000
1878	900
1878-CC	97,000
1878-S	4,162,000
1879	1,541
1880	1,987
1881	960
1882	1,097
1883	979
1884	10
1885	5

Morgan Dollars

DATE	MINTAGE
1878	10,509,550
1878-CC	2,212,000
1878-S	9,744,000
1879	14,807,100
1879-CC	756,000
1879-O	2,887,000
1879-S	9,110,000
1880	12,601,335
1880-CC	591,000
1880-O	5,305,000
1880-S	8,900,000
1881	9,163,975
1881-CC	296,000
1881-O	5,708,000
1881-S	12,760,000
1882	11,101,100
1882-CC	1,133,000
1882-O	6,090,000
1882-S	9,250,000
1883	12,291,039
1883-CC	1,204,000
1883-O	8,725,000
1883-S	6,250,000
1884	14,070,875
1884-CC	1,136,000
1884-O	9,730,000
1884-S	3,200,000
1885	17,787,767
1885-CC	228,000
1885-O	9,185,000
1885-S	1,497,000
1886	19,963,886
1886-O	10,710,000
1886-S	750,000
1887	20,290,710
1887-O	11,550,000
1887-S	1,771,000
1888	19,183,833
1888-O	12,150,000
1888-S	657,000
1889	21,726,811
1889-CC	350,000
1889-O	11,875,000
1889-S	700,000
1890	16,802,590
1890-CC	2,309,401
1890-O	10,701,000
1890-S	8,230,373
1891	8,694,206
1891-CC	1,618,000
1891-O	7,954,529

Morgan Dollars

DATE	MINTAGE
1891-S	5,296,000
1892	1,037,245
1892-CC	1,352,000
1892-O	2,744,000
1892-S	1,200,000
1893	378,792
1893-CC	677,000
1893-O	300,000
1893-S	100,000
1894	110,972
1894-O	1,723,000
1894-S	1,260,000
1895	12,880
1895-O	450,000
1895-S	400,000
1896	9,967,762
1896-O	4,900,000
1896-S	5,000,000
1897	2,822,731
1897-O	4,004,000
1897-S	5,825,000
1898	5,884,735
1898-O	4,440,000
1898-S	4,102,000
1899	330,846
1899-O	12,290,000
1899-S	2,562,000
1900	8,880,938
1900-O	12,590,000
1900-S	3,540,000
1901	6,962,813
1901-O	13,320,000
1901-S	2,284,000
1902	7,994,777
1902-O	8,636,000
1902-S	1,530,000
1903	4,652,755
1903-O	4,450,000
1903-S	1,241,000
1904	2,788,650
1904-O	3,720,000
1904-S	2,304,000
1921	44,690,000
1921-D	20,345,000
1921-S	21,695,000

Peace Dollars

DATE	MINTAGE
1921	1,006,473
1922	51,737,000
1922-D	15,063,000
1922-S	17,475,000
1923	30,800,000
1923-D	6,811,000
1923-S	19,020,000
1924	11,811,000
1924-S	1,728,000
1925	10,198,000
1925-S	1,610,000
1926	1,939,000
1926-D	2,348,700
1926-S	6,980,000
1927	848,000
1927-D	1,268,900
1927-S	866,000
1928	360,649
1928-S	1,632,000
1934	954,057
1934-D	1,569,500
1934-S	1,011,000
1935	1,576,000
1935-S	1,964,000
1964	30
1964-D	316,076

Eisenhower Dollars

DATE	MINTAGE
1971	47,799,000
1971-D	68,587,424
1971-S	11,133,764
1972	75,890,000
1972-D	92,548,511
1972-S	4,004,687
1973	2,056,000
1973-D	2,000,000
1973-S	5,608,381
1974	27,366,000
1974-D	35,466,000
1974-S	5,643,929
1976	117,337,000
1976-D	103,228,274
1976-S	7,059,099
1977	12,596,000
1977-D	32,983,006
1977-S	3,251,152
1978	25,702,000
1978-D	33,012,890
1978-S	3,127,788

Anthony Dollars

DATE	MINTAGE
1979-P	360,221,874

Anthony Dollars		Anthony Dollars	
DATE	MINTAGE	DATE	MINTAGE
1979-D	288,015,700	1980-S	20,400,000
1979-S	109,575,500	1981-P	3,000,000
1980-P	27,600,000	1981-D	3,250,000
1980-D	41,625,000	1981-S	4,000,000

SHRINKING MINTAGE FIGURES

The melting of Silver Dollars, which was extremely heavy in the last year also, has had a tremendous effect on the dollar market. This is a relatively unimportant topic for investors in bullion coins, but if you invest in numismatic quality Silver Dollars, you will want to learn about it. It has a definite bearing on the investment potential of any Silver Dollars you buy.

As we have pointed out, the number of surviving specimens of any particular date or mintmark cannot be judged on the basis of mintage alone. If we have two Silver Dollars, one of which was struck in 4 million specimens and the other in 6 million, it does not automatically follow that the former is scarcer on today's market. The relative scarcity in BU, let alone in all grades of condition, could bear little resemblance to the difference in mintage.

This is why we do not advocate making investments strictly on mintage numbers. The mintage totals are helpful in selecting your Silver Dollar investment coins, but if you look deeper than mintage figures you will have an edge on most investors. The average investor is not attuned to these fine points of numismatics. Therefore he misses many good purchases.

We advise you to study and contemplate this subject before doing any serious investment buying.

Obviously the value of any Silver Dollar, or other coin, depends much more on current availability than on totals originally manufactured. If a coin is difficult to get, its value will inevitably be driven up, even if it carries a high mintage figure. A large mintage means nothing if the coin is not offered for sale in shops and cannot readily be found at auctions. On the other hand, a date or mintmark with relatively low mintage, which is readily available, is not likely to rise as rapidly in price.

This will certainly seem confusing to a beginnner. How can a high-mintage coin be scarcer on the market than a low-mintage coin?

The explanation is in how many were melted. The surviving number of Silver Dollars of all dates and mintmarks is considerably less than originally produced. More than half of all Silver Dollars made by the U.S. Mint from 1794 to 1935 no longer exist. However, the rate of attrition has not been uniform from one date to the next. Some dates and mintmarks have perished to a greater extent than others. This has happened because most of the destruction of Silver Dollars has not been in the nature of natural loss. It has been intentional.

If natural loss were the only factor, or even the chief factor, the situation would be different. Mintage totals would be fairly reliable indicators of current availability. Natural loss, such as coins going down in a shipwreck (which occurred frequently in the late 18th and early 19th centuries), does not play any favorites with dates. Natural loss reduces the availability of all dates and mintmarks at a pretty constant pace. Of course, a coin struck in 10 million specimens would be expected to sustain more natural loss than one struck in 500,000, since there are more specimens to be lost. Nevertheless it would be unlikely, from natural loss alone, for a coin with high mintage to become scarcer than one with low mintage. The percentage of specimens in existence would vary somewhat from the mintage figures, but the low mintage dates and mintmarks would still be the scarcest coins.

Natural loss, has, compared to intentional destruction, played a very small role in the loss of Silver Dollars. This is especially true of Morgan and Peace Dollars, which (because of their relatively recent origin) seldom got involved in shipwrecks or lost in the sand of western Ghost Towns. If no intentional melting had occurred, the quantity of Morgan and Peace Dollars now surviving would probably exceed 90% of their original mintage.

The intentional destruction of Silver Dollars and other coins is abhorred by collectors. But, as objectionable as this practice has been (and still is), it has resulted in considerably stronger prices for BU specimens and — more significantly — created investment opportunities that certainly would not otherwise exist. Market values have not caught up with these uneven attrition rates. The current prices of BU Silver Dollars, especially in the Morgan series, do not fully reflect availability. They are still based largely on mintage totals, since this was the traditional criteria for pricing for many years. Heavy investment activity in recent times has taken some attention away from mintage figures and focused it upon . . . availability, where it ought to have been all along. But values are still adjusting, and they have a long way to go before realistically reflecting the true scarcity of each coin. The next five years are sure to witness more price adjustments in line with availability. Investors buying today can take advantage of this. We have indicated to you, in this book, some dates and mintmarks which are scarcer on the market than their mintage totals would suggest. We would further advise you to keep watch on the market, via dealer offerings and the price trends published in coin newspapers, to remain currently informed of availability and it effect on values.

Undoubtedly, you have seen other books on coin investment, which give purported "totals in existence" for coins of different dates and mintmarks. Such information probably gives these books added sales appeal, but it is not dependable. Whenever "totals in existence" numbers are published for any coin, they represent nothing more than an estimate on the compiler's part. It may be possible to give very rough, approximate figures with some assurance of reliability. But when an investment advisor states that (for example) 112,000 specimens remain in existence of a date of which 2 million were struck, this is merely a personal opinion which cannot be supported by hard evidence. It is simply impossible to become that precise. The publication of such estimates, when not labeled as estimates, are a disservice to investors — and to collectors as well. Whenever something is published, no matter how extreme or ridiculous, it tends to be accepted as fact by many readers. This is especially true in a field like Silver Dollar investing, where a majority of interested persons have little personal knowledge of the subject.

The truth of the matter is that nobody — dealer, historian, investment expert or otherwise — has information *nearly that precise* on totals in existence. Such information is impossible to obtain. Totals in existence of *very rare coins* can be tabulated fairly closely, with time and effort. This task involves searching through auction sale records and finding mention of different specimens that have been sold, then taking into account the numbers in institutional collections. Even then, an exact figure is not likely to be entirely trustworthy, but a much closer estimate can be made than for high-mintage coins. Of coins of which thousands or even just hundreds of specimens are in existence, there is absolutely no means of tracing them all — even if one had a lifetime to spend and ample research grants to finance his efforts. The best that can be done is for rough estimates to be made. When such estimates are published under the guise of fact, an unfair disservice is done, and the feeling cannot be avoided that such information is included merely to give these publications an aura of expertise that they do not deserve.

The feeling is likewise aroused that compilers of such data may have a personal interest in some of the coins.

You cannot reduce Silver Dollar investing to precise, exact, comfortable numbers. And, in a way, it is very fortunate that you cannot!

Beginning investors, especially those coming into Silver Dollars with no numismatic knowledge, would like to see trustworthy figures of this kind. They would like to have as many reliable numbers and percentages in front of them as possible. They are accustomed to working with such information in other fields of investment. They feel — understandably — that the less hard information available, the greater risk they take. The publication of "totals in existence" comforts them. It reduces guesswork. It seems to guarantee that certain dates and mintmarks are good investments. It's something to have faith in, which the vague statement that a particular coin is "scarce on the market" is not.

This very situation, this lack of solid information on numbers, is actually playing in your favor. If totals in existence were reliably recorded, and of free access to every investor, the number of "sleeper" coins would be considerably reduced. Nearly every Silver Dollar would already have reached its fair watermark of price. You would probably not have the opportunity to buy undervalued dates and mintmarks. It is precisely this lack of hard information that causes imbalances in prices — imbalances which, in time, correct themselves and result in profits for the investor. You can depend on the harder-to-get coins going up in value, as pressure from collectors and other investors will see to that. A coin cannot long remain undervalued. Buyers will come in to take these coins. When they do, the dealers naturally are obliged to pay more in replenishing their stocks. The upward price spiral begins, and can push on until the "underpriced" coin actually becomes "overpriced." Instances of this have been numerous in the Silver Dollar market within the past 10 years. The thinking investor is alert to all signs and signals. He becomes aware of the better coins and the better buys. He knows when to buy and does not let a good opportunity pass. By the same token he knows when to sell.

The more you learn about Silver Dollars, the more confidence you will invariably have in making investment selections. You will become your own expert and you will look to self-appointed authorities for direction. And you will see, very readily, the foolishness of most of the information currently being published about Silver Dollars.

As we have said, the loss of Silver Dollars is not proportionate with all dates and mintmarks evenly or equally. The loss ratio has been unpredictable throughout history and is hardly more predictable in 1985 than it was in 1882. Silver dollars continue to be lost, and most of this loss will result from intentional destruction. The big silver boom of late 1979 and early 1980 brought wholesale melting of Morgan and Peace Dollars in average circulated condition. There is no doubt that millions of specimens went into refinery furnaces during a six-month period. If another similar "rush" occurs, as there is every likelihood it will sooner or later, more heavy melting is sure to accompany it.

We are apt to think strictly in terms of Morgan and Peace Dollars when we talk of attrition by melting. These are the Dollars melted presently, because they have no premium value in average circulated condition (unless the date is very scarce). The next oldest series, the Seated Liberty Dollars, are not melted for their silver bullion content — though one or two may occasionally slip into bullion bags. These Dollars, which ceased to be struck in 1873, *do* have some collector value in average circulated condition. Look at the advertisements in coin magazines, and you will find dealers offering "type coins" of Seated Liberty Dollars in average circulated condition for three or four times the value of their bullion content. Nor are Trade Dollars melted for their bullion. These are collector coins even in low grade condition.

However, earlier generations looked upon average circulated Seated Liberty and Trade Dollars exactly as we now look upon Morgan and Peace. They were considered fair game for melting and many were melted. The same is true of earlier Dollars as well. Even Flowing Hairs and Busts, now worth hundreds of dollars even in mediocre condition, were melted at one time. Thus, attrition has done its work comprehensively on the whole Dollar series, going back to the 18th century.

It is natural to presume that the earliest Dollars, the Flowing Hair and Bust designs, would survive today in the lowest quantitites relative to their mintage figures. This is correct. But mere passage of time would not have brought about that circumstance. If intentional destruction of Silver Dollars has started only in the 20th century, it is quite likely (and in fact almost a certainty) that Busts and Flowing Hairs *would be more plentiful in relation to their mintage figures than Morgan and Peace Dollars.* The loss of Early Dollars by natural loss would not, could not, have approached the rate of attrition of Morgan and Peace Dollars by melting. They would still be reasonably scarce because of the low mintage totals. They would be extremely scarce in the higher grades of condition, from having remained in circulation so long. But they would be more plentiful in existence, in terms of specimens surviving vs. specimens minted, than Morgan and Peace Dollars. This may sound extraordinary but it is perfectly true. Silver coins are not fragile. They can do very well if left unmolested, in terms of survival. Silver coins much smaller and thinner than our Dollars have come through 2,000 years of burial in Asian deserts. Natural loss would have taken its toll of Early Dollars, but at a moderate pace. The chances are excellent that, if natural loss had been the only cause of destruction for Early Silver Dollars, the survival rate for Flowing Hairs and Busts would be 70-80% of their mintages. After all, America has been a continuous civilization since the Mint began operations. There is no reason why all our early coins — going all the way back to the administrations of Washington and Adams — should not have enjoyed a high survival rate, if their only enemy was natural loss.

The fact is that our Silver Dollars, from the very earliest times, suffered a quite unnatural loss, and to alarming proportions. The late 18th century, just three or four years after the Dollar was introduced, witnessed enormous quantities of the coin shipped abroad, to take advantage of the slight difference in value between gold and silver that prevailed in Europe. Foreign traders took kegs of dollars back to Holland, France, England and other countries, and converted them into gold coin of their native land. If they then converted the gold coins into native silvercrowns, they ended up with more silver than by keeping our U.S. Dollars. It was a profitable enterprise, so profitable that a kind of industry sprang up around it, profiteers who syphoned Silver Dollars out of the country. Nearly every cargo vessel weighing anchor at Boston, New York or the other big port towns, headed across the Atlantic, carried some Silver Dollars. Most of these coins never returned home. Some were melted down upon reaching the other side.

This state of affairs led to suspension of the Silver Dollar in 1804, as the coin could simply not be kept in circulation regardless of how many were manufactured.

Even in later times, Silver Dollars were deliberately melted. The government has probably melted more of its own Silver Dollars than have been lost to profiteers or private industry. The silver used in making Peace Dollars was derived from melting down Morgans from the government's stockpiles.

Generally speaking, the number of specimens in existence of any Silver Dollars is lower than that of other coins with comparable mintage totals. The Morgans as a whole had high mintage output, but this is deceiving as an indicator of current availability. Most of the dates from this series were extensively melted, and early melting (by the government as well as by commercial interests) naturally made no distinction between Uncirculated and Circulated. Since the government was in possession of exclusively uncirculated specimens, all the Morgan Dollars it melted were in that category.

With the Dollar series, you have a situation in which many coins are scarcer than the mintage totals indicate. Some of them have not reached realistic price levels. We have pointed them out in this book, and we urge you to give them consideration when planning your investment portfolio.

HOW DOLLARS ARE MADE

To most collectors and investors, the minting process is a mystery; the lack of knowledge aptly pointed out by the common practice among novice collectors of referring to coins as being "printed." Just by learning to describe coins as being "minted" instead of "printed," you have advanced a giant step toward becoming an experienced collector and are one more jump ahead of the majority of the collector-investors you will be competing with in the marketplace.

We are often asked, "Why should I bother to learn anything about the minting process? All I'm interested in is getting the right coin to make me a profit." Our answer is, in part, very simple — it is a waste of time to get the "right" coin in the "wrong" condition, due to some problem in the minting process, or if it has defects that you mistakenly assume are due to the minting process.

The last phrase in that answer is often the most important because it is by learning to detect damage that occurred after the coin was

A view of the proof press room at the San Francisco Assay Office. Only one of the coin presses is being operated.

Looking into a blanking press for Anthony Dollar planchets. Each of the smaller cylinders is a punch.

minted that you can often avoid buying a coin that is undesirable. Mishaps that occur in the minting process can often add spectacularly to the value of a coin, increasing the value by a hundred or a thousand times. But there are many more things that can occur accidentally, or intentionally, after the coin is minted that only reduce its basic value.

Before we look at some of the possibly valuable minting varieties, let's describe the minting process, so that you can better understand

Rolls of coin metal strip ready to be punched.

A rotating drum annealing oven, used to soften planchets before they are struck into coins.

why a coin looks the way it does and just how it is made.

First, the alloy must be made. For our silver dollars, a mixture of 90% silver and 10% copper was melted in large furnaces and poured into molds to form ingots. The ingots were then cleaned and passed through rolling mills which turned the ingot into a strip of coin metal of the proper thickness. This strip was passed through a blanking press which punched out the round discs, called planchets, upon which the coin was to be struck.

The rotating drum and fence from an upsetting mill, used to upset the edge of the planchet before striking.

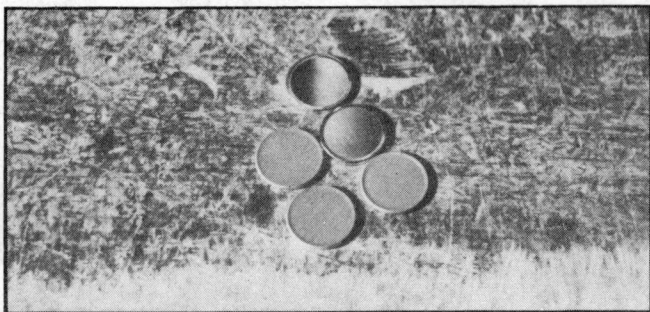

A group of proof planchets. The upper pair have been burnished to improve the finish before striking.

The planchets were then annealed by heating them, to make them be soft enough to be properly struck by the dies, then cleaned, and passed through an upsetting mill, which pushed back the edge of the planchet, forming a slight rim where the design rim was to be on the struck coin.

The processed planchets were then sent to the coin presses, where the planchets were fed between the dies and struck with 150 tons per square inch of pressure by the die pair to form the design on both sides of the coin, and the reeded edge. The final impact of the die pair is the end of the minting process as far as the collector is concerned. The struck coins were then sent to the counting room where they were inspected, counted, and placed in cloth bags which were sewn shut, ready to be shipped to the Federal Reserve Banks for further distribution to local banks and ultimately the public.

We have, in the preceding paragraphs, given a brief sketch of a very complex operation involving the skills of many people, ranging from the metallurgist to the die maker, the coin press operator to the electrician; all of whom are needed to produce a single coin. Even from this very con-

Front view of a coin press. The planchets feed down the sloping tube from left, are carried by the feed fingers (foreground) into the coining chamber, where they are struck by the dies. The heavy set screws holding the upper die can be seen on each side of the base of the feed tube.

An extremely delicate balance beam scale used to weigh coins.

densed description, you have undoubtedly learned several things you didn't know.

For example, even among those who know that coins are minted, there are large numbers of people who don't know that coins are struck on a cold planchet by the die pair, many assuming that coins are cast from molten metal. This misapprehension is common even among experienced collectors. It is a costly lack of knowledge, because many fakes and counterfeits ARE cast and knowing the difference can keep you from being victimized. A key piece of knowledge is that metal struck by a die pair has a completely different appearance from cast metal, or even metal that has been struck in two separate operations by a pair of dies.

The "art" of die making is actually a science, as are all other parts of the minting process and plays a very important part in the process of making a coin. Coin production is actually a form of mass production, since coins are turned out in quantity just like so many washers or screws, nuts, bolts or any of a thousand other mass produced items. Certain rules of physics, chemistry and other disciplines are applied and used in coin making, meaning that the coin conforms to the "laws" of those sciences, and the results for both normal strikes and varieties can be rigidly defined and classified.

To make a die, the usual practice is to first make a design in plaster. This is coated with a thin layer of copper, forming a "Galvano" which is used as a model in a reducing lathe to cut the incuse design into a piece of tool steel (Master Die) or in relief (raised) to form a Master Hub. The Master Die can then be used to make a Working Hub by pressing the Die into a softened piece of steel under several hundreds of tons of pressure. This process must be repeated two or more times, because the softened steel hardens from the pressure applied and the Master Die can penetrate only part way.

Once the Working Hub is completed, it can in turn be used to make hundreds of working dies in the same way. For the Morgan and Peace dollars, we know from well documented reports that this "hubbing" pro-

Die blanks ready to be made into dies.

cedure was repeated as many as ten times to form the big dies. The Master Die is never used to strike coins. Its only purpose is to serve as a model from which new working hubs may be made as necessary.

Prior to about 1840, before the hubbing process came into general use, dies were usually made one by one, by hand, resulting in many variations that do not appear on hubbed dies. Some of the work was done by an engraver, cutting away the die metal, taking as much as eight hours to form a single letter or number. Much of this work was done with letter and number punches and even some of the design such as the stars were added to the die with a punch, since a minute's work with a punch would save a day's work with engraving tools. One of the most common mistakes made by today's collectors, dealers and investors is to describe punching varieties as "recut."

A painting of workmen preparing coin planchets around 1900.

It is important to remember that a die is the mirror image of the coin. Where there is a raised (relief) design on a coin, there is a corresponding "recession" in the die, and where there is an incuse part of the design, there is a matching raised area on the die. The Hub is a replica of the coin with the identical relief image. The metal to metal transfer of the design in the hubbing process is vital to production of the masses of coins used by today's society.

While many coins are practically identical, year after year, because of the use of a Master Die, there is one frequent variation — the date. The practice varied, but very often the dies were made without a date, or with only a partial date, the final number or numbers being added to the individual dies. This explains why you may find a coin with the first three numbers in an even row and the final number above or below, tilted or otherwise out of line. The numbers were often applied with a "logo" punch, which had two, three or even all four numbers on a single punch. This explains why some dies have a matching location of the numbers from one die to another.

A final note on the importance of the minting process: significant variations occur from year to year and from mint to mint. Some silver dollar experts can, from a glance at the reverse, tell the year a coin was minted before turning it over to confirm the date; or by looking at the obverse, can tell which mint struck the coin before checking the mint mark on the reverse. This kind of expertise is gained only through long experience and you probably won't need to become that adept in order to profit from your coins. But it certainly wouldn't hurt to do business with that kind of knowledgeable dealer, so that you can benefit from his experience.

A display of a piece of coin metal strip after the planchets have been punched out.

MINTING VARIETIES

One of the most neglected areas of coin collecting, so far as the investor is concerned, is the variety. This is an area where some highly specialized knowledge is a necessity. Like anything else having to do with coins, it is one that can be learned, and one where knowledge can be especially profitable, mainly because so few collectors, dealers and investors take the time to learn what varieties are, how they occur, how to recognize and evaluate them and how to profit from them.

We use the term "variety," actually "Minting Variety" in its broadest sense. Most coin collectors, if they are even aware of varieties, limit their interest to a few, very narrow areas having to do with the die, such as some overdates. Anything else that happens to a coin is thought of as a "mint error." You will find that many dealers and collectors hold low opinions of anyone foolish enough to collect "errors."

After a number of years of research into the minting process, and years of writing about some of the things that can happen to coins, we feel that this approach to variety collecting is not only a negative attitude, but also an indefensible one, since it is extremely rare that some die varieties can be positively identified as to whether they occurred accidentally or intentionally. A large segment of the hobby would like to have you believe that it can in fact read the mind of a mint worker long dead and thus determine the difference between a variety and an "error."

Since it is obvious that such a distinction is totally impractical, we have suggested to the hobby that all variations from the "normal" be treated as minting varieties, and include within that broad base those which can be also readily described as errors. We feel it is pointless to waste time in arguing intent, accident or omission; time that can be better spent in adding to our collections.

Two of the most common varieties that you are likely to encounter in dollar collecting are the overdate and the repunched, or "over," mint mark. An overdate is a date with one or more numbers punched, cut or hubbed over a different number or numbers. 1880/79 is an overdate, 1880/80 is not. The letters indentifying the mint are often repunched, and on occasion, one letter is punched over another, either by accident or intentionally, to save an expensive surplus die so it can be used at a different mint. Some of the overdates and mint mark varieties can be quite valuable, and some of them, as you will see in our later chapters, offer the investor some "sleepers" that have been neglected by many collectors.

Mistakes in striking the dollar coins often lead to some startling prices. For example, a double struck dollar, a coin which has received two strikes from the die pair, may be worth $2000 or more; even for an Ike dollar that otherwise is worth little more than face value.

A "clip," a coin struck on a planchet that has a portion missing (from the process of punching the planchets from the coin metal strip), can add significantly to the value of a dollar. An Ike dollar with a small clip, about 5% of the total area of the coin, is worth more. Add an additional premium if it's a Bicentennial date. Values run even higher for the older dollars. Even the planchets on which the coins were struck are valuable. A silver dollar planchet for a Morgan or Peace dollar will bring approximately $200, while one of the earlier dollars will bring even more. A planchet for one of the Trade Dollars is a real rarity.

An off center strike dollar is also a rarity. The largest known off center Morgan is 18% off center and worth a four figure sum. Major Die Breaks ("cuds"), which show a raised irregular area of the coin metal extending across the rim into the field, are almost non-existent in the Morgan and Peace dollars. Consequently the minor ones that are known bring several hundred dollars for top grade coins.

This brings up another point. Very often a novice gets the impression that any minting variety will automatically make a coin very valuable, regardless of the coin's grade. This is false, as grade plays as important a role in variety collecting as it does in any other area of coin collecting. Simply stated, the higher the coin's grade, the more valuable the variety will be.

There are also many minting varieties that are very common, and many more coins that have been damaged, accidentally or intentionally, or altered. So it is necessary to learn the difference between mint process varieties and damage or alteration, and to learn the relative values of the different minting varieties. Another common mistake is to automatically assume that a coin you find with a possible variety is the "only" coin with it. Die variations repeat, exactly, on every coin struck by that die until some further change in the die occurs. Planchet varieties and striking varieties may be unique in themselves, but in the vast majority of cases they are very similar to many other nearly identical pieces.

As a general rule, any minting variety that has significant value will have the greatest value on a dollar. Most variety prices are on a sliding scale, ranging up from the cent through the larger denominations. This is because most coin collectors (and variety collectors) concentrate on the cent and because much larger quantities of cents are usually produced than any of the larger denomination coins. For the past decade, mintages in the billions are the rule rather than the exception.

Very often the first question asked about a minting variety is: "How did that ever get by the inspectors?" We often wonder the same thing, but we have to remember that inspectors are human and since the coins are usually inspected on a moving belt, any momentary distraction is enough to miss one or more "defective" coins. Today, the inspection belts are a thing of the past in U.S. Mints, which instead depend on mechanical sorters and such things as vibrating screens to catch the misstruck coins. In some instances, the machines are better than the human inspectors, but in others there are larger numbers of misstrikes escaping. We have to remember that, like any other mass production operation, the number of defective pieces is a fraction of the total punched. One percent of a billion coins is 10 million coins. Fortunately for variety collectors, the defect rate is well below 1%. We say "fortunately," because this makes them more valuable.

As an investor, if you take the time to learn about varieties and their values, you have the collector or dealer who looks down on "errors" working for you in many cases. Their attitude is often based on a lack of knowledge of the subject. Such dealers could be a source of bargains, as they sometimes sell a valuable variety for the normal numismatic value. As you can see from this limited discussion, the "foolish" variety collector often can make a substantial profit from coins that "regular" dealers ignore, their loss being your gain.

There are only a very limited number of coin dealers who are expert in minting varieties and we recommend dealing directly with them.

Needless to say, in the limited space available, we can only touch very briefly on some of the possibilities in investing in minting varieties. Consult the regular weekly column on U.S. minting varieties in World Coin News, and the column on paper money varieties in the Bank Note Reporter as in addition to as monthly columns and articles in Error-Variety News and COINS Magazine. There are also similar columns and articles in Coin World weekly, COINage Magazine and other publications in the numismatic field which we have listed in the chapter on Recommended Reading.

In the individual chapters on the different dollar series, we will point out and try to evaluate some of the significant varieties, keeping in mind that there are many unlisted varieties such as those we have suggested in this chapter which require additional skills and knowledge to find and profit from.

PROOF DOLLARS

A common mistake is the assumption that the term "proof" is a grade. Proof is a condition of a coin, and, to a limited extent, proof coins can be graded, just as circulation strikes are.

The general definition of a proof coin is one that has been struck with specially prepared and polished dies on specially prepared and polished planchets, resulting in a coin with a mirror-like field and preferably with what is described as "frosted" design. Once you have seen a proof coin and a normal circulation strike side by side, the differences are very obvious. With a little practice you can distinguish the majority of such coins. The term originated from the practice of striking several coins with a new die to "prove" the die and make sure the design would strike properly.

Proof coins are normally not struck for circulation and thus are primarily intended for either the collector, or as a presentation piece for some foreign dignitary; the latter the underlying cause for a significant number of proof strikes beginning in the last half of the 19th century.

Until 1964, all U.S. proof coins were struck at Philadelphia except for a few very proof coins struck for special purposes at the branch mints. Beginning in 1968, all U.S. proofs have been struck at the San Francisco Assay Office and all bear the "S" mint mark. The exceptions are a couple of notable varieties that occurred when the mint mark was omitted from dies sent to San Francisco from Philadelphia where all coining dies are made.

A proof die usually begins life in the same manner as a die intended for circulation strikes. The die is hubbed. A tool with the relief design is forced into the face of the die two or more times to fully impress the design into the die. The die is then hardened, after the mint mark (if any) is punched in by hand, and sent to the press room to begin work.

Current practice is to polish the conical face of a proof die before the hubbing operation. When the die is sent to San Francisco, workers use diamond dust to further polish the field and sandblast the design, giving it the rough surface that results in the frosted appearance prized by collectors. Once the die is in service, the rough design surface is maintained by periodically applying acid. Proof dies normally have a very low die life, with current practice resulting in mintages per die ranging downward from a maximum of five or six thousand coins for the smaller denominations. The usual average for the larger denominations is considered to be about 3000 coins.

After the initial polishing, the die is removed from service after one-third and two-thirds of its normal life and repolished. Since each of these polishing operations removes some field surface from the die, it reduces the design's depth and thus the struck relief on the coin, and may remove some of the shallower parts of the design. Typically, polishing is responsible for such things as a strand of hair separated from the head, a "broken" nose or other similar loss of detail.

The almost universal practice is to strike all proof coins twice, in some cases three times, in order to bring up the sharp outlines of the design to their utmost. Striking quality may vary widely due to a multitude of factors, ranging from the exact degree of annealing to the amount of humidity in the air. In general, proof coins are likely to have very well struck designs, and the edges of the rims are more likely to be sharp and angular, rather than rounded. Very often a proof will display a thin raised "lip" sticking up from the outside edge of one or more both rims, evidence of the extra pressure and additional strike or strikes, which forces the coin metal between the edges of the dies and the collar. This effect is known as a "wire edge." It may also be found on heavily struck circulation strikes, so do not automatically assume that a wire edge is "proof of a proof."

Very often you will find circulation strikes which appear at first glance to be proof quality, but if you examine the coin with a magnifying lens, you will soon see that the "bright" field has millions of tiny hairline scratches and is different from the more polished field of the genuine proof. The circulation strikes which most often cause this type of confusion are the first few strikes from a brand new die pair, before the dies have had a chance to wear.

Some proof coins are also found with what is described as a "matte" finish which is a dull, slightly rough surface, somewhat similar to the frosted surface on a polished proof. This type is considerably more difficult to produce and only very limited numbers have ever been struck.

As a rule, far fewer proof coins are struck than normal circulation strikes, as they are not used for money, but there are numerous instances where the only coins produced for a given year are proofs. In general, the lower mintages for proofs usually command higher prices than a top grade circulation strike of the same year, but again there are exceptions, so it pays to check the prices and grades listed. Even concentrating on one denomination, there are hundreds of dates and grades to remember, so it never pays to rely solely on memory.

Another general rule covering proofs is that given identical mintages of a proof or a circulation strike, the proofs will outnumber the available examples of the circulation strike in the top grades of condition. As we mentioned, proofs often went directly into the hands of the few collectors around, or into a dignitary's display case, while circulation strikes had no proud owners to pressure them.

Proofs require even more delicate handling than regular strikes, so pay heed to the material we have presented in the chapter on care and storage, particularly if you run into proofs that may have been stored in material containing PVC. This substance will ruin the coin if not properly removed. Best piece of advice is to never touch a proof with an ungloved hand if you can avoid it.

Especially with some of the older proofs, you may be offered coins that actually circulated, and in some instances are well worn, but are still unmistakable proofs. While each coin needs to be taken on an individual basis, you obviously will not pay a proof price for such a coin, and to determine the value will require close examination in order to determine the exact grade. Such a coin may be described as an impaired proof and while it may appear to be a bargain, it should be examined very carefully before purchase.

As you will see in later chapters, some of the low mintage proofs are underpriced on today's market, and suggest potential profits that can be made if you strive to locate and buy them. "Proof" does not automatically mean a rare and valuable coin, so never be awed by the term, but instead consider it as just one of the factors involved in deciding whether to invest in a given coin.

WHY YOU SHOULD INVEST IN DOLLARS

The question can be answered in a single sentence — "Because they have an excellent track record." While this is admittedly a generalization, there is considerable truth to the statement.

One needs only to study the current market for a few weeks to see that dollars are the most in demand; dollars continue to "lead" the price of bullion, and dollars have the best resale value.

This we feel is of special significance to the investor because one of the key attractions of an investment is the ability to get your money out, if you have an emergency, or if for some reason you decide to invest in something else. It is a plain truth that the dollar market is readily available, both for buying and selling, so that you can get in and get out readily. We don't recommend selling in a rush, but it can be done if necessary.

Dollars in essence are a form of bullion that can be readily bought, conveniently stored, and easily sold. With slightly more care, the more valuable dollars can also be invested in and offer an even better potential for return, since the collector coins are always (or almost always) "ahead" of the bullion market.

Actually, an investment in dollars is double barrelled. You have the benefit of the bullion content supporting their price, plus the fact that they have a relatively steady "minimum value" which remains well above the bullion content. The rarer the coin, the higher that minimum is, and the faster it will increase.

For example, if silver is selling at $12 an ounce, the minimum "buy" price for silver dollars from a dealer will be about $14, and the dealer will sell at about $16. The other lower denomination silver coins are probably somewhere around $10.50 per dollar face value. This means that a single dollar, compared to two half dollars, four quarters or ten dimes is worth about $3.50 more if you have to sell it. By the time you reach bag quantities, your spread is $3500, so it is obvious that, because of the premium attached to dollars, they are a good buy.

Almost every expert in the field of collecting and investing in dollars stresses buying the best grade possible and there are reams of statistics to back up this position. It is an axiom of coin collecting that almost invariably the top grade is the one most likely to increase in value, AND BY THE LARGEST AMOUNT, both in dollars and in percentage. The reasons are obvious, because the top grades are always the rarest. We keep modifying our "always" because there are exceptions, so if we don't "always" modify it, remember the possibility of exceptions.

Because of the millions of silver dollars that have been struck over the years, there are plenty available for all classes of investors. Even if you can't afford the top grades or rarest mintages, there are still dollars that can be collected for profit, primarily because of the quantity, and because of that premium over the bullion value. A dollar struck before 1965 contains 90% silver or about ¾ of an ounce. The smaller silver coins also contain 90% silver, and the weights are such that one dollar face of the smaller coins contains the same amount of silver as one silver dollar.

Almost any coin dealer will have dollars, even though their stock may be sadly lacking in other denominations, so the supply is readily available. Every series, every date, and almost every mint has been well documented, researched and published, so that there are untold quantities of reference material on the coin that you can study to learn more about the coins you own or intend to buy.

The dollar has been studied and reported upon to the point where its qualities are about as familiar and well-documented as they can ever become. There is a wealth of experience in grading the coins, in detecting counterfeits, in the characteristics of each series, often each mint, all available to you as an investor. Consider if you will the comparison between buying stock in a company on the basis of a prospectus running at best to a few pages to the volumes of material published on the dollar.

At this point, the astute investor will lean back and say, "But if all this work has been done, then all the bargains have been found, and there is nothing left for me." The supposition is false, as we have indicated several times. Despite all this material, all this information, few investors have made a skillful application of it in their buying. This automatically means that the person who is willing to spend any time at all in learning is going to be one step ahead of the rest of the pack as far as finding the good investments are concerned. We have mentioned varieties as but one aspect of this, but it is a truism that knowledge is one of the most powerful investment weapons you can bring to bear. Certainly, with this wealth of knowledge available, the chances of success by investing in dollars are much greater than in some other fields where little or no knowledge is available or where you must depend totally on advice of brokers.

Dollars are an investment that can "suit" a far greater variety of investors than most other commodities we can think of. If you are working with only a few dollars to invest. You can find the dollars that work for you at any level. If you need $10, you can sell a single coin, or if you need $10,000 you can sell enough coins just as readily.

This is because despite their status as an investment, the coins are actually still a medium of exchange, and in the worst case you could actually spend a silver dollar to buy something, because — with the exception of the Trade Dollars — all of them are still legal tender.

Invest money in a company drilling an oil well and you may wind up with dust. Buy dollars, and you are buying legal tender, plus bullion, giving you a double whammy in your investment planning.

The money hungry investor wants a profit, but there is fun to be had in buying dollars, because they are, after all, collectibles, and you may well be bitten by the collecting bug. This is the way many investors got their start. While this may not be an influence, there are many others to whom it will be. It's possible to enjoy investing when you are investing in dollars.

RARITY AND ITS CAUSES

The quotation, "What is so rare as a day in June?" comes to mind when we talk about rarity in coin collecting. An apt comparison would be to point out that to a farmer looking for rain on his parched land, a warm sunny June day is not exactly what he had in mind.

The same thing is true when we work with coins. The collector may be looking for a wide variety of different coins, for as many different reasons. For the investor, the one underlying thought is to find the coin that is — or will be — in the most demand, thus increasing the price and creating an investment profit. Unless there is a potential for profit, the reaction is the same as the farmer's at a sunny day. Since profit is one of the underlying causes even for the average collector, both the investor and the collector need to learn more about rarity.

One factor often overlooked is that a "rare" coin may have strong investment potential, or it may well fall into the "so what" class as far as the investor is concerned. A unique coin is one which has only one example extant. There are hundreds, even thousands of coins in the world which fit the definition of unique, but there is a wide variation in their value. We have to be extremely careful to avoid saying "the rarest" coin, because nothing can be rarer than a single coin. Obviously there are other factors affecting the value of a coin.

"Age before beauty." This is a rule that has an entirely different interpretation when it comes to coins. Beauty very often is the primary deciding factor, with age often, but not always, secondary. By beauty we mean a coin that is still in its mint state, unworn, undamaged.

"Out of sight, out of mind." Now there's a rule that directly affects coin value. Publicity, collector acceptance, collector interest, and continual discussion about a coin or group of coins, have very positive influences on the value. This often is a key factor in the price of one coin compared to other, similar coins.

"Penny wise, pound foolish." This is one that investors should post prominently. Buying the cheapest coin frequently results in a purchase that never gains significantly. Buying the best almost insures a potential profit. This can be read another way — don't buy at "fire sale" prices, because you may be buying a stolen coin, or one that is altered or counterfeited.

"Little things mean a lot." A wise saying that all coin investors and collectors should take to heart, because it's the little things that often mean the difference between a valuable coin that will increase in value and a space filler that will never do anything significant.

Let's list some of the major points that have an effect on rarity and the consequent value of the coin.

1. **Mintage**
2. **Survivors**
3. **Grade (condition)**
4. **Age**
5. **Publicity**
6. **Collector interest (Numismatic Value)**

Mintage is all important, as the first factor that should be checked for a given coin. The mintage figure for a given date and mint tells you a lot about the coin, but of course, is by no means all of the story. However, you know at the least, that the surviving total can be no larger than the mintage and that the number of "UNCS" has to be considerably fewer.

This is not to say that a coin out of a mintage of millions might not be rare. The chances are less, but remember, we have other criteria to consider than just mintage.

Survivorship is of key importance and is the main modifier of the original mintage. In many instances coins were never issued, or issued and recalled for melting down, or simply withdrawn from circulation and melted down. More recently, with the price of silver setting records, private interests were again withdrawing coins — as has happened several times in the past — and melting them into bullion. In recent history, the dollar coins have not been subject to melting in quite as large numbers as the smaller silver coins, primarily because the recent market has put a premium on dollars. However, when one considers the several major periods in our history when coins were being melted down for one reason or another, it is easy to realize that not a single mintage figure is accurate. They serve only as a guide to the maximum possible number available.

Coins survive. Yes, but rarely in the pristine state they attained in being struck. The moment a coin enters circulation it begins to wear. It is scratched, bumped, scraped, dropped, and mangled to a greater or lesser extent, and the deterioration grows with time. Attrition rates assume that a certain percentage of coins will disappear from the total mintage every year. This is not a smooth curve on a graph, as some of the factors involved in coin value have a bearing. For example, a dollar minted in 1794 might have disappeared at a fairly high rate for the first few years of circulation, due to shipwreck, indian attack, burial, intentional melting, etc. Now, nearly 200 years later, any 1794 dollar that still exists is likely to be carefully preserved and guarded, so that only a very small percentage of the survivors continue to disappear.

"Cabinet Friction" is a term often applied to the condition of early coins. When coin collecting first came into vogue the popular method of storing coins was to lay them on velvet or a similar material in many European countries. Every time the drawer was opened, the movement tended to slide the coin back and forth on the velvet, and this friction eventually showed as wear. High points of the coins were rubbed in a manner similar to circulation wear.

Wear takes us into grading, to which we have devoted a special chapter. Grading is no more, no less than determining the exact amount of wear that has occurred on the coin. It is of prime importance to the investor or collector, because a very tiny amount of wear reduces the value of a coin substantially. As you will learn, very frequently a modern coin that shows no wear can be far more valuable than a much older coin that exhibits considerable wear. The main reason why we specifically point out that age is not as important as most people think. If offered a choice, accept a MS-60 1934-S Peace dollar rather than a VF-20 1836 Gobrecht Dollar.

We're back to age which, as you see, is farther down on our list of specifications than you probably expected. There is no denying that age has at least an indirect effect on the rarity of a coin. The older the coin, the more likely that large numbers of the original total have perished, and that well-preserved survivors are in the minority. Age adds a certain prestige to a coin, but very often prestige doesn't pay off as an investment. The older a coin, the more likely it is to carry numismatic prestige, but the more difficult it may be to assemble facts and figures about the coin. The greater the age, the more other factors can come to bear on it.

The notoriety of the coin often has a far greater effect on the value than most people realize, or stop to think about. Some coins have had a substantial amount of publicity over the years, and become the target of strong collector attention. For instance almost anyone who has been exposed to the coin hobby for any length of time is aware of the premium attached to most of the coins struck at Carson City, NV, which bear the CC mint mark. At times this premium has no real relationship to the actual mintage, age, survivorship or any other factor, simply because the coins have received an unusual amount of publicity over the years, including that surrounding the General Services Administration sales of dollars found in the Treasury's vaults in the last decade.

The first three years of Morgan dollar production have gotten an overwhelming amount of publicity over the years, primarily because of the numerous varieties (including several significant overdates) and the design changes involving the tail feathers. The coins are very well known, but because of the relatively high mintages most are considered "common dates."

While collector interest is the last point that we discuss, there undoubtedly would be arguments that it should rank higher, and in the minds of some, should be first. As you have seen in this chapter, all of the factors work together, and it is often impossible to pinpoint the exact cause for a given coin having a higher value that some similar coin.

It is certainly true that collector interest can make or break a coin. One of the most recent examples of this was the introduction of the clad coinage in 1965, replacing most of the silver coins. Collectors for more than a decade totally ignored the clads, and only very recently have there been any significant moves toward actively collecting some of them. It is no different in the dollar series. The Gobrecht dollars, for example, are all relatively low priced, primarily because they have been considered patterns by most authorities over the years, automatically excluding them from the realm of the average collector, since pattern collecting is considered a very specialized and esoteric area of the coin hobby.

Many of the coins minted before the 1870s were restruck later by Mint personnel. Most such restrikes demand prices below the value of the genuine coin struck in the year of date or succeeding year. However, the 1804 dollar, the subject of serious and continuing controversy over the years, is a known and admitted restrike, not minted in the year of date.

We must point out that often all six of these points have a direct bearing on a coin's value. There are others, since inflation is today directly affecting coin prices, where earlier depression sharply reduced the values of rare coins. Each point must be considered in the overall "picture" of a coin, and it is well to study each coin in an effort to determine as best as possible which particular influence is having the sharpest effect on that coin. Each point affects the others as we have shown, so each must be evaluated individually, and as a group.

BUYING DOLLARS

There is an old, and well honored axiom in the coin hobby, which is "Buy the book before you buy the coin." When we quote it, we add one thing: Buy the book before you buy — or sell — the coin, a point that we will also dwell on in the chapter devoted to selling your coins.

The underlying message of this sage piece of advice is that it is dangerous to buy before you know enough to avoid making a bad buy. It is the same problem that you encounter when you go out and make any major purchase. Investment coins are just such a major purchase, because there is a great deal riding on your decision to buy a given coin.

Many of you are going to say, "Fine, but I don't have the time to spend learning all these things. I simply have some money that I need to get working for me." If that is the case, and you aren't just evading the need to learn what you are doing, then you are going to have to rely on someone to do the buying and selling for you. Your local coin dealer is one of the best possible sources of assistance and professional advice on your investments and, in many cases, will be the first person you are likely to turn to.

If you can't spend the time to learn the ins and outs of buying coins, at least take time to check out the person you intend to get some advice from. Is the dealer well known in the community? Does he have a permanent shop and how long has he been in business? Will he give you references? These, and a host of other questions, should be answered because you are hiring this person to serve as your investment advisor. Since this person is going to be closely acquainted with your financial affairs and spending your money for you, you need to know some things about him as well.

A local dealer is readily available for advice, suggestions and very often either has, or can get, the coins you should be investing in. If you happen to be in a town or rural area where there are no coin dealers, you will probably need to conduct your buying by phone or letter. There are hundreds of very reputable coin dealers across the country who do most or all of their business by mail and with a little searching you should be able to find one with whom you can do business. An increasing number of coin dealers are working especially with investors, often with established investment programs, scaled to your investment needs. Very often these programs will involve a fixed sum per month that the investment advisor places in coins that he is recommending, sometimes even working on an installment plan, so that you are able to purchase an expensive coin with payments spread over several months.

There are always a few bad apples in any industry and the coin hobby is no exception, so don't be taken in by flamboyant ads, screaming headline promises or just plain confidence game tactics that can cost you dearly. One of the first mistakes you can make is to respond to an ad in the "lay" press, even in some of the highly touted business publications. Although there are a few legitimate coin dealers who advertise in financial publications, the majority are usually offering overpriced coins that are worthless to either the collector or investor.

Your first step should be to get one or more of the coin hobby periodicals which we have listed in the chapter on recommended reading. There is a very important reason for this single piece of advice. These publications carefully screen their advertisers, and deny space to the con artists and the fast buck swindlers who infest the lay press. If you see an ad in a publication devoted exclusively to coin collecting and investing, you can be reasonably sure that the dealer's activities are at least within the law, even if his coins are overpriced and his investment advice unsound.

One of the best ways to check an ad for honesty is to read it. If the coin is described in glowing terms, but nowhere is the A.N.A. grade stated, this should arouse doubt. There are frequent ads for silver dollars, "nearly" or "over" one hundred years old. You will see that they offer you a small group of coins for a price usually two or three times that charged at a legitimate coin dealer's shop — IF you could determine what the grade of the coin is. The reader is led to believe that these coins are "UNCS," though this is not actually claimed. Usually they prove to be "VF" or less.

Responding to an ad like that is very likely to get you a set of coins that have been harshly cleaned, polished or buffed — which is known as "whizzing" the coin, from the expression "Gee whiz, what a beautiful coin." The coins you get, even if properly graded, are nearly valueless to the collector, certainly so to the investor. Obviously a lot of people are not aware of this because companies with important sounding names continue to run their ads in newspapers, national tabloids, and various magazines. Another warning is to avoid coins that have been "doctored" by gold plating them, at gold plated prices.

Another good piece of buying advice would be to proceed with caution when you do pick a dealer to work with. Start out by buying a few coins, even if the pressure of a sharply advancing market is urging a major investment right now. Check your purchases carefully. Ask for a second opinion by taking the coins to some well informed but impartial person. If you find that they are properly graded, reasonably priced, and as represented, then you can begin to step up your purchases, but caution should never be wholly abandoned. One of the commonest scams is to fulfill the first few orders correctly, and then when the con artist has gained your confidence, unload overpriced, overgraded coins on you.

All of this is going to cost you money. Very often you may have to pay for an appraisal of your coins, if you are not buying or selling through a dealer who gives you an opinion on coins bought from someone else. You are in the position of having to find not one but two honest men, either of whom could be cleaning your pockets. You can save yourself some, most or even all of this expense by learning to grade your own coins, learning to use price charts to go with the grades and learning when and how to buy.

Common advice from investment dealers is to buy when the market is falling, sell when it is rising. Try and estimate the peaks, sell just before the market tops, buy just before it bottoms, or just after it bottoms and starts back up. Coin prices are often much like stocks or other commodities. They may fluctuate fairly widely, but they very definitely do run in cycles. It will pay you to sit down and study these cycles and take advantage of them. Every time you buy, you are paying what amounts to the retail value of a coin, and every time you sell, you are receiving the wholesale value. In order to profit, you must let the marketplace work for you, and push the price up enough so that you can recover the premium, or difference between the retail and wholesale prices.

Coin prices are not fixed prices in most cases. Almost any dealer will bargain with you on the price of a coin. Rarely are sales made at the exact catalog price. If a coin is in especially good condition, it will be priced well above catalog, with a correspondingly lower price for a coin ranking a shade below average for that grade. Catalog prices should never be considered as hard and fast. They are intended merely as a guide to average prices all over the country for a coin in the approximate grade listed. Expect, and be willing to pay, the current market price for the coin you buy, and avoid any coin at a "bargain" or "fire sale" price, since no reputable dealer could afford to sell a coin for less than it is really worth. When you see a coin offered that you are interested in, check the description and grade against a CURRENT price guide or catalog to see if it is within reason. We suggest "The Official Blackbook Price Guide of United States Coins" by The House of Collectibles, 201 East 50th Street, NY, NY 10022. It is available for only $3.95 plus $1 postage and handling.

One of the most common mistakes that beginners in the coin hobby make is to price coins on the basis of an outdated catalog or price guide. Last year's catalog is obsolete and the figures tell you little about the present values of coins. So many times a collector or investor will — reluctantly — spend money for a catalog, and then base all his buy and sell decisions for the next decade on that one edition. This is not to say that books or catalogs or price guides should be thrown away as soon as the newest one comes out. The smart investor is always comparing today's prices with those of yesterday, five or ten years ago, watching for the trend, watching for some coin that is underpriced and ripe for a sharp move upward.

When you get a piece of good advice, or spot a potential investment coin, act. Very often a published comment from an authority will in itself push the price of a coin upward as readers rush to buy that coin. If you find a coin that is lagging, yet has other factors going for it, like fairly low mintage or a high destruction rate, the time to buy is now, and not after it has shot up. All of us are highly expert at looking back at coins that have doubled or tripled in the last year or two, but few learn to spot the coins that are going to do this NEXT year. Even fewer have the courage or capital to follow through, so you as an investor have an advantage if you learn what to look for and are willing to put your money down on your decision.

One more thought on references. Some of the books we list in Recommended Reading are written by coin dealers, from their own point of view. While the advice given is legitimate, it is often designed to create interest in coins the dealer is selling, rather than from a standpoint of strict impartiality. Accordingly, you should read with an open mind, and compare advice while considering the source. Our personal view centers around the ethics of placing ourselves in the position of saying that a given coin is worth so much, and then selling it to you at OUR price. For this reason, the publisher never entered into the buying and selling of coins, considering it a conflict of interest. There are several very good books on the market written by dealers, since very often they are the only ones with a sufficiently complete knowledge of the topic to write a book, but we will again remind you to always consider the source of any advice that you see or hear.

BULLION OR NUMISMATIC VALUE

A very important distinction that the investor needs to learn is the difference between the bullion value of a coin and the numismatic, or collector value. It is something that we mention frequently throughout this book because the two values are often substantially different.

There are three often used terms in connection with numismatic value that are essential to know and understand. They are "common date," "semi-key" and "key" as applied to coins. The three terms generally relate to the total mintage for that particular date and mint, although there are exceptions based on some of the other factors we have mentioned that relate to rarity. For the most part, you will consider these terms as directly related to total mintage.

A "common date" coin is one which has a high mintage and high survival rate. These are coins frequently bought and sold in bulk — by the bag — by the investor and are often the coins which are listed in price guides to give you a general idea of what a "type coin" of that design is worth. A little study of price guides and catalogs will show you that the majority of coins for a given series usually carry identical values. Silver coins (and gold) in the common date category are frequently sold for their bullion value, when the condition is sub-standard.

A "semi-key" coin is one with a lower mintage, often much lower than the common dates. They are rarely priced near the bullion value, usually have a higher value than a common date and fall in the scarce to rare area as far as numbers available. Typically, where you might be offered a roll of a common date, you might not find solid-date rolls of semi-keys.

"Key" coins are normally those with very low mintages, survival rates, and usually very high prices. They are almost invariably the coins in a given series which have the lowest mintage for that series. Some series may have only a single key coin. Varieties are not usually considered as key coins, although they actually fit the definition and are very often low mintage/high value coins. This is one of the reasons why we have attempted to list some of the varieties in this book, so that you will be aware of some of the important variety keys which most other books have ignored. Key coins most often fall into the "rare," "very rare" or "unique" categories. There are never enough of them around to fully satisfy collector and investor demand and the price structure reflects this.

As you can readily see, mintage and survivorship are two very important points in the relative value of a silver coin. This is translated in the marketplace to values that affect most of the grades you are likely to find. Common date coins in the lower grades almost never sell above the bullion value, or what the smelter can afford to pay for a coin to melt in his furnace and still be able to profit from the resulting bullion. (Coins struck before about 1870 are an exception to this statement.) This is frequently referred to as the "melt" value, which of course is lower than the quoted daily figures for the "spot" price of silver, or what refined silver is selling for on the spot market.

For this reason, the investor is rarely interested in the lower grade common date, known in the trade as "junk" bullion, although there are profits to be made in handling large quantities. These profits depend on having ready access to the market, so that you can get in and out (buy and sell) at a moment's notice.

In most cases, unless there is an extremely high mintage, top grade common date coins will bring at least double the bullion value. Top grade coins always demand a premium and, as we pointed out, silver dollar prices have stayed above the bullion content, in most cases, even for the lower condition grades. Our frequent advice is to buy the highest grade you can get, but don't ignore the lower grades if you can't find the higher ones.

Semi-key and key coin prices, even for the lowest grades, are substantially higher than the bullion value and, in almost all cases they will not reflect the daily fluctuations in the bullion market. Obviously, when we get a boom like that in early 1980, this puts a "floor" under the semi-keys and keys and tends to push them up at an accelerated pace. The rarer coins are so far above spot prices that only a major value realignment would force bullion prices up to that point. You can be well assured that semi-key and key coin prices will stay far above the bullion value.

There are two schools of thought, or at least two factors that play an important part in the relationship between bullion and numismatic prices. One is that key and semi-key coins "pull" the lower grade, lower value, coins up with them as they rise. The other is that the vast bulk of the common date coins exerts a "push" under the keys and semi-keys, so that as the common date values gain momentum, they ignite the rarer coins.

There are times when one or the other of these factors is probably responsible for what is happening to prices, and others, when both are at work. There are also times when the market will perform in a manner that defies explanation.

With every boom there's a bust. We would be negligent in our responsibility if we didn't warn you of some of the hazards and some of the possible problems that you can encounter. 1980 was a classic example of a cycle that went 360 degrees. For a brief moment, silver exceeded $52 an ounce on the spot market and then suddenly beat an alarming retreat. Investors who had bought in on the way up watched in horror as silver prices rapidly sank far below what they had paid. Little more than a year later, silver prices were back down at the $10 level.

In this kind of a situation, you are likely to find that there is "no market" for your investments. Nobody is willing to buy in a falling market, especially in large quantities, so your regular channels are often closed until the market has stabilized again. Obviously, as with any investment, you should not put yourself in the position of having all your capital tied up in one direction. We have felt that the $10 figure is about as low as silver can get, and we have been predicting that it will climb to the $100 level for some time. The investor who is willing to ride out fluctuations and wait for the market to climb again should ultimately recover his money and make a profit. Frequently we are approached for advice about selling silver and gold holdings, a topic we will discuss in the next chapter.

Probably quite a few more investors get involved in silver coins at the bullion value level than do at the numismatic value. Those with numismatic investments — semi-key and key coins — have seen nothing worse than a slight drop, in some instances even a climb in values for their coins, while the common date market declined disturbingly. It is certainly possible to diversify your investments within the framework of the silver dollar. Learning how to do this is an important step toward security for your whole investment program.

SELLING DOLLARS

When you come right down to it, your dollar investments are no more than dead weight until you sell them. Learning to sell at the right time is just as important — some may think more important — than learning when to buy. In the last chapter we noted the problems that many investors faced when the silver market dropped so fast in 1980 that there was no place where you could sell your silver — nobody who was willing to buy it at even a fair discount from "spot." The investor needs to recognize and, if possible, avoid that kind of situation.

If this kind of thing happened only to silver or silver coins, then we would have no purpose in writing a book for investors, since nobody would want to risk money in one hazardous way when all the others were safe. Even a rudimentary knowledge of other forms of investment shows that similar or perhaps even greater hazards abound in just about any kind of investment. If it were not for the fact that there is a streak of the born gambler in almost everyone, we wouldn't invest in anything. Investing has often been compared to a game of cards — if you know the game, and are holding the right cards, you are likely to win.

One of the benefits of investing in silver dollars is that with limited exceptions over which you have no control, there is a market for either small quantities or large quantities, so when it comes time to sell you can usually find a willing buyer. The key issue is when do you want to sell, more than where, because of this ready market.

If you buy a silver dollar today for $15 and sell it tomorrow for $16, you have made a profit, and can be considered an investor. If you buy 1000 silver dollars (a bag) today, and sell them five, ten or twenty years from now, you may sell each $15 coin for ten or a hundred times what you paid for it, almost certainly more than you paid as the price trend on all coins is upward. We like to consider investing as just such a long term commitment to your holdings. The in and out investor is more of a trader than an investor and, while profits can be made, this usually winds up as a nearly full time "job" with constant market watching and a great deal of paperwork.

We have pointed out some of the differences in bullion value and numismatic value. It is important that you as an investor know these differences. Our overall recommendation is that you expand, broaden and diversify your investing as you gain knowledge.

We have never suggested, and do not now suggest, that all your money should be in dollars. They should be just one of several forms of investment. This is a tip that many major corporations have long since learned, as you will note when you see some of the broad areas involved in diversification. We also have been saying for some time that unless you need the money, you should not be overly anxious to cash in your silver dollars and other coin investments. This advice holds for most other investments as well.

"But, when DO I sell?" is the question that comes next. We don't pretend to have a direct answer. It will require a bit of judgment on your part, to evaluate trends or market conditions that might prevail in the future. We will give some suggestions on strategy.

Assuming that you have tried to pick coins to invest in that are "wanted" and that you have kept them in as good condition as they were received, you should not have too much trouble finding a buyer. Again we turn to the local coin dealer, who may have originally sold you the coins. He is in business to make a profit, so unless it is a forced sale, you should recognize this spread between sell and buy prices and wait until retail values have climbed high enough to absorb the dealer's profit margin. A rare coin will perhaps call for approaching a major coin dealer, perhaps even a coin auctioneer, who may charge you as much as 20% of the sale price. Frequently, an auction sale is likely to draw a much higher price than you could otherwise get for it.

One of the best pieces of advice we can offer is to do business only with recognized individuals, with a permanent place of business. Whether selling or buying, you are taking a serious risk when you deal with the type who rents a motel room for a couple of days and runs flamboyant ads offering prices "up to" certain amounts. The prices offered are frequently below, or well below those offered by permanent dealers in the same area, and may not even approach those quoted in the ads. These fly-by-night buyers fast-talk you into dropping the grade of your coins (to add to their already substantial profit margin), or claim that the bullion market has "dropped" so they can't afford to pay the ad prices. With luck, these "travelling" dealers may give you honest value for your coins, but if you have a complaint, they will prove elusive to find.

The same advice goes for two other sources of coins that the small investor especially may run into. One is the local flea market. The other is the local auction. Unless you are ranked in the expert class, or know a great deal about the particular coins that you want to buy, a flea market is just as hazardous to your investments as a motel room dealer. You are most likely to encounter overgraded, overpriced coins being sold by sharpies who deliberately prey on the uninformed collector, or by fellow collectors who know even less about their coins than the fast-buck artists. Many legitimate coin dealers got their start at flea markets, but usually they didn't open a shop until they had "practiced" their trade on a number of flea market customers.

If you are anxious to sell, a local auction may be the place to do it, assuming that the commission rates aren't exorbitant, but they are about the last place I would ever recommend buying a coin. It has been our experience with numerous local auctions that the coins sold almost invariably are overbid, and frequently there isn't even a pretense of grading or quality standards. You are buying "as is," and have even less recourse than from a travelling dealer. The chance of picking up one, or a quantity of counterfeit coins is very great, particularly if a "guest" consignor is involved. Very often con men will "dump" a quantity of coins at a local auction house to be sold at the next auction, get a cash advance for them and be far away by the time the auction is held. In the case of counterfeit coins there is almost no chance of recovering your money.

The flea market or the local auction is likely to be a source of highly polished, harshly cleaned, "whizzed" coins that are not acceptable to the numismatic trade. The average person who wants to sell a few coins they have around the house can think only of cleaning and polishing them to "improve" their looks and (they think) their value. Unfortunately, there are many collectors and investors, with long experience in the hobby, who persist in cleaning coins. We know of one "collector" who specializes in silver dollars and who has, over the years, handled thousands upon thousands of them, and CLEANED EVERY ONE HE GOT HIS HANDS ON! The extent of destruction he has committed is astronomical. We had another "collector" come to us with a large quantity of coins, ranging from silver dollars to cents, that he had put in a *rock polishing tumbler.* The bullion coins were salvageable for their silver content, but the rest were worthless.

Needless to say, if you refuse to learn not to clean or polish your coins, you are going to run into serious problems, and probably serious losses when you get around to selling them. Very likely you will run into some hostility from potential buyers who know better than to buy cleaned coins, and who may suspect you of trying to cheat them by offering such coins for sale.

Whether selling or buying, shop around. If you have a number of coins to sell, check as many dealers as you can to find out who is paying the best price. This requires a bit of planning, as it must be done in a relatively short period of time so that all the quotes that involve common date dollars are based on the same, or nearly the same, "spot price." We don't necessarily recommend buying at the lowest possible price, but certainly, other factors being equal, we would urge you to get the highest obtainable price when you sell. If you have any serious doubts, based on your knowledge of the coins, delay selling until they can be resolved.

When buying you have the problem of making sure that you get the grade you pay for. Once you are certain of the grade, selling almost comes easy. If the dealer recognizes his own grade, or agrees with the grading, you will get what the coin is worth. The one precaution you need to take is to get the agreed-on price in writing, especially if you are selling a large quantity of common date dollars that the dealer is passing on to a broker. This assures that the price is "locked in" at the agreed-upon level and will not fluctuate further while the coins are in transit. You may regret doing this if the bullion price should start upward, but it seems more logical to guarantee yourself a profit, even if modest, than risk possible loss.

If you do decide that you want a dealer to handle the sale of your coins by mail, there are a couple of additional precautions. You can't just dump the coins in a box and mail them. First, you need an agreement from the dealer to accept them, preferably in writing so that there can be no question. A little known quirk in the postal laws allows anyone receiving any unsolicited item through the mail to accept it as a gift and relieves him of any responsibility to return it or pay for it. However, when a published buying ad states "ship for offer," or words to that effect, this law does not apply.

Ask any dealer for shipping instructions. He has had experience with the hazards of mailing coins, and can tell you exactly how they should be packed, wrapped, and insured. Always include a copy of a detailed list of the coins, denomination, date, mint mark and grade, so that if the shipment is lost you will be able to document your claim, and of course, so that the dealer can identify your shipment and any agreement made about it. This is a good practice to get into, even if you take the coins to a dealer just around the corner.

A common practice when buying is to attempt to pick off the best pieces and leave the lower grade, common date or "trash" coins. When you are a seller, you need to decide exactly what you are going to sell, and plan to resist any attempts to "high grade" the coins you are offering. Sometimes you can turn this to your advantage, if you have a few "duds" that you want to dispose of, by offering to include them in an "all or none" deal. If you know your prices, you can tell if the dealer is discounting the better pieces to offset the others.

One possible method of disposing of your investments is to sell them to other investors at "retail" prices. An ad in your local paper often will turn up eager buyers who are willing to take your coins at prices near or very near the current book values. This takes time and the expense of the ad, plus the hazard of strangers becoming aware of your investments. There are certain precautions you should take, such as avoiding the publication of your home address or phone number and examination of your coins on neutral ground, such as at the bank where you keep them.

Some dealers will also take coins on consignment rather than just buying them outright. It is a matter you should discuss with your coin dealer, to determine the possible advantages in waiting a bit for your money, as the dealer may offer you better terms, but the list of coins involved and the agreement must be in writing to avoid future problems. Also, the dealer's estimate of the length of time needed to sell your coins could prove over-optimistic.

Our last piece of advice is: back to the book. Remember, we quoted "Buy the book before you buy — or sell — the coin." Before you sell your coins, check them again to make sure that you didn't accidentally undergrade a coin, or let a variety slip away at the price of the normal coin. You can get hurt just as badly by selling a coin for a lot less than the value, as if you bought it for far more than the value, so never neglect a final check before making a sale. Don't let someone rush you.

DOLLARS AS COLLECTOR'S ITEMS

Very often throughout this book, we refer either to the collector or the investor, or both in the same sentence, primarily because both the collector and the investor have some of the same goals in mind. The underlying motive of many collectors is profit, although there certainly are dedicated collectors interested only in the thrill of the hunt or in studying and exhibiting his coins. There are a broad range of motivations between the two extremes of course, but perhaps the basic difference between the collector and the investor is that the collector derives some pleasure from ownership of coins while an investor may be entirely passive to their charms. The investor will purchase a coin for which he feels no emotion, simply for its profit-making potential. Most investors are about as fond of their coins as are stock investors of the paper that stock certificates are printed on.

We certainly are not implying that one reason is better than another for being involved in collecting or investing in dollars. We refer to coins as a hobby very frequently and to some this is certainly the significance of putting a collection together. It is purely a form of relaxation. The investor can treat dollars in the same way, investing not so much for the quick profit or financial advantage, as the diversion of concentrating on a topic, studying it, learning as much as possible about it, and learning to enjoy the fruits of that knowledge.

In previous chapters we have touched on some of the important facts that both the investor and collector should know, such as differences between common dates, key and semi-key coins. We feel that because there are so many collectors already in the hobby — an estimated 28 million people in the United States collect or have an interest in coins — that anyone seriously interested in investing should also consider the possibilities of enjoying some of the benefits of collecting coins as well. It is no crime for an investor to enjoy his coins.

In the coin hobby, anyone who gathers a group of coins together without any particular pattern or reason is generally referred to as an "accumulator" rather than a collector. Collecting implies that the coins are being put into a logical order of some kind with some basic purpose in mind. For example, a person who has a bank box full of a thousand unrelated coins would fall in the category of an accumulator. His neighbor, with a set of Peace dollars, one of each date and mint, would be considered a collector, because by putting together the set, or part of a set of a given series or denomination, he has obviously decided on some plan and is carrying it through. Whether he has done this for pleasure or profit would call for further inquiry.

Some collectors take life easy. They buy a coin now and then, go to a lot of coin shows, visit coin dealers regularly, and once in a while make a purchase when they spot a coin that fits their plan. Other collectors move at a feverish pace, make a near-obsession of the hobby, and cannot rest until they have every elusive coin in the series or denomination they are specializing in. Again there is a broad range of collecting activity between these two extremes. Specialty is perhaps a key word here, because the average collector who carries out the goals he has set for his collection becomes something of a specialist in the process.

The numismatic hobby includes an astounding array of collectibles, ranging from coins through medals, tokens, paper money, checks, bonds, stocks and even such exotics as food stamps and rationing tokens. The paper collectors often are separated from the coin areas, but all fall under the general umbrella of anything having to do with money, barter or trade. We know of no single person anywhere in the hobby who is expert or specializes in all areas of numismatics, but there are thousands upon thousands who are specializing in their own particular area of the hobby, and many of them may be considered expert on their topic.

Just in coins alone, it takes a specialist to handle U.S. coins, the coins of many individual foreign countries, ancient coins, varieties or any of a hundred other subdivisions. A number of people have spent decades or even most of their adult lives studying and collecting the U.S. dollars, or even a single part of them, such as the Morgan series.

Obviously, if this were a shallow topic, there would be nothing in dollar collecting to attract and sustain this kind of interest, especially among the caliber of specialists who have and are working with dollars. We cite this not as a warning to scare you off or give the impression that everything has already been learned but rather as an invitation to get involved.

There are still many unanswered questions about the dollars, still research to do, still new varieties to be found. The investor who wants to become a collector and get more deeply involved has plenty of virgin land to explore. Collecting skills can help the person interested in investing, because these are the skills that add to total knowledge of the topic, and add to the value of the knowledge. The better you know coins, the better you can invest in them.

There are no particular barriers to becoming an investor-collector, other than a lack of knowledge and unwillingness to learn. We would certainly recommend broadening your interest into collecting dollars because it always adds a sense of discipline to your investing. It may create problems when you buy a coin that you would like to keep in your collection when your investing instincts tell you to sell it, but these conflicts can keep you alert both to the collecting market and the investment market. The worst that would probably happen under these circumstances is that you would not sell the coin, and it would increase further in value in the future.

Goals in most instances are much the same for the collector and the investor. The collector wants the same high quality, top grade coins that the investor wants, so in most cases one welcomes the other because the demand is what is keeping the price trends moving upward for both. The collector who has a rare coin is happy both because he owns the coin and because it is steadily gaining in value, so it adds some new dimensions to buying a coin. For many collectors the thrill is in owning a part of history. Did Thomas Jefferson handle and examine the 1794 dollar in your collection, or perhaps it was George Washington? Did this coin come from a famous collection that is noted in the history of numismatics, or was part of some event noted outside the area of numismatics? For many other collectors, the thrill of being able to exhibit a set of coins, painstakingly gathered in years of collecting, and to see the admiration and envy in the eyes of the viewer is the ultimate in goals. In addition to these intangibles, there is also the attraction of a coin's artistry, design, and the role it might have played in awakening public interest in classical art.

Collecting is certainly not for every investor. Because of some of the factors we have suggested, many investors will simply not be interested, or will not have the time to spend, preferring instead to concentrate strictly on profit and loss figures. Even then, there is still a need to be aware of the role that collector interest plays in the value of dollar investments. Most coin dealers that you are likely to encounter are collector rather than investor oriented, since most entered coin dealing after being private collectors, so you need to understand this relationship. Investing in coins, even speculation, has been around for a long time, mostly in the guise of collecting. Only in the last couple of decades has there been any serious interest in serving the needs of the investor who is not a collector.

If pride of ownership means something to you, then you are going to be interested in the special significance that dollars have for collectors. Along with this is the point that we keep emphasizing that dollars are of interest to a broad spectrum of people. Even though they do not like the coin as a medium of exchange, you will find that a surprising number of people have quantities of dollars, on occasion some rather startling amounts, which are far more than you would expect from people who profess neither a collecting interest or a desire to make money.

FORECASTING PRICE TRENDS

Someone once said, "In order to look ahead, you must look back." This suggestion has special meaning for the investor. Before you can predict with any hope of success what your dollar investments are going to do tomorrow, you must study and learn from what they have done in the past. Hindsight is the clearest form of vision, and it is one of the most powerful tools in your investment arsenal. After we discuss grading, we are going to show you, coin by coin, what some of the important coins have done in the past, and make our predictions based on their reputations, so that you may decide as to how to wisely invest your money in dollars.

A handicapper who studies past racing results for horses or dogs is much more likely to pick a winner than the person who randomly picks and then heads for the betting window. Certainly the same thing is true of coin investments. Random selections, though they sometimes proved profitable in the 1970s, would be very dangerous today. You will find of course that the temptation is to jump on the bandwagon, join the crowd with the big money dollars that have multiplied in value in the past couple of decades. Our advice includes some of those "not" coins, and perhaps even more important for the small or moderate investor, the coins that have been "sleeping" in the past and are now ready to wake up and do big things for their sponsors.

Fortunately for the investor, there are literally bales of material on silver dollars. Books, magazines, catalogs, auction sales records, numismatic newspapers, price lists, articles — enough to fill a small library. Practically every move the dollar has ever made is documented; and with a little diligence, this documentation is available to the investor. If you are serious about investing, you need to have a reference library of this kind of material, or access to one. We have suggested some of the books you will need in a later chapter. To start out, you should have the most up-to-the-minute information available. This should include a subscription to one or more of the weekly coin publications. We recommend Numismatic News. It carries a weekly "Coin Market" report which not only shows up-to-the-minute values but includes a commentary on behind-the-scenes activities that you as an investor should be aware of. Once a month the Coin Market section is expanded to include even more detailed information about all U.S. coins. Prices are computerized and updated as quickly as changes are signaled in the market place, so you are kept about as current as possible.

For a more in-depth interpretation of coin market prices we suggest "The Official Blackbook of U.S. Coins" which is a must for every coin collector. It's available from The House of Collectibles, 201 East 50th St.,

NY, NY 10022 for $3.95 plus $1 postage and handling.

Based on what we, and you, can learn about the past and present market, we both can predict with increasing accuracy how a fair number of these coins will perform. We lay no claim to infallibility, and neither should you, but the main goal is to get your prediction average over the 50-50 probability mark, and keep it there. Taking stock of the many factors that can affect value is the mark of the prudent and successful investor. Undoubtedly, some readers who have gotten this far will say, "This is not for me. It involves some measure of risk and risk frightens me. I want something where I can be sure my money is safe and will earn a guaranteed income."

For such a person, dollar investing, and almost any other form of investing other than a passbook savings account, are unsuitable. Certainly there are other safer investments, but almost without exception the return is substantially lower than from investing in dollars. Under the right circumstances, dollar investing can yield some rather astonishing returns, measured in three and four digit percentages, as you will see when we look at the "track record" of the past couple of decades. With increased knowledge and selective purchasing, the level of risk diminishes.

If you are looking for a "get rich quick" opportunity, dollar investing is also not for you. Windfall profits are occasionally made when the market goes into one of its skyrocket leaps. But these, being very unpredictable, should not be the core of your investment strategy. You can find yourself in serious financial trouble by expecting too much too soon. If you merely accumulated dollars and other silver coins over the past decade, without regard to mintages, grade or past performance, you very likely would have made a profit — if you sold at the height of the bullion boom a year ago, as did thousands of haphazard investors who suddenly found themselves with substantial values in silver holdings.

You are going to receive a lot of advice about investing in dollars. Very often the advice is going to be conflicting. There are numerous books, dozens of newsletters, and various tip sheets and other literature for investors. In the final analysis, the decision is up to you. You are the one who must sift through this material, see how it fits your particular situation, since no two investors have exactly the same situation to contend with, and then act. The decision to act is certainly going to be influenced by many different factors. Don't get in the habit of following a single prophet, or being unduly influenced by zesty ad copy. A lot of investment analysts don't dig deep enough. They tend to appraise the coin without appraising pressures it might be under from various groups of buyers and sellers. It should also be kept in mind that world events have a day to day effect on the value of your investments.

For example, one of the "unknown" factors in dollar investing, to cite a single point out of many, is the number of dollars being held by foreign banks. Few people realize that in many foreign countries, coins are a prime commodity sold by banks, often far more than in coin shops as we know them. We happen to know that the German Central Bank has thousands upon thousands of silver dollars in their vaults, so many that you can find some of the scarcer semi-key and key coins by the the roll, whereas it is nearly impossible to find even a handful of examples here in this country. Around the world, a startling number of people and institutions hold American dollar coins as investments, hoards, accumulations and in collections. These factors are very often overlooked by almost everyone who has any connection with coins in this country. One of the wealthiest countries in the world in silver bullion is India where literally tons of the metal are being hoarded. A percentage of this is in the form of dollars that have escaped the melting pot. If silver had remained at the $52 level for any length of time a substantial percentage of this hoard would probably have come on the market. As we have predicted that silver will climb in the near future to the $100 mark, we may see this happen, with a corresponding effect on the common date silver coin market.

We have commented several times in our writing that merely a "sneeze" in Washington could have a 20 or 30 point effect on the stock market. The same thing is true of dollar investing, but the sneeze may be elsewhere. We advise the investor not to limit his reading and learning to the standard references but to be attentive to what is happening in the world. World events definitely influence your investments. But, do not develop anxiety over this and reach the point of selling your coins in preparation for world war and market collapse whenever disturbing news is published.

GRADING

Grading — the most feared, and often the most misunderstood, area of coin investing and collecting! To put it mildly, grading is one skill that an investor must learn for his own protection. You will commonly encounter dealers or collectors who will "overgrade" when selling and "undergrade" when buying. This takes on added significance when you understand that a difference of two grades — one each way in a round of buying and selling — may make a difference of thousands of dollars in the value of a rare coin.

We have mentioned several grades. There are other basic grades and the American Numismatic Association adds several numeric grades in between. These occur at the high end of the grading scale because of the necessity of showing differences between very similar graded coins, one of which is slightly better than the other. Slight grade differences can make whopping value differences.

"Why bother?" This is the first question asked by investors and collectors when they are confronted with the complex grading system. Really, what difference does it make whether a 100 year old coin is worn or as shiny as the day it was struck? There are numerous reasons, but one among them stands out as a primary criteria upon which coin collecting is based: fine condition contributes to rarity.

By this we mean that any coin struck for circulation tends to circulate and examples of the coin that did not circulate, remaining unworn and undamaged, are far rarer than the simple mintage figures indicate. A coin with a mintage of over a million may exist for the collector only in a handful of examples that truly grade MS-60 or Uncirculated. This is why you will find when reading coin price charts that low grade coins usually bring only a tiny fraction of the price of a top grade coin. Not only aren't they as physically appealing, they're more common. You will also frequently find that there are NO KNOWN EXAMPLES of a top grade coin for a given date and mint. All of them went into circulation and nobody bothered to save one in its pristine state so far as is presently known.

This is also why you will find that almost every expert on investing in and collecting coins will recommend that you buy the highest grade possible. The higher grades advance more rapidly in value than lower grades and this difference in the rate of increase becomes more pronounced with each passing year.

We have stressed circulation strikes in these statements, since proof coins generally are found in much higher percentages of the original mintage, mainly because they were intended to be collector coins and not circulate. It is usually difficult to compare circulation and proof mintage figures and arrive at appropriate estimates of availability.

Grading primarily has to do with the amount of wear that the coin has received. Included in wear are abrasion, dents, scratches, nicks, and other possible forms of routine or accidental damage. Intentional damage is another matter. The coin which has been deliberately scarred with a sharp instrument, holed for making into jewelry or testing the content or bent is automatically going to be bought or sold for its bullion value only. The wise investor would never buy a coin that has any deliberate damage, even if it's a rare "key" coin. The rarest coin will not appreciate enough to make it a prospective investment if grossly damaged. However, a collector might well buy such a coin, since it represents an inexpensive way to get a key coin, which he can someday replace with one in better condition if his finances improve.

Few dealers make a practice of buying such damaged and holed coins, or coins that have solder on them resulting from the coin being attached to a piece of jewelry, and skillfully repairing them. The honest dealer will list such repairs in his description of the coin, but you will be better off in the long run to avoid any coin that has been "repaired" since it is not a good or wise investment, even at a "filler" price.

The Official ANA Grading Standards are the accepted basis for almost all of the buying and selling of U.S. coins, so it will pay you to purchase a copy of "The Official ANA Grading Standards for United States Coins." It is available from almost any coin dealer and, if used with care and patience, settles all arguments about the grade of nearly any coin. The grades you will most commonly find listed are: About Good, Good, Very Good, Fine, Very Fine, Extremely Fine, About Uncirculated and Uncirculated. "Proof" is not a grade, but a condition or way of minting.

The standards are not identical, since each series had its own peculiarities, and often, as we noted before, there are significant differences in the way coins were struck at the different mints. Philadelphia has always made all of the dies for the branch mints and the complaint has been made by several authorities that generally poorer quality dies found their way to the branch mints (probably intentionally). Combined with sometimes lower quality planchets, they yielded coins which were not equal to the higher quality Philadelphia product. It is an interesting aside that even today there is a considerable amount of rivalry between the minting facilities and it is a topic that officials at the various mints will only comment on privately, or "off the record." Today, however, any such rivalry is not likely to result in coins of noticeably different quality.

What the investor needs to do is follow through on each series and take note of the specific wear points, which are usually the highest points of the relief design. By learning them, you can become as adept as the veteran dealer who grades and values a coin after a few seconds' glance.

This raises another vital point, and another rule: Never buy — or sell — a coin without first examining it with at least a 10X lens. We are talking about a magnifying lens, which can come in a variety of sizes and strengths. "10X" means that the lens will magnify the image 10 times at optimum clarity. The ANA standards call for a 10X lens so that is the accepted MINIMUM. The serious investor will also want a 3X to 5X for general scanning, and a 25X lens for close inspection of a coin for possible alteration or counterfeiting. The very advanced investor will want a 20X-40X stereo microscope to double check all his coins. This used to be a rather exclusive tool of the serious researcher, but is rapidly reaching the point of being considered standard equipment for anyone who spends a good deal of money on coins.

You will find that use of good magnification devices will give you a distinct advantage in a quarter or more of the transactions you make, as you will sometimes be buying from persons who have neglected to make more than a naked-eye examination. Trying to "eyeball" a coin calls for much keener than normal vision, so don't ever depend on the unaided eye to spot defects, wear points, "whizzing" or possibly a valuable variety. For that very reason, we stress the lens check when selling, to make sure you don't sell something you may have underestimated and above all, to make sure that the grade you have marked on the coin holder is correct.

We don't recommend tongs for holding a coin, as they are often awkward, and interfere with thorough examination of the coin. Best bet is to simply hold the coin between two fingers — but ONLY by the edge. NEVER pick up a coin with your fingers on the flat surfaces. The coin must be tilted and turned to get the light exactly where you want it, so we recommend avoiding devices which only allow examination of the coin by looking straight down at it.

Whenever possible, leave the coin in its holder but don't sacrifice a good look at the total surface for sake of leaving the coin in the holder. The main purpose of the holder is to protect the coin and whenever it is out of the holder it is vulnerable to damage from accident, so avoid as much *unnecessary* handling as possible. It is always a good idea when showing someone your coins to make sure that the coin is secured firmly in the holder, as most non-collectors are likely to either grasp the coin firmly by the flat surfaces — or drop it when you hand it to them. A drop from waist height to a tile or masonry floor is usually enough to drop an MS-60 coin a full grade as well. A tumble to a wood floor is less harmful, while that to a carpeted floor may cause no injury.

Here are the things to look for in grading U.S. dollars, divided by series:

THE "FLOWING HAIR" DOLLARS
MINT STATE (*Absolutely no trace of wear.*)

MS-70 (Perfect Uncirculated)
A flawless coin exactly as it was minted, with no trace of wear or injury. Must have full mint luster and brilliance or light toning. Any unusual planchet, die or striking traits must be described.

MS-65 (Choice Uncirculated)

No trace of wear; nearly as perfect as MS-70 except for some small blemish. Has full mint luster but may be unevenly toned or lightly fingermarked. A few small nicks or adjustment file marks may be present.

MS-60 (Typical)

A strictly Uncirculated coin with no trace of wear, but with blemishes more obvious than for MS-65. May lack full mint luster, and surface may be dull, spotted, or heavily toned.

CHECK POINTS: For signs of abrasion, look at high points of bust, shoulder and hair above forehead. Eagle's breast, head and top edges of wings. Shallow or weak spots in the relief are usually caused by improper striking and not wear.

ABOUT UNCIRCULATED *(Small trace of wear visible on highest points.)*

AU-55 (Choice)

OBVERSE: Only a trace of wear shows on highest points of hair above forehead.
REVERSE: A trace of wear shows on breast. Three-quarters of the mint luster is still present.

AU-50 (Typical)

OBVERSE: Traces of wear show on hair above and beside forehead.
REVERSE: Traces of wear show on breast and head. Half of the mint luster is still present.

EXTREMELY FINE *(Very light wear on only the highest points.)*

EF-45 (Choice)

OBVERSE: Slight wear shows on high points of hair from forehead to neck. Very light wear at eyebrow, shoulder and bust line. Stars fully detailed.
REVERSE: High points of wing, breast and head are lightly worn. Lines in feathers are clearly defined. Part of the mint luster is still present.

EF-40 (Typical)

OBVERSE: Wear shows on hair from forehead to neck, and lightly on the cheek and bust. Lightly worn at neck line in spots. Stars fully detailed.
REVERSE: High points of eagle are worn, but each detail is clearly defined. Head, wings and breast are lightly worn. Traces of mint luster can be seen.

VERY FINE *(Light to moderate even wear. All major features are sharp.)*

VF-30 (Choice)

OBVERSE: Three-quarters of flowing hair details show. Hair above forehead is worn but has some bold features. Parts of star centers, eyebrow and ear are very weak.
REVERSE: Feathers are worn but more than half of the wing details are visible. Some of the details in head and breast are clear unless weakly struck.

VF-20 (Typical)

OBVERSE: Half of the details still show in hair. Eyebrow, ear and bust are worn but bold. Parts of shoulder are smooth. Every letter and star is plainly visible. Star centers are nearly flat.
REVERSE: Head and breast are worn, but some feathers are visible. Half of details in wings and tail are clear.

FINE *(Moderate to heavy even wear. Entire design clear and bold.)*

F-12 (Fine)
OBVERSE: Some details show in hair ends and below ear. All letters, date and stars are visible. The ear and eye are clear. Hair at top of forehead is outlined.
REVERSE: Some feathers are visible in body, wings and tail. Breast and head are smooth. Eye is visible. Letters in legend are worn but clear.

VERY GOOD *(Well worn. Design clear but flat and lacking details.)*

VG-8 (Very Good)
OBVERSE: Entire head is weak, and most hair details are worn smooth. Date and LIBERTY are weak but clear. Parts of the eye and ear are visible. Stars are outlines.
REVERSE: Eagle is boldly outlined with only a few details showing in wings and tail. Breast is smooth. Some letters are very weak.

GOOD *(Heavily worn. Design and legend visible but faint in spots.)*

G-4 (About Good)
OBVERSE: Entire design worn smooth with very little detail remaining. Legend, stars and date are well worn but all visible.
REVERSE: Eagle worn flat but is completely outlined. Tops of some letters are worn nearly smooth.

ABOUT GOOD *(Outlined design. Parts of date and legend worn smooth.)*

AG-3 (About Good)
OBVERSE: Head is outlined with nearly all details worn away. Date readable but very weak. Stars merging into rim.
REVERSE: Entire design flat and partially worn away.

NOTE: Examples of this design are often weakly struck, particularly on the eagle's breast and feathers. File adjustment marks are frequently seen, and are a normal part of the manufacturing process. 1794 is usually weakly stuck at date, UNITED, and stars on left side of obverse.

THE "DRAPED BUST — SMALL EAGLE" DOLLARS

MINT STATE *(Absolutely no trace of wear.)*

MS-70 (Perfect Uncirculated)
A flawless coin exactly as it was minted, with no trace of wear or injury. Must have full mint luster and brilliance or light toning. Any unusual planchet, die or striking traits must be described.

MS-65 (Choice Uncirculated)
No trace of wear; nearly as perfect as MS-70 except for some small blemish. Has full mint luster but may be unevenly toned or lightly fingermarked. A few small nicks or adjustment file marks may be present.

MS-60 (Typical)
A strictly Uncirculated coin with no trace of wear, but with blemishes more obvious than for MS-65. May lack full mint luster, and surface may be dull, spotted, or heavily toned.

CHECK POINTS: For signs of abrasion, look at high points of bust, shoulder and hair above forehead. Eagle's breast and top edges of wings. Shallow or weak spots in the relief are usually caused by improper striking and not wear.

ABOUT UNCIRCULATED *(Small trace of wear visible on highest points.)*

AU-55 (Choice)
OBVERSE: Only a trace of wear shows on highest points of hair above forehead.
REVERSE: A trace of wear shows on breast. Three-quarters of the mint luster is still present.

AU-50 (Typical)
OBVERSE: Traces of wear show on hair above and beside forehead. Drapery has trace of wear at shoulder and bust line.
REVERSE: Traces of wear show on breast and left leg. Half of the mint luster is still present.

EXTREMELY FINE *(Very light wear on only the highest points.)*

EF-45 (Choice)
OBVERSE: Slight wear shows on high points of hair from forehead to the ear. Drapery is worn at shoulder and bust line.
REVERSE: High points of wing tips, breast and left leg are lightly worn. Lines in feathers are clearly defined. Part of the mint luster is still present.

EF-40 (Typical)
OBVERSE: Wear shows on hair from forehead to ear, and lightly on the cheek and bust. Drapery lightly worn at neck line in spots.
REVERSE: High points of wings are worn, but each detail is clearly defined. Left leg and breast are lightly worn. Traces of mint luster can be seen.

VERY FINE *(Light to moderate even wear. All major features are sharp.)*

VF-30 (Choice)
OBVERSE: Three-quarters of hair details show. Hair above forehead is worn but has some bold features. Parts of drapery are worn smooth.
REVERSE: Wing edges are worn but most central details are visible. Some of the details in left leg and breast are clear unless weakly struck.

VF-20 (Typical)
OBVERSE: Half of the details still show in hair. Forehead and bust are worn but bold. Parts of drapery are smooth. Letters and star centers are plainly visible. REVERSE: Left leg and breast are worn, but some feathers are visible. About three-quarters of details in wings and tail are clear.

FINE *(Moderate to heavy even wear. Entire design clear and bold.)*

F-12 (Fine)
OBVERSE: Some details show in hair ends, curls and left of ear. All letters, date and stars are visible. The ear and eye are clear. Bust is worn with few drapery lines remaining.
REVERSE: Half the feathers are visible in wings. Breast and left leg are smooth. Letters in legend are worn but clear.

VERY GOOD *(Well worn. Design clear but flat and lacking details.)*

VG-8 (Very Good)
OBVERSE: Entire head is weak, and most hair details and drapery are worn smooth. Date and LIBERTY are weak but clear. Parts of the eye and ear are visible. Stars are outlined.

REVERSE: Eagle is boldly outlined with only a few details showing in wings. Breast and leg are smooth. Some letters are very weak. Rim is full.

GOOD *(Heavily worn. Design and legend visible but faint in spots.)*

G-4 (Good)
OBVERSE: Entire design worn smooth with very little detail remaining. Legend, stars and date are well worn but all visible.
REVERSE: Eagle worn flat and only outlined. Tops of some letters are worn nearly smooth. Rim is full.

ABOUT GOOD *(Outlined design. Parts of date and legend worn smooth.)*

AG-3 (About Good)
OBVERSE: Head is outlined with nearly all details worn away. Date readable but very weak. Stars merging into rim.
REVERSE: Entire design flat and partially worn away. Legend merges with rim.

NOTE: Examples of this design are often weakly struck, particularly on the eagle's breast and feathers. File adjustment marks are occasionly seen and are a normal part of the manufacturing process.

1796: Small date and letters. The reverse is usually weak.
1797: 7 stars right, small letters. The reverse is always weak.
1798: 15 stars. The reverse is usually weak.

THE "DRAPED BUST — HERALDIC EAGLE" DOLLARS
MINT STATE *(Absolutely no trace of wear.)*

MS-70 (Perfect Uncirculated)
A flawless coin exactly as it was minted, with no trace of wear or injury. Must have full mint luster and brilliance or light toning. Any unusual planchet, die or striking traits must be described.

MS-65 (Choice Uncirculated)
No trace of wear; nearly as perfect as MS-70 except for some small blemish. Has full mint luster but may be unevenly toned or lightly finger-marked. A few small nicks or adjustment file marks may be present.

MS-60 (Typical)
A strictly Uncirculated coin with no trace of wear, but with blemishes more obvious than for MS-65. May lack full mint luster, and surface may be dull, spotted, or heavily toned.

CHECK POINTS: For signs of abrasion, look at high points of bust, shoulder and hair above forehead. Eagle's breast, head, edges of wings and clouds. Shallow or weak spots in the motto are usually caused by improper striking and not wear.

ABOUT UNCIRCULATED *(Small trace of wear visible on highest points.)*

AU-55 (Choice)
OBVERSE: Only a trace of wear shows on highest points of hair above forehead.
REVERSE: A trace of wear shows on the clouds. Three-quarters of the mint luster is still present.

AU-50 (Typical)
OBVERSE: Traces of wear show on hair above and beside forehead. Drapery has trace of wear at shoulder and bust line.

REVERSE: Traces of wear show on breast feathers and bust line. Half of the mint luster is still present.

EXTREMELY FINE *(Very light wear on only the highest points.)*

EF-45 (Choice)

OBVERSE: Slight wear shows on high points of hair from forehead to the ear. Drapery is worn at shoulder and bust line.

REVERSE: High points of wing edges, breast feathers and clouds are lightly worn. Lines in shield are clearly defined. Part of the mint luster is still present.

EF-40 (Typical)

OBVERSE: Wear shows on hair from forehead to ear, and lightly on the cheek and bust. Drapery lightly worn at neck line in spots.

REVERSE: High points of clouds and wings are worn, but each detail is clearly defined. Head and breast are slightly worn. Lines in shield are separated. Traces of mint luster can be seen.

VERY FINE *(Light to moderate even wear. All major features are sharp.)*

VF-30 (Choice)

OBVERSE: Three-quarters of hair details show. Hair at back of head is worn but has some bold features. Parts of drapery are worn smooth.

REVERSE: Wing edges are worn but three-quarters of the central details are visible. Clouds, head and motto show wear. Horizontal shield lines worn but separated.

VF-20 (Typical)

OBVERSE: Over half of the details still show in hair. Forehead and bust are worn but bold. Parts of drapery are smooth. Letters and star centers are plainly visible.

REVERSE: Head and breast are worn, but some feathers are visible. Some lines in shield are merged together. About three-quarters of details in wings are clear. Motto is complete.

FINE *(Moderate to heavy even wear. Entire design clear and bold.)*

F-12 (Fine)

OBVERSE: Some details show in hair ends, curls and left of ear. All letters, date and stars are visible. The ear and eye are clear. Bust is worn with few drapery lines remaining.

REVERSE: Half the feathers are visible in wings. Breast and head are smooth. Letters in legend are worn but clear. Clouds and top of shield who considerable wear.

VERY GOOD *(Well worn. Design clear but flat and lacking details.)*

VG-8 (Very Good)

OBVERSE: Entire head is weak, and most hair details and drapery are worn smooth. Date and LIBERTY are weak but clear. Parts of the eye and ear are visible. Stars are outlined with some tips worn flat.

REVERSE: Eagle is boldly outlined with only a few details showing in wings. Clouds, head and top of shield are smooth. Some letters in legend are very weak; parts of motto missing. Rim is full.

GOOD *(Heavily worn. Design and legend visible but faint in spots.)*

G-4 (Good)

OBVERSE: Entire design worn smooth with very little detail remaining. Legend, stars and date are well worn but all visible.

REVERSE: Eagle worn flat and only outlined. Only half of the stars are completely outlined. Rim is full.

ABOUT GOOD (*Outlined design. Parts of date and legend worn smooth.*)

AG-3 (About Good)
OBVERSE: Head is outlined with nearly all details worn away. Date readable but very weak. Stars merging into rim.
REVERSE: Entire design flat and partially worn away. Legend merges with rim.
   NOTE: Examples of this design are often weakly struck, particularly on the motto, shield, clouds and wing feathers. File adjustment marks are occasionally seen and are a normal part of the manufacturing process.

THE GOBRECHT "PATTERN" DOLLARS
   NOTE: Grading standard for the Gobrecht "Pattern" dollars have not been established by the ANA. Reasonably accurate comparisons for grading purposes may be made using the standards for the preceeding and following series.

THE "LIBERTY SEATED" DOLLARS
MINT STATE (*Absolutely no trace of wear.*)

MS-70 (Perfect Uncirculated)
A flawless coin exactly as it was minted, with no trace of wear or injury. Must have full mint luster or light toning. Any unusual striking traits must be described.

MS-65 (Choice Uncirculated)
No trace of wear; nearly as perfect as MS-70 except for a few minute bag marks or surface mars. Has full mint luster but may be unevenly toned.

MS-60 (Typical)
A strictly Uncirculated coin with no trace of wear, but with bag marks and other abrasions more obvious than for MS-65. May have a few small rim mars and weakly struck spots. Has full mint luster but may lack brilliance, and surface may be spotted or heavily toned.
   For these coins, bag abrasions and scuff marks are considered different from circulation wear. Full mint luster and lack of any wear are necessary to distinguish MS-60 from AU-55.
   CHECK POINTS: For signs of abrasion, look at high points of right leg, breast and hair above eye. Eagle's head, beak and above eye. Weak spots in design are usually caused by striking and not wear.

ABOUT UNCIRCULATED (*Small trace of wear visible on highest points.*)

AU-55 (Choice)
OBVERSE: Only a trace of wear shows on highest points of hair above eye, breast and right leg.
REVERSE: A trace of wear shows on head, beak and above eye. Most of the mint luster is still present, although sometimes marred by light bag marks and surface abrasions.

AU-50 (Typical)
OBVERSE: Traces of wear show on knees, breast and edge of hairline. Foot is separated from sandal.

REVERSE: Traces of wear show on talons, neck, head and tips of wings. Three-quarters of the mint luster is still present. Surface abrasions and bag marks are more noticeable than for AU-55.

EXTREMELY FINE *(Very light wear on only the highest points.)*

EF-45 (Choice)

OBVERSE: Slight wear shows on high points of knees, breast and hair at forehead. Drapery is worn at shoulder and bust line. LIBERTY is sharp and scroll edges are raised.

REVERSE: High points of eagle and arrows are lightly worn. Talons are clearly defined. Neck feathers are fully separated. Half of the mint luster is still present.

EF-40 (Typical)

OBVERSE: Wear shows on knees, head and shoulder. Drapery lightly worn on neck in spots. LIBERTY is complete and scroll edges are raised.

REVERSE: High points of eagle and arrows are worn, but each detail is clearly defined. Neck feathers and talons are distinct. Partial mint luster is visible.

VERY FINE *(Light to moderate even wear. All major features are sharp.)*

VF-30 (Choice)

OBVERSE: Wear spots show on shoulder, breast, knees and legs. Neckline is weak but has some visible details in center. LIBERTY and scroll are bold. Fingers at pole are flat but separated. All lines in shield are distinct.

REVERSE: Leaves are worn but three-quarters of details are visible. Most details in feathers and talons are clear. Center of horizontal lines in shield show a trace of wear.

VF-20 (Typical)

OBVERSE: Over half of the details show in the gown. Hair, shoulder and legs are worn but bold. Every letter in LIBERTY is plainly visible. Horizontal shield lines are weak at center.

REVERSE: Three-quarters of the feathers are visible. Arrow heads and talons are worn, but some details are visible. Half the details in the leaves are clear. Horizontal lines in shield show wear.

FINE *(Moderate to heavy even wear. Entire design clear and bold.)*

F-12 (Fine)

OBVERSE: Some details show in bottom folds of gown, hair, cap and at shoulder and breast. All shield lines and letters in LIBERTY are weak but visible. Foot and sandal are separated.

REVERSE: Some details in feathers are visible. Most of shield border is visible on right side. Talons are flat but separated. Letters in legend are worn but clear. Horizontal lines in shield heavily worn. For 1866-1873 pieces, IN and ST of motto are weak.

VERY GOOD *(Well worn. Design clear but flat and lacking details.)*

VG-8 (Very Good)

OBVERSE: Entire shield is weak, and most gown details are worn smooth. Four letters in LIBERTY are clear. Rim is complete.

REVERSE: Eagle shows only bold outline. Most horizontal lines in shield are gone. Legend and rim are clear.

GOOD *(Heavily worn. Design and legend visible but faint in spots.)*

G-4 (Good)
OBVERSE: Entire design is well worn with very little detail remaining. Date is weak but visible. Shield is worn smooth. Most of rim is visible.
REVERSE: Eagle worn flat but is completely outlined. Tops of some letters are worn nearly smooth. For 1866-1873 pieces, the motto is partially visible.

ABOUT GOOD *(Outlined design. Parts of date and legend worn smooth.)*

AG-3 (About Good)
OBVERSE: Liberty is outlined with nearly all details worn away. Date readable but very weak. Stars merging into rim.
REVERSE: Entire design flat and partially worn away. Legend merges with rim.
  NOTE: Pieces dates 1840 to 1859 are often found with weakness on upper left wing.
  1857 sometimes has a weakly struck head on the obverse.
  This type is often found in prooflike condition. The 1870-CC generally looks this way when Uncirculated.

THE "TRADE" DOLLARS

MINT STATE *(Absolutely no trace of wear.)*

MS-70 (Perfect Uncirculated)
A flawless coin exactly as it was minted, with no trace of wear or injury. Must have full mint luster and brilliance or light toning. Any unusual striking traits must be described.

MS-65 (Choice Uncirculated)
No trace of wear; nearly as perfect as MS-70 except for a few minute bag marks or surface mars. Has full mint luster but may be unevenly toned.

MS-60 (Typical)
A strictly Uncirculated coin with no trace of wear, but with bag marks and other abrasions more obvious than for MS-65. May have a few small rim mars and weakly struck spots. Has full mint luster, but may lack brilliance, and surface may be spotted or heavily toned.
  For these coins, bag abrasions and scuff marks are considered different from circulation wear. Full mint luster and lack of any wear are necessary to distinguish MS-60 from AU-55.
  CHECK POINTS: For signs of wear, look at high points of head above ear, left knee and breast. Eagle's head and left wing.

ABOUT UNCIRCULATED *(Small trace of wear visible on highest points.)*

AU-55 (Choice)
OBVERSE: Trace of wear shows on head above ear, left breast and knee cap.
REVERSE: Traces of wear show on high points of left wing and head. Most of the mint luster is still present, although sometimes marred by light bag marks and surface abrasions.

AU-50 (Typical)
OBVERSE: Traces of wear show on head above ear, left breast and knee cap. Shoulder and wheat show a trace of wear.
REVERSE: Traces of wear show on head and both wings. Three-quarters

of the mint luster is still present. Surface abrasions and bag marks are more noticeable than for AU-55.

EXTREMELY FINE *(Very light wear on only the highest points.)*

EF-45 (Choice)
OBVERSE: Wear visible on head above ear, left breast and leg. Traces of wear show on wheat and shoulder.
REVERSE: Wear shows on head and both wings. Half of the mint luster is still present.

EF-40 (Typical)
OBVERSE: Wear shows on head and leg, foot and breast. Slight wear visible on shoulder and wheat.
REVERSE: Head shows wear but eye is visible and beak is clear. Trace of wear visible on leaves at right. Partial mint luster is visible.

VERY FINE *(Light to moderate even wear. All major features are sharp.)*

VF-30 (Choice)
OBVERSE: Head is worn but coronet outlined, with some hair details above and below. Knee and leg show wear; both knee points are sharp. Left breast visible. Wear shows on shoulder and wheat.
REVERSE: Most details show on head. Three-quarters of details are visible in wings. Left talon has some separation. Trace of wear shows on ribbon under E of motto.

VF-20 (Typical)
OBVERSE: Very little hair detail visible around coronet. Wear shows on knee and leg but knee points are clear. Breasts, shoulder and wheat are worn.
REVERSE: Half of head details and almost three-quarters of wing details are visible. Lettering shows wear, and there are wear spots under E and M in motto.

FINE *(Moderate to heavy even wear. Entire design clear and bold.)*

F-12 (Fine)
OBVERSE: Coronet and surrounding details partially visible. hair knot shows details. Most stems of wheat are separated. LIBERTY is worn but readable.
REVERSE: Eye, ear and nostril visible on head. Half of wing feathers are visible. Talons show little or no detail. Motto readable but very weak.

VERY GOOD *(Well worn. Design clear but flat and lacking details.)*

VG-8 (Very Good)
OBVERSE: Hair at back of lower neck and over left shoulder is visible. Shoulder has a garment line at top. Some wheat stems are separated. Motto is partially visible.
REVERSE: Slight spot visible for eye. One-third of wing feathers show. Motto is partially readable. Rim is complete.

GOOD *(Heavily worn. Design and legend visible but faint in spots.)*

G-4 (Good)
OBVERSE: Eye is visible as a spot. Nose and mouth are visible. Shoulder is smooth. Very little detail remains in wheat. Motto is gone, and rim merges with stars in spots.
REVERSE: Eagle worn nearly flat but is completely outlined. Motto is gone and rim merges with letters in spots.

ABOUT GOOD *(Outlined design. Parts of date and legend worn smooth.)*

AG-3 (About Good)
OBVERSE: Design outlined with nearly all details worn away. Date readable but worn. Rim merging with stars.
REVERSE: Entire design partially worn away. Rim merges into legend.
   NOTE: Pieces made at San Francisco are usually unevenly struck; details of the wheat sheaf and parts of the wing may be weak.
   On proofs dated 1879-1883, flat spots are often seen on heads and stars.
   Oriental chopmarks (small Chinese characters) are found punched into many of these coins. Such chopmarks do not alter the grade but they must be mentioned whenever they are present.

THE "MORGAN" DOLLARS
MINT STATE *(Absolutely no trace of wear.)*

MS-70 (Perfect Uncirculated)
A flawless coin exactly as it was minted, with no trace of wear or injury. Must have full mint luster and brilliance or light toning. Any unusual striking traits must be described.

MS-65 (Choice Uncirculated)
No trace of wear; nearly as perfect as MS-70 except for a few minute bag marks or surface mars. Has full mint luster but may be unevenly toned. Any unusual striking traits must be described.

MS-60 (Typical)
A strictly Uncirculated coin with no trace of wear, but with bag marks and other abrasions more obvious than for MS-65. May have a few small rim mars and weakly struck spots. Has full mint luster but may lack brilliance, and surface may be spotted or heavily toned.
   For these coins, bag abrasions and scuff marks are considered different from circulation wear. Full mint luster and lack of any wear are necessary to distinguish MS-60 from AU-55.
   CHECK POINTS: For signs of wear, look at hair above eye and ear, edges of cotton leaves and blossoms, high upper fold of cap. High points of eagle's breast and tops of legs. Weakly struck spots are common and should not be confused with actual wear.

ABOUT UNCIRCULATED *(Small trace of wear visible on highest points.)*

AU-55 (Choice)
OBVERSE: Slight trace of wear shows on hair above ear and eye, edges of cotton leaves and high upper fold of cap. Luster fading from cheek.
REVERSE: Slight traces of wear show on breast, tops of legs and talons. Most of the mint luster is still present, although sometimes marred by light bag marks and surface abrasions.

AU-50 (Typical)
OBVERSE: Traces of wear show on hair above eye and ear, edges of cotton leaves and high upper fold of cap. Partial detail visible on tops of cotton blossoms. Luster gone from cheek.
REVERSE: Traces of wear on breast tops of legs, wig tips and talons. Three-quarters of the mint luster is still present. Surface abrasions and bag marks are more noticeable than for AU-55.

EXTREMELY FINE *(Very light wear on only the highest points.)*

EF-45 (Choice)
OBVERSE: Slight wear on hair above date, forehead and ear. Lines in hair well detailed and sharp. Slight flat spots on edges of cotton leaves. Minute signs of wear on cheek.
REVERSE: High points of breast are light worn. Tops of legs and right wing tip show wear. Talons are slightly flat. Half of the mint luster is still present.

EF-40 (Typical)
OBVERSE: Wear shows on hair above date, forehead and ear. Lines in hair well detailed. Flat spots visible on edges of cotton leaves. Cheek lightly worn.
REVERSE: Almost all feather gone from breast. Tops of legs, wing tips and feathers on head show wear. Talons are flat. Partial mint luster is visible.

VERY FINE *(Light to moderate even wear. All major features are sharp.)*

VF-30 (Choice)
OBVERSE: Wear shows on high points of hair from forehead to ear. Some strands visible in hair above ear. There are smooth areas on cotton leaves and at top of cotton blossoms.
REVERSE: Wear shows on leaves of wreath and tips of wings. Only a few feathers visible on breast and head.

VF-20 (Typical)
OBVERSE: Smooth spots visible on hair from forehead to ear. Cotton leaves heavily worn but separated. Wheat grains show wear.
REVERSE: Some leaves on wreath are well worn. Breast is smooth, and only a few feathers show on head. Tips of wings are weak but lines are complete.

FINE *(Moderate to heavy even wear. Entire design clear and bold.)*

F-12 (Fine)
OBVERSE: Hairline along face is clearly defined. Lower two cotton leaves smooth but distinct from cap. Some wheat grains merging. Cotton blossoms flat but the two lines in each show clearly.
REVERSE: One-quarter of eagle's right wing and edge of left wing are smooth. Head, neck and breast are flat and merging. Tail feathers slightly worn. Top leaves in wreath show heavy wear.

VERY GOOD *(Well worn. Design clear but flat and lacking details.)*

VG-8 (Very Good)
OBVERSE: Most details in hair are worn smooth. All letters and date are clear. Cotton blossoms flat and leaves merging in spots.
REVERSE: Half of eagle's right wing and one third of left wing are smooth. All leaves in wreath are worn. Rim is complete.

GOOD *(Heavily worn. Design and legend visible but faint in spots.)*

G-4 (Good)
OBVERSE: Hair is well worn with very little detail remaining. Date, letters and design clearly outlined. Rim is full.
REVERSE: Eagle worn nearly flat but is completely outlined. Design elements smooth but visible. Legend is all visible; rim is full.

ABOUT GOOD *(Outlined design. Parts of date and legend worn smooth.)*

AG-3 (About Good)
OBVERSE: Head is outlined with nearly all details worn away. Date readable but worn. Legend merging into rim.
REVERSE: Entire design partially worn away. Rim merges into legend.
NOTE: Some of these dollars have a prooflike surface; this should be mentioned in any description of such pieces. Portions of the design are often weakly struck, especially in the hair above the ear and on the eagle's breast.

THE "PEACE" DOLLARS
MINT STATE *(Absolutely no trace of wear.)*
MS-70 (Perfect Uncirculated)
A flawless coin exactly as it was minted, with no trace of wear or injury. Must have full mint luster and brilliance or light toning. Any unusual striking traits must be described.

MS-65 (Choice Uncirculated)
No trace of wear; nearly as perfect as MS-70 except for a few minute bag marks or surface mars. Has full mint luster but may be unevenly toned.

MS-60 (Typical)
A strictly Uncirculated coin with no trace of wear, but with bag marks and other abrasions more obvious than for MS-65. May have a few small rim mars and weakly struck spots. Has full mint luster but may lack brilliance, and surface may be spotted or heavily toned.

For these coins, bag abrasions and scuff marks are considered different from circulation wear. Full mint luster and lack of any wear are necessary to distinguish MS-60 from AU-55.

CHECK POINTS: For signs of wear, look at high points of cheek and hair. High points of feathers on right wing and leg. Weakly struck spots are common and should not be confused with actual wear.

ABOUT UNCIRCULATED *(Small trace of wear visible on highest points.)*
AU-55 (Choice)
OBVERSE: Trace of wear shows on hair over ear and above forehead. Slight wear visible on cheek.
REVERSE: High points of feathers on right wing show a trace of wear. Most of the mint luster is still present, although marred by light bag marks and surface abrasions.

AU-50 (Typical)
OBVERSE: Traces of wear visible on neck, and hair over ear and above forehead. Cheek shows slight wear.
REVERSE: Traces of wear show on head and high points of feathers on right wing. Three-quarters of the mint luster is still present. Surface abrasions and bag marks are more noticeable than for AU-55.

EXTREMELY FINE *(Very light wear on only the highest points.)*
EF-45 (Choice)
OBVERSE: Hair around face shows slight wear, but most hair strands are visible. Lower edge of neck lightly worn.
REVERSE: Top of neck and head behind eye show slight wear. Central wing and leg feathers slightly worn. Half of the mint luster is still present.

EF-40 (Typical)
OBVERSE: Slight flattening visible on high points of hair; most hair strands clearly separated. Entire face and lower edge of neck lightly worn.
REVERSE: Wear shows on head behind eye and top of neck. Some flat spots visible on central wing and leg feathers. Partial mint luster is visible.

VERY FINE *(Light to moderate even wear. All major features are sharp.)*

VF-30 (Choice)
OBVERSE: Hair details weak around face. Upper wave of hair shows light wear. Hair above ear worn but single strands well defined.
REVERSE: Feather detail on right wing very week. There is wear on leg feathers and neck. Motto shows a trace of wear.

VF-20 (Typical)
OBVERSE: Very little hair detail visible around face. Wear shows on upper wave of hair. Hair above ear worn but some single strands are clear.
REVERSE: Details on right wing worn but the three horizontal lines of feather layers show. Flattening visible on leg feathers and neck. Motto and talons lightly worn.

FINE *(Moderate to heavy even wear. Entire design clear and bold.)*

F-12 (Fine)
OBVERSE: All hair around face is smooth. Slight wear shows on hair at back of neck and bun. Rays show a trace of wear.
REVERSE: All feathers on right leg are worn away. Lower third of neck feathers visible. Only the lowest horizontal line of feather layers will show. Parts of PEACE and E PLURIBUS weak but readable.

VERY GOOD *(Well worn. Design clear but flat and lacking details.)*

VG-8 (Very Good)
OBVERSE: Hair is flattened and rays have weak spots. Part of motto is weak. Rim is complete.
REVERSE: Most feather details worn away, with flattening on right leg, wing, and upper neck and head. Portions of rays, PEACE and E PLURIBUS missing. Rim is complete.

GOOD *(Heavily worn. Design and legend visible but faint in spots.)*

G-4 (Good)
OBVERSE: Date, letters and design clearly outlined. Well worn with very little detail remaining. Rim merges with letters in spots.
REVERSE: Eagle worn nearly flat but is completely outlined. Rim merges with letters in spots.

ABOUT GOOD *(Outlined design. Parts of date and legend worn smooth.)*

AG-3 (About Good)
OBVERSE: Head is outlined with nearly all details worn away. Date readable but worn. Legend merging into rim.
REVERSE: Entire design partially worn away. Legend merges into rim.
    NOTE: In grading this type of dollar, consideration must be given to the following characteristics:
    1921 — Struck in higher relief, and usually seen with hair weak in the center of the obverse. The reverse is often weak in the center.

1922-1928 — Struck in low relief and lack sharpness of details and lettering.

1934-1935 — Generally low relief but obverse design shows sharper details.

THE "EISENHOWER" DOLLARS
MINT STATE *(Absolutely no trace of wear.)*

MS-70 (Perfect Uncirculated)
A flawless coin exactly as it was minted, with no trace of wear or injury. Must have full mint luster and brilliance or light toning. Any unusual striking traits must be described.

MS-65 (Choice Uncirculated)
No trace of wear; nearly as perfect as MS-70 except for some small blemish. Has full mint luster but may be unevenly toned. A few minute nicks or marks may be present.

MS-60 (Typical)
A strictly Uncirculated coin with no trace of wear, but with no blemishes more obvious than for MS-65. May have a few small rim mars and weakly struck spots. Has full mint luster but surface may lack dull, spotted or heavily toned.

CHECK POINTS: For signs of abrasion, look at high points of cheek and jawbone, center of neck, edge of bust. On reverse, the head, high points of ridges and feather in wings and legs.

ABOUT UNCIRCULATED *(Small trace of wear visible on highest points.)*

AU-55 (Choice)
OBVERSE: Only a trace of wear shows on highest points of jawbone and center of neck.
REVERSE: A trace of wear shows on high points of feathers in wings and legs.

EXTREMELY FINE *(Very light wear on only the highest points.)*

EF-45 (Choice)
OBVERSE: Slight wear shows on cheek, along jawbone and on high points at edge of bust. Hair lines are sharp and detailed.
REVERSE: High points of head, legs and wing ridges are lightly worn. Central feathers are all clearly defined.

VERY FINE *(Light to moderate even wear. All major features are sharp.)*

VF-30 (Choice)
OBVERSE: Wear spots show on hair below part, and along cheek and jaw. Hair lines are weak but have nearly full visible details. Slight wear shows at center of neck and along edge of bust.
REVERSE: Wear shows on head, and feathers in wings and legs but all details are visible. All central tail feathers are plain. Wing and leg ridges are lightly worn.

THE "ANTHONY" DOLLARS
NOTE: Grading standards for the Anthony dollars have not been established by the ANA. Reasonably accurate comparisons may be made by using the standards for the Eisenhower dollars.

USING THE INFORMATION IN THIS BOOK

The information in this book is designed to help you select the most profitable Silver Dollars for investment and avoid those with questionable potential. Thousands of statistics are provided on mintages, price levels and percentages of value changes. While these are all useful to the investor if properly evaluated, they can be worthless or even misleading if misinterpreted. In coin investment, the facts do *not* speak for themselves. They tell much, and what they tell is worth knowing. But they cannot be relied upon, in themselves as an investment guide. The chief ingredient in a successful investment is the skilled investor, not necessarily experienced or a coin expert but willing to learn intelligent coin selection. We caution you against doing any serious investing before reading this *entire* book, rather than the charts alone. Very likely, some readers will concentrate upon the charts and figures, assuming this to be the "total substance" of the book. If they fail to read and heed our advice given in the text, they will not be prepared — merely from being familiar with numbers in the charts — to invest successfully.

We have included discussion of a great deal of investment strategy in this book. Our suggestions should not be looked upon as "a way to beat the market." There are no new, secret, or mystic formulas for coin investing. No one has the inside track on a method superior to others. Everyone (or nearly everyone) who successfully invests in Silver Dollars and other coins uses the basic approaches and strategies given in this book. These have not only been proven the most favorable over a long period of time, but are the *only logical* methods for investment in the 1980s.

During the 1970s, when many new investors were getting into coins, circumstances were radically different. Many of these investors bought haphazardly and blindly, having no knowledge of the subject or desire to seek advice. They committed blunder after blunder, buying wrong dates, coins in less than the best condition grades, and unpopular groups. They bought such items as mixed date rolls. They bought, generally, whatever the local coin shop was selling — regardless of what it was. They believed (apparently) that a dollar invested in coins was a dollar invested in coins, no matter what you got for your money. Yet the majority of them profited, because of the remarkable increases in values of nearly all classes and conditions of coins from 1970 to 1981. You could buy blindly then and still succeed. *This is not going to be the case in the mid to late '80s.* Handsome profits are still to be made in coin investing as, we believe, they always will be. But they will be yielded, in the 1980s, on carefully selected purchases *only.* Those who buy haphazardly in the eighties stand virtually no chance of profiting, or even getting their capital back. The coin market of the 1980s is not the coin market of the 1970s.

This is not a belief that we have originated. It is shared by other market analysts and nearly everyone in the coin profession. It is further reflected by the current state of the coin market, the bullion market, and, even to some degree, by trends in domestic politics. The whole economic structure of the U.S. is likely to be different in the eighties than in the seventies. Much good may come of this. It surely will for those skillful enough to take advantage of situations as they develop.

Make no mistake. The readjustment now taking place in the coin market is a healthy one. It will appear even more so when viewed two or three years from now. The number of coin hobbyists is continuing to increase; it could reach 40 million by 1990. The number of coin investors is increasing. But more importantly, for investors, coin values are beginning to reflect numismatic popularity and demand to a greater degree than they had in recent years. This is the trend of the 1980s. The seventies was a decade of investor pressure atop bullion-buying pressure, atop rumor and panic and wild emotion. Values of numismatic coins were knocked out of balance in the seventies. Though nearly all coins advanced in price, most of them sharply, the relative advances from one date to another were unrealistic. They did not reflect traditional price structures in the numismatic market. They bore little relation to mintages or availability. They were influenced far too strongly by fad, bandwagoning, and persons who bought and sold while keeping one eye fixed on the "spot" price of silver.

In examining the charts in this book, it would be tempting to invest along lines that were profitable to investors of five or six years ago. This would be a bad error. The investment strategy for use in the eighties must be orchestrated to suit current conditions . . . even though, at times, it will appear to be the exact opposite of what worked in the '70s. The serious investor who knows or is willing to learn a little something about coins will have his day in the '80s. He will have an advantage over uninformed buyers of miscellaneous coins. His skills will carry him through. He will have aid from other skilled investors, and from the numismatic community; whereas those who persist in buying haphazardly will find that, unlike the 1970s, no one will come to their rescue. They will be salvaged only if enormous price increases occur in the silver bullion market. They will not, and cannot, be saved again by the actions of other investors.

The old method of selecting coins to buy for investment, popular in the sixties and seventies, was to choose those showing the most significant price gains in the year (or two years, or five) prior to purchase. The belief was that these were "the coins going up," while those advancing at less rapid pace were considered automatically less attractive. This was strictly a Wall Street philosophy. It is very dangerous to apply this kind of logic to coin investment. Coins that have made the most substantial recent gains are not necessarily the best to invest in. Much more significant is the current price vs. present demand, desirability, and availability in MS-60 condition. Whether the coin has advanced briskly to reach the current price, or performed laggardly, is not really pertinent. In stocks, this probably *would* make a difference. But coins are, first and foremost, collectors' items. A coin is not in danger of going out of business. All the popular coins stand to be just as popular, or more so, in the coming years. Considerations used in selecting stock purchases — such as the possibility of a new invention making the company's product obsolete — do not apply to coins. It is an entirely different ballgame. Forget Wall Street philosophy when you invest in coins!

Though collecting tastes can and do change slightly over the years, these changes are very significant and can generally be predicted. An example of such a change in the Silver Dollar series is the increased popularity of Carson City Dollars, following the G.S.A. Carson City sales of the 1970s. But this shift in collector demand, for all the hoopla it has generated, really amounts to a little drop in a big bucket. It has not caused any serious alteration in the price structure of Silver Dollars. It has not brought panic or the storming of coin shops. And it will, in time, be quietly absorbed, as all other coin collecting trends and fads are. Viewed over the long range, it has little significance. Nothing that can possibly happen could have a *gross effect* on the popularity or relative values of 75-100 year-old collector coins. These coins are so staunchly established in their collector appeal that they cannot be shaken. As more collectors come into the hobby, they will gain further in popularity and demand, as a certain percentage of new collectors will naturally specialize in Silver Dollars. Just as their predecessors, they will value the scarce dates and mintmarks more highly than the common. They will value specimens in BU condition more highly than Circulated. This basic structure of coin collecting — and, consequently, of coin values — cannot change. The point will never be reached where common coins are preferred over scarce ones, or scratched and marred specimens sought for above "Uncs."

Thus, *the foundation for investment strategy is firm*. It is much firmer and more dependable — and more inviting to put money into — than that for most other kinds of investments. There is no question whether the basic commodity will continue in popularity. That point is settled. The question is only *which* coins have the best prospects of making the healthiest advances. Thus, the major consideration facing most investors in other fields — will the bottom fall out — is removed from coin investment.

To choose the best Silver Dollars for investment, you must follow the same approach used generally in coin investment. It is quite simple, at least in theory. This is, to select coins that appear to be undervalued in the present market, in relation to the values of other dates in their group. To do this, coins of one group (such as Liberty Seated, or Morgans) must be compared against others in the same group — not against all Silver Dollars. This is important. The different groups of Silver Dollars do not possess equal collector popularity. Also, factors contributing to the scarcity or desirability of coins in one group do not necessarily prevail among the other groups. Many examples could be given, but this will become just as apparent by reading the chapters devoted to the individual groups.

You will find, in all of the larger groups, some coins that are obviously underpriced or, at any rate, not as fully priced as their companions. You must become adept at spotting them; go wrong here and the odds of making a successful investment purchase are cleaved in half. Even if you follow the remainder of our advice religiously, and get a brilliant BU specimen, you will very likely not have a profitable investment coin. Coins that are overpriced or fully priced usually take years to advance substantially. Such a coin might not become profitably salable until 15 or 20 years after purchase. *Properly chosen* investment Dollars should be salable at a profit in five years or, in some cases, less. It is impossible for us to provide a reliable timetable. During the boon year of 1979, many Dollars bought for numismatic investment became salable at a profit six months later. This was of course extraordinary, but as it occurred in the past it could certainly happen again. We recognize this possibility, but it cannot be used as a basis for investment buying. The investor ought to be carefully choosing and buying coins that show the best possibility of turning a profit *within five years.* Well selected Dollars will do this, even if the market moves along at a modest pace. Nothing sensational need happen for a profit to yield itself after holding 5 years. Just the normal course of events will see to that, including the increase in numbers of coin hobbyists and the natural readjustment in values of coins that are currently underpriced.

How do you spot an undervalued Dollar? It isn't too difficult, if you take care to avoid the mistakes usually made by beginners when they attempt to do this. Anyone who has had experience as a coin collector, even if he knows nothing about investment, has a big head start. But even those with knowledge of neither coins nor investment can succeed.

First there are the mintage figures. We have provided mintage figures on all the coins listed in this book — every Dollar coin ever struck by the U.S. government for general circulation, excepting gold dollars (these are discussed in "The Official Investors' Guide to U.S. Gold Coins," also published by The House of Collectibles). Mintage figures are informative and should be used as an ingredient in selection. They must not, however, be relied upon too heavily in themselves, to the exclusion of other considerations.

Generally speaking, a coin from any given group will be scarcer on the present market than one which had a larger mintage. This is not invariably the case, because of melting, uneven ratio of loss, or other factors. When we confine ourselves to speaking of "Uncs," it becomes even less so. More "Uncs" could possibly have been saved of one coin, than of another with higher mintage.

Some factors involved in *present availability* are so obscure and abstract that they can be the subject of nothing more than guesswork. It's a matter of your guess being as good as mine, or as that of any expert's. *However,* others are well identified, and can be applied very usefully by the investor. They are discussed at greater length within this book. To mention one, there is the often overlooked fact that San Francisco struck Dollars have a tendency to be scarcer in "Unc" than those from other Mints with similar mintage totals. This is especially true of the earliest issues. It is an established matter of historical record that *paper money was unpopular in California for the first 20-25 years after its introduction, which occurred during the Civil War.* Any history of California will confirm this. The populace was accustomed to trading with bullion, as the state's economy was built on the Gold Rush of '49. It preferred, of course, gold over silver. But it preferred silver considerably over paper notes, which were virtually unpassable in many parts of California until the late 1880s. Thus, silver Dollars circulating in California tended to receive more use, and more handling, than elsewhere. Naturally, the majority were from the San Francisco Mint. Also, there were fewer coin collectors on the West Coast to preserve "Uncs" as they came out, compared to those on the East Coast who put away Philadelphias.

You cannot, perhaps, become expert on all the factors involved in estimating current availability in a day or two. But once you know the major causes and effects, and have picked up some rudimentary knowledge of coin collecting (as provided by this book), you are well along the road. The more skilled you become, the greater is your edge on uninformed investors. The *highly skilled* investor can occasionally spot "sleeper" coins long before they become noticed by others, and thereby take advantage of the opportunity to buy them at low prices. But you need not wait until you reach this level of virtuosity, before making investment purchases.

This basic precept of coin investment, Dollars or other denominations, is that coins eventually reach a fair and equitable value level, in relation to other coins of their group. An investor seeks to buy the undervalued coins, and hold them until the market has readjusted to a point where they become fully priced. In the time taken for this to happen (which, as we say, should be a minimum of five years for well selected dates), the fully priced and even overpriced coins of that group will probably advance somewhat, too. Therefore, when the underpriced coins have finally attained fair value levels, they will have come up considerably from the price paid for them. Whenever a coin doubles in value within five years, it rates as profitable. The exact amount of profit depends, of course, on the rate of national inflation and costs involved in selling it. But it would be extremely unlikely that a coin would gain 100% in value over five years and not pay an investment profit. Inflation would need to rise at an alarming rate for this to be the case.

Generally speaking, mintage figures for the earlier Dollars are not as indicative of current availability as those on later groups. Dollars struck before 1850 came into a world destitute of coin collectors and largely unconcerned about them as objects of art. There was, also, extensive melting in the years preceding coin collecting. Quantities of our silver Dollars were exported abroad in the early 1800s, to be exchanged for foreign gold coinage, and most of these Dollars ended up in smelters' hands. Destruction rates (and techniques) varied over the years; estimates can never be strictly depended upon. But it is not necessary to *know precisely,* in order to make investment selections. Much of this information will never be reliably known, by anyone. This does not prevent profits from being made in Dollar investing, by utilizing the information which is available.

We suggest, as one of the practices to be used in selecting coins for investment, to take good notice of values in the earlier years of our charts (1955 and 1960). While this may seem incidental, it can be a surprisingly accurate barometer of future performances — more so, quite often, than price levels of more recent times! The 1955 and 1960 figures are almost pure collector prices. Some investors certainly were buying Dollars at that time, but they had very little influence on the market. Thus, these antiquated prices, while certainly obsolete so far as valuing coins is concerned, indicate levels of collector demand between one coin and another. They show which coins were the most popular with collectors, and in *nearly all cases* these very same coins are still the most popular. Values no longer reflect this, as the more valuable coins of 1955 and 1960 are not always the most valuable today. But that, essentially, is the result of unselective investor buying and selling during the late sixties and throughout most of the seventies. These coins were purchased by investors without regard for their collector popularity or scarcity. This resulted in the values becoming imbalanced, as they still are in many instances. If collectors were still in control of the Dollar market, as they were in 1955 and 1960, the coins that were most valuable in those years would still carry the highest values today. There would, of course, be percentage differences in the rates of advance, as even collector buying, while far less erratic than investor buying, does not proceed at a perfectly even pace. There would still be investment opportunity. But, because of the present situation, in which some coins are overvalued and others seriously undervalued, the investment possibilities are much greater.

We advise you to give attention to these 1955 and 1960 levels of value from coin to coin. Most Dollars will, we feel convinced, reestablish the old value relationship with others in their groups. This will happen because the new breed of investors, now coming on the scene, are likely to structure their portfolios along the lines of *traditional numismatic popularity.*

As for the other information in this book, most of it is self-explanatory, or has been explained in the sections containing it. It is all important for the investor, and we strongly urge you to read it, think about it, and (if necessary) re-read it, before making investment purchases. If you follow the advice and adopt the suggestions we have laid out, there is little doubt that you will join the growing army of those who have MADE MONEY WITH SILVER DOLLARS.

THE "FLOWING HAIR" DOLLARS

OBVERSE   **REVERSE**

In late 1791, following President George Washington's annual message to Congress, a Senate Committee, headed by Robert Morris, was appointed to implement the establishment of a mint and to set standards for our coins.

The committee followed most of the specific recommendations of Alexander Hamilton, Secretary of the Treasury, but differed in one significant area. The members decided to alter the proposed dollar's silver content by increasing its total weight to 416 grains. With a silver content of 371.25 grains, this made the fineness a peculiar figure of .892, or 1485 parts silver out of 1664 total parts.

At the time, one ounce of gold was worth 15.1 ounces of silver. The specifications for the new dollar made the silver worth exactly 15 ounces to the ounce of gold and this over-valuation of silver, in relation to foreign bullion standards, was to haunt the U.S. Government for more than three-quarters of a century. It resulted in an immediate flow of the newly struck coins out of the country where they were exchanged for gold or for properly valued foreign coins at a profit.

The new law establishing these standards was signed on April 2, 1792. The cornerstone for the new mint was laid in July. Several patterns were struck late that year and beginning in February, 1793, the first half cents and cents were struck. It was not until March 3, 1794 that the required bond for the chief coiner and assayer were reduced to $5000 and $1000, requirements which were met so that the mint could legally strike gold and silver coins.

However, behind the scenes, there were some secret changes being made and the 1794 and 1795 dollars, while officially listed (to this day) as being .894 fine silver were actually produced by mint officials to a standard of .900 fine. While the total weight met specifications, the fineness was actually greater than intended, a factor which increased the number of coins that left the country and fell into the hands of the smelters.

In later series, we will divide the dates into three classes — Common, Semi-Key and Key. If we were to go only by the mintage, the 1795 would be thought of as a "common date," but as we note in the Variety section at the end of this chapter, there are a significant number of varieties, several with probable mintages of less than 1000. Because of the age of this coin we need to at least consider it as a Semi-Key.

SILVER $1 — FLOWING HAIR, COMMON DATE
THERE ARE NO COMMON DATES OF THIS VARIETY

SILVER $1 — FLOWING HAIR, SEMI-KEY
THERE ARE NO SEMI-KEYS OF THIS VARIETY

SILVER $1 — FLOWING HAIR, KEY
UNCIRCULATED CONDITION

Year	Mintage	1955	1960	1965	1970	1975	1980	1985
1794	1,758	2000.00	6500.00	12500.00	12500.00	75000.00	85000.00	58000.00
1795	203,033	150.00	325.00	950.00	1300.00	6500.00	15000.00	41000.00

	% of increase:		
		1955-60	325%
		1960-65	97%
		1965-70	3%
		1970-75	491%
		1975-80	23%
		1980-85	1%
overall % of increase:		1955-85	4505%

These are the only two dates for which Flowing Hair Dollars were produced. Midway into 1795 the Flowing Hair design was replaced by the Draped Bust. In that year, however, production of Silver Dollars was considerably greater than in 1794, with the result that Flowing Hair Dollars dated 1795 are not as scarce as their illustrious predecessor. From all standpoints the 1794 Flowing Hair Dollar ranks as one of the outstanding U.S. coins: legendary, charismatic, with a rarity that need not be measured by attempts to count "quantities in existence." The mintage figure tells it all: 1,758 coins. Even if every single coin had survived, this would be a scarce coin, scarcer than most other Silver Dollars. One need only consider the numerous pitfalls to survival, and the span of nearly 200 years between 1794 and today, to realize how truly scarce it is. When we talk about specimens surviving today in uncirculated condition, we are down to small numbers indeed.

How many? What is the total of existing 1794 Flowing Hair Dollars in all condition grades, and the total of those preserved in uncirculated condition?

This had been a favorite subject of numismatic writers, historian, researchers, and publishers of investment literature. It is nothing more than a guessing game, as there is no way of arriving at reliable figures. Any owner of an uncirculated 1794 Flowing Hair Dollar — collector or investor — would like to say he has one of only twelve, or ten or eight. The best he can say is that he has a very rare classic coin which passes through the market only occasionally. Anyone with even a rudimentary knowledge of numismatics cannot fail to be impressed with the rarity of such a coin. We start with a total of 1,758 coins, more than 190 years ago, and it starts going down almost immediately. Early Silver Dollars, including the 1794, face a high destruction ratio from the very beginning. They had only to be released into general circulation and the onslaught began. Not everyone was content to regard them as money and nothing more. Chiefly the intentional destruction in the earliest years derived from two sources.

On one hand were the speculators, who seized any opportunities to profit from silver bullion. It just happened that opportunities were very favorable in the 1790s. This big coin with a face value of $1 contained about three-fourths of an ounce of pure silver. In Europe, the value of silver was somewhat higher than in the United States. If you exchanged Silver Dollars at par in Europe, for local currency, you received equivalent face value with the inevitable broker's fee deducted. But if you SOLD Silver Dollars in Europe to buyers of scrap silver, you received MORE than the equivalent face value in local money. This local money could then be converted back into U.S. coinage at a fair profit. Do not imagine for an instant that the possibilities of this situation escaped our forefathers. Anyone traveling to Europe loaded his trunks with Silver Dollars — as many as he could acquire. They ended up in the melting pots of Germany, England, Holland and other nations, and the rate of destruction must have been enormous. In a short time the Silver Dollar came to be regarded as a speculation piece and appeared less and less in actual circulation. No one really missed it from circulation, as it was nothing more than a "new novelty." Commerce had been carrying on for over a century with foreign crowns and the Dollar-like coins, mostly from Mexico and Spain. they were STILL legal tender at the time of the 1794 Silver Dollar, and they remained legal tender until well into the nineteenth century. Had the government removed legal tender status from them, this would have provided an incentive to preserve U.S. Silver Dollars. Why did the early federalists choose not to protect our Silver Dollar? Mainly because it would have risked chaos. Not enough Silver Dollars were in circulation to serve the needs of the business and banking communities. Without foreign silver crowns to depend on, commerce and industry could have ground to a smashing halt — the last think anybody wanted in a new emerging nation. So the Silver Dollar was at the mercy of anyone to use for whatever purposes he might wish.

The 1794 Silver Dollar — and other pioneer Dollars — also faced destruction from another direction. Since the face value of the Dollar was equivalent to the amount of silver bullion it contained, silversmiths melted it as a way of obtaining silver. The 1794 Silver Dollar was turned into spoons, forks, serving dishes, trays, goblets, tea kettles, and all manner of other household objects. We can be quite certain that silversmiths wasted no time taking out of circulation for this purpose all the Dollars they could find. Before the availability of a domestic Dollar, they had been melting French ecu, the Spanish 8-reales coins, and other miscellaneous foreign coins. That was not nearly as convenient as melting U.S. Silver Dollars. The foreign coins varied in fineness; if several types were melted together, you obtained silver of an unknown grade. If you melted Silver Dollars whether one or a hundred, the fineness would not vary. Use of Silver Dollars (along with other U.S. silver coins, but primarily Dollars) became so widespread in the smithing business that the term "coin silver" was adopted, in reference to merchandise made from them. Coin silver was the backbone of the U.S. silversmith industry during the entire first half of the nineteenth century, accounting for destruction of an unknown — but certainly huge — quantity of our early silver coins. It was only at mid-century that American silversmiths switched to the sterling standard, which is .012 finer than coin silver (.912 as opposed to .900).

Thus you had Silver Dollars being syphoned off to Europe, where they were melted. Those escaping the speculators then had to escape domestic melters. And what chance did they really have, under the circumstances? If it was today, instead of the 1790s, they might have fared better. At least they would be distributed faster and over a wider geographical area. In the 1790s, most of the population was concentrated in a few large cities along the eastern shore; that was where the Silver Dollars went, and that was where the silversmiths were.

By 1800, six years after minting, surviving totals of the 1794 Silver Dollar could have been only a fraction of the already-small 1,758 originally struck. The destruction did not end there. Profiteering continued for a short while thereafter; melting by silversmiths continued for a long while. Now, this may seem hard to grasp, living in an age which pays such deserved homage to the 1794 Flowing Hair Dollar. But do you really believe that a silversmith in 1810 or 1820, acquiring Silver Dollars to be melted, would have set aside a 1794 as a "collector's item?" No, he would not have. It was three-quarters of an ounce of silver and that was all he cared about. So the population of 1794 Flowing Hair Dollars decreased further as the years passed. The number of people out to destroy them far surpassed those with an interest in preserving them. Did ANYONE want to preserve them? Yes, we know that a handful of coin collectors were active, and the mint itself wanted to keep specimens of its work for posterity. There were no coin dealers. If coin dealers had existed, it would have been a different story. The dealers would have served as an opposing force, to those bent on destruction of the 1794 Dollar. Each dealer would have saved multiple specimens. As it was there was nobody saving more than a single specimen, as the only savers were coin collectors; they were satisfied with one apiece. Coin collecting was much too minor a hobby, in those days, to have greatly aided in preserving the 1794 Flowing Hair Dollar. Not only did the U.S. boast very few active collectors, but some of them specialized in foreign or ancient coins and paid no attention to what could be obtained in daily circulation.

It is hardly any wonder that the 1794 Flowing Hair Dollar won an EARLY reputation as a scarce coin. By 1850 it was already expensive in terms of the prices of that day. There were still no fulltime coin dealers (they came along slightly later), but a definite market had developed in old, scarce coins. Curio dealers were selling them — these were the predecessors of what we now call "antiques dealers." Many shopkeepers, engaged in various lines of business, were selling coins on the side, coins they had received from customers. It was all very disorganized, of course, and values bore little relation to rarity. But everyone knew, even if they did not know mintage figures or historical background, that the 1794 Flowing Hair Dollar was an extraordinary coin. It was the first U.S Silver Dollar (almost everybody knew at least that much), and you just didn't find them floating around. By the time collectors had multiplied and started to feverishly search their pocket change, there was only a slim chance a 1794 Dollar would turn up. The coin was then decades old. If you wanted one, you had no choice but to buy it. Even that was difficult. And if you were lucky enough to find one offered for sale, the odds were ten to one that its date would scarcely be readable. Or that a wide gaping hole had been punched through it somewhere along the line, by someone who wanted to see if it was solid silver. The population of 1794's had not only been decimated: the survivors were wrecks, but for a very fortunate few. The mint itself naturally owned a few "uncs." The big collectors of the day (such as Stickney of Philadelphia) would have one. If any further uncirculated specimens were in existence, they were unknown to their owners, stored away in jars of "savings" by those who placed no trust in banks. They were just "money." And they were likely to repose in those jars for many, many years.

It is no wonder that when coin auctions started, in the 1860s, bidders were fighting tooth and nail over good specimens of the 1794 Flowing Hair Dollar. Nobody knew precisely how rare it was, but it was an awfully glamorous coin — a coin people wanted even if they took no particular interest in other early Dollars. Auction sale competition fixed a firm market value on this titan of numismatics. Those who might have shuddered at paying the "huge" sum of $50 or $75 for an uncirculated specimen saw these prices — and higher ones — easily obtained in open bidding. So they got bolder. More people started bidding, and bidding higher sums. Before long it was a $500 coin. Then it was a $1000 coin. The price history of the 1794 Flowing Hair Dollar has essentially been one of continual price spiraling — not at a steady percentage, not too readily predictable, but continual. It was a coin that could be counted upon to go up in value, even if you did not know how far, or how soon. Simple mathematics showed that it could not be otherwise. Each year brought more collectors into the coin hobby. This brought more money into the coin hobby, and meant heavier competition for the cream of the cream. If reliable statistics were available on the lifetime price history of the 1794 Flowing Hair Dollar — that is, from the time it began acquiring a market value right up to 1985 — they would undoubtedly show an increase for every five-year interval: higher in 1895 than in 1890, higher in 1900 than in 1895, and so on. The chain breaks, however, when we reach the present day. From a price of $85,000 in 1980, this masterpiece of numismatics fell to $58,000 on the 1985 market. Even for a superstar, losing $27,000 in five years hurts. It is the first taint on the 1794's record. Previously, its price had struck at $12,500 from 1965 to 1970, but a backslide? An actual decline? A decline of TWENTY SEVEN THOUSAND DOLLARS, for a coin that most collectors consider themselves unworthy to touch? That is so serious that one might easily conclude that the 1794 Flowing Hair Dollar will never be quite the same again. It has tasted defeat. It is, in the view of some, a fallen "blue chip" investment: a Rock of Gibraltar that slid into the sea.

What does the recent price decline of the 1794 Flowing Hair Dollar really mean? Is it a blow to coin investment? Does it mean that no coins are beyond the grasp of the red ink?

There are many ways of analyzing what happened to the 1794 Flowing Hair Dollar in the years from 1980 to 1985. Many theories, many explanations, and many potential conclusions for the future. You can see bad in what occurred (losing $27,000 ranks as rather negative for most people), or you can see good. Actually there were various factors and influences at work here, and it would take a whole book to explore them in depth. We can begin by confidently stating that the 1794 Flowing Hair Dollar is not finished as an investment coin. Nor as a collector's coin, for that matter. We can just as confidently state that it will regain its lost ground and then some. Given its almost unblemished credentials, it has the potential to be a $100,000 coin before too many more pages fall from the calendar. It could be a $100,000 coin today, without that slight derailment of the past five years. At $85,000 in 1980, it was within easy grasping distance of six figures. Some coins are now selling for $100,000 which, when you critically investigate their strong and weak points, are not as deserving of that price as is the 1794 Flowing Hair Dollar.

The humiliation of a $27,000 price decline should never happen to a coin of such regal status; it ought to be above such things. That it DID happen is clear proof of the gigantic sums of money going into (and coming out of) rare coins. Any coin can be manipulated; any coin can fall victim to a shift in buying patterns. We know that any coin can, because the rarest and most valuable coins in the world have fluctuated in price. When the Garrett specimen of the Brasher Doubloon was auctioned in 1979, it brought $725,000. The following year, another specimen — about equal in condition — was sold for $600,000. If you want to look at it that way, that represents a $125,000 decline in one year. Which makes the 1794 Flowing Hair's $27,000 slide in five years seem infinitesimal.

Let's see if we can make some sense out of this.

In the first place, before anybody can analyze figures and try to make them meaningful, you have to realize that coins of great price are not rigidly firm in their market values. When we say that the 1794 Flowing Hair Dollar fell from $85,000 in 1980 to $58,000 in 1985, these are established market values. Yet they are not as "established" as the market values of Silver Dollars from the 1890s and early 1900s that sell for under $100 apiece. As George Orwell put it in *Animal Farm,* all animals are created equal, but some are more equal than others. Some established values are more established than others. It all depends on frequency of sale. A coin in the under-$100 price bracket will be sold many thousands of times within a five year interval — in shops, at shows, at auctions, through mail-order. It will be advertised thousands of times. There will be buying ads and selling ads. There will be literature and more literature. Numerous dealers have these coins and each one is guided in the price he charges by what the OTHERS are charging. This is how a price becomes firmly established, so firm that you know instantly whether you are getting a 5 percent discount or paying a little too much. When a coin is scarcer it is sold less often, and the price becomes somewhat looser. Scarcer still, and the price is not really boxed in at all. Take the 1794

Flowing Hair Dollar. In the course of five years, ANY five years, there are not too many sales. Of these, some are unrecorded (one collector selling to another, an investor selling to a collector, etc.) and do not contribute to pricing information. Months may pass with no recorded sales; maybe a year, if we are talking about uncirculated specimens. So a dealer cannot say, "Look, you're getting a bargain on this $85,000, because X's coin shop down the street wants $90,000." Most likely X's does not have one. Most likely nobody else has one at the moment, so far as announced offerings are concerned. This invites a fluctuation in price, from one sale to the next. The seller plays upon the coin's rarity and the very real possibility that another opportunity to purchase one may not arise until far into the future. The buyer hesitates, looking at an old auction price, and says, "Well, just because it brought X amount of money back then, how can I really be sure I should put that much into it?" Which, of course, is a very reasonable attitude when you're contemplating such a large expenditure. The fact of the matter is that the "established market value" on a coin such as the 1794 Flowing Hair Dollar does not lock the coin into that value — at least not for very long. This can easily be proved. Just have a gala auction. One of the numismatic greats has slipped to the other side, and a collection known throughout the world is being put under the hammer. The catalogue is lavish, the publicity is handled by Madison Avenue, the luminaries of numismatics fly in from all over the world. Can you bet that the 1794 Flowing Hair Dollar, saddled with a lar, saddled with a declining "book price" of $58,000, will not sell for $100,000? Or $200,000, for that matter? Will everybody at the auction think in terms of the $58,000 book price, or will he take the opposite tack and reason that the auction makes the price (not the other way around)? Anyone who has followed coin auctions for any length of time knows that celebrated coins do not run true to their "established market values." Sometimes they sell for less. Sometimes they go through the roof.

But for the purposes of our study, we will assume — flatly and beyond the glimmer of a doubt — that the 1794 Flowing Hair Dollar is worth $27,000 less today than it was worth in 1980. If you bought it for $85,000 in 1980, you now have $58,000 worth of numismatic investment; actually quite a bit less, after the inflation rate is figured in. Your $85,000 worth of buying power in 1980 has shrunk to perhaps $35,000 worth of buying power at the moment, so your feelings toward the 1794 Flowing Hair Dollar are not apt to be complimentary. Quite likely you are asking a lot of questions, not the least of which is: will I make money on this coin, or even achieve break, if I keep holding. The answer to that one is an unqualified YES. Now, for the answers to some of your other questions.

Yes, the investment brokers and analysts and almost everybody else was telling you in 1980 that this was a sure-thing coin to buy. It was a coin among coins, a coin that would rise above any kind of market pressures or bad economic times because it had so much going for it. Roosevelt Dimes or Buffalo Nickels might go into a tailspin, but never — never — a coin as monumental and revered as the 1794 Flowing Hair Dollar.

Well, that kind of advice runs precisely contrary to the principles of sound Silver Dollar investment. You do not buy a coin on reputation. You do not buy a coin because of what it has accomplished in the past, because of its popularity, or because it is enshrouded in some kind of saintliness. None of this will do anything for you in the way of assuring a profit. There are many analysts who tell you that it WILL — that these are the coins to acquire, at all costs. But events prove them wrong again and again. You see this sort of advice so frequently because it is easy advice to give; it does not require any real analysis at all. Sure — buy the great coins. But buy them as a collector. If you buy them as an investor, make sure they deserve your investment capital at the time of making the investment. There are times when they do. There are times when they don't. The great coins can get overpriced, just as much as the unheralded ones. And when a great coin gets overpriced, it is just as bad to buy as ANY overpriced coin. Its greatness will not save it by pushing it up in price. Supply and demand are the equalizers. When a coin is overpriced, it is out of bounds for investment. The same thing applies to a coin which is not actually overpriced, but "fully priced." This means it is selling for just about what it deserves to — no more, no less. It is a healthy coin and out of bounds for investment buying at the moment. You have to catch coins when they're undervalued. Undervalued does not necessarily mean undervalued in relation to past performances. Some coins have eternally been undervalued. It means undervalued in relation to the price at which they should be selling in light of all factors (the most important of which is: the current prices of similar coins with similar mintages). If you bought the 1794 Flowing Hair Dollar for investment in 1980 at $85,000, you were buying a coin when it was not undervalued, which is one of the cardinal rules of investment success. A glance at the statistics on our chart will show WHEN it was appropriate to have bought the 1794 Flowing Hair Dollar. After the price had remained lodged at $12,500 from 1965 to 1970, it had obviously been swallowed up into the ranks of undervalued coins. It deserved to be selling higher. It deserved to have moved up from $12,500 in 1965 to at least $20,000 in 1970, but it did not. If you bought it in 1970, you were, in effect, buying a $20,000 coin for $12,500. And you were handsomely rewarded, because by 1975 it had not only surpassed $20,000 but left it far behind — it reached $75,000. Now, what sort of picture was presented in 1975? To the investor with $75,000 to spend that year, the 1794 Flowing Hair Dollar might have seemed to present magnetic attractions. What more could you want than an investment which rose 500% in five years? Not too many Wall Street stocks did half that well. Well, the problem SHOULD have been obvious. By registering that fantastic gain — the gain which made this coin look so irresistible for investment — the 1794 Flowing Hair Dollar had pulled itself up into the fully priced category. It had worked wonders for those who already owned it, but it was no longer in a position to do anything for the latecomers. Buying it at $75,000 you were catching it at the top of the market. It was not, in reality, a coin advancing in price at 500% every five years. It was a coin which scored this one great advance in one five year period, and an advance which really should have been spread over ten years. A price of $30,000 in 1975 would have been more realistic, then $75,000 in 1980. Of course, it did have a little steam left. It got to $85,000 in 1980, adding $10,000, before stalling and then turning the other way. Once again it was fully priced at $85,000, just as it had been at $75,000 five years previously. Possibly overpriced, though this is a matter of conjecture. In any case, it looked like anything but a winner carrying an $85,000 pricetag. What could an investor have possibly hoped to get out of the 1794 by putting $85,000 worth of 1980 dollars into it? If he was thinking in terms of a five year profit, this would have necessitated an increase to about $170,000 by 1985, a very lofty hope. If he was thinking of long term investment, $85,000 was still too much to spend under the circumstances. The coin was obviously entering a period of price adjustment. It was not going to continue rising — not even at the modest pace of advance it score between 1975 and 1980. This should have been clear to everyone familiar with the standard accepted strategy of numismatic investment. But of course, there were some who bought, who could not resist. It was, after all, a "blue chip," and the advice to buy far outweighed any other.

So there was a collision course. New investors buying the coin at $85,000 ran directly into the old investors, who bought it for $12,500 in 1970. They passed each other on the way to the coin shop. The old investors had their profit in their pockets. They knew the coin was leveling off, and they wanted to sell. There were other Silver Dollars to buy, Silver Dollars that had much more growth potential. Do you see what happened? An increased quantity of 1794 Flowing Hair Dollars was passing through the market — not mountains of them, obviously, but more than one would usually be available. This was the signal for the price to start declining. When big money is involved, a price adjustment will be fairly substantial. The bigger the price, the bigger the adjustment — depending, of course, on just how far out of line the value was to begin with. Between 1980 and 1982 (the 1982 figures are not shown on our charts, but we have them on record for comparison purposes as we do for all coin prices from the 1950s to today), the price went from $85,000 to $57,500. In the next three years, 1982 to 1985, it inched back up to $58,000. In other words this huge decline of $27,000 was suffered NOT in five years, as one would think from looking at the chart, but in a very brief two years. Then, another leveling off ensued, similar to that in which the 1794 Flowing Hair Dollar found itself from 1965 to 1970.

By now you can probably draw your own conclusions. At $75,000 in 1975 the coin was fully priced. At $85,000 in 1980 it was fully priced. Therefore, it cannot be fully priced at $58,000 in 1985. If $85,000 was a fair price in 1980 (fair in a numismatic sense, that is — not fair for investment), the 1985 price should be around $100,000 or slightly more. Just the ordinary increase in capital spent on rare coins, along with general inflation, should have served to boost the price to that level. Since the price slid back, and by a sizable amount, we can confidently conclude that the 1794 Flowing Hair Dollar is now — today — squarely in the underpriced category. What does this mean to you, from an investment standpoint?

There are many analysts (and others too numerous to mention) who would take these statistics and proclaim the 1794 Flowing Hair Dollar a perfect five-year or "short term" investment for those with substantial capital. If it should be selling for $100,000 right now, then it should be selling for $125,000 or more in 1990. Take $58,000 and compare it against $125,000 and you have — no doubt about it — a set of numbers that definitely inspire investment confidence. Our own personal appraisal of this situation is that the 1794 Flowing Hair Dollar has excellent potential for turning the short profit, which (admittedly) is rare for a coin of this high a price. You very seldom find $58,000 coins that stand a good chance of doubling in value within five years. To stay on the conservative side, which has been our goal and motivation throughout preparation of this book, we will call the 1794 Flowing Hair a *sure* winner as a long term investment (ten years or longer) and a *probable* winner for the short term. Our hesitancy about it short term performance is based entirely on the question of whether it can regain a fair price level that quickly. Sometimes a big coin will be a slow mover in that respect. It is more difficult to anticipate what a big coin will do, because one does not know the abstract elements of the next five years: how many specimens will be passing through the market, how many will appear in prestigious auctions. That the 1794 Flowing Hair Dollar achieve its rightful price level is a foregone conclusion — it WILL. The only point to be settled is the length of time involved. It should be there by 1990, but if by the year 1990 it is still somewhat shy of being fully priced, there is no doubt that the next few years will find it going over the top. If you can afford an investment of this proportion, and if you can safely put it aside for ten years, this coin presents a very low risk factor. You may very well be able to sell it profitably in a much shorter timespan. It is not a BEST BET and we are certainly not going to refer to it as a "blue chip." It is simply a very attractive coin to buy, based on the circumstances of the moment. We are going to project a price of $150,000 to $200,000 by 1995.

Keep in mind that we are advocating uncirculated condition, which will not come easy unless you have some luck on your side. It will be largely a matter of watching the weekly ads in numismatic periodicals to see what transpired. Sooner or later you will have the opportunity to purchase one. Do not expect to get one for precisely $58,000. As we said, prices of super coins do not run like clockwork. If it is $60,000 and in strictly graded uncirculated condition, you are not being overcharged. Possibly not even if the price is slightly higher. Of course, the market value may already be on the upswing by the time you read this, and it might be impossible to get any uncirculated specimen for less than $65,000. This is why it is smart and essential for survival, to read the coin collecting periodicals and keep in touch with what's going on week by week.

The 1795 is the only other Silver Dollar with the Flowing Hair motif. It had a considerably larger mintage and is more plentiful than the 1794 in all grades of condition, though it would be rash to attempt to estimate just how much more plentiful. The relationship in mintage figures is probably not a very accurate indication of the relationship in quantities surviving. The mintage figures give a better than 10-to-1 ratio so far as production is concerned. Normally, one can trust mintage figures to at least roughly indicate quantities of surviving specimens. Here it is difficult because of the circumstances discussed above: the overt, excessive, reckless destruction of Silver Dollars during the late 1700s and well into the 1800s. Percentage-wise, one would have to believe that a greater ratio of 1795 Flowing Hair Dollars were sacrificed, thereby leaving the "quantities in existence" below 10-to-10. There are perhaps six or seven surviving 1795's for every 1794, in the various condition grades. Why should the rate of destruction have been higher on the 1795 Dollar than the 1794? Simply because the coin was much more readily available. This cannot actually be proved. It is just a theory, but it seems a reasonable one, especially if you take frequency of sale as supportive evidence. Flowing Hair Dollars of 1795 do NOT occur for sale ten times more often than those of 1794.

The price history of the 1795 Flowing Hair Dollar is quite a bit different than that of the 1794. It has never commanded as high a price, nor as much adulation. In the early years, going back to the dawning era of serious coin collecting in this nation, it was really looked upon as nothing more than just another coin. It was not the first issue of its types and everyone knew it was not particularly scarce compared to the 1794; furthermore, both were vastly overshadowed by the 1804 Silver Dollar. It was undoubtedly still possible to find 1795 Dollars in general circulation as late as the 1840s. When coin dealers started selling them a decade later, it was impossible to get a premium over face value for circulated ones. They had to be "uncs," and, even at that, the traffic would not bear a very substantial price. In the minds of many collectors at that time, this was a "common" Dollar. It showed up in quite a few collections in which the 1794 was lacking. We know this from old auction sale records. It also showed up sometimes in multiple specimens. Gradually the price increased, but it was a long while before this became an expensive coin. Interestingly enough (if you like statistics, the 1795's price traditionally ran less than 10% of the 1794's. When the 1794 sold for $300, you could get the 1795 for around $25. When the 1794 was at $1000, the 1795 was just nudging $100. Back in 1955, the 1794 had reached $2000 but the 1795 was available at just $150, an extremely wide price differential. This pricing pattern was very closely aligned to the differences in quantities minted. If specimens of the 1794 and 1795 had survived in equal ratios, then the 1955 price spread would be fair and square. Very possibly the collectors and dealers of those earlier decade thought that they HAD survived in equal ratios. In any case they labored under the assumption that the 1795 was somewhat more plentiful than is actually the case. This, plus the fact that it lacks the glamor of the 1794, it served to keep the price down. If you check auction sale catalogues of the 1950s, you will find many instances of 1795 Flowing Hair Dollars in uncirculated condition selling for bargain basement sums.

Today that has all changed. The scale has now tipped so far in the opposite direction that the price of the 1795 is unfairly high, in relation to the current market value of the 1794.

Once again we have an instance of the effects of speculative buying, on the value of a Silver Dollar. It is very easy to see just what happened and why, even though it should not have happened. The 1795 Flowing Hair Dollar was clearly undervalued in 1960, 1965, and 1970. When its predecessor (the 1794) began making giant price strides in the early seventies, the 1795 seemed more undervalued than ever. Certainly its price would readjust, sooner or later, in line with that of the 1794. So, while the heavily bankrolled investors bought the 1794, those with less capital turned their attentions to the 1795. When it climbed from $1300 in 1970 to $6500 in 1975, it had earned a sizable investment profit and still looked seriously underpriced compared to the 1794 — which was selling for $75,000. The pace of investment buying picked up and, not surprisingly, hobbyists were more than willing to pay the increasing price. Often, hobbyists will back off when investment buying results in a large price increase. In this case, they well knew that the higher price — even though largely caused by investment buying — was entirely justified. They also knew that the coin would be getting even costlier in the future. With demand coming from both sides, the 1795 chalked up another good gain from 1975 to 1980, reaching $15,000. This marked the second consecutive half-decade in which it turned an investment profit. Then came the crushing blow: the years from 1980 to 1985. While the 1794 was declining in price from $85,000 to $58,000, the 1795 was gaining from $15,000 to a herculean $41,000 — a considerably higher price than anyone thought it would reach by 1985. This dramatic and shocking turn of events brought the two Flowing Hairs to within a scant (for them) $17,000 price differential, whereas in 1980 the price difference had been $70,000! It would be hard to find — in the entire coin market — any other example of such extreme alteration in value alignment over a five year period. Analysts were left stunned. The usual explanation offered for sharp price rises and declines, that of increased or decreased interest in the SERIES, would not work here. This is a series of just two coins. If you take them together, they were selling for a combined price of $100,000 in 1980, and for a combined price of $99,000 in 1985. A mere 1% difference in aggregate value from 1980 to 1985! Yet one coin gained $26,000 and the other lost $27,000! It almost looks as if some prearranged, well orchestrated plan was at work here. The numbers "fit" so well. The overall amount of money being spent on Flowing Hair Dollars was virtually the same between 1980 and 1985 — it was simply channeled away from the 1794 and into the 1795.

Many possible explanations suggest themselves. At $85,000, the 1794 was coming (temporarily at any rate) to the end of its road as an investment coin. Those buying for short term gain would not trust it at that price, and even most of the long term investors felt skeptical. Generally in this kind of situation they would look to another series, such as Draped Busts. This time they apparently looked no further than the coin listed directly beneath it. They bypassed the 1794 and poured investment capital into the 1795, which continued to give the impression of of being undervalued at the $15,000 for which it was selling in 1980. Another potential explanation which has been voiced, but in which we cannot place any confidence, is that buyers recognized that the 1795 had to be considerably scarcer than previously believed. This can hardly be taken seriously, as the relative availabilities of the 1794 and 1795 have been known for many, many years. They have not changed very much — hardly at all — since the 1800s. There is no new research or information on the side of the 1795. There is no new anything, except new bundles of money coming into the marketplace from buyers who want the 1795 but do NOT want the 1794. What has happened is that these two coins have now gotten so close in price that almost anyone who could afford the 1795 at $41,000 could also afford the 1794 at $58,000. Yet the more common 1795, which for eons of time was the "poor man's" Flowing Hair Dollar, is still receiving more attention. It has taken the play totally away from the much rarer, more historic, more-everything 1794. At the current rate of value changes, the 1795 would surpass the 1794 by 1987. However, we strongly advise against betting on it. It just won't happen. The situation as it now exists represents the effects of some very bizarre buying activity; it is a freak market at the moment so far as these two coins are concerned. The 1794 is underpriced at $58,000 and the 1795 is well beyond its logical range at $41,000. Some type of adjustment on a grand scale is in order, and should be shaping up before too much more time passes. They very same individuals (or others like them) who saw the 1795 as irresistible at $15,000 back in 1980 will now recognize the 1794 as being just as irresistible at $58,000. The buying emphasis will switch; it has to. Those who bought the 1795 Flowing Hair for $15,000 in 1980 can sell right now and walk away with a very enviable profit. If they know what they're doing, they will do precisely that — and use the proceeds to purchase 1794 Flowing Hairs. The next few years are going to see quite a few 1795's coming out of hiding. The market will be over supplied for a while, and that over-abundance cannot fail to bring about a decline in price. Not a crash, not a collapse, but an inevitable readjustment down to a more sensible level. While the present holders are selling, there will not be enough buyers for 1795 Flowing Hair Dollars to support the price. Smart investors will not be touching it, and collectors on the whole are probably going to wait until the price get MUCH better. Much as we hate to forecast gloom, we see the 1795 Flowing Hair Dollar going from its present level of $41,000 to a price of $35,000 by 1990. We would not be too surprised to find it slipping under $30,000. by all logic it should only be in the $20,000 to $25,000 range today.

There are two distinct varieties of the 1795, but as they carry the same retail market values we have not listed them on the chart. These are in the category of artistic varieties, which occurred very frequently on coins of the early mint. Die engravers were provided designs from which to work. They followed the designs insofar as all major elements were concerned; if the design called for a spread-wing eagle facing right (as in this case), they engraved a spread-wing eagle facing right. In the minor or accessory details there was, often, some variation from one die to another. This was not intentional but, at the same time, there was no real effort to prevent it. The die engravers had that much latitude in which to operate. Some dies for the reverse side of the 1795 Flowing Hair Dollar show two leaves on each branch beneath the eagle, while others show three. There are also other slight differences between these two dies, clearly reflecting the workmanship of two different engravers who did not attempt to duplicate each other. Naturally there are no separate mintage figures, and we judge from the frequency with which specimens of the two varieties are sold, it is difficult to proclaim one to be scarcer than the other. In the earlier days of numismatics, a collection of Silver Dollars was a date and mint mark collection, and either variety of the 1795 was sufficient. Today, the specialists want both of them — so if you talk in terms of demand it will be split more or less down the middle. There are, however, still some buyers who do not care which variety they get: these are the "type" collectors who merely want one coin representing each different design. With the 1795 still running a bit behind the 1794 in price, most type collectors choose the 1795. So far as the investment potential of the varieties is concerned, we would have to say it is unfavorable on both sides. This is just not an investment date at the present time, in any grade of condition.

A few further observations on the Flowing Hair Dollar may not be unwarranted.

The diameter of this coin varies slightly from one specimen to another. To someone who has possibly collected (or invested in) modern coins, this may come as a shock. We are accustomed to coins being standard in size but such was not the case in the early days of the mint. Variations occurred on the early coins of all denominations, but as the Silver Dollar was physically the largest coin it showed the greatest variations. The differences in diameter from the smallest Flowing Hair Dollar to the largest are no more than one mm. This sounds tiny indeed, and it is, but if you take a 39 mm. specimen and a 40 mm. specimen and place one atop the other it is very noticeable. However the original weights were almost precisely identical. These differences in diameter occurred because the coins were struck without tight fitting collars and the pressure varied from one strike to the next. Some European mints were using steam-driven machinery in the 1790s, but not in the United States. We had, by comparison, a rather primitive operation going. Our coins were being struck on manually operated screw presses, one at a time. The planchet or "blank" was inserted, and the pressman threw the lever to strike the coin. This squeezed the upper and lower dies together against the planchet, as in a vise. Of course, the planchet had been heated and softened so the designs would take better. One pressman exerted more force than the another, because he was stronger, or had more energy. Quite likely, coins struck early in the day — when the workers were well rested — were struck with more force behind them, than those produced later in the day. Thus, in every batch of coins, there would be differences in the depth or strength of impression, and in the diameter. With greater pressure exerted in the striking operation, the planchet spread out further, similar to stepping on a ball of clay. If light pressure was applied, it spread hardly at all. Nobody was concerned with this at the time, of course, as it had nothing to do with the fineness or weight.

The weight DID matter, since a coin (any coin made of precious metal, silver or gold) had intrinsic value. The original concept was that the metal contained in a coin had as much value, as metal, as the coin's face value. In other words, a Silver Dollar was worth one dollar of silver. Of course, this did not always hold precisely true, as silver (and gold) could vary in market value from time to time. Profiting on the manufacture of coins, such as is done by the mint today (to the tune of multi-billions), was unheard of. Thus the weight had to be closely controlled from coin to coin. The mint did not want to issue any overweight coins, for obvious reasons. It did not want to issue underweight coins, either, as this would cast doubt on the integrity of our coinage and open the way for multitudes of problems. Underweight coins would make EVERY coin suspect, and merchants would go back to weighing them as they had in the past. Of course, a certain degree of tolerance was allowed, as it was impossible to make every coin identical in weight down to the hundredth of a gram. The official weight was 26.9 grams and this was strictly maintained. Any slight differences that occurred did not affect the 26.09 reading. Before striking (NOT afterward), each planchet was weighed by a mint worker who did this, and nothing else, the entire day. A balance scale was used with a 26.9 gram counterbalance, and it was very easy to see whether the balance was perfect or not. Other scales with appropriate counterbalances were on hand to weigh the planchets used for coins of other denominations. When an underweight planchet was discovered (we do not know how frequently this happened), it was set aside. At day's end, these planchets were carried back to the smelting rooms, where they would be melted down. There was no way to add weight to an underweight planchet; you had to make the planchet all over again. There was, however, a way of removing weight from an overweight planchet. The mint elected to do this, rather than melt its overweight planchets. It was operating on a tight budget and had no choice but to save money wherever possible. Overweight planchets were passed on to a special workman known usually as an "adjuster" (though to his co-workers he was more often referred to as a "scrap"). It was the adjuster's job to remove a tiny bit of metal and bring down the weight of each overweight planchet to its fair tolerance range. This involved fractions of a gram, as the weight would never be off by a full gram or more. The accepted method of removing excess weight was to scrape the surface of the planchet, using a rasp or file. This yielded silver dust, which could be collected and recycled, though it is not known whether the mint made any effort to collect it. Sometimes the scraping was more in the form of gouging, in which a dental-like instrument was used to remove a chunk of metal. As you can well imagine, speed was the keynote, the physical appearance of the finished product ranking secondary to that consideration. If a worker took ten minutes to adjust the weight of a coin, it would have been necessary to have a dozen or more persons doing this job, and the mint could not afford extra salaries (it was so short of money that its security system consisted of one dog, which was let out at an appointed hour each night to roam the yard and search out possible prowlers; in spite of this, no attempt was ever made to rob or burglarize the mint, though embezzlement occurred often). Once a coin's weight had been adjusted, it would carry the adjustment marks with it into circulation. The striking process would not obliterate them, as they would show on the design and — to a certain extent — on the blank field. As the coin's design wore down with handling, evidence of adjustment likewise faded away. Nevertheless it is usually possible, even on a very worn specimen, to detect whether or not the planchet was adjusted.

Since adjustment marks (as they are called) were a part of the normal minting process of that time, specimens struck with adjusted planchets are not deemed inferior. Adjustment marks do not enter into the condition grade. A coin can have adjustment marks and still rank as uncirculated. The strength of impression is more important than the presence or absence of adjustment marks. An uncirculated specimen of a Flowing Hair Dollar with good strong strike will be a highly admired coin, with or without adjustment marks. It will sell for a higher price than a weak strike without adjustment marks. Do not confuse a weak strike with circulation wear. They give the same initial impression — that the design is not as crisp and sharp as it could be. With a magnifying glass (sometimes even without one) it is easy to tell the difference. If you have a specimen with some circulation wear, portions of the design will be good and sharp while small details have gotten "soft" or totally disappeared. When the problem is a weak strike, it is weak on the whole design, on both sides of the coin.

Toning, or changes in surface coloration, is very widespread on the Flowing Hair Dollars. Coin for coin, there is probably more extensive toning to be encountered on Flowing Hairs than any other Dollars. One can only speculate that this occurred because so many specimens were stored in jars or boxes along with other coins for extended periods of time. Also, storage in the old wooden coin cabinets encouraged toning, especially when these cabinets were made of acidic woods or treated with chemical preparations. Unfortunately it is rare — very rare — to find handsome toning on Flowing Hair Silver Dollars. The luscious reds, blues, violets and other shades seen on the Morgan and Peace dollars hardly ever occur on Flowing Hairs. Mostly the toning on Flowing Hair Dollars detracts from, rather than contributes to, their appearance. It is generally mud gray without brilliance or highlights, making the coin look as if it were made from modeling clay. If you did not know better, you would say the coin was not really silver but lead (do not dismiss this possibility out of hand — some lead fakes were made). This grayness results from oxidation of the copper, with which the silver was alloyed. It is only 10% copper, approximately, but this is more than enough to bring about a complete color change. The copper has actually turned black, but, being mixed with nine parts silver for every part of copper, the overall result is gray instead of black. You may be repulsed by the sight of such specimens, but this is the norm, not the exception. They are worth the full market value, and the occasional specimen with quality toning is worth a little more. Do not attempt to clean them. Some toning will remain and the coin will have a polka-dot appearance — much worse than ordinary bad toning. Watch out for cleaned specimens when you buy. If the coin has been "whizzed" (cleaned with electrically driven brushes), it is not worth the full value. You can detect cleaned specimens in various ways, the easiest of which is by their surface splotchiness. They would not have acquired that kind of appearance in ordinary aging and handling — they were tampered with.

What else should you look for in purchasing Flowing Hair Dollars?

Two points to be considered are the possibility of faking or reengraving.

Faking, of course, can never be totally discounted as a possibility whenever rare coins are involved — and both of the Flowing Hair Dollars are in that category (the 1795 may not be particularly rare, but at $41,000 one can rest assured that it has attracted the notice of a few fakers). We would not say that the number of fakes is greater than of later-date Silver Dollars in similar ranges of price. They do turn up from time to time. In the early days, when the Flowing Hairs were found in circulation, circulation fakes were made. These were made by the casting process, using genuine specimens to produce the casting molds. Pure lead or a combination of various base metals was used for the fakes themselves, covered in a thin layer of silver. The silver coating would either be electroplated, as in the tableware industry, or applied merely by dipping. Electroplating is a much older process than one may imagine. In this fashion the faker would produce spendable "silver" Dollars at an expenditure of perhaps ten cents for materials and another ten cents for labor, 80¢ being clear profit. Obviously, the chances for success were much brighter in the earliest days of Silver Dollars, than they became subsequently. Not many people were intimately familiar with the appearance and feel of real Silver Dollars, and thus would be more likely fooled by a fake. We do not know just how extensive fakery was, on the Flowing Hair Dollar, because most of the evidence is gone: the vast majority of circulation counterfeits have been destroyed over the years. A fairly good indication is provided, though, by the existence of so many circulated Flowing Hair Dollars with holes and test marks. This is true of the Draped Bust Dollars that followed them, too. Such extensive suspicion would not have flourished if people were not being victimized by large numbers of circulation fakes. Weighing was one means of detecting fakes, or attempting to. It was far from ideal. In the first place, some fakes were of the proper weight. Lead is similar in weight to silver, and a careful faker would use just enough led to arrive at the correct weight — even if that meant making the coin a little thicker than it should be. If the fake had a core of tin, zinc, nickel or some other metal, the weight would be short. Another obstacle was the type of scales used in weighing. Most merchants did not have the sophisticated gram scales used by the mint.

They had only merchandise scales that weighed in ounces or penny-weights, and these did not give accurate readings for detecting fakes.

Collector fakes of the Flowing Hair Dollars were made at a much later period and, presumably, are still being made. Some of these were cast, others made by striking with counterfeit dies. Collector fakes (so called because they were designed to be sold at a premium over face value) are of the same silver content as the genuine coins, so they cannot be exposed by weighing or specific gravity testing. If cast, they will normally show the familiar casting bubbles, which are not found on genuine coins. If struck, it then becomes a matter of comparing them against genuine specimens to detect differences in the engraving. Some Flowing Hair fakes have turned up which are extremely good, but sooner or later they are all identified. There is not much danger of buying one through normal dealer channels. You can be quite sure that a dealer, faced with the outlay of many thousands of dollars for a coin, will give it a close inspection before purchasing it.

Genuine Flowing Hair Dollars are sometimes found with evidence of reengraving. The term "reengraving," as applied by numismatists to doctored coins, is used improperly, as the coin was not engraved in the first place — the DIES used in striking the coin were engraved. In any event, a reengraved coin is one in which certain areas of the design have been reworked with an engraver's tool to make them clearer. This has a long history. The ancient coins of Greece and Rome were being reengraved 400 years ago for the Renaissance collectors. It was considered a perfectly acceptable practice in that day; the buyers knew it was being done and they approved. If fact sometimes they ordered reengraving on coins they already owned. Reengraving on American coins did not begin until some years following the Civil War, when the rising prices of old, rare coins made this sort of activity profitable. Mostly the targets were coins with some light circulation wear, which could be passed as "uncs" with reengraving and sold for twice as much. Sometimes, but seldom, it was used on uncirculated specimens having weak strikes. Reengraving never became as widespread on U.S. coins as it was on ancient coins, since the original "relief" or depth of impression was not as high. Ancient coins were almost like sculptures, and reengraving could work wonders in restoring their original appearance. Reengraving is not difficult to detect — it slips by because many people do not look for it. One must recognize that reengraving is a possibility with early Silver Dollars. The chief evidence of reengraving is areas of depression in the field, next to outlines of the design. For example, in the Flowing Hair Dollars one would scan (with a 5X glass) the area around Liberty's face, as this would be the most likely area to be reengraved. Next the hair would come under examination, and finally the eagle on the reverse side. If the field of the coin in direct proximity with Liberty's profile is depressed, or recessed slightly beneath the remainder of the field, this is evidence of reengraving. It is caused by the engraving tool wearing down, or eating into, that portion of the surface. The design is not actually "raised up" in reengraving (that is impossible), it is given the illusion of raising, by depressing the area around it.

THE "DRAPED BUST — SMALL EAGLE" DOLLARS

OBVERSE   **REVERSE**

Although the exact figures seem to be questionable, one of the best guesses is that somewhat less than 70,000 1795 Draped Bust — Small Eagle Dollars were struck in the last couple of months of that year. One source gives a mintage figure of 42,738, but R. W. Julian, in a census conducted in 1963, determined that about 69,000 Bust Dollars were actually struck in the final three months of 1795.

The new design is generally attributed to Gilbert Stuart and evolved because of foreign criticism of the Flowing Hair Dollars. At that time, the Government had no bullion of its own with which to strike coins and depended entirely on private stocks of bullion which were brought to the mint to be struck into coins. These private sources were the only supply available until the 1830s when government stocks of bullion for coinage were established. A sharp decline in private bullion acquisition in 1796 dropped the total number of dollars struck that year well below the total 1795 mintage (203,033) and it wasn't until 1798 that production again reached the six figure mark.

The 1795 Bust Dollars continued the illegal .900 fine alloy and 416 grain weight. The new Mint Director, Elias Boudinot, a Congressman from New Jersey, ordered an immediate change to the official standard. From 1796 through 1798, the dollars continued to weigh 416 grains, but the silver content was reduced to the proper .894 fineness.

For the investor interested in the history and availability of Bust Dollars, a very significant fact is that, during the period from 1798 on, the majority of dollars struck left the country almost immediately (for Europe or the Orient) which has a direct bearing on the availability of the 1798 Bust Dollars.

None of the Draped Bust — Small Eagle Dollars can be considered as Common Dates, or even Semi-Key dates, so despite the seeming disparity in the mintages, we must class them all as Keys.

SILVER $1 — DRAPED BUST/SMALL EAGLE, COMMON DATE
THERE ARE NO COMMON DATES OF THIS VARIETY

SILVER $1 —DRAPED BUST/SMALL EAGLE, SEMI-KEY
THERE ARE NO SEMI-KEYS OF THIS VARIETY

SILVER $1 — DRAPED BUST/SMALL EAGLE, KEY
UNCIRCULATED CONDITION

Year	Mintage	1955	1960	1965	1970	1975	1980	1985
1795	42,738	135.00	325.00	850.00	1700.00	5500.00	18000.00	15500.00
1796	72,920	135.00	250.00	600.00	1450.00	4750.00	12000.00	11875.00
1797	7,776	160.00	425.00	950.00	1600.00	5000.00	12500.00	11875.00
1798	327,536	150.00	325.00	725.00	1300.00	5000.00	10500.00	18250.00

1795 % of increase:	1955-60	141%
	1960-65	136%
	1965-70	94%
	1970-75	235%
	1975-80	162%
	1980-85	8%
overall % of increase:	1955-85	9814%

The Draped Bust Dollar made its debut midway into the year 1795, when a sizable quantity of the "old" style (Flowing Hair) Dollars had already been struck. Though the obverse (front side) was pretty thoroughly reworked, the reverse remained as it had been for the Flowing Hair design. This was the "small eagle," without heraldic symbols. It was redrawn for use with the Draped Bust design, but in the process only very minor details were changed and these, apparently, not intentionally. It was simply the difference between the work of one artist and the work of another. In the earlier days of numismatics, the Draped Bust design was referred to as the earliest Silver Dollar that a non-wealthy hobbyist could collect. This applied for many years, but today they have all reached five figures in uncirculated condition — not too far behind the Flowing Hairs. If you are intent on buying one for less than a thousand dollars, you have two choices (neither very appealing): a specimen on which the date is unreadable, or one punched with a testing hole. Or, as will more likely be the case, a specimen on which the date is unreadable AND which has been punched with a testing hole. Obviously, this is not the way to go for an investor!

Uncirculated Draped Bust/Small Eagle Dollars are not as rare, on the whole, as the Flowing Hair type — and most times they are better looking. You will not encounter the characteristic mud-gray toning of Flowing Hair Dollars as frequently on Draped Busts. Bright uncirculated specimens may not be the rule, and they are certainly not common, but they can be found without any great difficulty. The quality of strike tends to be better, too. Whether this was due to better striking or better dies is hard to determine. You will see some Draped Busts that appear as if they were struck yesterday, but this is very unusual for a Flowing Hair Dollar. The Draped Bust/Small Eagle series was not a long one; being only half a series. In 1798 the switchover was made to the large, or "heraldic" eagle for the reverse side. Only four dates were involved, and in only two of those four years — 1796 and 1797 — was the Draped Bust/Small Eagle type struck exclusively. In 1795, it overlapped Flowing Hairs; in 1798 it overlapped Heraldic Eagles. The Draped Bust type continued (with the changed reverse) until 1803. Then it — and Silver Dollars as a coin denomination — went on the shelf.

Production was stepped up on the Draped Busts but, as you can see, not by a great deal. During the first three years, the mintage totals fell under 100,000, including the ultra-low production year of 1797 when less than eight thousand came off the presses. Then in 1798 the output exceeded the combined total of all Draped Bust Dollars struck previously — the first year in which production topped on quarter of a million. You would presume this to be the least expensive of the four dates, since it is by far the most plentiful. In fact, it is the most expensive at the present time. But we will reserve discussion on that subject until a bit later. There is no question but that the mint wanted to make more Silver Dollars during that period than it actually succeeded in making. The stumbling block was the availability of silver bullion. Silver was still being obtained secondhand from scrap articles, which the mint bought from the public through newspaper announcements. Not too much could be obtained in that way, and for a while it looked as though the supply was diminishing. After all, there was a limit to the number of candlesticks, cups, and other meltable articles that could be found in Philadelphia. In addition, there was public apathy to contend with. When the government first announced establishment of a mint, in 1792, the request for scrap silver met a fairly enthusiastic response. Some public spirited citizens brought in large quantities of it. They were under the impression that they were doing their part, until the mint set up a regular supply channel for silver bullion. When years passed, and the mint was still asking for scrap silver, many people began to lose interest. They concluded the government was using them as a crutch instead of trying to locate a source of silver. Even the dealers in scrap silver were not selling to the government. They preferred to sell to silversmiths, as there was less red tape and they received payment quicker.

The investor will, of course, be curious about the attrition or destruction ratio of Draped Bust/Small Eagle Dollars. Mintage figures are not entirely informative unless one has at least some rough idea about preservation rations. Generally speaking, this series had a low preservation rate, second only to the Flowing Hair Dollars in that respect. The age of these coins has very little to do with it. Age by itself will not destroy a coin. We know that in the course of circulating, some coins are lost or accidentally destroyed in one way or another (going down in shipwrecks, for example — which was not an uncommon occurrence in those days). Some coins are destroyed in fires, and of course fires are very prevalent in early America with its woodframe houses and combustible furnishings. But destruction or loss through these means is a measured loss which will affect all coins almost equally. The pioneer Silver Dollars suffered far greater losses because of the intentional melting by profiteers and silversmiths, as detailed in the discussion on Flowing Hair Dollars directly preceding this section. It was still going on in the time of the Draped Bust/Small Eagle Dollar. Also, one must realize that the Draped Bust Dollars were not quite as enticing to contemporary collectors. If anyone was going to save Dollars from a hobbyist standpoint in the 1790s, his first target was obviously going to be Flowing Hairs, as they were the original Dollars of the species. This meant less intentional preservation for the Draped Busts. If we sound like we KNOW what the exact preservation ratio was — we don't. No one does. It was low, by all evidence, speculation and theory. Having made that observation, we cannot get any more precise. One thing we do know is that the Draped Busts stayed in circulation for ages. This was largely because no Silver Dollars, of any kind, were struck in the years from 1805 to 1835. Many specimens were handled so much, over those 30 years, that they became worn to the point of being unrecognizable. You will find them at coin shows, selling for one-twentieth the price of an "unc." At first glance they look like unstamped metal discs; only by looking closer can you begin to distinguish a design. The date, of course, is long since gone, but so long as it can be determined that a Draped Bust is on one side and a Small Eagle on the other, the "type" is identifiable. These coins did not get that way gradually in the course of 190 years. They were already worn smooth by 1835. But even specimens with just moderate circulation wear were ranked as plain "old coins" for many years. You will even — as hard as this may be to believe — find old auction catalogues, from the 1870s and 1880s, in which Draped Bust Dollars in circulated condition sold for LESS THAN FACE VALUE. Yes, they were still legal tender (just as they remain today) and spendable at one dollar. Yet they were sold for prices like 70¢ and 80¢, as the "prices realized" clearly indicate. How could this happen? Very simple. The early auctions were strictly "unreserved." Everything was sold for the highest bid, no matter how ridiculous the highest bid happened to be. It was not unusual for a few coins, in any auction, to sell for less than face. These were coins that nobody really wanted, but someone placed a bid — finally — just to get them as spendable money. The auctioneer had to sell them, as he would otherwise be violating the rules of the sale. (Today an auctioneer would simply withdraw a lot on which the bidding is too low.) It may be hard to think of Draped Bust Dollars falling into that category, but the evidence is there. When they were well circulated, they were just coins. When they were uncirculated, well, maybe you could get five dollars apiece for them in the 1870s. That was a lot of money for a coin in those days, especially a coin that was not noted for extreme rarity. When the dealers bought them, they would pay approximately 25¢ over the face value.

The Draped Busts gained considerably in stature toward the close of the nineteenth century, mainly because of the multiplicity of coin hobbyists. Popularity of the 1804 Dollar helped, even though it had a different reverse design. The publicity surrounding that super coin led many hobbyists to collect Silver Dollars and particularly the Draped Busts. They were available, and with the exception of the 1804 you could aspire to a complete run of them. Of course, the collectors of the late 1800s were not aware of all the varieties that we now know to exist, but this might have been a help rather than a hindrance. Early collectors like a date collection. There was help on the way from numismatic researchers, too. A great deal of study was being undertaken on Draped Bust Dollars and its results published in the coin journals of that era. This was the tip of the iceberg; the twentieth century brought about truly mountainous research, which is still continuing and — apparently — still increasing. Almost all known specimens of Draped Bust Dollars have been carefully examined for possible die variations, and many efforts have been made to estimate the rarity of one variety vs. that of another. This series was one of the most prolific, so far as varieties are concerned. More dies were used in striking, and it appears that no two are alike. If you take the Draped Bust series as a whole, including the Heraldic Eagle reverses which began in 1798, it carries far more varieties and more MAJOR varieties than any other group of Silver Dollars. As we said, the early collectors were not fully aware of this, but as more and more die varieties became known, the Draped Bust Dollars attracted greater attention. Everyone want to examine their own specimens — and those in the stock of their local coin dealer — to see if he could find an unrecorded variety. In addition to the major varieties found mentioned in auction sale catalogues and numismatic literature, the minor ones are legion, occurring every year and usually in quantity. Some of these do not involve the engraving itself but are in the nature of "die crack" or "die break" varieties, which are sometimes referred to as "stress varieties." It is sometimes possible to trace the development of a crack on a die through the coins produced from that die. There will be early specimens in which the crack is small, and late ones (possibly dating from the same year, but obviously struck late in the year) in which the crack has widened or gotten longer. It can be identified as the same die because the crack starts in precisely the same place on both coins. When dies crack, they crack at random points, and it would be most unlikely for two dies to crack at exactly the same spot — especially in a situation, such as we have with the Draped Busts, when the total number of dies in use was not too great. Of course, the mint should have disposed of any working dies that cracked, as soon as the defect was noticed. Once again it was a matter of finances. The die itself was not worth much money, but the time and labor that went into producing a new die was costly. Meanwhile, fewer coins would be struck, without the die in service, and production would fall behind schedule. Most times a cracked die remained in use until it actually split in two. This of course could happen in a split second, as the presence of a crack meant the die was weak and could split at any time. Die cracks are largely the result of the constant temperature changes to which they were exposed, in striking the heated planchets.

Of the so-called major varieties (the only ones which space permits us to mention), there are two for the 1795, three for the 1796, three for the 1797, and two for the 1798 at this point. The words "at this point" must be emphasized, as the consensus of opinion on what constitutes a major variety tends to vary. There are not differences in the market values from one variety to another, of any of the four dates, and no really reliable information on which is scarcer. Of course there has been, and continues to be, speculation on relative scarcities, which may lead the investor to choose one variety over another. On the surface this would seem like a way of doubling a coin's investment potential: getting a date that shows good prospects of turning a profit, and getting it in the scarcest variety. Of course if you pay the standard market price — no premium — you can't do yourself any harm. Whether you will do any good is very questionable. When varieties have a long history of moving together as a unit in value, they are likely to continue doing so. Even when this is not the case, and a value spread eventually develops among them, it is very difficult to forecast which variety or varieties will benefit from it. In nine cases out of ten this seems to happen without logical cause. A variety specimen may, for example, command a higher than normal price in a well publicized auction sale. The result if taken, by some, to indicate that this particular variety is more valuable than its counterparts, and a mild increase in overall market value can follow. In reality the specimen sold at auction might have brought just as much if it were a different variety; its variety status may have had nothing to do with the price. This is a clear cut example of trying to read too much into statistics! Also, book publicity can increase (temporarily, anyway) the value of a variety coin. These are chance factors and really outside the scope of investment strategy. When you buy a variety coin for investment, you had best be certain that the coin — regardless of its variety — has the necessary profit potential. The truth of the matter is that relative scarcity of different varieties of a coin is very difficult to pin down. It seems as though one need only check through stacks of auction sale catalogues, to determine the frequency of sale of each different variety. In many instances, no attention will be called to the variety, and it is either not pictured in the catalogue or pictured in a photograph of such low quality that the variety cannot be identified. This is true even of costly Silver Dollars, which deserve to be described in exacting detail. When you add to this the fact that varieties are sometimes incorrectly identified, calculations become anything but informative. We advocate buying by date in cases where two or more varieties OF THE SAME PRICE exist, but be sure the coin does carry proper identification as to variety. This is vital for your own information in the event a price spread does develop, as well as being an important factor in selling the coin.

We will point out a few of the varieties which can be found on the Draped Bust/Small Eagle series.

       small date/small letters
       small date/large letters
       large date/small letters

No specimens have as yet been discovered with large date/large letters, though it is entirely conceivable that this could happen.

Visually these are very minor varieties. Even when one is aware of their existence they are difficult to spot. Unless you are very familiar with the series, comparison coins are needed to make a positive identification. The "small date" is only fractionally smaller than the "large date," the "small letters" barely smaller than the "large letters." In comparing two coins of different varieties, the difference can be noted, but a lone coin may be very confusing. When any wear has developed, the confusion becomes still greater, and this is why incorrect identifications are sometime encountered.

These varieties occurred because of the method of producing coin dies. The designs were engraved directly on the dies, but the accessory work — date and lettering — was added by means of punches. Apparently two different styles of punches were in use, the "large" style and "small" style. As the dies passed through this phase of the operation, it was a matter of pure chance whether they would be impressed with the large or small style punch. As the date and lettering were on different punches, they could receive a "small" date and "large" lettering, or the other way around; or the date and letter could both be small or both large. There were four possible combinations but, as we noted above, no "large/large" specimens have yet come to the attention of numismatists. If it so happened that none were made, this again was the result of pure chance.

Total mintage given by mint records was 72,920 for 1796. If production of the three varieties was equal, slightly fewer than 25,000 of each would have been manufactured. We can be quite sure it was not equal, but we do not know how unequal.

At this point some readers are almost certainly asking the following question:

If 72,920 specimens were struck, how could it happen that none with "large date" and "large letters" have been discovered? There are various possible explanations. The most plausible is that the punches with "large date" and "large letters" never got on the workbench of the same workman simultaneously. One workman had the "large date" punch while another had the "large letters" punch, and each had both the "small date" and "small letters" punch. The difference between the date and letters in these varieties is exclusively in their size. In style they are perfectly alike.

For 1797 the varieties were:

10 stars at left/6 stars at right
9 stars at left/7 stars at right, large letters
9 stars at left/7 stars at right, small letters

Now things begin to get a bit more complex. There is only one version of the "10 stars left/6 stars right" variety, as it is not known in different sizes of lettering. On the "9 stars left/7 stars right" variety, specimens are known in both large and small lettering. Hence, a total of three varieties — with, once again, no differences in the retail market values.

As you will see from the illustration of the Draped Bust obverse (or front of the coin), a curved column of stars was placed at either side of Liberty's portrait. This was purely for decorative effect, though some have believed that the stars represented states in the union or other symbolism. Without the stars — or SOMETHING at either side — the design would have lacked balance, in addition to having very large open fields. In the preparation of this design it was indicated only that stars be at either side of the portrait, following the curvature of the coin. There were no specifications on the number of stars. As the area to be filled on the left side was larger than on the right side, more stars would naturally be used on the left (the alternative being to use the same number but to space those on the left at greater distance from each other). Just as with the date and lettering, the stars were punched in after the die was engraved. There was real latitude here, in the number of stars to be punched. They could be spaced closely or set farther apart, so long as balance was achieved on both sides of the design. Thus, some obverse dies ended up with ten stars on the left, and others with only nine; while some had seven stars on the right, and others six. It is interesting to note that the combination always adds up to 16; no specimens are known with nine stars on the left and six on the right. Perhaps the workmen were told to use 16 stars, without being told how they should be divided. However, as we will soon see, this directive (if it ever existed in the first place) was abandoned. In the 1798 striking, some specimens have a total of 15 stars and others a total of just 13. The stars are always the same in style and size, the difference being only in their number. Varieties of this sort are meaningless to the general collector, who wants dates above all else. They are of interest wholly to specialists who concentrate on one date or one series and try to acquire every known variation. There are no 1797 varieties concerning the date, as occurred on the 1796. On all known specimens the date is of the same size. However, varieties with "large letters" and "small letters" do occur on obverses having nine stars to the left and seven to the right. They do not occur on obverses with ten stars to the left and six to the right. Once again we must refer to the theory of the workman's bench for an explanation. The workman punching dies with "ten stars left/six stars right" undoubtedly had only one set of letter punches available to him. His coworker punching the other style of obverse had both letter punches and used them at random.

In 1798 there were two major varieties:
15 star obverse
13 star obverse
As no overdates were struck in 1798, we know that fresh dies had to be used. This meant repunching the stars and a different pattern developed than in the previous year. Perhaps there had been a turnover in employees and new workmen were involved.

Before the year 1798 drew to a close, the Small Eagle was removed from the reverse side and replaced with the Heraldic Eagle. This is not considered a variety but a whole new type, or design, and these coins are discussed in the following section.

Neither the price histories or current market values of the Draped Bust/Small Eagle Dollars seem to make much sense. Prices are not in line with mintage figures or availability. One thing thing that can be readily observed from the price histories is that investors made their initial big move on these coins in the years between 1965 and 1970. The figures alone — with no other supportive evidence — show the market slipping away from collectors in the 1965-70 period and into the control of investors. In both 1965 and 1970, the 1797 was the highest priced Draped Bust/Small Eagle Dollar. It had historically been the highest prices thanks to having the smallest (by far) mintage of the four dates, and would have continued in that position without the influence of speculative buying. By 1970 the 1797 had been surpassed in value by the 1795, of which six times as many specimens were struck. It reached $1700 while the 1797 — still rising in price but not as rapidly — stood at $1600. What happened was quite obvious. Investors entering the Silver Dollar field between 1965 and 1970 studied the list and many of them apparently considered the 1797 too high priced for an early profit. This was certainly erroneous reasoning on their part, as the 1797 deserved an even higher price in relation to its availability and was clearly the coin to buy among this group. In any case, they looked for another favorable date — a coin with a lower price but still a relatively low mintage. Only one out of the remaining three answered the purpose: the 1795. It was next lowest in mintage to the 1797, and you could buy it for $100 less. The fact that six times as many specimens were struck seems not to have occurred to investment buyers of the mid and late sixties. They liked the 1795, they bought it, and they drove it to the top of the heap by 1970. Surprisingly enough it was still there in 1975, though in the years from 1970 to 1975 all of the Draped Bust/Small Eagle Silver Dollars scored sufficient gains to turn handsome investment profits. Having registered investment-size gains in three consecutive half decades, the 1795 was once again heavily bought in the years from 1975 to 1980 and attained the astounding price of $18,000 by the decade's end. This was not only higher than it deserved to be, but much higher than it merited in relation to the 1797 — which reached only $12,500 by 1980. The difference of $5500 in the relative values of these coins should have been in favor of the 1797. The time for a readjustment had come — was overdue. It arrived in the early eighties, but in a most unlikely form. Any skilled observer making investment forecasts in 1980 would have tabbed the 1797 to rise to the top by 1985, with the 1795 holding steady or slipping back somewhat to more reasonable territory. The 1795 did indeed slip back, dropping from $18,000 to $15,500 in the 1985 market, at which sum it is still fully priced and out of bounds for investment at the present time. Beyond this, the price movements of the Draped Bust/Small Eagle Dollars were chaotic. The 1797 did not gain from the 1795's retreat, as it should have. It, too, lost ground. Having been undervalued in 1980 it has become more undervalued at its 1985 price of just $11,875. It is now tied with the 1796 for the lowest price among Draped Bust/Small Eagle Dollars in uncirculated condition — in spite of having the lowest mintage in the series. To top off this bizarre turn of event, the 1798 — which has the HIGHEST mintage and has long been regarded as the most common date in the group — has ascended to the first place in market value. The 1798 is now commanding $18,250, while no other Draped Bust/Small Eagle Dollar is even as high as $16,000.

One could be excused for concluding that these coins have been bought and sold very haphazardly. Haphazard buying did occur, even on coins worth more than ten thousand dollars. In fact they are often the most vulnerable targets of such buying. Investors with large capital but no knowledge of numismatics or of coin investing are drawn to them. In 1980 the 1798 was the lowest priced date in the series, which it should be. It was bought by many investors strictly on grounds of having the lowest price, without making any further investigation into its potential. Though there was enough buying activity to send the price up by almost $8000, no profit resulted for those who bought in 1980. In fact, nobody who bought ANY of the Draped Bust/Small Eagle Dollars in 1980 had a profit by 1985. Had at least the majority of investors recognized the 1797 as the coin to buy, it could easily have climbed to a profitable level while the others were adjusting. As it was, investors were at cross purposes, defeating each other and, ultimately, themselves. Those now holding the 1798 are on the threshold of a profit — but the final push into profitable ground will not be easy. The 1798 is so overpriced at $18,250 that it cannot gain any further support from new investment purchases. No wise investor would touch it at $18,250, and collectors cannot be expected to buy it at that kind of sum either. Instead, we believe most of those now holding the 1798 will decide to sell and take a small loss for the sake of purchasing more attractive investment coins. As this occurs the price will gradually deflate, and the 1798 should come down within the next several years. We are going to predict it falling to $15,000 by 1990, which will still leave it somewhat overpriced. However for the Draped Bust/Small Eagle series as a whole we think the prospects are bight during the next five years. There is a super coin here, the 1797, which at this moment ranks as one of the most favorable of all Silver Dollars for investment purchase. We are designating it among our BEST BET selections and project its value to rise from the current level of $11,875 to $22,500 or $25,000 by 1990. Nothing extraordinary needs to happen for the 1797 to achieve that kind of price advance. It is necessary only for buyers to begin thinking straight and avoiding overpriced coins. If they buy this series properly, most of their funds will be going into the 1797 and it should benefit very handsomely.

As for the other two coins in this group, the 1796 is shaping up as a favorable long term investment. We could not honestly consider it attractive for the short term at its current price of $11,875. This is precisely as much as the 1797 now commands, and we do not see these coins rising at an equal rate in the next five years. The 1797 can expect a much faster spurt of value increase because it is so seriously undervalued. For the 1796, a rise to $15,000 or $17,500 by 1990 would be more within the realm of possibility, but from there the price could and should improve dramatically in the following five years. We think you will realize a profit on the 1796 by 1995, if bought at the prevailing 1985 price in uncirculated condition.

The 1795 ranks as a borderline coin at the present time. The mintage is relatively low, and it has certainly demonstrated the ability to return profits to its holders. We are of the opinion that the current price, though it represents a decline of $2500 within the past five years, has still failed to bring the 1795 back down to investment territory. Some investors will automatically be buying it, just because of its price decline (some investors will buy ANY coin that has declined in price). We don't look for it to get above $20,000 by 1990, with a future projection of $30,000 by 1995. Admittedly these are conservative numbers and it could do better. But frankly if you are interested in Draped Bust/Small Eagle Dollars for investment, everything points so strongly in favor of the 1797 that it seems almost pointless to look further.

THE "DRAPED BUST — HERALDIC EAGLE" DOLLARS

OBVERSE   **REVERSE**

Starting in 1796, the Heraldic Eagle design was introduced for the reverse of U.S. coins, beginning with the quarter eagle or $2.50 gold piece. By 1798, all our gold coins had the new design and pressure mounted to introduce it on the silver dollar.

The Mint Director actually ordered that all of the silver coins receive new designs, but the dollar, being the prominent trade coin, got the new reverse first. As nearly as can be determined, the switch was made about the end of January, 1798, so the majority of the 327 thousand dollars listed for that year are the new design, probably around 290 thousand.

It is with this series that we find two new factors to contend with — the proof coin and the restrike. Actually, one and the same in this case, because the only actual proofs for this series are restrikes, made some years later. Up until about 1817, there are no true proofs known, although there are several "Presentation Pieces," as Breen calls them, including a 1795 dollar and others made to more stringent specifications than the circulation strikes. As you will see, proof coins play an increasing role in investment possibilities as we progress through the dollar series.

The Heraldic Eagle reverse came about as a move toward adding some prestige to our coinage, both to express our national pride and to close the rather embarrassing gap in artistic quality between our coins and those of Europe which dominated world trade. The year 1798 marked a significant turning point in world trade as foreign gold and silver coins began flowing into this country in sharply increasing numbers. With more silver bullion available, more silver coins could be struck. For a time, the subsidiary silver was the prime effort — mainly to show as large a quantity of coins as possible for the scant supplies of bullion available. With increased trade, the dollar got the nod as the coin to strike. The 416 grain weight continued, as did the .892 fineness. Traders continued to ship dollars overseas as fast as they could get their hands on them, a problem that led to suspension of striking dollars in early 1804. They were not to be resumed until 1836.

Again for this series we must consider all dates as Key coins. Despite the large mintages, the survivorship is extremely low. As you will note, this series has experienced an extreme case of "leveling," to the point where all of the current prices are equal. This is surely a result of heavy investor buying and, to some degree, heavy investor selling. While it may present a picture of confusion, the skilled investor is not discouraged by these situations.

Year	Mintage	1955	1960	1965	1970	1975	1980	1985
1798	190,000	85.00	140.00	350.00	825.00	2300.00	6000.00	7250.00
1799	423,515	85.00	140.00	250.00	775.00	2500.00	6000.00	7250.00
1800	220,920	100.00	140.00	230.00	700.00	2500.00	6000.00	7250.00
1801	54,454	135.00	175.00	275.00	700.00	2500.00	6000.00	7250.00
1802	41,650	110.00	135.00	260.00	725.00	2500.00	6000.00	7250.00
1803	85,634	100.00	125.00	260.00	725.00	2500.00	6000.00	7250.00
1804, Type I	8	5000.00	10000.00	10000.00	10000.00	150000.00	150000.00	200000.00
1804, Type II	7	3125.00	8000.00	29000.00	29000.00	125000.00	400000.00	250000.00

Series % of increase:		
	1955-60	39%
	1960-65	115%
	1965-70	7%
	1970-75	383%
	1975-80	179%
	1980-85	-16%
overall % of increase:	1955-85	5546%

Jefferson felt a strong sense of personal involvement, because he had contributed so much to the Independence of 1776 and then to establishment of the mint in 1792. He held a very low opinion of persons who assaulted the Dollar, destroying it for their own personal gain; but aside from holding a low opinion there was little he, or anybody else, could do. The public complained that not enough Silver Dollars were available for commerce and banking. For years the government listened to these complaints, and looked at the costs it was incurring in manufacturing Silver Dollars (it did not make a profit on coin production in those days, as it does now). It was receiving criticism from all sides in addition to losing money. Finally, in 1804, with Jefferson in the third year of his first term, the decision came: no more Silver Dollars. The mint would strike for further Silver Dollars, period. This was not announced as a temporary measure. It was not an interruption in Silver Dollar production. It was a complete, final, no-clause termination of the Silver Dollar after ten years of problem-plagued production. And it is entirely likely that the Silver

Dollar would never have returned, if extensive supplies of silver bullion had not been located. We know that the ax fell on the Silver Dollar in 1804, not in 1803 as is often supposed. The evidence for this is NOT the existence of those very few Dollars dated 1804, as they are now known to have been stuck at a later date. It is, rather, the records of the mint itself, which indicate that 19,500 Silver Dollars were manufactured in 1804 before production was halted. For many years, this statistic puzzled numismatic historians. If nearly twenty thousand were struck that year, how could they be so rare? This is a much higher mintage figure than for the 1797 Dollar, which is not in the same league with the 1804 in terms of rarity or price. Various theories were put forward. As it was impossible that 19,500 Silver Dollars dated 1804 reached circulation, it was popularly supposed that the mint did indeed produce them but then melted the whole batch — with the exception of the handful that somehow got out. If the Dollar was going to be scrapped anyway, why waste silver on it, when the metal could be put to better use in silver coins of lower denominations? Twenty thousand Dollars will make 200,000 Dimes or 400,000 Half Dimes. Recycling the coins was the accepted explanation, for many years, for the 19,500 mintage figure. Later investigations revealed that no recycling was done, so far as can be determined. It also revealed, even more importantly, that no Dollars dated 1804 were struck in 1804. The entire output of 19,500 pieces consisted of backdate Dollars, presumably (but not positively) all carrying the 1803 date. If the mint was fairly certain, when 1803 was at a close, that the Dollar's days were numbered, would it really have bothered preparing more dies? Would it have even bothered punching Jefferson felt a strong sense of personal involvement, because he had contributed so much to the Independence of 1776 and then to establishment of the mint in 1792. He held a very low opinion of persons who assaulted the Dollar, destroying it for their own personal gain; but aside from holding a low opinion there was little he, or anybody else, could do. The public complained that not enough Silver Dollars were available for commerce and banking. For years the government listened to these complaints, and looked at the costs it was incurring in manufacturing Silver Dollars (it did not make a profit on coin production in those days, as it does now). It was receiving criticism from all sides in addition to losing money. Finally, in 1804, with Jefferson in the third year of his first term, the decision came: no more Silver Dollars. The mint would strike for further Silver Dollars, period. This was not announced as a temporary measure. It was not an interruption in Silver Dollar production. It was a complete, final, no-clause termination of the Silver Dollar after ten years of problem-plagued production. And it is entirely likely that the Silver Dollar would never have returned, if extensive supplies of silver bullion had not been located.

We know that the ax fell on the Silver Dollar in 1804, not in 1803 as is often supposed. The evidence for this is NOT the existence of those very few Dollars dated 1804, as they are now known to have been stuck at a later date. It is, rather, the records of the mint itself, which indicate that 19,500 Silver Dollars were manufactured in 1804 before production was halted. For many years, this statistic puzzled numismatic historians. If nearly twenty thousand were struck that year, how could they be so rare? This is a much higher mintage figure than for the 1797 Dollar, which is not in the same league with the 1804 in terms of rarity or price. Various theories were put forward. As it was impossible that 19,500 Silver Dollars dated 1804 reached circulation, it was popularly supposed that the mint did indeed produce them but then melted the whole batch — with the exception of the handful that somehow got out. If the Dollar was going to be scrapped anyway, why waste silver on it, when the metal could be put to better use in silver coins of lower denominations? Twenty thousand Dollars will make 200,000 Dimes or 400,000 Half Dimes. Recycling the coins was the accepted explanation, for many years, for the 19,500 mintage figure. Later investigations revealed that no recycling was done, so far as can be determined. It also revealed, even more importantly, that no Dollars dated 1804 were struck in 1804. The entire output of 19,500 pieces consisted of backdate Dollars, presumably (but not positively) all carrying the 1803 date. If the mint was fairly certain, when 1803 was at a close, that the Dollar's days were numbered, would it really have bothered preparing more dies? Would it have even bothered punching new dates into the old dies, which must have been fairly worn by then? Most likely mint officials said, "Well, we'll keep going ahead with production until word comes to stop, but we'll just continue using the 1803 dies." There was nothing in the regulations to prevent this. There was no rule that coins must bear the date of the year in which they were produced, and it is evident that this was not the first (nor last) time that outdated dies were kept in use without being repunched with the current year. Mint statistics on yearly production were designed ONLY to indicate output in a calendar year, not to show the specific quantities of coins struck with one date or another. So the best conclusion to be drawn is that the actual output of 1803 Silver Dollars was not the 85,634 indicated by mintage figures, but something in the neighborhood of 105,000. As this is a relatively small difference in a mintage that stood at close to one hundred thousand, it does not have a great bearing on investment strategy. But it does serve to show the workings of the mint in those primitive times, and to clear up at least one mystery surrounding the great 1804 Dollar.

The switch to the Heraldic Eagle design for the reverse side was not, of course, restricted to the Dollar, but was made on the whole series of silver coins. It was considered more in keeping with the European approach, which was to have clearly recognizable national symbols on at least one side of the coin. Also the European "crowns" (the equivalent to our Silver Dollars) were fine works of art, while the Small Eagle design seemed plain by comparison. Demise of the Silver Dollar just a few years thereafter meant a very brief lifespan for the noble Heraldic Eagle. When the denomination was reintroduced, the eagle was totally restyled. Many collectors consider the Draped Bust/Heraldic Eagle our finest Silver Dollars in terms of artistry. This of course is a debatable point as the Morgans are also beautifully designed.

For the collector of varieties, the Draped Bust/Heraldic Eagle series is a playground not to be equaled. Investors are urged not to concern themselves too much with the varieties, as there has been no difference in market price arising from the varieties of AND of the dates — with the exception of the 1804 as we will soon discuss. The others have moved along in the trade as date coins exclusively and give every indication of continuing in this fashion well into the foreseeable future. Still it is worthwhile for the investor to be aware of the varieties that exist and have been identified as "major," as opposed to the minor ones to which attention is rarely called in sales offerings.

These are are follows:

For 1798 there are four major varieties:

 Knob 9

 Ten arrows

 Thirteen arrows with wide date

 Thirteen arrows with compressed date

The "knob 9" variety, occurring on a portion of the run from 1798, involves the numeral 9 in the date, which on these coins has a blunted or knobbed appearance. As usually the dates were being punched on the dies, and one of the punches apparently carried this irregularity. Technically, the variety was in the punch and then transferred to the coin, rather than originating with the die. It is not instantly recognizable unless one is familiar with it, and on coins with circulation wear it becomes still less easily noticed.

The so-called "arrow" varieties relate to the reverse side. As this was the first use of the Heraldic Eagle reverse it was inevitable that some discrepancies would exist from one die to the next. Artists were basing their engravings on the Great Seal, but as was customary in the early days of U.S. coinage there was no attempt at precise duplication. One of the components of this design is the sheaf of arrows clutched in the right claws of the eagle, symbolizing national defense. On one or more of the dies, the eagle holds ten arrows, while on one or more of the others they add up to 13 (they are not easy to count, being so tightly bunched, but numismatic researchers enjoy this sort of challenge). This is another of the many varieties which cannot be noticed unless you are specifically looking for it. This variety was part of the engraving and not added by means of a punch.

The "wide date" and "compressed date" varieties involve the spacing between numerals in the date. Here, again, there is little actual difference, but it can be noticed by comparison. The numerals were not punched in individually but set together into a single punch so that the date could be impressed into the die with one operation. Slight variations in spacing were so likely that it is surprising they did not occur more often. It is impossible to say whether one or the other represents an early type. The popular assumption is that both were made at approximately the same time, probably by two different workers.

Varieties for 1799 included the following:

 Overdate with 15 stars on obverse

 Overdate with 13 stars on obverse

 Irregular date with 15 stars on reverse

 Irregular date with 13 stars on reverse

This is one of the more interesting groups of varieties to occur in a single year on an early Silver Dollar. For one thing it includes the first known striking of an overdate on a Silver Dollar, and that in itself is a milestone. There had been no overdates in the Flowing Hair series (none was possible in 1794, as that was the first year of issue), and none in the Draped Bust/Small Eagle series. As a rule, overdates occurred less frequently on Silver Dollars than on silver coins of lower denominations. On early Quarters and Halves they are particularly numerous, going all the way up to the mid 1800s in fact. Much speculation has been entered into, in an attempt to explain the infrequency of overdates on Silver Dollars. One theory is that the large size of the coin, and hence the correspondingly larger size of the numerals in the date, discouraged overdating: it made overdates too obvious. Overdating was the practice of changing the date on a coin die (not on the coins themselves, as all work was always done on the dies) by revising the old die to give the current date. This was customarily done — and presumably with full approval of mint authorities — whenever an outdated die was still in good condition without cracks or serious wear. Rather than engraving a new die, the new date was punched over the old. Since the old die has received some wear, the newly punched date would always be more legible than the one it replaced; but rarely did it cover the old date so effectively that it could not be seen at all. This was largely a matter of the numerals involved and how well they matched each other. The simplest task was in changing just one numeral (such as in this case, changing 1798 to 1799), and the success ratio was greater if the numerals had the same general contour. For example, an "8" would go very well over a "6" without leaving much telltale evidence. Some combinations were bad, such as "7" over "6" and "4" over "3." And of course if two digits had to be changed — going from 1809 to 1810, for example — that was really difficult to camouflage. For many years collectors automatically assumed that overdate varieties were scarcer than the regular date. As the market values are identical this should not be a cause for great concern.

The "irregular date" varieties on the 1799 are of interest as they represent non-overdates which are, nevertheless, a bit out of the ordinary. Normally a date on a coin is either an overdate or a standard date. In striking the 1799 Draped Bust/Heraldic Eagle Dollars, at least one die was used in which the date was out of register. This can only be accounted for by the punch numerals being hastily aligned. Being accustomed as we are to uniformity in coinage dates, these coins are rather easily recognized. It was certainly not the norm for coins to have shoddy dates at that time. This was a rare exception. At least two different reverse dies were used in combination with the "irregular date" obverse die, resulting in still further varieties.

Beyond those mentioned above, varieties also occurred on the 1799 Dollar with regard to the numbers of stars. This, as we noted earlier, was in evidence in the Draped Bust/Small Eagle series as well. However, there was an important difference so far as the 1799 Dollar was concerned. In the preceding series the varieties involving differences in the numbers of stars ALWAYS dealt with the obverse (or front) of the coin, since the Small Eagle reverse motif did not have stars. The new reverse motif, the Heraldic Eagle, had stars of its own, strewn across the blank field above the eagle. These were slightly smaller than the stars on the obverse but, like them, were also applied by means of a punch. They were not engraved into the die. Punching did the work much faster and also assured that every star would be identical in size and shape, which freehand engraving would not likely achieve. Of course, punching did not guarantee that the same NUMBER of stars would appear on every die. In the 1799 reverses we find some specimens with 13 stars and others having 15; there are none recorded with 14 stars. This could lead to the assumption that only two reverse dies were in use, but in fact the number was undoubtedly greater. Nearly half a million coins were struck that year, and it would be hard to imagine two dies lasting that long.

Differences in the number of stars occurred on the obverse, too, some having 13 and others 15. These are the stars framing the portrait of Liberty at either side of the design.

In addition to the overdates of 1799 and the irregular dates, some specimens are known in which the date is entirely normal. These could easily be assumed to be the most plentiful of the lot, but, if so, it has not been reflected in the prices.

The varieties to be found on Silver Dollars dated 1800 are:

Ten arrows

Twelve arrows

Wide date with misaligned 8

Fractured date

"Americai"

There are no known overdates on the 1800 Silver Dollar. Hardly surprising, as that would have necessitated repunching three of the four numerals in the date (to change 1799 to 1800). All of the 1800 output was struck from fresh dies but, as you can see from the above list of varieties, there was hardly much uniformity among them. The varieties that year were not only numerous but included exotic types that had not previously occurred.

The varieties known as "ten arrows" and "twelve arrows" relate to the number of arrows held in the right claw of the eagle, on the reverse side. Normally there are 13 arrows in the portrayal of the Heraldic Eagle, and some specimens of the 1800 Silver Dollar do show the 13 arrows. In striking, the obverses and reverses were used interchangeably. Thus, you can find any of the obverse varieties in combination with any of the reverse varieties, or in combination with a normal 13 arrow reverse. The number of possible combinations is greater than one might imagine.

The "wide date with misaligned 8" variety is one of those plentiful oddities — this one odder than usual — which occurred due to the practice of punching in the date separately from engraving the die. Spacing of the four numerals comprising the date was at the workman's discretion. In this instance the die puncher not only spaced the numerals more widely apart than was normal, he also impressed the "8" out of register. The lower part of the "8" hangs down beneath both of the numerals on either side of it. At first glance this looks like an overdate — as if the "8" was not punched at the same time as the rest of the numerals. Of course it cannot be an overdate. This has to be ascribed to nothing more than human blunder. Once something like this was done, it could not be undone. They only way to fix an improperly punched die was to melt the entire die and start over again: which proved to be much too time-consuming. This would be allowed only if a serious error occurred in the basic engraving. We do not know if such errors ever did occur. Differences in the number of arrows on the reverse side were not considered serious errors, if indeed they were regarded as errors at all. Quite likely nobody noticed them until collectors came on the scene.

The "fractured date," often called "dotted date," likewise involved the punching of the date (on a different die, of course — there was just no luck punching the date 1800). This one looks so unusual. The coins bearing this variety seem as if they should be worth a premium price. If there was any great collecting interest in oddities among early U.S. coins, they undoubtedly would be. But the fact is that they are not discernibly scarcer than the other varieties, and sell for the same price. In the "fractured date," the numerals are broken, giving the appearance of having been crushed under a weight. There are clear breaks in them, to such extent that some collectors refer to them as "dots." There are various ways in which this could have happened, but it would be much more easily explainable if only one numeral was "fractured." As the fracture affects all four numerals, one is led to believe that cracks developed in the die, running through the numerals and splitting them apart. This theory is so widely accepted, as the cause for the "fractured date" variety, that it is sometimes termed "die crack date."

The "Americai" variety, even more bizarre, involves the reverse side of certain specimens struck from a particular die. In these specimens the word "America" appears to read "Americai," as if a letter "i" had been mysteriously added at the end. Varieties of this sort (which are not really uncommon on coins of lower denominations, but rare on Dollars) were an obvious source of embarrassment for the mint. They were noticeable, and they appeared to arise from ignorance rather than accident. Into this class fall the "Likerty" and "Libekty" errors well known to collectors of lower denomination silver coins. They seem to betray a distinct lack of literacy among employees of the mint. The so-called "spelling error varieties" on our early coins were not really spelling errors. They resulted either from broken letters or some other causes that had nothing to do with misspelling. In the case of "Americai," one can only presume that the "i" was really a plain strip of metal along the side of the letter- punch. It was not intended to be impressed into the die, and perhaps it got there because of excess pressure being applied — as in pounding down a rubber stamp too hard and getting a blurred impression. It is certainly not a real letter "i."

Varieties of the 1801 Draped Bust/Heraldic Eagle Dollar were:
Proof restrike
Minor varieties not generally recognized in catalogues
Essentially, 1801 was a variety-free year. The proof restrikes were not made in 1801. They originated probably in the mid 1830s when the mint struck its few specimens of the 1804 Dollar to include in proof presentation sets. At this same time, proof restrikes were made of the 1802 and 1803 Dollars as well. The reverse die used in striking proofs of the 1801 Dollar has been positively identified as that also used in striking the original run of 18044 Dollars. The 1801 proof restrike is an extremely rare coin for which no price history is available, and it is therefore not included on the above chart. We are likewise unable to offer any investment advice on it. The existence of fakes is likely.

There are several major varieties the following year, 1802:
Overdate with wide date
Overdate with compressed date
Non-overdate with wide date
Non-overdate with compressed date
Proof restrike
The proof restrikes are, like all of those manufactured of Draped Bust/Heraldic Eagle Dollars, in the class of ultra rarities without a pricing history. Quantities struck are not known but it was likely less than ten of each date were made (1801, 1802, and 1803 — there were none struck of the earlier dates).

This (1802) was another "overdate" year, that is, a year in which the mint kept old dies in service by repunching the new date over that of the previous year. We know that at least two overdate dies were used, as they exist with both "wide" and "compressed" dates — actually there may have been more than two. The low mintage on this coin should not be taken as an indication that only a few dies were used; mintage totals and the number of dies in use seldom corresponded. There were high-mintage years in which the mint apparently went through numerous dies. This was all a matter of circumstances. A die could suffer a bad break after being in service only a short time. Of course, 1802 was not an ideal year for an overdate. In punching "2" over "1," the vertical ascender of the "1" remained plainly visible. This yielded one of the most recognizable of all overdates. In some specimens, particularly uncirculated ones, it almost seems as if the "1" had been punched over the "2" because of it clarity.

Varieties occurring on the 1803 Silver Dollar were:

Large 3
Small 3
Proof restrike

No overdates were struck in 1803, which is surprising. There were at least two good working dies left over from 1802, but perhaps the mint was getting some criticism about the previous year's overdate. (There is no record of the government ever complaining to the mint about the appearance of these coins, but this might have been done quietly.) The "large 3" and "small 3" varieties have been the topic of considerable discussion. Some commentators regard them as so similar that they should not be classified as major varieties, and it is really difficult to take issue with that position. The terms — "large 3" and "small 3" — suggest a noticeable difference in the size of the numeral, when in fact it can be detected only by the closest examination. If one wants to be technical, it is not even a real difference in size, so much as in shape or bulkiness. The "large 3" is slightly thicker than the "small 3." In terms of their height, one would need to measure down to the hundredth of a millimeter before discovering any difference; and even then there may be none. The other three numerals are apparently identical. This is a perfect example of the sort of variety that was of absolutely no interest to early collectors. Varieties of this sort were called "flyspecks."

The proof restrike, as already stated, was one of a series of such restrikes made probably in the mid 1830s and in very limited numbers.

The final year for the Draped Bust/Heraldic Eagle Dollar, 1804, was the glory year. According to the best available current information, the mint continued striking Silver Dollars for at least several months into 1804, arriving at a production total of 19,500 (this is not an estimate but based on the actual mint records). This entire total must have been struck from 1803 dies, as no 1804 Silver Dollars reached circulation or were reported to exist in any way, shape or form at that time. It is not hard to believe that the 1803 dies had some life left in them, as 1803 was not a high production year. Then, at some point in 1804 (we do not know the date), production of Silver Dollars ceased. At the time of termination, no Silver Dollars dated 1804 were struck. This much is ascertained beyond reasonable doubt. One question (and a good one) does remain: even though no Silver Dollars were dated 1804 were struck in 1804, had dies been prepared in 1804 Dollars? This is one of the great "missing links" in the chair of numismatic history. There are two popular schools of thought. Theory #1 is that the mint prepared 1804 dies (or at least an obverse die — it could reuse the reverse of the 1803) in the normal course of events, just as it prepared new dies every year, but withheld placing them in use because of the doubtful future of the Silver Dollar. Delving deeper into this, it was possible that the government (i.e., President Jefferson) wanted to proclaim that no Silver Dollars were manufactured after 1803, in which case the use of the old dies was imperative. It would have been easy to conceal the 19,500 production of the 1804, if desired. These could be accounted for as "stock" Dollars on hand at the mint since the previous year, as there was no way of determining the year of mintage from the coins themselves. Theory # is that no dies were prepared for the 1804 Silver Dollar, owing to the fact that the Silver Dollar was a doomed coin. Supporters of this theory conjecture that mint officials were expecting to receive word at the end of 1803 to stop striking Silver Dollars. When it did not immediately arrive, they simply continued striking with the 1803 dies into the following year. Certainly there was much speculation, throughout 1803, that production of the Silver Dollar would cease.

After well over a century of debate on this essential question, there is no proof, evidence, or even strong weight of opinion on either side of the fence. Most numismatic experts believe that dies for the 1804 Dollar did exist in 1804, but there is ample margin for doubt. A good case can be made either way. The mint would be more than happy to supply the answer, but its records do not include this information, and those who had personal knowledge of what was going on in 1804 did not survive long enough go be interrogated by numismatists. The 1804 Silver Dollar did not become known to the public until 1843 (though it was certainly made somewhat earlier), and at that juncture it was known to just one member of the public and his own circle of friends. That was the celebrated Mr. Stickney of Philadelphia, the first great coin collector in this country. He acquired — directly from the mint — the first specimen to reach the hands of a collector, in May of 1843. He was not informed of the coin's history but, being a collector, was well aware that no Silver Dollars dated 1804 had ever been found. He knew it was rare, but he did no know how rare (he might have believed, in fact, that it was rarer than it actually was). He was not sure if it was made in 1804 or at a later date. He knew he wanted it, and that the mint was the only place to get one. So he swapped a valuable coin from his collection (a coin missing from the mint's collection) for an 1804 Silver Dollar. We can at least presume he knew of the existence of more than one specimen, as the mint was not about to lose its only one if the coin was unique.

It was at that point — 1843 — that the 1804 Dollar's career as a celebrity was launched, gradually at first and then gathering steam. It was another twenty years before it received really widespread publicity, but this was due only to the lack of numismatic publications, societies, and other means for dispersal of information. The Stickney specimen became known to other collectors, and of course THEY wanted one. Since Stickney had been successful in getting one from the mint, they tried their luck. Of course there were not enough to go around. Demand became so strong for the 1804 Silver Dollar that in 1859 the mint decided to strike a few more of them — just a very few — to show that it was really on the side of the collector after all. Of course it faced a dilemma. On one hand there were numerous collectors (not to mention dealers and speculators) who wanted to have a specimen. On the other there were those who already possessed one, and who would no longer own such a great rarity if the mint started churning them out in quantity. The decision was to limit the new production to such a small quantity that it would not greatly interfere with the coin's rarity status. It is believed that only seven new specimens were made, classified as restrikes. In any event, seven have been traced; if any further ones were made, they are hidden somewhere. This fell far short, of course, of providing one for everybody. But it did serve to stir up a great deal of additional press coverage for the 1804 Silver Dollar. For the first time they were in the marketplace, dealers were getting their hands on them, and the price was going up. It is not known how much the mint charged for them, or if indeed they charged anything (they may have been given them in trade only, as in Stickney's case). It would have been unseemly for the mint to place itself in a position where it could be accused of profiteering. Coin dealers, being far less moralistic, charged what the traffic could bear. And it could bear an awful lot.

So we know that the 1804 Dollar existed by 1843, and we know that another small supply was made in 1859. How early did the 1804 actually exist? How much time elasped between its time of manufacture and the acquisition of Stickney's specimen? Originally it had been believed that Stickney got his almost as soon as they were made. Either that, or they had been stored in the mint's vaults since 1804. We now know that neither of these theories was correct. The first striking of the 1804 Silver Dollar occurred either in 1804 or 1835 — it cannot be pinned down any closer than that. It was prompted by the government's decision to resume making Silver Dollars for general circulation, which let to the 1836 Seated Liberty Dollar designed by Gobrecht. The government made a practice, in those days, of presenting proof sets of its coins to foreign dignitaries. Since the Silver Dollar was definitely coming back into production, officials want it represented in these proof sets. The new Gobrecht design did not yet exist, so the old Draped Bust type was used (very likely there might have been speculation, at that time, that the Draped Bust would be revived for circulation). The newly struck 1804 Dollar was not the only Silver Dollar to be used in these presentation gift sets. Some included the 1804 while others had specimens of the 1801, 1802, and 1803 Dollar — all of which were proof restrikes made at the same approximate time. Original proofs could not be used, as none had been made. If you want a proof Silver Dollar in the 1830s, there was no choice but to make one. To the best of all tangible data, it seems as though eight specimens of the 1804 Silver Dollar were struck in 1834/1835. This, combined with the seven made in 1859, gives a grand total of 15. That may be an accurate figure and it may not be. Needless to say, no specimens were ever in circulation.

The 1804 has always been the most expensive Silver Dollar, but it is not the rarest. The 1866 Seated Liberty "without motto" is known to exist in just two proof specimens, making it at least seven times rarer than the 1804. The 1873-S Seated Liberty were presumably struck in 700 specimens, but this coin is believed to be totally extinct today: there is no record of even on surviving 1873-S Dollar. Several of the early Gobrecht trial Dollars are rarer than the 1804 Silver Dollar. And if statistics were available (which they are not), it is entirely possible that the restrikes of the 1801, 1832 and 1803 Dollars are ALL rarer than 1804. This gives us more than half a dozen Silver Dollars which are probably rarer than the

1804. Yet it is the 1804 which has been, and undoubtedly always will be, the king of Silver Dollars. It has not only rarity but reputation and tons of press clippings. It has the distinction of selling for more than a thousand dollars at a time when most Silver Dollars were worth their face value and nothing more. It was the first Silver Dollar to break the $10,000 price barrier, and then the first to break $100,000. It has now broken the quarter-million mark, and will eventually be hitting half a million and then a million. Will it become the first U.S. coin to sell for a million dollars? Probably not, but of course this depends greatly on circumstances. The Brasher Doubloon (a gold coin, and not a regular mint issue) has already brought more than $700,000, far better than the best recorded sale of the 1804 Silver Dollar. This occurred in 1979 when the market was at a peak high. In any case, the first U.S. coin to sell for a million dollars will NOT be the first coin of any kind to reach that plateau. A price of more than one million dollars was paid several years ago for an ancient Greek silver coin. Nevertheless, while the 1804 Silver Dollar is not the most expensive coin in the world, it is certainly the most expensive coin for which a reliable price history can be published. Other coins in this range of price are sold so infrequently that it become impossible to state their current value at any given time — the last previous sale might have been years earlier when the market was in a totally different condition. Despite the rarity of 1804 Dollars they do reach sale with which might be called a surprising frequency. It is unusual for more than a couple of years to pass without the sale of an 1804 Dollar, and in some years there are two or three sales. This is largely because a number of specimens have gravitated into the hands of investors, who have bought them specifically for the purpose of releasing them on the market when the time is right. If the time becomes right within a few months after purchase, they are sold that quickly. While they do appear for sale by auction (as in the Garrett sale of Bowers and Ruddy, now known as Bowers and Merena), it is more usual for their sale to be handled by a dealer asking as agent for the owner. Outright sales from a private owner to a dealer are seldom, if ever, made on this coin. Rather the coin is consigned to a dealer — one of the major ones, of course — and he and the owner agree upon a price. The coin is then offered publicly, and when the sale is made a commission is retained by the dealer. In this way the owner (seller) can do much better than in making an outright sale to a dealer. A dealer buying outright would be tying up a great deal of capital, without being certain of his proceeds, and therefore would offer something less than could otherwise be obtained. Sometimes an owner, especially if he happens to be an investor, will attempt to do the selling on his own, by running ads in the numismatic press.

Looking at its price history (both types — the 1830s version and the 1859, which are identified as Type I and Type II), it is apparent that the 1804 Silver Dollar has made a great deal of money for some (if not necessarily all) of its owners. The fact that the Type I could be bought for a little as $10,000 in 1970 seems remarkable today, when that sum will not even pay the commission on a sale any longer. As you will see on the chart, the Type I has not always been the price leader — nor is it today, as the 1859 restrike is outselling it by $50,000 based on the latest tabulations. The gap was $150,000 in 1980, with the Type II ahead at that point, also. It may seem hard to believe that a later restrike would do better than the first version in terms of dollars and cents. Could the one less existing specimen of the Type II be the deciding factor? More likely the real explanation is that buyers drew no particular distinction between the two. They are both 1804 Dollars, both are very glamorous coins, and hardly anybody is in position to say which he would "rather" have. Specimens of the two types are very seldom on the market simultaneously, so there is no choosing involved.

The 1804 Silver Dollar in both its types will always be regarded as an investment coin; it is too famous, too beloved to ever slip from the ranks of acknowledged investments. There will always be coin investors who will buy it, when they can afford it. Saying anything negative about the 1804 Dollars seems unthinkable — if any coin could be canonized, this would probably be it. Yet, in an investment book such as this, the compiler must be objective. What is the real investment status of the 1804 Silver Dollar at the present time? Since the late seventies this coin has ranked as a favorable item ONLY for long term holders. It cannot be considered an attractive short term investment under the present conditions. A short term (that is, five years) profit would necessitate a rise to approximately $400,000 by the Type I by 1990, and to $500,000 for the Type II. While such increases are not beyond the bounds of possibility, they are too optimistic to be anticipated by an investor. Gains of this sort would occur, presumably, only if the 1804 Dollar rode the crest of a great overall price surge among ALL rare coins — all Silver Dollars, all gold coins, all U.S. coins across-the-board. Such a surge did occur in 1979 and 1980, but as you will see from out charts, the effect was not quite what one might have predicted. It benefited the Type II splendidly, boosting it up to nearly triple its value within five years and returning a handsome investment profit to those who had bought at the 1979 level of price. But for the Type I it did nothing at all, as the retail market value remained precisely the same during that half decade. It has now reached $200,000 — meaning no profit, still, for those who have been holding since 1975. This does not mean that individual sales have not occurred at higher prices within that ten-year period; they obviously have. This is the average price at each five-year interval, and it is the average price or "established market price" which must become the guideline for investors. Any coin is capable of an extraordinary single sale, under the right set of conditions. If the average price does not appreciably increase, your chances of making that one good sale are slim. If you have bought the 1804 Type I for $150,000 in 1975, you would not yet be at the break even point. Considering the sum total of national inflation between then and now, you would experience a loss of rather sizable proportions. The buying power of the dollar is about half today what it was in 1975. Thus, to just break even you would need to sell the coin for at least $300,000, AFTER commissions and other expenses. With a current market value of $200,000, a $300,000 sale would be unlikely (though not impossible). As for the Type II, if you bought it for $125,000 in 1975, you presumably sold at the top of the market in 1979 or 1980 when you could have netted a clear profit (after inflation and after commissions) of better than $100,000. If you did not choose to sell at that time, you MUST have sold thereafter, unless you were totally out of touch with activities in the rare coin market.

We like the 1804 (either type) as a long term investment coin, because it always profits — in one way or another — from general prosperity. It will hit the half million dollar mark, and it will hit the million dollar mark — sooner or later. If you buy it, and can afford to keep that kind of capital tied up for an extended period of time, you will profit on it eventually. With luck the "eventuality" might only be a couple of years. We are not going to make any specific value forecasts on the 1804 Silver Dollar for 1990 or 1995 or at any point in the future, as this would amount to nothing more than taking stabs in the dark. We would say, though, that if you have the opportunity to purchase one and do decide to purchase it, you should take extreme caution. Get papers on the coin, know its provenance (history of its previous owners), and know the person from whom you buy. There have been fakes AND stolen specimens on the market. With a coin in this price range, no sort of trickery can be ruled out.

We will now examine the investment standing of the other, less-lofty Draped Bust/Heraldic Eagle Dollars. As we have pointed out, the numerous varieties that exist from date to date are not an influence upon value. Therefore we will discuss these coins in terms of date only, with the general suggestion that any variety is just as good as another so long as the specimen is in strictly graded uncirculated condition AND exhibits the variety clearly. Even if you do not care about the variety (and there is really no reason why you should, as an investor) someone to whom you sell the coin in the future may care about it very much.

One thing that immediately arrests the eye, in examining our chart, is that all other Draped Bust/Heraldic Eagle Dollars (other than the 1804) are currently standing at the exact same retail price figure, $7250. Not only that, but they all rose the exact same amount from their 1980 levels, having been bunched as a unit at $6000. Only when we go back to the 1975 column of figures can we find any variations in the prices, and even then it is of the most minute nature: all the coins were at $2500 except the 1798, priced at $2300. So we have a situation, not at all unique in the world of coin investing as a whole, in which a group of coins has traveled together at the same levels of price for a period of one full decade. What causes this to happen? There are various factors which contribute to unit pricing or "herd" pricing, but in almost all cases where this occurs it is irrational and against the long-standing tradition of price movements within the rare coin marketplace. Prices can get bunched and remain bunched for so long that it appears perfectly normal for a whole list of coins to carry the same price. Yet in reality this is a situation which in normal circumstances should not occur in the first place, since the supply and demand varies at least somewhat (if not greatly) from one coin to another. The only logical explanation for bunched prices would be if the coin were being sold primarily in sets, which would make it difficult to calculate the demand from coin to coin. We know that the Draped Bust/Heraldic Eagle Dollars are not being sold in sets. Every sale is for an individual coin; and every coin has its own level of availability. Therefore, the prices should not be the same. The fact that they are the same can, however, be useful to an investor. Instead of passing over this group as sluggish, a skilled investor will first of all realize that the current bunched pricing cannot last very much longer. After then years it is bound to give sooner or later, and the break—when it comes—cannot fail to benefit those who have invested wisely. These bunched prices are nothing more than a holdover from the outmoded investor buying patterns of the 1970s, when everyone seemed to be buying by "type" rather than by "date". Very foolish, but such was the status of numismatic investing and particularly Silver Dollar investing in those times. In a sense this was the fault of those who gave investment advice via newsletters, books and other literature. They did not trust their readers to comprehend detailed advice about dates, mint marks and varieties, so they simply said, "buy Standing Liberty Quarters," or "buy Draped Bust Dollars." They let the reader take it from there. They went into coin shops and bought whatever dates happened to be available. This meant that the level of demand for any particular date fell far, far below the demand for plain type coins. This type of uneducated buying on the part of Silver Dollar investors has greatly diminished in recent years, and hopefully the present book will do its share in totally eradicating this very unproductive approach. Coins have to be invested in by DATE, and sometimes by mint mark or other consideration. The Draped Bust/Heraldic Eagle series comprises no mint marks and only six dates are involved (if you delete the out-of-range 1804). It can be analyzed in no more than a few minutes, and the conclusions to be reached are fairly obvious.

The "old school" of investors would ask "do you like Draped Bust/Heraldic Eagle Dollars for investment?"

To which we would answer: there is no series, among Silver Dollars, that we either like or do not like. There is no good series or poor series. There are good coins and poor coins, and it is the coin which matters — not the series from which it comes. If you talk about any series as a whole (and this applies to other denominations of coins, too, not just Silver Dollars), you are talking about some coins which will be going up in price and other which will be holding steady or declining. The series as a whole may fluctuate 10% or 15%, but at the same time certain coins within the series are rising by 100% in value. So it is definitely a losing proposition to think in terms of series or designs or types. These are useful for classifying coins, but not for investing in them. You cannot simplify coin investment to the point where a consideration of dates can be eliminated. It is impossible, in spite of the many attempts! We can virtually guarantee you that if you — today — invest in any group of Silver Dollars as a series, you will not have a profit by 1990. We can also make the same guarantee that if you carefully select your investment purchases by DATE, you WILL realize a profit by 1990.

As simplistic as it may seem, the correct approach for Draped Bust/Heraldic Eagle Dollar investment is to follow the mintage figures — up to a point. This is not what some readers like to hear, and it is not what they are accustomed to hearing from investment advisors. They would like to believe that the analyst has some exclusive, secret information, some technique of investing which will place his readers ahead of the pack. And, of course, there are investment analysts who want to believe that they DO have such information. They don't, and it is just a game when anyone pretends to have exclusive strategy or exclusive data. The Draped Bust/Heraldic Eagle series is a perfect example of how the standard investment formula can be utilized to advantage. We have six coins selling for the same sum of money. One of these coins is ten times more plentiful than one of the others, according to the mintage figures. Availability of the others in the group ranges in between the extremes of high and low. When price spreading develops on this series, it is certain to bring about higher prices for the dates with lowest mintage, and may even cause a fallback in price on the higher mintages. The 1802 had the lowest mintage (not counting the 1804, which is outside the realm of this analysis) at 41,650. It is just slightly lower than the 1801, with a recorded mintage of 54,454. These are, without question, the dates to buy from this group. Having climbed only $1250 in the past five years, any doubts about them being overpriced — and such doubts were voiced in 1980 — should by now be dispelled. They were, perhaps, fully priced at the $6000 for which they sold in the 1980 market, but between 1980 and today they slipped into the underpriced category. This is not to say that every date in this series is underpriced. The 1799 with its mintage of close to half a million specimens cannot be regarded as underpriced at $7250; it is fully priced if anything and possibly even a bit overpriced. The same holds true for the 1800, though its mintage was only half that of the 1799, was still produced in too large a quantity to be considered an investment coin at the present time. So we are narrowing the field: we have placed the 1801 and 1802 on the side of those which merit investment attention, and the 1799 and 1800 on the side of those which are not attractive at the moment either as short or long termers. This leaves two coins, the 1798 and the 1803. Our opinion on the 1798 may come as something of a surprise. Its mintage of 190,000 was not significantly less than that of the 1800, which we have placed in the unfavorable category (the 1800 had a recorded mintage of 220,920). Nevertheless the 1798 has characteristics which are lacking in the 1800, and which, in our opinion, renders it favorable for investment purchase. It would appear, for one thing, that the 1798 is somewhat scarcer than the mintage figure would indicate. There is no way to actually prove this, but we have tangible proof of one thing: its price performance. If we go back to 1965, we find that the 1798 was outselling all the other Draped Bust/Heraldic Eagle Dollars by a fairly considerable margin. It was then commanding $350, while its nearest rival among the other five stood at $275. This is a difference of roughly 20%, which would translate into well over a thousand dollars at the current price levels. Then in 1970, five years later, the 1798 was still leading the pack, selling for $825 while its closest companion brought $775. It is not difficult to believe that the demand for this coin could be somewhat higher on grounds of being the first year for use of the Heraldic Eagle reverse design (though it was not, of course, the first year for the Draped Bust). It was also a year of mixed production in which some of the output comprised Small Eagle reverses and some Heraldic Eagle. Taking all this into consideration, the 1798 does give the appearance of being thinly priced at $7250 and in line for a healthy increase within the near future. So we have three attractive investment buys from this group — the 1798, the 1801, and the 1802.

As fas as the 1803 is concerned, there will be some who point to the mintage of less than one hundred thousand specimens and automatically conclude that here must be a coin of some merit. But this is a case where we are going to split the series right down the middle, placing three of the six coins on the "good" side and three on the "bad." The 1803, despite its mintage of 85,634, does not strike us as a particularly inviting investment item. It would be more favorable than either the 1799 or 1800, but not favorable enough to turn a profit. One problem with the 1803 is that the mintage figure is WRONG. As you will recall in our discussion of the 1804 Dollar, we noted that the mint reported a striking of 19,500 Dollars for the calendar year 1804, but that dies reading 1803 were used. This total must be added to the stated mintage figure for 1803 to arrive at the actual number of Silver Dollars produced bearing the date 1803, and by doing this we see than the quantity is not below 100,000. It gives this date a mintage of nearly double the 1801, and well over double that of the 1802. So we would advise you to bypass the 1803 for now, and possibly review its market standing a few years hence. If it is still at the current figure after some of the other dates have begun moving upward, it may THEN be a good investment buy.

Our price projections on the recommended coins in this series are as follows:

For the 1798, we look for a price of $15,000 by 1990 and $27,500 to $30,000 by 1995.

For the 1801, we envision a rise to $17,500 by 1990and easily to $30,000 by the year 1995.

For the 1802, we likewise see a climb to $17,500 by 1990 and possibly as high as $35,000 in 1995.

The 1801 and 1802 are being designated among our BEST BET selections as Dollars that we particularly recommend for purchase.

As for the remaining coins in this group, we look for a price of $8000 on the 1799 by the year 1990. The 1800 should do somewhat better, getting to $10,000 by 1990, but this will still leave it considerably short of profitable territory. The 1803 should get to around $12,000, very close to the profitable range but not quite good enough. In other words we are predicting read spreads to open up in the prices of these coins within the coming years. It will be much more difficult to make profitable investments in them, after the spreads have developed. At this point they are still dormant so far as their pricing pattern is concerned, so this definitely looks like the time to strike.

THE GOBRECHT "PATTERN" DOLLARS

OBVERSE   **REVERSE**

As we remarked earlier in this book, the Gobrecht dollars hold a special place in our coinage because of their curious history. So far as can be determined, they actually were intended to be circulating coins and part of them are accounted for in that fashion in the mint's records, despite the fact that all were struck as proofs. For many years, all were classed as patterns until research uncovered their true status buried in the mint's files.

SILVER $1 — GOBRECHT PATTERN, COMMON DATE
THERE ARE NO COMMON DATES OF THIS VARIETY

SILVER $1 — GOBRECHT PATTERN, SEMI-KEY
THERE ARE NO SEMI-KEYS OF THIS VARIETY

SILVER $1 — GOBRECHT PATTERN, KEY
PROOF STATE

Year	Mintage	1955	1960	1965	1970	1975	1980	1985
1836	1,000	185.00	690.00	1350.00	1900.00	2700.00	5500.00	7200.00
1837			NO SILVER DOLLARS WERE STRUCK IN 1837					
1838	25	525.00	950.00	2750.00	3750.00	4500.00	8000.00	12500.00
1839	300	300.00	750.00	2750.00	3750.00	4500.00	4800.00	9000.00

% of increase:		
	1955-60	273%
	1960-65	187%
	1965-70	37%
	1970-75	24%
	1975-80	56%
	1980-85	57%
overall % of increase:	1955-85	2742%

These three coins comprise the first issue — or, it may be more correct to say, the prototype issue — of the Liberty Seated Dollar. They are not referred to as Liberty Seated Dollars because that term was not in general use at the time. Instead they are referred to as Gobrecht Patterns. Christian Gobrecht, a Dutch/American artist, was their designer. The word "patterns" denotes the fact that the designs were not finalized during the period that these coins were issued. In numismatic terminology, a "pattern" is a coin whose design has not been approved for general production. Pattern coins are always struck before a new design is introduced. Often, there are various patterns for the same coin, by the same designer or different designers. The Gobrecht Pattern Dollars are in a class by themselves, however, among Silver Dollar patterns. All of the other Silver Dollar patterns (and there were many) were stuck on a strictly experimental basis with no intention of releasing them to the public. The Gobrecht Patterns were not only struck in relatively large quantities as proofs — large for patterns, at any rate — but also in circulating coins or "business strikes." This was never before, or after, done with Silver Dollar Patterns. Various factors contributed to this situation. Silver Dollars were returning to the mint lineup after an absence of thirty years. It was natural that they should be brought back with an appropriate flourish. The number of coin collectors had greatly increased in that period of time, and catering to collectors with Gobrecht proofs was one way of deriving widespread publicity for the coin. Also, one would have to assume that the Gobrecht Patterns were in a slightly exalted position compared to most proof coins. Most proofs have a very doubtful status at the time of striking; the artist is not aware whether his design will be accepted or rejected. In the case of the Gobrechts, it is apparent that a firm commitment existed. The mint knew that the Gobrecht design — with possible minor changes — would be the next Silver Dollar. Therefore it could afford to be a bit more flamboyant with it than under normal circumstances. As coin collectors are well aware, the

Liberty Seated design was not used only on the Dollar. The later Morgan and Peace designs were restricted exclusively to the Dollar, but Gobrecht's Liberty Seated was placed in general use on our silver coins. The smaller denominations simply carried scaled-down versions of the Dollar design. This was the last time in the mint's history that all our silver coins were uniform in design.

To say the least it was a colossal change-over. All our silver coins had previously carried portrait heads of Liberty, and nothing else, from the mint's inception. Now, with one sweeping flourish of Congressional action, they were all removed, to be replaced by a totally different kind of design. (They remained, however, on copper and gold coins, as the Liberty Seated design was for use on silver coins exclusively.) It was considered a controversial move. Some observers considered the new design a great improvement. Others found it too suggestive of British coins, as the Liberty Seated figure closely resembled Britannia Seated. Critics chided the government for lack of originality. Gobrecht's reputation as an artist was instrumental in eventually winning general acceptance for the design. Once the Liberty Seated motif became firmly entrenched, it remained in use longer than any other silver coin design in history.

Needless to say, collectors were anxious to get the early or trial strikings. For all they knew, the Gobrecht design might now win final approval, and they would have something really unusual. Even if it did enter into general production, strikings from the later years would not be as desirable. There was no way of knowing, either, if the mint intended to go on striking proofs. Proof strikings of Silver Dollars were far from a standard item in those days. No proofs whatsoever were struck in the mint's early years, as the objective was merely to get as many coins as possible into circulation. The first Silver Dollar proofs of which there is any record originated very shortly before these Gobrecht Patterns. In 1834 or 1835, the mint struck proofs of the Draped Bust Dollar bearing dates of 1801, 1802, 1803 and 1804. Only a handful of each were made and hardly any collectors had the opportunity of owning one — the original position of the mint was that it was making them "for presentation purposes only" (i.e., for inclusion in mint sets presented to visiting heads of state). Until the Gobrecht Patterns, these few scattered proofs were the only existing proof specimens of any of our Silver Dollars. When one thousand specimens of the Gobrecht Dollar were struck in 1836 (mostly proofs), collectors saw this as an opportunity which might never occur again. They could not know that the striking of proof Dollars would become commonplace. Nor did the mint know, at that time. It got heavily into the proof business largely because of collector response. If these Gobrechts had not received a favorable welcome, the chances are quite good that the idea of proof specimens would go on the shelf. In a sense it was the Gobrecht Patterns which led, in a direct ancestral line, to the modern proof sets of today.

Another thing that collectors did not know, when the Gobrecht Patterns began to be struck in 1836, was that the design would be modified twice. Those who bought the 1836 proofs had a version of the coin which would never be struck again. The same was true of those who bought in 1838 (none were struck in 1837). The 1838 version represented a revision over that of 1836, but when large-scale manufacture began in 1840 it was with a third version of the design — one which had not been previously struck as a trial pattern. For a "type" collection of Silver Dollars to be absolutely complete, it must include the 1836 and 1838 Gobrecht Patterns, as well as one of the later specimens from 1840 onward.

In addition to the two major types among the Gobrecht Patterns, there were also a number of relatively minor types created by way of experimentation. These have been exhaustively studied and classified, and several of them have even arrived at their own levels of market value. Prices stated on the above chart are for the most readily available versions.

The chief difference between the Gobrecht Patterns and the coin as finally introduced in 1840 involved the reverse side. The Liberty Seated obverse (or front) received moderate alterations but was basically unchanged. The reverse side was to picture an eagle, which had become the standard symbol for the backs of our silver coins. No specific directions were given on how the eagle should be depicted. Earlier there had been two versions of the eagle on our Silver Dollars. At first the so-called Small Eagle was used, a standing eagle viewed from the front with wings spread. This was the subject of extensive criticism as the eagle was said to look undernourished and anything but the symbol of a proud noble country. Next came the Heraldic Eagle, also called Large Eagle, which was really the U.S. seal with "E Pluribus Unum" on a banner. In terms of nobleness, no one could fault the Heraldic Eagle. This design had served for a long period on our silver coins by the mid 1830s, and Gobrecht was given approval to redesign the eagle. His first eagle, used on all the Gobrecht Patterns, was shown in flight, and in profile — both of which were new concepts. There was no heraldic symbolism. It was an extremely attractive eagle but, alas, it did not survive the pattern stage. When finally struck for general circulation, the Liberty Seated Dollar had a Heraldic Eagle on the reverse. It was, however, a sort of compromise Heraldic Eagle — more naturalistic and less official-looking than the previous one. That fine flying eagle can be seen only on the Patterns. Collectors were later to comment that he represented the market prices on these Patterns flying skyward.

The principal difference in design, from the first version of the Pattern to the second, involves the stars. Stars had been a component in the designs of earlier Silver Dollars. It was decided to retain them, but Gobrecht received no specific instructions on where or how they were to be placed. In the first version of the obverse, stuck in 1836, there is an absolutely plain "field," without stars or lettering. Liberty is seated amid nothing but an expanse of gleaming silver — very eye-arresting, but also very unconventional for a U.S. coin. Two different reverse types were used in 1836. In one, the flying eagle is surrounded by small stars, as well as by the words "UNITED STATES OF AMERICA, ONE DOLLAR." In the other, the wording remains, but the stars are missing. Gobrecht himself was apparently not a great fan of stars, but his employers were. For the second version of the Pattern, Liberty is framed by a semi-circle of stars in the upper portion of the design. This was likewise issued with a "stars" and "no stars" reverse side. By the time the coin was struck for general circulation, the stars had vanished from the reverse, but they remained on the obverse. The newly designed eagle on the reverse made stars unnecessary, as the design left very little blank field.

The most common of the Gobrecht Pattern Dollars — "common" being a very relative word, as they are all scarce — was struck in 1836. This was the only variety to be released in both proofs and business strikes. Other types will occasionally be found with circulation wear, but these are NOT business strikes. They are "impaired proofs." They were struck as proofs, not to be released into general circulation, but for one reason or another they reached circulation. It is not extremely unusual to encounter circulated proofs among early coins, especially those of higher denomination which represented a substantial face value. The scenario probably went this way: someone acquired a proof specimen, retained it for a while, then passed it along to a young collector or other relative. The second owner may have been far more intrigued by what it could buy ($1 was quite a sum of money) than how attractive it looked, or how scarce it was. These proofs, like all U.S. proofs, were legal tender. They could be spent just like regular coins and quite obviously some of them were spent. Once having reached open circulation, it was one chance in a thousand that anybody would recognize them as proofs, or even care for that matter. So they traveled around and received wear just like any other coin. In describing such specimens, the standard ANA condition scale is normally used, even though it was not intended as a means of grading proofs. If the coin is just lightly circulated it will be listed as PRF-50 or PRF-55. Or, with more circulation wear, it can be PRF-40, PRF-30 and so on down the line. Needless to point out, such specimens are very unsatisfactory for investment purposes. They are not popular as collectors' items and their values are erratic. Dealers sell them for whatever they can get, which is usually not too much. The "impaired proof" is also used of proof coins that have not actually been circulated but have sustained an injury, such as from mounting in jewelry.

No statistics are available on the breakdown between proofs of 1836 and business strikes. The total mintage as indicated on our chart was an even 1,000. Speculation has ranged far and wide. Some coin historians believe it was split right down the center: 500 proofs, 500 business strikes. Others think the business strikes outnumbered the proofs, possibly 600/400, possibly 700/300. No one seems to think that the proofs were in the majority. Since 300 proofs with no business strikes were issued in 1839, the final year of Gobrecht Patterns, it is quite possible that at least 300 were likewise issued in 1836. This coin is not as scarce on the market as the 1839, and we know there were 300 of those.

Discussing mintage figures in relation to proof coins is, as we must take special note to advise beginners, very different than in discussing business strikes. The ratio of preservation is always higher with proofs. This holds true regardless of the denomination or age of the coin, or any other circumstances. The 1839 Gobrecht Pattern, for example, would be a coin of extreme rarity if the 300 struck specimens were placed into circulation. We have, in fact, in the Silver Dollar series an example of a coin which had a higher mintage and which is now apparently extinct. There were 700 specimens struck of the 1873 San Francisco Liberty Seated Dollar and all of them have disappeared. If the 1839 had been a business strike, with that kind of minimal mintage, no more than a dozen at the most would be likely to exist at the present time — and possibly none in uncirculated condition. Proofs were intended to be preserved and most of them succeeded in being preserved. Some loss occurred and, as we have said, some specimens trickled into circulation. But it would be a reasonable estimate, in the case of most early proof Dollars, that at least 50% of the original mintage still exists in proof state. This in itself is not a strike against the Gobrecht Patterns for investment purposes. Their prices would be considerably higher if they were business strikes — not only outside the reach of most investors, but so high that reliable value histories would be difficult to research.

The 1836 version struck for circulation had the so-called plain obverse, as did all specimens of that year: Liberty without stars. The reverse had stars around the eagle in a pattern that roughly amounts to a small circle inside a larger circle. At first a small controversy developed over this coin. Being the first Silver Dollar in three decades it was subjected to close scrutiny, both by the public and press. Gobrecht, being accustomed to prominently autographing his works of art, placed his name beneath the portrait on the obverse. Not only was it conspicuously positioned, between the portrait and the date, the lettering was of rather large size. This immediately drew criticism, insofar as the previous designers of Silver Dollars had not placed their names — nor even initials — on their coins. To pacify Gobrecht somewhat, the mint allowed him to keep his name on the coin, but to move it from the lower field to the platform or base on which Miss Liberty sits. This seemed more appropriate: if the design were viewed as a sculpture, it would not at all be unusual for the sculptor's name to appear at the base. The balance of the 1836 striking was done with this revision, but criticism continued. After going out of production for a year in 1837 (mainly for the purpose of weighing all the various pro and con reactions), the obverse as reintroduced in 1838 did not bear Gobrecht's name at all. This was the first painful blow dealt to him by the mint. The second was turning thumbs down on his flying eagle. The name appeared as "C. GOBRECHT F." The initial "F" stood for "fecit," meaning, in literal translation, "C. Gobrecht Made This." The word "fecit," frequently abbreviated down to "F," had traditionally been used by Italian violin makers of the 1600s and 1700s, then was adopted by craftsmen and artists in general.

Both of the 1836 varieties mentioned have a plain edge. This, in a way, was a holdover from the pioneer Dollars, but its days were numbered. The early Dollars (Flowing Hair and Draped Bust) were given plain edges so that the edges could be imprinted with wording. They read "ONE HUNDRED CENTS/ONE DOLLAR," which followed the practice of European mints placing value designations on the edges of "crowns." By the 1830s, most European governments had abandoned doing this, and the U.S. did not want to seem old fashioned. The question then was: what to do with the edge? Leave it plain with no lettering, or decorate it in some way? The finalized version of the Liberty Seated Dollar had a reeded edge, but in 1836 there had been no decision one way or the other. Most of the striking was with a plain, unlettered edge. Some proofs were struck in which the designs were identical, but the edge was reeded. ("Reeded" simply means a series of closely spaced vertical lines running entirely around the edge, creating ribs or "reeds" between the lines.)

Another variety of the 1836 striking has the plain edge, a plain reverse side (that is, no stars surrounding the eagle), and the designer's name set into the base of the obverse portrait. This is a very scarce type on which market value is difficult to determine due to infrequent sales. It is generally regarded as a restrike, struck at some date later than 1836. Speculation as to the date of manufacture runs as late as the 1850s. No evidence is available on which to base a reliable estimate. It may very well be that two or more different restrikes were made. Quite possibly the "original restrike" (an awkward expression, but in this case a valid one) was produced in the off year of 1837, when there is no recorded mintage. This could have constituted the first stage of experimenting with a plain, starless reverse side. The fact that the 1838 and 1839 proofs had plain reverses would seem to corroborate this theory.

All of the later proofs — those of 1838 and 1839 — have stars around the obverse. Some of them were very obviously experimental, based on the small number of strikings. There are two varieties of which only two or three specimens are known (though it is not known how many were originally struck). The first of these very rare types has a plain edge and is classified as a restrike. The second has stars on the reverse, along with a plain edge and is likewise listed as a restrike. Some numismatic historians are of the opinion that ALL the specimens dated 1838 and 1839 are later restrikes, but this seems unlikely.

One thing you will note about the Gobrecht Pattern Dollars is their variations in toning or surface coloration. They are found in a wide variety of color shades, and also in specimens that exhibit no toning whatsoever. Most of these coins were kept for many years in the old-style coin cabinets of the 1800s: wooden cabinets with sliding drawers, each drawer set with recesses into which the coins were laid. Some cabinets had fabric (usually velour) linings in the drawers, but others were bare wood and the coins came into direct — and very prolonged — contact with the wood. Depending on the type of wood, and the oils or other preparations used in finishing it, this gave a characteristic toning. In purchasing for investment, a premium price should not be paid for toning, regardless of how attractive it may be. Get good toning, if you can, on a specimen selling at the established market price; or forget about toning if necessary. It is unwise to pay a premium as you are not likely to receive a premium when the coin is eventually sold.

Status of the Gobrecht Pattern Dollars for investment must be considered separately from an examination of the ordinary Gobrecht Liberty Seated Dollars. It is a very small group with its own price history and special features. For one thing, when investing in Gobrecht Patterns you will be buying proof state coins rather than uncirculated business strikes. This is not necessarily a plus or minus, but you must be certain the coins ARE proofs and are not circulated or damaged in any way. This is especially true so far as the 1836 is concerned. If the design is not very sharply struck, against a clear and brilliant field, the specimen is undoubtedly not a proof.

Just looking at the price histories and current market values, it is apparent that these coins are badly out of alignment. The value breakdown is logical in terms of placement: the coin with least mintage is the most valuable, the coin with second least is in second place, and the coin with greatest mintage has the lowest value. But the value spreads — that is, the difference in value from one coin to the other. The 1838 had a recorded mintage of 25, as opposed to one thousand of the 1836, and the difference in price is $12,500 vs. $7200. The 1838 is not even selling for twice as much as the 1836, even though it is 40 times scarcer! If the 1836 is worth $7200, the 1838 should — if we go strictly by mintage figures — be worth close to $300,000. The question is: how much should we trust the mintage figures? And, even if they are accurate, what do they really tell us with regard to the prices? There is obviously more here than meets the eye. Values do not get 4,000% out of alignment without a good reason.

For one thing, the figure of 25 is suspect, as representing the total quantity of 1838 Gobrecht Patterns. It may be accurate in terms of the first strikings or original strikings, on which the mint was keeping books. The mint did not include any of the restrikes in its official tabulations, so far as we know. The quantity of restrikes is not known, but quite likely they far exceeded 25. There may have been hundreds of them. This would certainly be an explanation for the lack of a wide price spread. Restrikes were made of the 1839, too, bringing the total manufactured to well beyond the stated mintage of 300. We do not know the total quantities produced of these coins, and lacking this information it becomes difficult to utilize standard numismatic investment strategy.

Also, as stated earlier, it is not known what portion of the 1836 mintage comprised proofs, and what portion were business strikes. Even if we say that 500 were proofs (the figure was probably much lower), the mintage figure of 1,000 becomes very misleading. Suppose only 300 or 200 were proofs? And further suppose that 60 or 70 restrikes were made of the 1838, which is well within the scope of possibility? Looking at it this way, there is no longer any vast difference between the two coins in terms of availability. Yes, the 1838 looks underpriced at $12,500. A mintage figure of 25 and a price of $12,500 just do not seem to belong together. But after analyzing all the circumstances and possibilities, one begins realizing that the price may not be low at all. Historically the price of this coin has been more or less in line with that of the 1839. Undoubtedly it deserves to sell for a bit more than the 1839, and today it has reached the point of doing just that. It is outselling the 1839 by $3500. Perhaps this is as large a price spread as can be anticipated. Our own personal feeling is that the relationship in prices between these three coins will not materially change within the next ten years. We see them all rising in value, but at more or less an equal pace, leaving the 1838 at about 25% higher than the 1839 and roughly 40% higher than the 1836. This forecast runs contrary to some of the published predictions. Analysts have paid a great deal of attention to that 25 mintage figure, some even working it down by trying to calculate the number of specimens that have been lost over the years and those unavailable to the coin market (specimens owned by the mint collections or by various institutions). In doing this you could easily delude yourself into believing that only ten or a dozen specimens could ever occur for sale. If that were the case, $12,500 would represent one of the best investment buys in the current silver coin market. We think the real figure, on numbers of specimens in private hands and subject to sale, would be closer to 50 and possibly higher. It is a confusing coin, to say the least.

What is the investment potential of the Gobrecht Patterns? If the price spreads remain essentially as they are structured today, will values rise strongly enough in the next five or ten years to yield a worthwhile profit? This is the second important question to be asked by the investor. We know that the Gobrechts have been favorites of investors; they have a standing with collectors and investors alike. When we examine their price histories, however, we discover that they have seldom returned worthwhile profits within a five year holding period. This did not occur on any of the three dates from 1980 to 1985, even though all of them rose in value. Between 1975 and 1980, the 1836 scored a sufficient gain to return an investment profit, but the other two failed to accomplish this. Thus in the past ten years, there was one instance of investment profit on this group. Their best period (so far as years covered by the chart are concerned) was from 1960 to 1965, when random or across-the-board buying of Gobrecht Pattern Dollars would have achieved a good return. They went profitless from 1965 to 1970, and again from 1970 to 1975, though these coins have a very admirable record of never going DOWN in price. They rise, continually and perpetually, but the pace of gain is not too exciting. Their price performances, just like their mintage figures and quantities in existence, are also subject to analysis. Some persons would say, based on this data, that the Gobrechts are undervalued; that they should be worth more today, based on the values they carried in 1965 and 1970. Others will certainly theorize that they peaked in value rather early in the game and were overpriced in 1965 and 1970. If that was the case, their moderate increases between then and now represent a justified leveling off. We tend to support the latter of these two positions. They MAY be in for a substantial price increase within the next five years, but the available information does not build up one's confidence in that direction. When all is said and done it will probably be the investment community itself that will decide the fate of the Gobrechts. Collector buying in itself is not apt to do anything too drastic to their prices, not in five years or ten (or in fifty, for that matter). The collector demand runs at a fairly predictable pace, as the principal demand comes from "type" collectors of the Silver Dollar series. It is then a question of the investor buying patterns of the next several years. A groundswell of enthusiasm could find them scoring handsome gains. This has certainly happened to many proofs in the past: a big boost up the value ladder thanks to heavy investment buying activity.

Our own projection on the values for Gobrecht Pattern Dollars is as follows:

For the 1836, we see a value of $10,000 by 1990.

For the 1838, our prediction is $17,000 in 1990.

For the 1839, we look for a value in the area of $13,000 by 1990.

None of these advances would be sufficient to return a profit. However, we would advise those who bought the 1839 in 1980, or around that time, to keep in touch with market developments. This coin does not require too much movement to get into the profitable area — at which point we would suggest selling. It is not the sort of coin that we would want to hold for further appreciation in the future. To do better in the years ahead, it would need to maintain or slightly surpass the pace at which it climbed in the early eighties. This is unlikely, due to the fairly good value spurt it enjoyed at that time. This is a coin (one of many in the Silver Dollar series) which should be cashed in and forgotten about, the capital to be used in acquiring coins with more attractive investment potential.

THE "LIBERTY SEATED" DOLLARS

OBVERSE   **REVERSE**

Despite the fact that the Gobrecht Pattern Dollars were intended as designs to be used for a series of circulating coins, they were not used when the Seated Liberty Dollars were first issued in 1840. Designer Christian Gobrecht had in the meantime become the mint's Chief Engraver.

The obverse design used is similar to the Gobrecht Patterns, but the eagle reverse was dropped to resurface later on the cent. The weight, which had been at 416 grains since the 1794 dollar, was reduced to 412.5 grains (the original weight proposed by Alexander Hamilton) with a fineness of .900, so that each silver dollar from 1834 through 1935 contained .77344 troy ounces of silver.

The Liberty Seated Dollars were struck for a total of 34 years, the first dollar series to contain more than a handful of dates, permitting us for the first time to break down the issues into the three general classes. The series is noted as well for the fact that, while it includes some high mintage coins, it also has at least one mint and date for which there are no known examples, that being the 1873-S. Mint records show that 700 dollars were struck that year at San Francisco, but none of them are known to exist today.

One significant change was made in the design. In 1866 a ribbon, with the motto: "IN GOD WE TRUST" was added above the eagle's head on the reverse. In 1873, the Liberty Seated series was discontinued along with the 3 Cent piece and the half dime by the law which established the Trade Dollar.

As with almost all of the dollar coins — and the Anthony Dollar is a classic example — the Liberty Seated Dollars were not exactly a popular item with the public and many of them never left the hands of the Treasury Department. Some in fact turned up in bags of dollars mixed in with the plentiful stocks of Morgan and Peace Dollars that were sold to the public for face value during the early 60s.

The series is described by at least one author as one that has been seriously neglected by the collector, a point which should grasp the investor's attention. As we will show you on our pricing charts, there are indeed some bargains here, which undoubtedly will be attracting investor and collector interest in the next decade.

The series is relatively easy to grade. Once the investor has learned the key points in identifying the grade, he should be able to protect himself from the misgraded, or "between grade" coins fairly readily. There are two noted restrikes, both occurring shortly after the originals were struck, and both readily identified, as described in the Varieties at the end of this chapter.

An exception to the grading standards should be noted. You will find "soft" strikes — coins which are not struck up well — for the Philadelphia issues of 1854-1857, the Carson City (CC) Dollars and the 1859-S from San Francisco.

The very top grade coins are extremely difficult to find and priced accordingly, so our recurring advice is to enlist the aid of a specialist when investing in the best coins, or have the specimen authenticated and graded by the American Numismatic Association.

For the first time, the investor needs to concern himself with mint marks, beginning with the 1846-O struck at New Orleans. The mint mark letters are always located directly below the eagle, so this spot should be checked immediately after confirming the date. A mint mark letter can make a substantial difference in the value of a coin, since it is the key to determining where the coin was struck, and thus reading the actual mintage from the charts.

LIBERTY SEATED DOLLARS — COMMON DATES

Year	Mintage	1955	1960	1965	1970	1975	1980	1985
1841	173,000	$35.00	50.00	75.00	150.00	600.00	800.00	850.00
1842	184,618	27.50	40.00	82.50	150.00	600.00	800.00	850.00
1843	165,100	27.50	40.00	60.00	150.00	600.00	850.00	850.00
1846	110,600	25.00	45.00	62.50	135.00	600.00	900.00	1200.00
1847	140,750	25.00	40.00	60.00	150.00	550.00	800.00	1800.00
1849	62,600	27.50	47.50	60.00	150.00	550.00	800.00	1800.00
1857	94,000	32.50	60.00	80.00	275.00	650.00	1000.00	1750.00
1859	256,500	30.00	50.00	65.00	160.00	530.00	800.00	1850.00
1859-O	360,000	21.00	38.00	65.00	135.00	500.00	800.00	875.00
1860	218,930	31.00	50.00	65.00	135.00	530.00	800.00	1775.00
1860-O	515,000	21.00	39.00	52.50	100.00	500.00	800.00	1200.00
1861	78,500	35.00	60.00	85.00	165.00	525.00	900.00	2000.00
1865	47,000	25.00	50.00	80.00	200.00	550.00	900.00	1650.00
(Motto Added on Reverse)								
1866	49,625	20.00	45.00	80.00	185.00	575.00	1000.00	1625.00
1867	47,525	18.50	40.00	55.00	185.00	550.00	1000.00	1625.00
1868	162,700	18.50	35.00	55.00	130.00	500.00	1000.00	1350.00
1869	424,300	18.50	29.00	45.00	125.00	500.00	1000.00	1350.00
1870	416,000	18.50	29.00	42.50	115.00	500.00	1000.00	1350.00
1871	1,074,760	17.50	26.00	35.00	110.00	500.00	1000.00	1550.00
1872	1,106,450	17.50	26.00	35.00	110.00	500.00	1000.00	1100.00
1873	293,600	17.50	29.00	45.00	125.00	525.00	1000.00	1575.00

LIBERTY SEATED DOLLARS — COMMON DATES

% of increase:		
	1955-60	70%
	1960-65	48%
	1965-70	144%
	1970-75	264%
	1975-80	73%
	1980-85	54%
overall % of increase:	1955-85	5789%

This is the first series of Dollars which can be broken down into Common Dates, Semi-Keys and Keys. It is also the first in which mint marks enter the picture, as the Silver Dollar had previously been struck in Philadelphia at the only mint. The period of the Liberty Seated Dollar was long and production totals varied considerably from one year to another, and from one facility to another. Thanks to these circumstances, it is a series with much to offer the investor. There are both expensive and relatively inexpensive investment-grade coins among the Liberty Seated Dollars. There are some with bright prospects for a short term gain, and many that look like solid winners over the longer term. Both business strikes and proofs are available to the investor. We will of course deal with them separately. Proofs will be charted and discussed following the Common Dates, Semi-Keys and Keys of the business strikes. In this series, all values for business strikes are given for uncirculated condition.

The Liberty Seated Dollar has a rather interesting history as a collector's series. This was the Gobrecht design, introduced originally via the patterns of 1836 and then brought into general production following certain modifications in 1840. The major change was the restyling of the eagle on the reverse. There are two distinct types of the Liberty Seated Dollar. The Type I is without the motto "IN GOD WE TRUST." This motto was added in 1866, and those struck from 1866 to the conclusion of the series in 1873 are known as Type II. Several great rarities are included. In 1866, the year of the change-over to Type II, a very few specimens were struck without the motto, in proof state only. Then of course there is the celebrated 1873-S. The coin is beyond rare. It is known to have been minted, but no specimens can be found today. Strikings of the Liberty Seated Dollar originated at the Philadelphia, Carson City, New Orleans and San Francisco mints. Despite the fact that three subsidiary mints were involved, the majority of production came from Philadelphia.

During the period of the Liberty Seated design, the weight of our other silver coins was changed, bringing about the use of arrows at the date to indicate the weight change. This was NOT done with the Dollar. The Liberty Seated Dollar retained the same weight and specifications throughout its entire history, from the 1836 patterns to 1873.

Liberty Seated coins in general had a long-standing reputation of being only moderately popular with hobbyists. This was particularly true of the smaller denominations. The Liberty Seated Dollar was always clearly a cut above the Dime, Quarter and Half Dollar in collector attention. Compared to other Silver Dollars, however, it ranked well behind both the Morgan and Peace types, and even behind the Draped Bust. There were many more people collecting Liberty Seated Dollars than Draped Busts, but this can be ascribed to the great difference in price. All things being equal, the Draped Busts would have been the recipients of more collecting activity. In recent years the situation has changed, and the Liberty Seated Dollar has now acquired its deserved level of attention and popularity. The very fact that this is a late phenomenon, however, means that some of the prices are still a bit below what they should be — an ideal situation for the investor! They have some catching up to do, and most likely the next five to ten years will see them making the necessary upward adjustments.

Why was the Liberty Seated Dollar outshone for so many years by other designs in the Silver Dollar series? While this question may not have great bearing on the current investment potential of these coins, it cannot fail to arouse the curiosity of some readers — especially those who are not coin collectors. Traditionally, collectors tended to regard this period (1840 to 1873) as a sort of Middle Ages in the history of Silver Dollars. They saw the dawning years of the Silver Dollar as the classic period, admiring the Flowing Hairs for their beauty and historical background. The Flowing Hairs were supposedly the Dollars for aesthetic collectors of 30, 50, and more years ago. The so-called Renaissance in Silver Dollars was brought in by the Morgan design in 1878, the series which became the single most popular group among all the Silver Dollars. To the earlier collectors, or at least to many of them, the Liberty Seated series was just a "filler" to bridge the gap between classical Dollars and the much-loved Morgans. So much attention was spread in both those directions — and toward the Peace Dollar, too — that the Liberty Seated suffered essentially from being in the wrong chronological time-period. It got comparatively little "press," compared to the other Dollars. This was most noticeable in the late 1800s and early 1900s, when coin periodicals seemed to give up on the Gobrecht Dollar. Why publish commentary about it, they seemed to be thinking, when only a limited circle of readership would be interested? So they concentrated on the Morgan, Flowing Hair, and Draped Bust Dollars, all of which had an assured reader appeal. Even the Trade Dollar got a better press.

In examining the series itself, one may easily jump to the conclusion that the coins themselves are at fault. There are very few "varieties" in the Liberty Seated series, compared to those encountered in the Morgan Dollars. It gives the appearance of being a group with limited potential for original research or study, or for putting together a collection that could be termed unique. Actually this could hardly be a factor in the long-standing unpopularity of these coins. One must remember that our ancestors in the coin hobby were not as devoted to varieties and intense study, as are the numismatists of today. Just the reverse in most cases: they were glad to have a series in which a date and mint mark collection could serve as a full collection. Most coin dealers were not even calling attention to varieties, nor pricing specimens separately because of them. There are, however, other reasons that could be advanced to explain why these coins failed to arouse great enthusiasm. If we turn back the clock to the time they were being issued, 1840 to 1873 (counting the business strikes as apart from the earlier patterns), some clues come into focus. Coin collecting was growing at a very healthy pace in that era. It was a small hobby without any professional dealers in 1840. In 1873 there were thousands of collectors as well as numerous dealers in all the major cities. Coin auctions had come on the scene, too. The Liberty Seated Dollars were readily available for anyone to collect during those years. A nearly complete collection could be assembled just from "finds" made in everyday circulation. It was even possible to get bright uncirculated specimens of the older dates from bankrolls. All places of business kept rolls of Silver Dollars on hand, and by searching these rolls you could get virtually any date you wanted in uncirculated condition, except for the rarities (and even they must have been turning up, from time to time). In a sense it was the vast availability of Liberty Seated Dollars which contributed to their lack of collector popularity. The attitude toward coin collecting was very different than it became in later years. Recent and current coins were considered fit only for those who were not "serious" collectors. Anyone who collected from finds made in pocket change was in the non-serious category. The only coins worthy of being collected were the classics: those no longer in general circulation, which had age and some measure of scarcity behind them. These, of course, had to be purchased from the coin dealers or obtained by swapping with fellow collectors. Needless to mention, the early coin dealers did their best to promote this line of reasoning — if everyone collected the coins they found in change, the dealers would be out of business. They were careful, extremely careful, to play down recent and current coins, for fear that these issues might become too popular. They offered proofs of the Liberty Seated Dollar, because proofs were not available in circulation. Beyond proofs, they would offer only the rare dates. The philosophy of some coin dealers in those days was, roughly, "When someone has reached the point of entering a coin shop, make sure he gets interested in — or stays interested in — coins that have to be BOUGHT, no found." Of course this applied to all the Liberty Seated coins, not just to Dollars. the Dollar was in a rather different position, however, because of its high face value. If someone took a Dollar out of change to place in a collection, this was a large sum of money to tie up. So, in effect, the Liberty Seated Dollar was ignored by the more advanced collectors who went for Flowing Hairs and Draped Busts, and by the low-budget collectors who could not afford to collect Dollars in any way, shape or form. It was a vicious circle and it was not effectively broken until the Morgan design came on the scene in 1878. At that point, the attitude toward "current and recent" coins was changing. Everyone saw the Morgan Dollar as a masterpiece of designing, and this helped to popularize it. It became so popular, within a relatively few years after its introduction, that virtually everyone collecting "current and recent" dollars was specializing in Morgans. The Liberty Seated series was virtually all but forgotten. Of course there WAS some collecting activity on Liberty Seated Dollars, but these individuals were considered die-hards by numismatists at large. Most collectors could not understand why anyone would want Liberty Seated when Morgans were around. So it continued, well into the twentieth century. The Liberty Seated series gradually gained in popularity and in price, but the pace of advance was not equal to overall growth of the coin hobby. More of the new hobbyists were interested in Morgan and Peace Dollars; and those who could afford bigger and better things seemed to turn instinctively toward Flowing Hairs, Draped Busts, or Trade Dollars. The Gobrecht Liberties just got lost in the shuffle. They did not truly break the cycle and work their was into the mainstream until the 1960s. In the past twenty years they have done enormously well in making up for lost time. Partially this has been due to the writings of the late Kamal Ahwash, who authored numerous books and magazine articles on Liberty Seated coins of all denominations. He also established himself as a dealer specializing in Liberty Seated coins and served the growing numbers of collectors and investors whose interests ran in that direction. Major auction sales of the 1970s and 1980s showed that the rarer Liberty Seated Dollars could attract just as much attention as the best Morgans, Draped Busts and Flowing Hairs. Another indication of the growing clout of Liberty Seated Dollars is the prices charged for "type" specimens (that is, the dealer's choice of date, for a coin to be included in a "type" collection). Not too many years ago, a type specimen of a Liberty Seated Dollar could be obtained for just a few dollars more than a Morgan type or Peace type. Today the price spread on type specimens between the three designs is considerable, even for coins in low grades of condition. The Liberty Seated Dollar has come of age!

We will not go quite so far as to state that the Liberty Seated series offers the most investment potential of all the Dollars. This would not be entirely accurate. As a whole, they ARE the most underpriced Dollars, and if you want to use that as a criterion of the best investment group — well, then so be it. More is involved, however, than the basic fact of the Liberty Seated Dollars being more underpriced than Morgans or Peace Dollars. In general the Morgans are not an underpriced series, but the investment potential within Morgans is just as great or possibly greater. This is largely due to the heavier volume of buying and selling that occurs on Morgans. You can normally depend on price adjustments to occur quicker with Morgans because of the very active market. These comments can also be applied to the Peace Dollars, though the Peace series is not quite in the same league as the Morgans.

One will certainly want to examine the mintage totals on these Common Date Liberty Seated Dollars and try to derive as much information from them as possible. There are no known inaccuracies in the mintage figures, as given in mint records. This may seem difficult to believe in light of the current retail prices, which show low-mintage coins selling only fractionally higher than those with substantial mintages; and, in a few cases, no higher at all. This is the fault of buying patterns, not the result of availability. In a sense it's a left-over effect from the days of this coin's unpopularity, an imbalance still in need of correction and which CAN be counted upon to correct itself in the coming years. The variation in mintages among these Common Dates is greater than 20-to-1. The variation in price is only 2½-to-1.

A very good analysis can be made of the Common Dates, better in fact than of the Semi-Keys and Keys, because with the exception of just two dates (1859-O and 1860-O) these are all Philadelphia strikings. Thus the level of preservation should have been roughly equal from one coin to another right down the line, allowing of course for a slightly lower ratio of preservation on the early dates. When attempting to estimate quantities remaining in existence, especially those in MS-60 or uncirculated condition, the time factor does enter the picture. Here we have coins issued from 1840 to 1873. Though this is not really an enormous span of time (the Lincoln Cent has gone from 1909 to the present), it covers an important era so far as coin collecting is concerned. The growth of coin collecting in those 32 years meant that the later-date coins were receiving somewhat greater hobbyist attention, and a slightly better ratio of preservation. For everyone who put aside uncirculated coins in 1841, there were perhaps five collectors doing so by 1873. Of course, not all of them were interested in Liberty Seated Dollars. Furthermore, not all the coins preserved by these early collectors continued to be preserved: some of them, unfortunately, ended up in circulation at a later date. Still, you can depend on later coins having a higher preservation ratio in uncirculated condition. It is difficult to say what exact percentages are involved. This amounts to little more than a guessing game. Investment analysts commonly guess, but we do not. We will present a few observations which are not in the nature of guesswork, and leave it to the reader to take things further if he so chooses. Looking at the first two dates in the lineup, we see that the 1841 had a mintage of roughly ten thousand fewer than the 1842. These are both Philadelphia coins. By all logic the 1841 should be preserved in fewer overall specimens than the 1842, and fewer in uncirculated condition as well. There were less to begin with and they were issued at approximately the same time. Of the 1843 there were about eight thousand fewer struck, than of the 1841. The two year difference would not be a factor in their preservation ratio, so it would be reasonable to assume that the 1843 is scarcer than the 1841 in all condition grades. The 1846, struck in fifty thousand fewer specimens than any of the preceding Common Dates, should be scarcer than any of them. Here we have a five year time factor, but that is not nearly enough to off-set a mintage differential of 50,000. Then, coming to the 1849, we find a mintage of only 62,000, far less than any of the earlier Common Dates. Once again, even though the date is nearly a decade after inception of this series, it must be presumed that this coin is quite a bit scarcer than its predecessors. All of these are relatively simple conclusions to reach, for anyone even slightly familiar with coin collecting. Now we will give an example of a more complicated case, in which a clear-cut decision is difficult. The 1867 had a striking of 47,525, the second lowest of any Common Date Liberty Seated Dollar. Theoretically this should make it the second scarcest on the market. But is it? Not necessarily. We have a time-gap of 18 years between it and the 1849, which was struck in a quantity of 62,600. That is a rather small difference in mintage figures, and the fact that the 1849 was issued almost two decades earlier might — MIGHT — cancel out the difference. If we were going to make an estimation (knowing full well that there is nothing concrete to back it up), we would surmise the 1849 to be slightly more plentiful overall, that is, in all condition grades going down to "average." However the 1849 is probably scarcer than the 1867 in uncirculated condition. Having started off with an edge of fifteen thousand specimens, there should be more existing specimens of the 1849 in the world today. But the 1867 should have enjoyed a higher rate of preservation in uncirculated condition, simply because there were many more coin hobbyists active in 1867 than in 1849. This may seem like a very technical point. It is the substance of sound investment strategy. If you miscalculate availability, you are very likely to buy the wrong coins.

We hasten to add that calculations of this sort become more complex when coins of different mints are involved. The usual preservation rate was different, from the coins of one mint to those of another. This was strictly because of geographical location. Coins released in San Francisco were going into an area with far fewer collectors than coins released in Philadelphia. A San Francisco mintage could be quite a bit higher than a corresponding Philadelphia mintage, and the existing totals of "uncs" may be about the same. We have a good example in the Liberty Seated Common Dates. The 1859- O ("O" signifies New Orleans) had a mintage of 360,000. The 1859 from Philadelphia was struck in 256,500 specimens or roughly one hundred thousand fewer. Considering the difference in the number of collectors in the two areas, it would be unreasonable to believe that existing totals in uncirculated condition are approximately the same. Even the 1860-O with its mintage in excess of half a million could not be termed a really plentiful coin in "unc." It is scarcer in that condition grade than either the 1869 or 1870 Philadelphia, both of which had mintages of less than half a million. Of course there

THE "LIBERTY SEATED" DOLLARS / 127

are always intangibles involved which can throw off such calculations. Coins are not always preserved in the ratios they should have been, under the prevailing circumstances. Yet, by and large, an application of the foregoing logic will, in the majority of cases, reveal which coins are the scarcer.

There is not a great deal to be said about the investment history of Common Date Liberty Seated Dollars. They received virtually no investment attention in the first half of this century, with the possible exception of the rarities. The Common Dates were just not being bought for investment, even though the opportunities seem irresistible in light of later developments. Many of the Common Date "uncs" could be bought for less than $10 in the 1930s, and this was for coins with a $1 face value and an intrinsic value for their bullion content. Circulated specimens were selling for $2 and $3 unless they were on the "unc" borderline. Investors would not touch them as there was not enough overall public support for them. Today we would seize such coins, fully confident that such vast underpricing would soon be corrected. Investors of that era did not see them as being underpriced — they saw them fully priced in relation to existing demand, and they were correct. Even if bought for those modest sums in the thirties, these coins would have taken several decades to register an investment profit. In 1960, none of the Common Dates were selling for as much as $75. They had advanced, of course, from their price levels of earlier years, but the values were still quite thin in relation to availability. Did investors come in at that time? No. There was, by that time, a long standing tradition of leaving these coins alone for investment purposes. As you will note on the chart, the rate of increases between 1960 and 1965 certainly justified the hesitancy on the part of 1960 investors. The Morgan and Peace Dollars were doing very nicely in that half decade, but not the Common Dates from the Liberty Seated Series. However it was quite a different story in the years from 1965 to 1970, and then significantly so from 1970 to 1975. In the later sixties most of these Common Dates began rising at a worthy pace. This was not totally the result of increased investment purchasing, but rather the one-two punch of more investment buying coupled with growth in the coin hobby. The Liberty Seated Dollars were gaining greater popularity among hobbyists and this inevitably contributed to higher prices across-the-board. The fact that prices rose sharply on all the coins in this group is evidence that collectors were doing their share of the buying. We know that investors were buying them, too, but the actual level of investment purchasing was slight compared to what it became in the half decade that followed (that is, from 1970 to 1975). The upward price push of Liberty Seated Dollars from 1965 to 1970 proved the long-needed encouragement to investment buyers. This finally removed all doubts that the coins lacked the ability to score well in the marketplace. This was all that was needed to bring more investors into the series, though it was not the sort of stampede buying that occurred on Morgans. Most of it was rather judicious buying being further supplemented with a continuing growth in the volume of purchases made by collectors. This served to balance out the market fairly well and prevented drastic price spreads from developing. Nevertheless if the series is viewed as a whole it will be evident that the price advances, from 1970 to 1975, did not truly reflect availability of each coin. Instead the prices were gradually heading together as a group, with a differential in 1975 between $500 for the lowest priced coin to $650 for the highest. This was a much smaller percentage difference than had existed at any time previously on our chart. Finally by this time the analysts and publishers of coin investment newsletters were tipping the Liberty Seated series and various dates within it. The only real problem with the investment buying of that time was the failure of many investors to make a careful selection of dates. They were unfamiliar with the Liberty Seated Dollars and many took an oversimplified approach to buying them, under the assumption that one date in the group was just as good as another. Essentially, all the dates had been seriously underpriced and most of them continued to be underpriced even after the gains of 1970-1975. This in itself was not (and never is) justification for buying coins within any series without regard for dates and availabilities. The presumption that all coins in a group will increase in value at the same pace is usually incorrect. Even when it does prove to be correct (which will be about 15% of the time), one cannot lose by buying the best investment grade coins in the lineup. They will always advance as well as the lesser coins, and you have approximately an 85% chance that they will do better. Investors could have done much better on the coins in this group from 1975 to 1980. Looking at the rate of advances, it gives the impression that they could have succeeded only by buying the late dates toward the bottom of the chart. Actually, the late dates scored well ONLY because of the misdirected buying on the part of investors. With better all around planning and selection of dates to buy, there could have been good profits on the earlier dates. Some dates that definitely deserved to score investment-size profits in the years from 1975 to 1980 failed to do so, only because of unskilled buying.

The values remained fairly well bunched in 1980. The lowest price in the Common Dates was $800 and the high was $1000, both of these figures being shared among many different dates (a difference of only 20% between the highest and lowest). Things opened up considerably in the ensuing five years. As the market stands currently, the lowest price is $850 ($50 higher than the 1980 low), but the highest has touched $2000 (precisely double the highest recorded price of 1980). For anyone with investment instincts this tells a lot. The price spreads that developed in those years did not accurately reflect availability or collector popularity. They left some dates underpriced, some fully priced, and possibly (though this is hard to say with Liberty Seated Dollars) a couple overpriced. In any event, the group is now wide open and the investment grade dates should be quite apparent. Their prices are out of alignment with the other coins in this lineup, and buying activity in the next five to ten years should EASILY raise them to their deserved price levels.

On the whole, the increases for Liberty Seated Common Dates were very impressive from 1980 to 1985, especially in light of the slump which hit coin collecting during several of those years. A number of the dates doubled in price and only a few recorded very slight increases or none at all. Not one of the dates decreased in value from 1980 to 1985. Collector buying alone could not, of course, account for this kind of development. The collector demand would not increase that rapidly on coins of this nature; and, even if it did, it would show itself in a more even, less radical breakdown of prices. Investors were buying the Common Dates pretty heavily in the past five years, and they were not (in the main) buying them across-the-board as they had done in preceding years.

The reader at this point is likely to be wondering: if so much investment buying of Common Date Liberty Seated Dollars was occurring in the years from 1980 to 1985, could there now be a problem with the quantities of specimens held by investors? In other words, if investors are now largely in control of this market (which we can acknowledge to be true), what dangers are there of large quantities returning to the marketplace and resulting in a temporary surplus? We would have to assume that a few of the dates, at least, are over-held by investors ("over-held" means that a fairly dangerous quantity is in the hands of investors — enough to upset the market if they were all sold within a short period of time). However we do not see any mass exodus of these coins from the portfolio of investors. Some investment holders are certain to continue holding, even though they could sell at the present time and realize a profit. This is invariably the case with any coins that have registered a profit, and it might hold true even more so in the case of Liberty Seated Common Dates. As the series was clearly undervalued for so long a period of time, some investors will certainly conclude that further room exists for upward price movement on ALL the dates. And they will continue holding and watching the market, selling only if the prices on their particular coins stagnate or begin to slide downward. It is very unlikely that any large-scale wholesale selloff will occur. The average investor in this series has a mixed portfolio, and if he has succeeded in profiting on some of the dates he will very likely want to build up this portfolio further, rather than liquidating it. There are no danger signals on the horizon that would lead anyone, and surely not en masse, to dispose of Liberty Seated Common Dates. Price projections on most of the coins in this group for 1990 as well as 1995 are favorable. We can further believe that many of those who bought them for investment in 1980 and the early eighties were thinking primarily in terms of the long haul, without any intention of selling in the mid eighties regardless of their price movements. Of course there will be SOME investor selling, as there always is (it occurs constantly and is a normal, routine phase of the Silver Dollar market). In our view this cannot help but BENEFIT the new investor who buys these coins today. As we see it, unless something goes drastically awry, profits from the liquidated coins will be immediately returned to the Liberty Seated series and placed into dates which show the most current investment potential. There is no shortage of these. Hence it should be a case of the seasoned investor helping the novice with good profits on all sides. We cannot imagine investors slipping back into the old unproductive buying patterns that prevailed in the seventies. The science of coin investing has come too far to even entertain such a possibility.

One of the BEST BETS in this group is the 1849, which we have already mentioned. Its mintage of 62,600 is the lowest in the Common Date lineup among coins struck before the Civil War. Not until we get down to 1865 do we find a Common Date Liberty Seated Dollar with a smaller mintage. Although the price made a strong advance between 1980 and 1985, rising from $800 to $1800, there should still be room for much greater advance. Any way you analyze this coin it comes up underpriced. Match it against the 1847, whose mintage was 140,750. That's more than twice as many. Yet the 1847 is selling for just as much: $1800. The 1861 had a higher mintage and is selling for $200 more than the 1849. The cruelest cut of all is the fact that the 1859, with a mintage of more than a quarter million, is selling for a higher price than the low-mintage 1849. More than four specimens were struck of the 1859 for every one of the 1849, and the 1849 has the investment advantage of being a decade earlier (in other words, it should have had a lower preservation ratio in uncirculated condition). A reasonable price at the present time on this coin would be $2200 to $2350, in light of the prices being obtained for other dates within the group. Considering that the group as a whole tends to be undervalued, a more logical price on the 1849 would be as much as $2500. We feel confident that by 1990 the 1849 will come up to around $3500 with a very good chance of hitting the $4000 mark. It should do as well price wise as any date in the Common Date lineup. Our projection on its value by 1995 is $7000 to $8000, which would classify it as favorable for both the short and long term.

Two more BEST BETS from this group are the 1841 and 1843. The mintages on these are not nearly as low as the 1849, standing at 173,000 and 165,100 respectively. But the current retail market values: only $850 each, seem utterly appalling. These are the lowest prices for any Common Dates, and certainly not the highest mintages. If the prices were anywhere within reason, the two dates with mintages exceeding one million — the 1871 and 1872 — would have the lowest price tags. Instead, one of these coins (the 1871) is selling for $1550, nearly twice as much as the 1841 and 1843. This is a clear example of imbalanced prices. The situation worsened on these coins from 1980 to 1985. The 1841 scored an advance of only $50 while the 1843 remained static at the $850 level. They both deserved to climb well over $1000. At the present figures they are seriously underpriced and very favorable for investment buying. The only question is how long they will take to achieve a reasonable level of price. Considering the pace of buying activity on this group as a whole, we have little doubt that the year 1990 will find these imbalances completely, or nearly completely, erased. The 1841 should be at the $1750 mark by then with an excellent chance of hitting $2000. If it seems too optimistic a forecast, it is only a slight advance over the price at which the coin should be selling right now. It would not be overpriced at the moment at $1300 or $1400, so an increase to $1750-$2000 would simply make up for lost ground and add a bit extra for normal inflation. Our projection on the 1843 is precisely the same as for the 1841. We think both coins will attain the same levels of price in 1990, and our feeling about their price for 1995 is in the range of $3500 to $4000. Hence we view them as somewhat more favorable for the short term than for the long. This is because we look for them to be almost fully priced by 1990, leaving not as much room for advance between 1990 and 1995.

We are saying "no" to the 1861, the highest priced date in the lineup. It looks fully priced to us at the moment, in terms of price vs. availability. It will gain somewhat in the coming years just from the overall upward sweep of this group, but we do not see it coming anywhere near the profitable category by 1990. Its price is now $2000, and we feel it would be lucky to reach $3500 by 1990. The three coins following it on the chart ALL have lower mintages and lower current prices. We are not tabbing any of this trio as a BEST BET, but we do recommend them as favorable coins to buy. These are the 1865, 1866 and 1867. Of course we are referring to the 1866 with motto added on the reverse side. This date also exists without the motto (the old style), but is very rare. The mintage figures are very similar on the three, varying by no more than about two thousand among them. The prices are likewise similar, going from $1625 to $1650. There should be no difficulty in all three getting beyond $3000 by 1990. Our projection for their prices in 1990 is for all of them to be at $3250, which would place them in the profitable category. You are advised to pay little heed to the past performances on these, as they are really not indicative of what the future holds. They have historically been underpriced, and even the surges of 1975 and 1980 did not bring them to a reasonable price level in relation to other coins in this series.

There is a borderline coin in this group, one we do not specifically recommend but which we point out for those who may want to take a long shot. This is the 1868 from the Philadelphia facility. At first glance it does not look appealing. The price is $1350 with a mintage of more than one hundred and fifty thousand, and to make matters worse the date is late. Yet you will notice that the coins directly following it on the chart — the 1869, 1870, 1871 — have higher mintages and either identical or higher prices. This places the 1868 squarely in a position where it could make a substantial value gain in the coming years. A certain number of investors will see this coin as being undervalued in relation to the others and they will buy it. Any upward movement could be interpreted as a signal for further buying. We don't know! We would not want to bet on the prospects of the 1868, between now and 1990. It might do very well.

Of the New Orleans strikings (only two are included in the Common Date lineup), one is unfavorable for investment and the other is so attractive at the present that we are awarding it our BEST BET designation. The coin to buy among this pair is the 1859-O. True enough, the mintage is high at $360,000 but as a subsidiary mint production you can be quite certain that it had a low preservation ratio — especially in uncirculated condition. The current price of $875 is meager, with an advance of only $75 since 1980. This one should be getting up around $1750 by 1990, which would render it profitable unless the rate of national inflation reverts to double digits. Just compare the current price of $875 to that of the 1860-O. The latter had a mintage exceeding half a million, and is now selling for $1200. If the $1200 valuation is justified for the 1860-O, the 1859-O should now command around $1700 or $1800. So all we are really saying is that it will reach its fair 1985 price by 1990.

There are no adjustment marks to be encountered on the Liberty Seated Dollars. By the time they were placed in production, the mint was using planchets of uniform weight and the archaic practice of removing excess metal was no longer necessary. You will encounter weak strikes, but they are not as numerous as to be found on earlier Silver Dollars. Actually, many of the "weak strikes" on Liberty Seated Dollars are really worn dies. The steam-driven striking machinery of that era was fairly dependable in striking each coin with the same pressure. It may be difficult at first to recognize these coins (weak strikes/worn dies). If really noticeably weak they may give the appearance of slight circulation wear until examination is made with a magnifying glass. The series is notorious for being "baggy," that is, showing a profusion of nicks and scratches which collectors refer to as "bag marks."

LIBERTY SEATED DOLLARS — SEMI-KEY DATES

Year	Mintage	1955	1960	1965	1970	1975	1980	1985
1840	61,005	40.00	60.00	100.00	175.00	685.00	900.00	850.00
1844	20,000	30.00	55.00	100.00	225.00	635.00	1000.00	1825.00
1845	24,500	30.00	55.00	100.00	225.00	635.00	1000.00	1825.00
1846-0	59,000	40.00	60.00	75.00	175.00	675.00	750.00	3875.00
1848	15,000	30.00	50.00	100.00	240.00	650.00	900.00	2100.00
1850-0	40,000	32.50	57.50	85.00	165.00	660.00	3200.00	3625.00
1853	46,110	35.00	80.00	150.00	300.00	725.00	900.00	850.00
1854	33,140	65.00	110.00	175.00	360.00	775.00	1200.00	4375.00
1855	26,000	60.00	100.00	135.00	400.00	850.00	1500.00	3750.00
1856	63,500	40.00	70.00	110.00	300.00	650.00	1000.00	1900.00
1859-0	20,000	40.00	115.00	175.00	325.00	675.00	800.00	875.00
1862	12,090	27.50	55.00	95.00	250.00	575.00	1500.00	2300.00
1863	27,660	25.00	55.00	90.00	220.00	550.00	1200.00	1900.00
1864	31,170	25.00	52.50	80.00	200.00	550.00	1000.00	1650.00

LIBERTY SEATED DOLLARS —

Semi-Key % of increase:		
	1955-60	87%
	1960-65	61%
	1965-70	127%
	1970-75	161%
	1975-80	70%
	1980-85	101%
overall % of increase:	1955-85	5996%

The Semi-Keys all have mintages under 75,000. As you will note, however, several of the dates classified as Common Dates had lower mintages than a few of these Semi-Keys. Once again we must point out that the categorizing of coins as Common Date, Semi-Key and Key is based on long standing tradition within the numismatic hobby. It does not always follow strict logic.

One may wonder why so many low-mintage dates occur in the Liberty Seated series. Taking the Semi-Keys and Keys together, they account for about as many dates as the Common Dates. After not striking any Silver Dollars since 1803, the argument could certainly not be made that an ample supply was already in circulation. The fact of the matter is that when the Liberty Seated series began, the quantity of Silver Dollars passing through ordinary circulation had dwindled to an extremely small number. In some parts of the country, especially the expanding midwest into which few Dollars had circulated originally, it was difficult to find any at all. This was largely the result of intentional melting. Ordinary wear and tear in circulation had nothing to do with it; Silver Dollars that had managed to escape the melting pot continued to be passed in circulation until they were worn smooth. Actually the reason for the low mintage figures in many of these years was the advent of the gold Dollar in 1849. Production of the Silver Dollar would almost certainly have been higher in the 1850s and 1860s, had the gold Dollar coin not existed. Contrary to a widely held belief, the gold Dollar was not struck primarily in the west and circulated in that area. It had a substantial output at the Philadelphia mint, and the objective was to distribute it as evenly as possible throughout the country. The gold Dollar was smaller and easier to handle than its silver counterpart. Also, it had the lure of being made from gold. That, in the 1850s and 1860s, was a strong recommendation indeed.

As with the Common Dates, this Semi-Key grouping consists chiefly of coins from the Philadelphia mint. Three New Orleans strikings are also included, but none from either the Carson City or San Francisco facilities. Comparatively little output occurred at the western mints, and all of it now falls under the heading of Key Date. In terms of time period the Semi-Keys range from 1840 — the first year of the series so far as regular circulating coins are concerned — to 1864. It is quite an interesting group, with some unusual and downright bizarre price movements in recent years. When investment interest began on the Liberty Seated Dollars, the level of buying was about parallel from the Common Dates to the Semi-Keys. Very soon thereafter, in the period from 1970 to 1975, investor attention shifted noticeably to the Semi-Keys. The pattern here was a logical one. At first, investors were hesitant about the Semi-Keys because of their higher prices. There was some doubt about the overall ability of Liberty Seated Dollars to score noteworthy price increases, as the series had a reputation of being the least popular of all the regularly issued Silver Dollars. While the levels of values did seem low in relation to mintage figures during the 1960s, investors preferred to test out this series with the Common Dates and await further developments. When the group showed itself capable of scoring good gains, there was greater confidence in the Semi-Keys and in the Key Dates as well, and a greater share of investor capital began to be channeled in that direction. This pattern was not only maintained but intensified in the years from 1980 to 1985. While the Common Dates enjoyed very satisfactory growth in some cases, during that half decade, the Semi-Keys were turning in some performances that could only be termed remarkable: such as the 1846-O gaining from $750 to $3875. This was one of the big overall gainers among all Silver Dollars in that period and it served to give the Semi-Key group considerable investment publicity. These have been very talked-about coins and the general consensus of opinion on them is favorable. Liberty Seated Dollars are no longer the black sheep of Silver Dollars and these Semi-Keys have done just about everything possible to prove themselves. The question to be answered today, of course, is: has their rate of price increases within recent years taken them to the stage of being "fully priced," without room for further investment profit? The answer would be yes if one talks in terms of the group as a whole. You could have made a simple date collection of them in the 1970s, just as a numismatist would, and profited handsomely in the ensuing years. This would not have required any investment strategy beyond ascertaining the fact that all Liberty Seated Semi-Keys were undervalued and due for substantial increases. You would have profited even more by being selective. Today, this sort of buying is no longer feasible, as the future prospects for these coins as a group are not as bright as they were a decade ago. There is still, however, ample opportunity within the Semi-Keys for those who will choose the most favorable dates, based on availability and current retail market prices. The chart as presented above should make this a relatively simple matter. Some of the recent price movements have left certain dates clearly undervalued at the present time in relation to the values attached to other dates. In fact the prices coin-by-coin are more imbalanced than they were in the 1980 market. This is an indication of extremely heavy buying mixed with fairly brisk selling. Obviously there was a good deal of switching-off on the part of speculative buyers. This is evidenced by such performances as that of the 1850-O, which ballooned from $660 to $3200 in the years from

1975 to 1980, but then gained only an additional $425 by 1985. It is not unreasonable to believe that the 1990 market will find greater price parity among the group, with values more truly reflecting availability. We do not anticipate that the prices will be totally fair by 1990 — if ever — but they should be heading in that direction. This is really all the investor needs to realize worthwhile profits.

With a group of coins whose mintages are as similar as these (ranging from twelve thousand to sixty-three thousand), one must be particularly cautious in making analysis. The difference of a few thousand in mintage between coins of similar date is often meaningless. Then, too, it is important to take into consideration the higher preservation ratio of coins with later dates, as they tended to be put aside in greater numbers by hobbyists. On the whole this is not a group on which the beginning investor should trust himself to make a correct application of the investment strategy presented in this book. We have analyzed these coins date by date, and the results of our findings follow. To many of the more seasoned investors among our readers it may appear that we are being too conservative in our future projections. This is intentional, as we want to leave the least possible margin for error. We would rather err on the side of underrating coins than overrating them.

One of the outstanding dates in this group, and a definite BEST BET, is the leadoff coin: the 1840. It has the distinction of being the first Liberty Seated Dollar in the revised Gobrecht design (that is, with the Heraldic Eagle on the reverse side, replacing the Flying Eagle used in the trial strikings of 1836 to 1839). This alone counts for something, as some collectors want first-year-of-issue coins. More important is the fact that the mintage is certainly not high at 61,005, even though the casual observer may consider it high in relation to other coins in this array. As we said, when mintage figures are this similar they require greater interpretation. What strikes us most about the 1840 is that it declined in value from 1980 to 1985, losing $50 to its current level of $850. This was undeserved, especially in a market in which the Semi-Keys as a whole were scoring so well. Actually it had reached $1200 in 1982 (which is not shown on our chart), so the present value represents a decline of $350 within a three year period. Investor selling could not be the explanation for this decline. Investors who bought the coin in 1975 when it stood at $685 would not have achieved a profit in 1982, so it is very unlikely that they would have sold. Given these circumstances the average investor would want to wait a few more years to see which direction the coin would go. There is really no logical reason for the decline but we have the feeling it will be followed in these next five years by a strong rebound. At $850 this coin is at least 50% underpriced in relation to the Semi-Keys as a lot, if you take them price by price in relation to their availability. We think it will not only make up this shortage in the years from 1985 to 1990, but will add some additional increase owing to the growth in both collector and investor buying. From its current plateau of $850 we foresee the 1840 rising to $1750 in 1990 — a most conservative prediction, as it could get to the $2000 mark with no trouble at all. Some investors could miss this one if they pay undue attention to the mintage figures. The next eight coins in the Semi-Key lineup all have lower mintage figures, and they could easily attract attention away from the 1840.

Another BEST BET among the Liberty Seated Semi-Keys is the unheralded 1853. You do not hear a great deal about this coin. We do not recall it ever being "tipped" by anyone or even discussed in the investment newsletters. Yet it obviously has a good deal going for it. The current price is $850, with a mintage of 46,110. You need only compare the mintage total and price against those of some of the other coins in this group. The 1856 has a mintage of 63,500 and a price of $1900 — more than double the price, with a mintage of seventeen thousand MORE specimens. At that rate the 1853 should now be selling for about $2000, making it extremely undervalued at $850. It compares favorably against the higher priced dates, too. The 1854, selling for $4375, had a mintage of 33,140. That's approximately three-fourths the mintage of the 1853, which means the 1853 should be selling for about three-fourths as much as the 1854. If the 1854 is worth $4375, the 1853 is then worth roughly $3100 — a very far cry from the $850 at which it now stands! Of course one cannot try to get too exacting in these calculations, or place 100% faith in their results. The coin market never runs THAT true. But when a coin that should be bringing $3100 is available at $850, it looks extremely alluring for investment. We could hardly be accused of being overly optimistic if we predicted a price of $3000 for the 1853 by 1990. That would bring it ONLY to its fair level of 1985 value; the fair level by 1990 should be higher. Yet, for the sake of staying within conservative bounds, we are going to make a projection of $2000 by 1990. Even with that increase, far less than what this coin is obviously capable of, it will land firmly on the profitable side of the fence. You could easily term this one a "sleeper," in that it has been overlooked by so many people. We doubt if it will be overlooked any longer by 1990. Our long term forecast on the 1853 is for a price in the vicinity of $4400 by 1995.

There is a great bargain to be found among the New Orleans strikings. The first two New Orleans dates on the list have been heavily bought, and both of their prices have been run up beyond $3000. The 1846-O with a mintage of 59,000 is now at $3875 while the 1850-O, struck in 40,000, has reached $3625. While not really overpriced at these levels, both coins would have to be deemed fully priced and out of range for investment purchase at the present time. The 1859-O presents a sharp and really inexplicable contrast. Its recorded mintage is 20,000, far less than either of the above. It is now selling for $875, up from a very weak $800 of 1980. Strangely enough — if you probe deeper — this coin was once at $1750, twice what it is bringing on the current market. That figure was reached in 1982 and it did not, by any stretch of imagination, represent overpricing at that time. From that figure it should have easily hit $3000 by the time the 1985 prices were tabulated, but instead it went in the opposite direction. As we see it, this is an instance of freak pricing and not much more. It would be difficult to assign an explanation to this price tumble. Were investors caught up in the 1846 and 1850 New Orleans strikings that they failed to notice what was happening with the 1859-O? Why didn't groups of investors rush in to buy, when the prices started going down? Wouldn't it have been an attractive buy at $1000 or even $1500? Apparently no one got the message. At $875 this coin is as much as 70% underpriced. It should start taking off very quickly, so you are well advised not to wait on this one if you choose to add it to your investment portfolio. We see the price getting up to $2500 by 1990, with a very good chance of exceeding $3000. This is our prediction regardless of the price activity on the 1846-O and 1850-O. We look for the 1859-O to hit $2500 whether its companion coins from the New Orleans facility go up or down in value the next five years. Personally we anticipate them to go up, but only fractionally. The levels at which they stand now would not allow for a substantial increase. Needless to say, the 1859-O is a BEST BET selection and one of the best in the entire Silver Dollar market at the present time.

Although we are not giving it the designation of BEST BET, we have positive feelings about the 1862. This wartime Dollar had a mintage of just 12,090, the lowest mintage of any of the Semi-Keys. While it has scored good price gains, it has not received anything comparable to the attention it really merits. Its current price of $2300 is far from being in the lead in this group, though with the lowest mintage it deserves to be at, or at least near, the top. The 1854, also a Philadelphia coin, is selling for nearly twice as much. The 1862 is also being outsold by the 1846-O, 1850-O, and the 1855 Philadelphia. It is fifth on the price list while ranking first on the mintage list. Even though this coin has a definite potential to hit $5000 by 1990, something that has not yet been achieved by any of the Semi-Keys, we will place our prediction in the range of $4250 to $4500. This would be sufficient to turn an investment profit.

The remainder of the coins in this group are too fully priced to warrant investment consideration. For example, the 1863 at $1900 and the 1864 at $1650 are selling at approximately their correct levels based on availability and other considerations.

LIBERTY SEATED DOLLARS — KEY DATES

Year	Mintage	1955	1960	1965	1970	1975	1980	1985
1850	7,500	40.00	110.00	150.00	300.00	675.00	1200.00	3625.00
1851 (A)	1,300	300.00	800.00	1000.00	1000.00	3000.00	6000.00	12500.00
1852 (B)	1,100	275.00	690.00	1500.00	2750.00	3500.00	6000.00	12000.00
(Motto Added on Reverse)								
1870-CC	12,462	80.00	155.00	325.00	500.00	900.00	1500.00	2450.00
1870-S (C)	Unknown							
1871-CC	1,376	250.00	925.00	2000.00	2400.00	3800.00	5800.00	7500.00
1872-CC	3,150	200.00	525.00	1150.00	1400.00	2225.00	3250.00	8750.00
1872-S	9,000	85.00	185.00	250.00	385.00	850.00	2500.00	3300.00
1873-CC	2,300	235.00	900.00	2250.00	2800.00	6500.00	8000.00	9500.00
1873-S	700	UNKNOWN IN ANY COLLECTION						

LIBERTY SEATED DOLLARS — KEY DATES

% of increase:		
	1955-60	193%
	1960-65	101%
	1965-70	42%
	1970-75	75%
	1975-80	60%
	1980-85	74%
overall % of increase:	1955-85	4540%

The Key Dates are an alluring lineup. These are coins that any collector would like to own. Their scarcity can hardly be disputed; only one date has a mintage above ten thousand and a number of them are under two thousand. For the investor there is obvious potential here, however the investor cannot take a hobbyist's approach. He must draw distinctions based on what these coins have done in the marketplace and what they are likely to do in the future — which is often two very different things. They are fabulous coins, but not all of them are fabulous from an investment viewpoint.

With the Key Dates the situation is quite a bit different than we encountered on the Common Dates and Semi-Key. In those groups we had a preponderance of Philadelphia strikings with a few scattered New Orleans mint marks mixed in. Here there are three Philadelphia coins out of a total of ten, the remainder being from the Carson City and San Francisco mints. It is interesting to note that no New Orleans strikings are among the Key Dates, despite the fact that this was a subsidiary mint noted for relatively low year by year production. The total of ten coins is reduced, for practical purposes, to eight. The 1870-S and 1873-S are included on the chart merely for the sake of making our listings complete. They are unavailable, both of them being unknown. These are not only two of the most legendary Silver Dollars, but two of the fabled rare coins of any denomination. While no really helpful investment information can be gleaned from them — as there are no price histories — the 1873-S does provide us with one interesting shred of data. Mint records indicate that 700 specimens were struck at the San Francisco facility in 1873, yet the coin has vanished. If the mintage figure is correct and 700 specimens were indeed manufactured, the total extinction of this coin does not agree with the popularly held theories about ratios of preservation. If a coin from 1873 is going to be extinct with 700 specimens made, then a coin struck in 7,000 specimens should only exist in ten specimens, while 70,000 in original mintage would yield 100 surviving specimens in ALL grades of condition. From all the research and study that has gone into rare coins and especially Silver Dollars, it is apparent that the ratio of preservation is much — MUCH — higher on most coins. You would not, under normal circumstances, expect to have just 100 specimens surviving from a coin of which 70,000 were minted. You would certainly be surprised to find NO surviving specimens from a mintage of 700. This just does not make sense, if we look at the normal preservation ratios that apply to rare coins. There must be more to the story of the 1873-S than meets the eye. If 700 specimens were struck and RELEASED INTO CIRCULATION, it is utterly unthinkable that none would survive today. At least a few collectors would have acquired them. There were dealers active in 1873, too. Even pure luck should have preserved a couple of specimens, in cookie jars or savings boxes. Failing all that, a fortune hunter with a metal detector should have — by now — found one on the California beaches. The fact that none whatsoever have surfaced leads one to a choice between the following conclusions:

Theory A The 700 were struck but not released. All of them were remelted at the mint. (if not released, they had to be remelted. If these specimens were simply stored away by the mint, they would have surfaced by now. There have been people over the years who have had a remarkable ability to find "unknown" coins among those stored by the mint.)

Theory B They were never struck in the first place. The mintage figure is correct in stating that 700 Silver Dollars were struck at the San Francisco facility in 1873, but all of them bore the date 1872.

There is yet another possible theory: the mint records are incorrect. It is simple to jump to that conclusion, but anyone familiar with mint records should be convinced that errors of this magnitude — saying a coin was struck when it really wasn't — are almost unknown. The closest you can get to this among Silver Dollars is the production total for 1804, which states that the mint struck 19,500 Draped Busts. We know for a fact that it did not strike ANY Silver Dollars dated 1804 in 1804 (it struck a few of them later, in the 1830s). The figure of 19,500, if accurate, was for Dollars struck with 1803 dates.

What happened to the 1873-S Silver Dollar? They seem to have just disappeared. Until one is actually located, or at least a reliable record of someone having seen one, many of the experts will refuse to believe that the coin ever existed. We are not aware of any fakes of this coin, either, though it is not impossible that some may exist. Undoubtedly there would be fakes if the circumstances were more favorable. When a coin is THAT rare — to the point of being totally unknown — any specimen coming to light is automatically suspect, and subjected to close scrutiny. Also, the logical way of faking this coin would be via a date change on a genuine Liberty Seated Dollar of a different date, and that too presents a problem. The ideal "victim" would be an 1878-S, as the digit "8" can be changed to "3" by removing just a bit of metal. However, no 1878-S Liberty Seated Dollars were struck. The design was not in use after 1873. The only two Liberty Seated Dollars available from the 1870s are the 1870 and 1872. Changing a "0" or a "2" into a "3" is difficult. Even with the prospect of creating a half-million-dollar coin, the fakers have apparently been sufficiently discouraged. There is, of course, one other alternative: applying a fake mint mark to an 1873 Philadelphia Dollar, which is a relatively common coin. While this could be done without much trouble, fake mint marks are easily detected. They come loose when the coin is dipped in acetone (nail polish remover).;

Regarding the 1866 Philadelphia, this is also a very glamorous, legendary coin. It is in a different category than the 1873-S in two major respects. First, the mint records for 1873 clearly state that 700 Silver Dollars (presumably dated 1873) were struck at San Francisco. The 1866 Philadelphia Dollar is not mentioned at all in mint records. Secondly, the reverse situation prevails in terms of existing specimens. No specimens are known of the 1873-S, which the mint claims it produced, but two ARE known of the 1866 — which the mint gives no record of. These two are proofs struck for inclusion in proof sets. Whether they represent the total originally manufactured, or whether more were struck that are no longer traceable, we do not know. It would seem unlikely for only two proofs to be made, after going to the pains necessary to strike proofs. A reasonable guess would be that between six and a dozen were struck, as was done with the 1804 Dollar when struck as a proof for inclusion in sets. Thus there is a chance for an 1866 turning up somewhere. It would be impossible to value this coin as there are no sale records. It could be valued only by placing it before the public in an open sale, to discover how high the bids would go. Based on scarcity it should be the most valuable Silver Dollar, if we discount the possibility of an 1873-S being discovered. This would not guarantee it a higher price than the 1804, however. The 1804 has considerably more reputation.

Restrikes were made of two of the Key Date coins, the 1851 and 1852. Mintage figures given in the above chart are for the originals only. Totals produced of the restrikes are not known. Nor is it known when they were manufactured, which could have been closely contemporary with the originals or a number of years thereafter. The restrikes were exclusively proofs. The 1851 restrike is known to have utilized a remade obverse die, as the date is positioned differently than on the original business strikes. On the business strikes the date is a fraction of a millimeter higher than on the restrikes. Otherwise they are identical. Pricing information on these restrikes will be found in the next section, dealing with proof strikes of the Liberty Seated Dollar. There is no danger of confusion for the investor who wants to buy the 1851 or 1852 in MS-60 uncirculated grade. He will not find the restrikes in that condition grade. Any MS-60 specimens of the 1851 or 1852 which are not proofs have to be the originals.

The Key Date Liberty Seated Dollars have an impressive record of turning investment profits. If you follow our chart from the 1970 column to the 1985 column, you'll see that some dates registered investment-size gains in each period, while others did not. From 1980 to 1985 the winners included the aforementioned 1851 and 1852, the former going from $6000 to $12,500 and the latter turning in an almost duplicate performance: $6000 to $12,000, and the 1872-CC with its climb from $3250 to a very lofty $8750. During the same period the 1850 tripled in value, from $1200 to $3625. But then there were sluggish coins in the group, such as the 1873-CC with its modest gain from $8000 to $9500 and the 1872-S, managing a rise of only $800 to its current level of $3300. All told this was much better than many analysts had expected, back in 1980. With prices already well into the four-figure range, it seemed to be asking a lot to anticipate any 100% or higher increases. Today that same question can be asked again: how much further room is there for rapid growth among these Keys? At their present levels, can any of them be counted on to double in value within the next five years or rise as much as 200% by 1995?

For the person who wants long term investments, especially beyond 1995, it is entirely likely that ALL the Key Dates are favorable. They are now on solid footing, and the fact that the Liberty Seated series remains a bit undervalued should help them out. The underpricing is more noticeable on the Common Dates but it can still be beneficial to these Keys. As the "commons" climb in value, their growth should spill over to all the other coins in the series. This is not speculation. It would be nothing more than a continuation of what has been happening in the Liberty Seated Dollar market for the past ten or fifteen years. If there is any one series of Silver Dollars which can truly be termed coins "of the future," it is the Liberty Seated design.

We outline some specific observations.

The 1851 and 1852, in our opinion, are not overpriced at the present time, but priced somewhat high in terms of investment potential. These are very scarce coins in uncirculated condition, more so than they have traditionally been given credit for. They were historically underpriced. The 1851 was too low at $1000 in 1965, too low at $1000 in 1970 (no price gain in five years), still unreasonably low at $3000 in 1975. The jump to $6000 in 1980 began bringing it within a fair range. Now, at $12,500, it seems to be just about in line with availability and demand. This would point to a gradual increase between now and 1990, bringing it to the $15,000 range or possibly $17,500. An increase of that size would merely keep it level with inflation and the overall growth in the coin collecting hobby; it would not signify any real change in the level of demand. Our feelings about the 1852 are roughly the same. This coin had a slightly smaller recorded mintage (1100 as opposed to 1300) and at the present its price is $12,000. One could build a case for it, perhaps, arguing that its 200 fewer mintage should translate into a higher price than that of the

1851. When mintages are this close, however, they are not too instrumental when calculating relative values. The number of existing specimens in uncirculated condition could be about the same. We have the feeling that the 1852 will continue moving in price at the same rate as the 1851, reaching a level of $15,000 to $17,500 by 1990.

The 1850 is not particularly appealing at the moment. It stood out like a green flag for investors in the 1980 market with a price of $1200, having advanced from $675 five years earlier. Numerous investment buyers recognized this as a coin to get, and the growing demand between 1980 and 1985 pushed its value to $3625. It is still slightly undervalued, we believe, but is now so close to being fully priced that it can no longer be deemed suitable for short term investment. If it had merely doubled in price between 1980 and 1985, we would recommend it for purchase, since it should be approaching $5000 by 1990. As things now stand, a rise to $5000 will leave it well short of the profitable territory. This one should, however, do much better in the more distant future.

Although some analysts may consider this going out on a limb, we rank the 1872-S as a favorable investment coin for both short and long term gain. This coin presents one dilemma. There is nothing to compare it against, to determine with any degree of accuracy whether it is underpriced — and, if so, by how much. It is the only San Francisco striking available on the market. To accurately gauge its true value, it must be compared against another Liberty Seated Dollar from the same minting facility. The only two others — the 1870-S and 1873-S — are not exactly suitable for comparison purposes, as there are no sales records. But even lacking this kind of support for the 1872-S, we still view it as an attractive investment coin. The mintage was just nine thousand and it is likely that only a small percentage of specimens survived in "unc." If the preservation ratio bore any similarity to that of the 1873-S, it was a much scarcer coin than anyone had suspected! Actually the 1872-S is not as difficult to get as (for example) the 1851 and 1852. But there is quite a difference in the prices as they stand right now. Those two have topped $12,000 while the 1872-S is selling for not much more than one-third as much, $3300. Furthermore, its increase in the past five years was moderate. It climbed from $2500, gaining just $800, while other coins in this group were adding thousands to their prices. By all odds it should be ready for a more significant advance in the next few years. Our projection for the 1872-S is for a figure of $6000 to $7000 by 1990, then going to $12,500 to $15,000 by 1995. We will not rate it as a BEST BET, as the projected rate of increase is not quite high enough to qualify for that distinction. Still, it should be a worthwhile Dollar to have in your portfolio.

The lowest price among the Key Dates is $2450 for which the 1870 Carson City is selling. It also has the highest mintage with a figure of 12,462 (the only Key Date whose mintage exceeds ten thousand). This is a questionable coin on which a prediction is difficult. It does not appear to be fully priced at the current sum; it should be at least $3000 right now. But what does it have the potential to do between 1985 and 1990? To fall within the profitable category it would need an increase to almost $5000, depending on the rate of national economic inflation (if inflation holds around 6% through the next five years, it could be profitable just by hitting $4500). The unpredictability of this coin is partly the result of it being a "CC" striking. As veteran coin collectors and investors are well aware, the Carson Cities are subject to heavy buying and selling spurts. This has been occurring ever since the government's sales of CC Dollars in the early seventies. At first the publicity of those sales helped the value of CC Dollars to rise rapidly. Periods of declining public interest and stagnating prices followed. Some people, especially investors, feared that the government was not telling the whole story — that it had caches of huge quantities of CC Dollars stored away, which would send prices tumbling when released for sale. There is still some speculation in that direction, but the likelihood is very slim that the government still owns — or would consider selling — any Liberty Seated Dollars from the Nevada facility. This one has to be ranked in the borderline category. With just a mild boost it could do extremely well.

If you are intent on adding a Carson City striking to your portfolio of Liberty Seated Dollars, the 1871-CC is probably the better choice. A big plus in favor of the 1871-CC is that its mintage is similar to mintage totals of several other CC Dollars in this group, thereby enabling it to be valuated with greater accuracy. The current prices as they now stand leave the 1871-CC undervalued in relation to the 1872-CC and 1873-CC. The 1872-CC was struck in 3,450 specimens as opposed to the 1,376 struck of the 1871-CC. Yet the 1872-CC is running higher in price, $8750 vs. $7500. The mintage figures, if interpreted literally (which we know is not always possible), would give the 1871-CC a fair value level of close to $20,000. The 1873-CC also serves as a comparison coin, for those interested in judging the potential of the 1871-CC. Some 2,300 specimens were struck of the 1873-CC and it now carries a $9500 price. The mintage is midway between that of the 1871-CC and 1872-CC yet the price is higher than both of them. If $9500 is a fair price with a 2,300 mintage, then the 1871-CC would be fairly priced at around $15,000. We have one comparison coin showing the 1871-CC as deserving of a $20,000 price, and another giving its true value level at $15,000. In either case this is well above the $7500 for which the 1871-CC is now selling. Even if it takes the next five years to reach the level of value which it should have today, it would return a good investment profit. We are forecasting a climb to $15,000 by 1990. Beyond that we envision it passing both the 1872-CC and 1873-CC in value by 1995. We look for the 1871-CC to be selling for $35,000 in 1995, at which time we anticipate prices of $25,000 on the 1872-CC and $30,000 for the 1873-CC. This, though a radical readjustment based on the current standings, would bring these coins more directly in line with their availability. The 1871-CC is being tabbed a BEST BET. It is, unfortunately, the only Key Date Liberty Seated Dollar that can be termed a BEST BET at this time.

LIBERTY SEATED DOLLARS — PROOF DATES

Beginning with this series, significant numbers of proof coins were struck which are offered for sale regularly. To avoid confusion, we have separated the proof figures from the circulation strikes for a better comparison. For most proofs prior to 1859, actual mintage figures are lacking.

Year	Mintage	1955	1960	1965	1970	1975	1980	1985
1840	(10)	$135.00	375.00	750.00	1000.00	1500.00	3200.00	3800.00
1841	(10)	125.00	340.00	700.00	900.00	1400.00	3200.00	3800.00
1842	(12)	120.00	325.00	600.00	900.00	1400.00	3200.00	3800.00
1843	(12)	120.00	325.00	600.00	900.00	1400.00	3200.00	3800.00
1844	(12)	125.00	325.00	650.00	900.00	1500.00	3200.00	3800.00

Year	Mintage	1955	1960	1965	1970	1975	1980	1985
1845	(10)	115.00	315.00	650.00	900.00	1500.00	3200.00	3800.00
1846	(20)	110.00	310.00	600.00	800.00	1400.00	3200.00	3800.00
1847	(12)	110.00	310.00	500.00	800.00	1400.00	3200.00	3800.00
1848	(10)	110.00	310.00	700.00	900.00	1400.00	3200.00	3800.00
1849	(12)	110.00	325.00	600.00	850.00	1400.00	3200.00	3800.00
1850	(15)	115.00	340.00	700.00	950.00	1500.00	4500.00	6000.00
1851	(10)	450.00	1100.00	2000.00	2750.00	4250.00	7000.00	15000.00
1852	(10)(A)							
1853	(B)	375.00	900.00	1250.00	1500.00	2500.00	4800.00	5375.00
1854	(25)	115.00	250.00	800.00	1200.00	2500.00	4100.00	4750.00
1855	(60)	115.00	225.00	850.00	1200.00	2500.00	7000.00	12500.00
1856	(40)	95.00	185.00	550.00	900.00	1700.00	5000.00	10000.00
1857	(50)	85.00	145.00	400.00	750.00	1500.00	5000.00	10000.00
1858	80	285.00	600.00	1500.00	2000.00	2500.00	5000.00	12500.00
1859	800	55.00	95.00	200.00	350.00	700.00	5000.00	8175.00
1860	1,330	45.00	90.00	125.00	275.00	700.00	5000.00	8175.00
1861	1,000	60.00	97.50	150.00	300.00	700.00	5000.00	8175.00
1862	550	37.50	95.00	150.00	400.00	700.00	5000.00	8175.00
1863	460	40.00	97.50	150.00	400.00	700.00	5000.00	8175.00
1864	470	40.00	92.50	150.00	400.00	700.00	5000.00	8175.00
1865	500	37.50	85.00	150.00	400.00	700.00	5000.00	8175.00
1866	2	—	—	13000.00	15000.00	—	50000.00	75000.00

(Motto Added on Reverse)

Year	Mintage	1955	1960	1965	1970	1975	1980	1985
1866	725	38.50	75.00	150.00	350.00	700.00	4500.00	7950.00
1867	625	32.50	72.50	140.00	350.00	700.00	4500.00	7950.00
1868	600	32.50	75.00	140.00	350.00	700.00	4500.00	7950.00
1869	600	33.50	75.00	125.00	350.00	700.00	4500.00	7950.00
1870	1,000	30.00	55.00	110.00	300.00	700.00	4500.00	7950.00
1871	960	27.50	55.00	90.00	300.00	700.00	4500.00	7950.00
1872	950	27.50	55.00	90.00	300.00	700.00	4500.00	7950.00
1873	600	32.50	75.00	100.00	350.00	700.00	4500.00	8250.00

NOTE: (A) Breen lists original examples from one obverse, matched with three different reverses, as well as the restrikes for this date.

(B) Breen believes that all of the known 1853 proofs are restrikes.
Other figures in ( ) are estimates of survivors.

LIBERTY SEATED DOLLARS — PROOF DATES

	% of increase:	1955-60	126%
		1960-65	114%
		1965-70	54%
		1970-75	65%
		1975-80	397%
		1980-85	59%
Overall % of increase:		1955-85	9068%

This was the first series of Silver Dollars for which proofs were regularly struck. In the 34 years during which this design was in use, not a single year was skipped without proofs. Neither the Mexican or Civil Wars interrupted them. Nor did the occasional criticism (which waned as the years rolled on) that the mint was becoming overly commercial. A regular, continuous series of proof Dollars would never have been considered in the earlier days of the mint. First, there was not enough collector interest; second, in the days of Flowing Hairs and Draped Busts, the mint was finding it difficult getting Dollars in circulation and keeping them there. The silver shortage would have generated storms of protest, if the mint had attempted to strike proofs. This action would have been denounced as a "waste of silver" in the press. To go from this kind of situation, to one in which proofs were struck annually, shows the extent to which circumstances changed. In a way it was a memorial to the influence exerted by the coin collecting hobby, both directly and indirectly. Directly, because the mint was well aware of the growth of coin collecting and the salability of proofs. Indirectly, because the importance of coin collecting in other countries led those governments to strike proofs as a matter of routine. These foreign proofs served as an impetus for the U.S. mint to strike proofs of its own. Another factor was involved, too. Visiting foreign dignitaries often presented the U.S. President with a set of their country's proof coins, lavishly displayed in custom built cases. It would be good protocol for the President, in turn, to do likewise. Proof sets became popular items to exchange, in the days when they had a reasonable value. Today, with proof sets containing no silver or gold coins, they do not rank highly as a suitable presentation item. It is believed, though with no really firm evidence, that the first striking of proof Dollars was strictly for that purpose. These were the proof restrikes made in the 1830s of the 1801, 1802, 1803 and 1804 Draped Busts (technically the 1804 was not a restrike, as there had been no originals). Very few of each were made and at that time the future of proof Dollars was much in doubt. The mint did not really become proof oriented until the Gobrecht Pattern Dollars, which started to be struck in 1836 and continued to 1839. Here the situation was just the reverse of what had prevailed earlier. A majority of the Gobrecht Pattern specimens were struck in proofs, with only a limited number made as business strikes for actual circulation. The number of Gobrecht proofs struck is not specifically recorded, but it was at least in the hundreds. This compared to a striking of perhaps eight specimens each of the 1801, 1802, 1803, and 1804 Draped Bust proofs. Obviously the mint did not intend for all the Gobrecht proofs to go into proof sets, though this was the destination of a portion of them. The balance was struck with just one group of people in mind — the coin collectors, whose numbers had been gradually increasing through the years. Lest this be thought a purely profit-motivated venture, it also represented a show of pride by our government in its coins. Undoubtedly, some of these proofs would fall into the hands of European collectors, who were accustomed to beautifully designed coins. As the design was the work of a great artist, it was a perfect coin with which to promote the artistry and collectability of U.S. coins.

There was yet another reason for the mounting interest in proofs on the part of the U.S. mint. By the time of the Gobrecht Patterns — and of course in the 1840-1873 era of the regular Liberty Seated Dollars — the mint had the capability of striking high-quality proofs for the first time in its history. The equipment it was using in the days of the Flowing Hair and Draped Bust Dollars was not conducive to high quality proofs. At that time (1794 to 1803), all striking was done using hand-operated presses. This was satisfactory — though far from speedy — on business strikes destined for circulation. Striking proofs in this fashion is another story. One of the characteristic features of a proof coin is the strength and depth of its impression. This is achieved not only by the use of fresh dies without the slightest trace of wear, but by striking the coin twice instead of once. In mechanical striking, with tight collars around the dies, the second strike is always perfectly aligned without any ghost image or "shift." This is difficult to achieve in non-mechanical striking. If the press lever is thrown back to raise the upper die for a second strike, it will usually not meet the coin at precisely the same alignment. The alternative to this was to hold the lever forward and just throw more pressure on it, such as by having two pressmen work the lever instead of the customary one. You could strike passable proofs in this manner, but they were not as convincing as proofs struck by machinery. For one thing, excess pressure caused the planchet to spread out wider than it should, resulting in a very thin "pancake" coin. By the time of the Gobrecht Patterns, the mint was utilizing steam driven presses, which enabled it to do anything the European mints (which had steam presses much earlier) were doing. Later, with the installation of electrical presses, the quality of proofs was improved even further.

Totals struck in the early years indicate no great desire to make Liberty Seated proofs widely available to the public. In 1859 it suddenly jumped to a robust 800. For the next two years, one thousand or more proof Dollars were struck each year, and for every year thereafter the total was well up into the hundreds at minimum. This, then, was the dividing line between what could logically be termed private proofs (for use largely in mint sets that were to be given away rather than sold), and collector proofs. Many efforts have been made to estimate the yearly totals from 1840 to 1857, the period in which the mint did not keep records on its striking of proofs. As the opinions vary greatly from one source to another, and are largely within the realm of guesswork, we have omitted any references to specific quantities. Several points can however be made with assurance. Quantities struck in the early years (that is, 1840 to 1857) were in most instances considerably lower than those of 1858 onward, which can be deduced simply from the sharp differences in surviving totals. The figure of 800 given by the mint for 1859 must have far surpassed any previous year's output. It is not unreasonable to believe, however, that in a few of the earlier years (particularly 1856 and 1857), the quantity struck may have fallen between 100 and 200. In the very earliest years, the 1840s, the output could not have approached 100 per year, but was probably within the range of 25 to 50 during most of those years. This is about as precise as one can get. There appears to be more surviving specimens of the 1846 than of any other proof Dollars from the 1840s, so it can be concluded that the 1846 had a larger production. It is doubtful that the mint struck any of these proofs in predetermined numbers, or they were struck consecutively at a given time. Quite likely the striking was occasional throughout the year, as the supply on hand declined and more were needed. Perhaps a few more proofs would be struck each time a new set of dies was placed in production. If they had all been struck on the same day, or in the space of a few days, it is likely that the mint would have some specific record of them. The impression given is that they were made in a very casual offhand way and that the mint director was not concerned with recording the quantities. This changed in 1858 with the implementation of a record keeping system. Of course there is much speculation to be found in numismatic literature. One theory is that the mint purposely chose to keep no records on production, or kept secret records never incorporated into its Annual Reports, for the purpose of making these proofs seem scarcer than they really were. Possibly the mint wanted the recipients (the foreign dignitaries) to believe that no additional proofs were in existence, beyond those included in the deluxe presentation sets. If it really wanted to hide the fact that these coins were being acquired by private individuals, that would have been difficult to do. It is known that in 1843 the pioneer collector Stickney obtained one of the 1804 proof Dollars from the mint. He could hardly have been the only collector getting proofs from the mint, though Stickney publicized his acquisition while the others did not. Just how many proofs of the early Liberty Seated Dollars went into the hands of collectors, at the time of their striking or shortly thereafter, is another question that cannot be answered. All we know is that the mint was not adverse to dealing with collectors. Of course this raises the question: what sort of value would collectors have attached to Liberty Seated proofs when the coins themselves were current? Stickney knew he was getting something far out of the ordinary in his 1804 Dollar. None had been struck for circulation, so it was strictly a case of a proof. Since the Liberty Seated Dollars were in production for general distribution, this was quite a different situation. It would be easy enough to assume that most collectors would be taking "uncs" out of circulation, as this represented a way of obtaining the current coins at their face value. We must realize, however, that the business strikes — whether uncirculated or circulated — were "just coins" to most collectors of that era. They were not considered worthy to be included in a collection. Any serious hobbyist who wanted to include Liberty Seated Dollars in his collection would certainly prefer the proofs. They would provide him something that the average person (non-collector) was not picking up in change. After all, anybody working at a bank could put aside "uncs." They were the easiest to get.

Published records of mintage totals for the later years are in all probability accurate. By that time the mint had its regular customers who came to Philadelphia and bought proof coins directly from the mint. Not surprisingly, some of those who frequented the mint were dealers, who knew that the passage of a few years would bring about an increased market value. It is very doubtful if the mint ever had any difficulty in selling them. Those which remained on hand into the following year continued to be sold until the supply was exhausted. Of course the mint kept a few sets for itself, for posterity. These are now the property of the Smithsonian, which inherited all of the mint's collections. Quantities sold are all the more impressive when one considered the coins included — there were gold pieces with face values of $20, $10 and $5, making $35 with just three coins. There was no problem in charging a healthy premium over and above the face value, as the coins were specially prepared and handsomely packaged. The cases were made of wood and set with velvet and not the polystyrene cases of later years. Just as the growing numbers of collectors aided the mint in selling proof sets, it also worked the other way around: proof coins generated interest in coin collecting. Proof coins were often given as awards in scholastic competitions, etc., and many a collection probably had its beginning in that fashion.

Some general observations need to be made on the subject of proof coins, for the benefit of new investors who do not have a background in coin collecting. For one thing, "proof" refers to a manufacturing process, not to a condition grade. There are two types of coins: business strikes (which circulate as money) and proofs (which are never intended to reach circulation, but which do, nevertheless, have the same legal tender status as business strikes). A proof is a showpiece specimen intended to show the coin at its absolute finest. It is made from fresh dies using specially polished planchets, and, as we have said, the design is struck twice to achieve maximum depth and clarity on the small details. To anyone even slightly familiar with coins, a proof can be recognized without much difficulty. There are occasional cases, however, especially with early coins such as the Liberty Seated Dollar, when a brilliant "unc" can be mistaken for a proof. In the advertisements of coin dealers, and in auction sale literature, you will sometimes find Liberty Seated Dollars described as "possible proof," "probably a proof," or "proof-like." The expression "proof-like" is really not in the same category. It signifies a specimen which has been positively identified as a business strike, but which is fine enough in terms of strike to give the appearance of a proof. It is not difficult to see how this could happen. When a new set of dies was placed in use for regular business strikes, the first few dozen coins would naturally be sharper and bolder than the ones which followed. By the same token the 500th coin struck from a set of dies would be finer than the 10,000th. This was not just a matter of deterioration of the dies, though of course they did deteriorate gradually from the brutal pounding they absorbed. The dies attracted dust and grime and this worked its way into the fine areas of the design. They were supposed to be cleaned periodically, but a cleaned die never struck as well as a brand new one. If you have a Liberty Seated Dollar struck from a very fresh die, a business strike can indeed fool you into believing you have a proof. You may even be able to lay the business strike alongside a specimen known definitely to be a proof, and a magnifying glass may be required to reveal the difference. In terms of dollars and cents, it is another story. If the specimen is questionable — if it cannot be identified as a proof beyond all doubt — it is not worth a proof price. You should keep this in mind when buying. The "possible proof" is not a bargain because it can be bought for 30% less than a confirmed proof. It may be worth a substantial premium over the value of a normal "unc," but you would not be getting a proof and you may still be paying too much! Do not forget that the difference in market values between a proof and an uncirculated business strike is considerable.

Just as there are business strikes which masquerade as proofs, there are inferior specimens of proofs. While proofs were not intended to be circulated, some would invariably get into circulation one way or another. This was not the fault of the mint — it did not accidentally include some proofs in bags of business strikes, so far as is known. It happened after the coins reached the public's hands, and it is still happening today (you will find modern proofs in pocket change occasionally). For the original owner, who had presumably acquired the proof at a premium over face value, there would be no thought of spending the coin. But a subsequent owner — such as a member of the family who found such coins in an attic — had no investment in them. If he likewise had no interest in coin collecting, and no knowledge that these coins carried a premium value on the hobbyist market, he would very likely spend them. This occurred with proofs of all denominations. Then it became a matter of chance as to what happened next. If the coin was quickly spotted by a collector as it traveled around in pocket change, it might be preserved in uncirculated condition (the only acceptable grade for proofs). If not, it would eventually acquire signs of wear just like business strikes. In fact it acquired them faster, because the designs were raised higher from the surface and more vulnerable to rubbing. The correct term for such specimens is "impaired proof." The impairment could also be an injury rather than circulation wear. These, in addition to those designated as "possible proofs," are not for the investor.

Proofs differ greatly from business strikes in terms of their survival rate. For this reason it is vital to refrain from comparing mintages of proofs and business strikes. Such comparison will always give the impression that proofs are much rarer than they actually are, and, in most instances, underpriced. Proof Dollars survived in a much higher ratio than specimens of circulating coins. They were not intentionally melted, as their owners would not very likely be selling them for melt value. While some did get into circulation, this accounted for just a fraction in any given batch. One starts with the assumption that all proofs went originally into the hands of persons who knew exactly what they were, and who valued them. From there, possibly 10% to 20% of the struck total met with some kind of accident or were later channeled into circulation. Of the remainder, we could guess that perhaps another 10% disappeared through natural loss, such as by fire and flood. But even taking account of all these possibilities, the surviving total on MOST proof Dollars should be more than half of those originally struck. In many cases it would be quite a bit higher than half, even if we speak strictly in terms of specimens still in optimum proof state. This is a considerably higher ratio than would apply to any business strikes from a comparable period of time. Generally the percentage of existing uncirculated specimens, from any business strike, is well below 10%. It is higher than this on some of the later Dollars of the Morgan and Peace groups, because they did very little actual minting. Still, it is never as high as the ratio on proofs.

Also there is the matter of toning (surface coloration) on proofs. You will note that proofs, on the whole, exhibit a greater variety of toning than business strikes. In many cases the toning is also more intense. The popular conception is that this process began with the manufacturer — that the special polishing of the planchets made them more receptive to exquisite toning. More likely, proofs have acquired more toning and better toning due to their method of storage. The early proofs usually were stored in wooden coin cabinets and could acquire toning from the oils and natural acids of the wood. They remained in these cabinets for many years without any type of protective shielding; the early collectors did not use envelopes or holders. Not as many business strikes were housed in this way, as many collectors of business strikes could not afford cabinets. Proofs went into more elite collections, and these were the ones normally maintained in coin cabinets. (You can still find these old coin cabinets in antiques shops from time to time. They are very expensive today — even when empty!)

For all their obvious scarcity and high prices — not a single one out of 34 years' worth selling under $3800 — the Liberty Seated proofs are available on the market. Some dates may require waiting and searching, but almost any coin dealer with a well-stocked inventory will have at least a few Liberty Seated proofs on hand. They appear regularly at auction sales, sometimes a "run" of them comprising 15, 20 or more, though it is very unusual to find a complete set of the early ones. Locating them will not be a problem for the investor. He need only keep in touch with the market, by reading the weekly issues of the various numismatic newspapers, and by subscribing to the catalogues of the major coin auction houses. Therefore your investment selections should be based on the coins having the greatest potential, not on those which are most likely to be available at the moment.

As investment items the Liberty Seated proofs profited greatly from the increased interest in (and confidence in) proof coins which began in the late sixties and intensified during the early to middle seventies. Many investors in those days were restricting themselves exclusively to proofs and the result was, in many cases, a much sharper price rise on proofs than the corresponding business strikes of the same coins. At the time, speculation arose that this investor enthusiasm for proofs would prove to be of short duration and be followed by a disaster in the market, such has not been the case. The overall rate of price increase on proof coins in general slowed somewhat in the years from 1980 to 1985, compared to what it had been earlier, but there were no signs of wholesale selling or price collapses. Many of the prices, including some of those in the Dollar series, increased so strongly in the 1975 to 1980 period that very little room was left for further significant advances. We have examples here among the Liberty Seated Dollars, with the coins struck from 1859 onward rising from $700 to $4500 and $5000 in 1980. There could hardly have been any greater justification for investors buying proofs! The prices did not retreat from these levels. They were unable to register profitable advances for those who bought at the 1980 figures, but the advances were still well within the encouraging category. It is believed that more investors are buying proof Dollars today than ever before. If this is not reflected in the price movements, it is ONLY because so many proof dates were seriously underpriced in the early to middle seventies. They advanced by leaps and bounds at that time as they were starting from very meager prices. Today, being at much higher levels, the pace of advance cannot be quite that great. Still it can be profitable and it WILL be, if one makes his selections judiciously.

There are many good dates in this group and they are all rather obvious. It is not difficult to see what has happened here, or even WHY it happened. In the earlier years shown on our chart, the early dated not only outsold the later ones but outsold them by wide margins. This held true up to 1975. In 1960 the early dates were over $300 while none of the later ones had reached $100. In 1965 the early dates topped $600 while the later dates had gotten into the $100-$150 range. By 1970 the early dates had climbed to $800 and $900, while the late ones were at prices of $300, $350 and $400. In 1975, all of the early dates had gotten at least as far as $1400 with some doing better, while the later dates became bunched at a common price of $700 — half as much. Then the situation radically changed. By 1980 the late dates were ahead of the early ones, and currently they are outselling the early dates by roughly 2-to-1. This sort of turn-around is very rare in the Silver Dollar market, for proofs or business strikes. In this case a pricing pattern that had been maintained for well over 50 years (long before our chart begins) was erased. This would be understandable, if the traditional, long-established price structure was wrong — if it did not reflect the scarcity of the coins involved. In this instance the traditional pattern was perfectly accurate, and the current situation is in disarray. The late dates do NOT deserve to be selling for twice as much as the early ones. They do not deserve to be selling for any more, or even for as much. They should be priced considerably less than the early dates, which are much scarcer coins. How did this shift in values come about? Obviously it was no accident; nothing ever is, in the world of coin prices. You can clearly see what was responsible. As the year 1975 began, the level of investment buying was heavy and concentrated on the early dates. That was when the apple cart overturned. The new investors, entering the market from 1975 onward, took a diametrical tack from that of their predecessors. They carried the science of investment strategy a little too far. Looking at this lineup of proofs, they saw that official mintage figures began only with the 1858 date. They saw the blank column of mintage figures prior to that date. They reached a conclusion based not on logic and the realities of the rare coin market. They dismissed the early dates, on grounds that the lack of mintage figures would stand in the way of future price increases. They put their trust in the later dates, those with tangible availability data. Their reasoning ran as follows:

(1) Because the later dates have mintage figures, other investors will be buying them. Other investors may not buy the early dates.

(2) I can apply investment strategy to the later dates because I have something to work with.

(3) How do I know that the early dates did not have mintages just as great, or greater, than the later dates? Maybe they are overpriced.

Of course, this was incorrect, and it serves as a perfect example of what can happen when investment buying is misdirected. Because numerous investors were thinking along the same lines, and buying the same coins, quite a few of them DID score short term profits, in the years from 1975 to 1980. This market was manipulated to a much greater extent than any other Silver Dollar group has ever been. Those who continued buying after the prices had gotten high in 1980 showed even less investment skill. Apparently there were many who DID continue buying, as if the sky was the limit on the prices of late-date Liberty Seated proofs. Those still holding are well advised to rethink their position. All of the late dates are now seriously overpriced. They cannot maintain these inflated levels indefinitely. By 1990 they may be reduced drastically.

The lack of a mintage figure on a coin, or group of coins, should not rule it out for investment buying. True, it is more difficult to gauge the real value of such a coin, in terms of determining whether it is overpriced or underpriced (or just simply "fully priced"). But there are other sources of evidence, such as the number of specimens passing through the market. Even the price histories should — in this case — have told investors that they were attacking from the wrong angle. The early dates are unquestionably scarcer on the market than the later dates. We do not (and cannot) know for a fact that they had lower mintages, but the relative levels of scarcity would certainly point to that conclusion. But even if the mintages were identical, the important thing is that the current scarcity levels of the early dates far surpass those of the late dates. They were either struck in lower quantities or preserved in MUCH lower quantities, and there is absolutely no difference one way or the other. Estimates have been made that as few as 12 specimens exist of the 1842, 1843 and 1844, while only ten exist of the 1840 and 1841. While these are only estimates, they would contrast very sharply with any reasonable estimates on surviving totals of coins such as the 1860 or 1861. Out of a thousand or more specimens struck, no one would estimate the existing total at 10 or 12. More likely it is well over 500.

This extreme and unreasonable imbalance in prices creates rare investment opportunities, for those who can afford coins in this range of price.

It would be easy to state that the early proof dates are favorable for investment while the later dates are not, but one will want to explore the prospects a bit more deeply. Relative scarcity levels on the dates from 1840 to 1849 inclusive are similar, and all of these dates are considerably undervalued. If you wanted to choose just one, the logical selection would be the 1840. It was the first proof striking of the revised Liberty Seated Dollar with Heraldic Eagle reverse, and is easily as scarce (in surviving specimens) as any other date from the 1840s. Yet it can be obtained in proof state at the same price as all the others. Making further selections from this lineup — that is, the 1840s dates, is not as easy. There is very little to separate these coins in terms of scarcity and profit potential; they are all distinctive and it is difficult to say which are better than others. In this respect the price histories may be helpful. You will note that in 1975, the 1844 and 1845 were selling at $1500 while the others stood at $1400. Very often when underpriced coins readjust themselves, dates that had previously been the highest priced become higher once again. This is far from a sure thing, but it reflects that the 1844 and 1845 have the ability to sell for higher sums than their companion coins. Of course, the ideal approach would be to add this entire group to your investment portfolio. In our opinion, if Liberty Seated proofs appeal to you, the entire decade's worth, from 1840 to 1849, falls within the BEST BET category. All of them should gain sufficiently in value by 1990 to realize a very satisfactory investment gain. To accomplish this they need only to reach the price levels at which the later dates now stand. Our feeling is that the 1990 market will find most of the 1840s dates selling for at least $7500, with the 1840 outdistancing the pack somewhat. Our projection of the 1990 price for the 1840 is $8000 to $9000.

Nothing reassuring can be said of the later dates. All of them are overpriced with the possible exception of the 1853 and 1854, which now stand at $5375 and $4750 respectively. Some have pointed to the 1851 as a possible investment item, since it is known to exist in very limited quantity. However, with the price now at $6000 it is almost twice as expensive as the dates from the 1840s, which are no less scarce and have the advantage of earlier dates.

Some readers, after digesting our comments on the Liberty Seated proofs, may say: yes, the current values are very much out of line, but this is not so unusual for a long list of proofs. Proofs tend to get out of balance in value, and what assurance is there that this pattern will not continue for many years into the future, even though it may be unjustified?

We would agree that the prices of proofs do not, on the whole, readjust themselves as predictably as those of uncirculated business strikes. This is largely because they are very expensive coins, bought mainly by the investment community. The overall influence of collector buying is modest. Still, gross imbalances such as these can be counted upon to correct themselves in the normal course of events. Investors cannot keep hammering away at the late dates, now that they have reached such high price levels. We look for heavy investor selling on the late dates, with much of the acquired capital being channeled into dates from 1840 to 1849. This is where the potential lies today, and where it should be for at least several years.

THE TRADE DOLLARS

OBVERSE   REVERSE

The coinage act of 1873 brought a halt to the production of the 412.5 grain silver dollar for five years and introduced the Trade Dollar, part of our effort to compete with other countries for the Oriental trade. The coin was the first dollar produced to a 420 grain weight standard, although it conformed to the dollar's standard diameter of 38.1 mm. The .900 fineness (90% silver) was also continued so that the coin, in effect, contained a bonus of silver.

The authorization also made the coin legal tender in the U.S. for sums up to $5, which caused the coins to circulate in this country as well as to be shipped abroad. But the increasing amounts of silver being produced by western mines drove silver bullion's value down to the point where Congress repealed the legal tender status in 1876 and the mint was ordered to strike only trade dollars needed for export.

In the dying gasp of the coin, San Francisco in 1877 produced more than three times as many (9.5 million) Trade Dollars as did Philadelphia (3.04 million). In the last year of circulation strikes — 1878 — no coins other than proofs were struck at Philadelphia, while San Francisco churned out 4.2 million. Output from then until 1885, when the coin was officially dropped from production, was limited to proofs. The last two dates are very controversial, with the general belief that they are actually restrikes made several years later.

Trade Dollars are frequently found with "chop marks," the stamped symbols added by Oriental money changers to certify authenticity of the coin. This led to a law permitting redemption of Trade Dollars only if they were not stamped or otherwise mutilated. 7.7 million (about 20% of the total number of trade dollars struck) were redeemed and melted down by the Government, to return as Morgan Dollars and subsidiary silver coinage in the 1880s and early 1890s.

Because of this redemption, the number of remaining Trade dollars with chop marks, which are considered to reduce the value of the coin, was artificially increased, with a consequent drop in the number of available unmarked coins. The influx of foreign silver, especially the German stocks released after the Franco-Prussian War, was helping to drive down the price of bullion and holders of the coins were willing to sell them at almost any discount in fear of total collapse. Since they could not be spent, they were in danger of becoming valueless if silver dropped alarmingly. Modern investors might regret being born too late to take advantage of this opportunity.

Several million of the U.S. trade dollars went into foreign melting pots as well, especially in Japan and India, further reducing the stocks of coins available to the investor today.

TRADE DOLLARS — COMMON DATES

Year	Mintage	1955	1960	1965	1970	1975	1980	1985
1873	397,500	$12.50	37.50	65.00	175.00	400.00	600.00	1000.00
1873-CC	124,500	50.00	95.00	140.00	285.00	550.00	700.00	1450.00
1873-S	703,000	45.00	70.00	80.00	170.00	375.00	600.00	1175.00
1874	987,800	12.50	22.50	35.00	100.00	350.00	500.00	700.00
1874-CC	1,373,200	35.00	60.00	90.00	185.00	450.00	600.00	975.00
1874-S	2,549,000	15.00	27.50	35.00	137.50	375.00	500.00	700.00
1875-CC	1,573,700	22.50	42.50	70.00	175.00	450.00	600.00	900.00
1875-S	4,478,000	15.00	22.50	30.00	95.00	350.00	500.00	700.00
1876	456,150	12.50	22.50	32.50	110.00	360.00	500.00	700.00
1876-CC	509,000	30.00	47.50	80.00	175.00	450.00	600.00	900.00
1876-S	5,227,000	11.00	20.00	30.00	95.00	350.00	500.00	700.00
1877	3,039,710	12.50	17.50	30.00	95.00	400.00	500.00	700.00
1877-S	9,519,000	10.00	17.50	32.50	95.00	350.00	600.00	700.00
1878-S	4,162,000	11.00	17.50	25.00	95.00	350.00	500.00	700.00

TRADE DOLLARS — COMMON DATES

% of increase:	1955-60	77%
	1960-65	49%
	1965-70	156%
	1970-75	180%
	1975-80	40%
	1980-85	54%
overall % of increase:	1955-85	3982%

The Trade Dollar, our heaviest Silver Dollar ever struck had little popularity with collectors or investors for many years. Many collections of Silver Dollars did not include the Trade Dollar, as it was not a regular issue in the standard Dollar series. Today, it is not only found in nearly all Silver Dollar collections, but is a favorite specialty of hobbyists. A number of superb collections of Trade Dollars have been built, some of which have been recently dispersed in the auction rooms. As an investment series it began to attract attention in the middle sixties, then was bought heavily by investors in the early seventies. Today its standing with investors is almost equal with the Morgan Dollar, though of course the much fewer number of Trade Dollars makes for less overall investment activity. As investment coins they are bought in both uncirculated and proof state. Mintage figures are available on all the Trade Dollars with the exception of the 1875 "S over CC" variety. While these figures are helpful in plotting investment strategy, one must realize that vast quantities of Trade Dollars were melted. Most of this destruction occurred while the coins were current or shortly thereafter. It diminished in the twentieth century, and today it is rare for any Trade Dollar to be melted for its silver bullion content, as circulated specimens all have premium value unless their condition is horrendous. This melting occurred in various ways, chiefly as follows:

(1) Enormous quantities of Trade Dollars reached the Orient, principally Japan, where they were instrumental in our early commercial trade with Japanese import/export firms. Some of them found their way back to the U.S.; in fact some specimens probably made numerous Pacific crossings. In general, the Japanese were more interested in the Trade Dollar as bullion than as a unit of money, and it was frequently melted rather than exchanged.

(2) In the U.S., wholesale melting began in 1887 (two years after the last specimens were struck), when the Trade Dollar's legal tender status was revoked. As it could no longer be passed as money in the U.S., owners of Trade Dollars could retain them as silver bullion speculation, or melt them. Some went into the hands of hobbyists but this accounted for a mere fraction of the total owned by U.S. citizens. The Trade Dollar was attractive to melt because it contained a bit more silver bullion than ordinary Dollars.

(3) The mint itself melted Trade Dollars. There was one publicized melting, which occurred while the coin was still current. In 1878, the mint melted 44,000 Trade Dollars. It is not known whether the batch consisted entirely of the same date, or of different dates; there has been much speculation on this point. There may have been unpublicized meltings in addition. As the 1878 Carson City Trade Dollar is considerably scarcer than its 97,000 mintage figure would indicate, a popular theory is that the 44,000 melted Trade Dollars were from that facility.

The Trade Dollar had a colorful and unusual history, and has been the focus of numerous books and other writings. It was (and still remains) the only U.S. coin ever specifically struck for commerical purposes. Representing such sharp departure from normal mint practices, the Trade Dollar was subjected to widespread criticism in the press. Charges ran from the coin being "politically motivated," to a "reckless tampering with U.S. coinage." The Trade Dollar was introduced in 1873, which was the final year of the Liberty Seated Dollar. Both coins were struck that year, but from 1874 until 1877 only the Trade Dollar was produced. The original intention was for it to replace the standard Silver Dollar. It was soon realized that this would be impossible, as the Trade Dollar disappeared too rapidly from domestic circulation and a shortage of Silver Dollars ensued. Next it was decided to strike both Trade Dollars and regular Silver Dollars simultaneously. This was done in 1878, the year of the Morgan Dollar's introduction. The Morgan Dollar was the same weight as the old Liberty Seated Dollar, 26.73 grams. The Trade Dollar was 27.22 grams. Almost immediately it became evident that two Silver Dollars, with the same face value but containing different amounts of silver, could not subsist side by side. No one wanted the Morgan Dollar as they felt they were being shortchanged; if the government could put more silver in the Trade Dollar, they protested, why not in the Morgan also? So the Trade Dollar came to a halt as a circulating coin in 1878. It continued to be struck in proof specimens for a number of years thereafter. According to the mint, the last year of striking was 1883. However about a quarter century later, existence of Trade Dollars dated 1884 and 1885 became known. None with a later date has yet appeared. It is not specifically known whether these specimens dated 1884 and 1885 were actually struck in those years or at a subsequent time. The general belief is that they were struck in the years indicated.

The Trade Dollar came about largely as the result of developments following the opening of Japan to foreign commerce, which occurred in the late 1850s. Prior to that time, Japanese products had traveled westward through the Orient. Eventually some of them reached Europe, especially Paris, which was the center for Japanese merchandise in the 1700s and early 1800s. By then, however, they had incurred such huge charges levelled by the many agents along the way, that their retail prices were very high. Finally the Japanese government consented to direct import/export trade with the western world, though it was highly distrustful at first of western intentions. Naturally the U.S. was to play the primary role, as it had access to the most direct route to Japan (across the Pacific).

This flurry of western trade brought coins into Japan that had never been seen there previously: coins from all parts of Europe and both North and South America. This made for a booming trade in currency exchange. Numerous businessmen set themselves up in Japanese port towns to change these foreign coins into Japanese money. All exchanges were based strictly on bullion values, as no trust was placed in face values (the Japanese knew that governments could crumble and money could be demonetized). Here the U.S. Silver Dollar — which was the Liberty Seated at that time — was at a distinct disadvantage. It contained slightly less silver than the corresponding "crowns" of European nations (in Europe, a "crown" was the equivalent of what we called "Silver Dollar"). Businessmen who paid in Silver Dollars found that they would be accepted only at a discounted rate. Much was riding on the success of our trade relations with Japan, so the government was persuaded to intervene. The Trade Dollar represented an effort to compete on equal terms with the large size silver coins of Europe. It was not only heavier, it proclaimed both its weight and fineness directly on the coin: 420 Grains, .900 Fine. This appears prominently on the reverse side beneath the eagle (it was feared that many Orientals would mistake this for simply a new design, if the specifications were not visible).

The Trade Dollar did succeed in improving our trade position in the Far East. Its demise had nothing to do with lack of effectiveness in that regard. Criticism at home, plus the gradual reliance of Japanese traders on paper banking, brought about the end of the Trade Dollar. Interestingly enough U.S./Japanese trade increased enormously in the years following termination of the Trade Dollar, reaching colossal proportions in the 1890s. It was largely as a result of this increase that the U.S. passed a law requiring all imported items to be marked with their place of origin.

Millions of Trade Dollars were in circulation in Japan at any given time — not in circulation among the general public, but among bankers, money changers, and import/export merchants. At the same time there was at least an equal quantity of large size European silver coins circulating in Japan, not to mention those of Mexico and South America. Knowing full well that the Japanese were unfamiliar with these coins, counterfeiters produced countless fakes and poured them into Japan by the ship load. This paved the way for another kind of enterprise: the money changing operation which not only converted coins into local currency, but certified them to be authentic. Coin experts evaluated each coin passing through their hands, and placed their stamp on it as a mark of approval. These stamps were in the form of very tiny Japanese characters, which in most cases were the initials of the money changer or his special symbol. Even if a coin had been previously certified by another money changer, it would still be routinely stamped by each one through whose hands it passed; one money changer was not legally responsible for the opinion of another. Thus, numerous Trade Dollars exist carrying these stamps, and are known as "chop mark Dollars." The stamping was called "chopping;" probably because the money changers used a work table similar to a butcher's chopping block. Some chop marked Dollars have one or two marks; others are literally covered with them, both front and back, to the point where they overlap and can hardly be counted. Though chop marked Dollars were traditionally unwanted by collectors, being considered defective, there is now a great enthusiasm for them and sometimes they command a premium price. Naturally, the vast majority of chop marked Dollars never returned to the U.S. After making the rounds of the money changers they were melted. So there is a certain scarcity factor as well as historical appeal. Though the investor will encounter some chop marked Dollars, they will probably fall outside his sphere since most specimens are NOT in uncirculated condition. When chop markings occur on an uncirculated Trade Dollar (very unusual), it is still graded uncirculated, and the value depends on the number and placement of the marks. One or two well-struck marks in the field of the coin may result in a premium price, or at least no reduction of price. When the markings are on the portrait, there is usually a sizable discount. Fake markings are found, both on genuine Trade Dollars and fake ones. Also, chop markings are occasionally — VERY occasionally — seen on Liberty Seated and Morgan Dollars.

William Barber, better known for his portrait profile of Liberty used on lower denomination coinage, was the designer of the Trade Dollar. Only one design was used, and no alterations were made in the course of the series. It was decided to retain the Liberty Seated concept, but Barber totally repositioned and revamped the earlier Gobrecht rendering. Gobrecht's figure held a "cap of liberty," while Barber's holds an olive branch. The eagle on the reverse was considerably reworked, too. The heraldic shield was removed, though he continued to carry the arrows and branch. For all practical purposes it was a totally different coin. The slight difference in weight is accounted for by a very minute difference in thickness; in diameter the Trade Dollar is no larger than standard Silver Dollars. The extra weight is too minimal to be detected by hand weighing, except for a person who is extremely familiar with Silver Dollars.

After gaining Congressional approval for the Trade Dollar, the mint pushed forward with high hopes. Production was assigned to three mints: Philadelphia, San Francisco and Carson City, with a go-ahead on both business strikes and proofs. However, only the Philadelphia facility was authorized to strike proofs. In the first year alone, more than one million business strikes rolled from the presses. As you might expect, San Francisco did the largest striking of Trade Dollars throughout the coin's lifetime, exceeding the combined total of the other two mints. As the coin were mostly destined for the Orient, San Francisco was the logical place to manufacture them. They could be transported the short distance to the port and loaded for their trip across the Pacific. Those struck in Philadelphia were mostly made available to banks in the eastern part of the country. Some of the Carson City output was intended for storage, but it is not precisely known to what extent the mint wished to store them.

In its early days it was certainly a coin which generated curiosity. You would think coin collectors — whose numbers were not exactly meager by 1873 — would have put aside any specimens they could get. This was apparently not the case. There seems to have been more negative than positive feeling on the part of collectors about the Trade Dollar. They objected to the discontinuance of the regular Silver Dollar series. There is no doubt that hobbyists could have acquired Trade Dollars in the 1870s, if they wanted to. Banks had them, and they could even be found in ordinary circulation in some parts of the country (especially in California). As for coin dealers (who were also on the scene in 1873), they seem to have paid no attention to the business strikes, but they did make an effort to stock the proofs. These at least had the glamor of low mintages and were worth a gamble.

Though everyone interested in coins knew that Trade Dollars were being melted heavily during the 1870s and 1880s, this did not arouse any significant collecting enthusiasm. When the Morgan Dollar made its debut in 1878 it quickly pushed the Trade Dollar farther into the background. Efforts were made to sell Trade Dollars to collectors for fractional sums over face, even as little as $1.10, but there were few takers. Demand for these coins by collectors gradually increased but the pace was very slow. Even as late as the 1920s there were coin dealers who did not stock any Trade Dollars with the exception of proofs. Prices on a number of the Common Dates were under $10 in the 1940s for uncirculated specimens, while a few dollars could buy a Common Date in circulated grade. During the 1960s, Trade Dollars came in for intense study and also received an impetus from the removal of silver contained in our coins, which occurred in 1964. As the U.S. coin containing the most silver, of any ever struck, the Trade Dollar was drawing some attention from investors as well as hobbyists. If silver was going to be the winning investment that so many believed, then surely the Trade Dollar would benefit from its price increases. As you will see, the Common Dates did very well in the years from 1965 to 1970, which witnessed the first wave of investment in the group. At this stage, investment buying was still very disorganized, but the price increases were strong nevertheless. Some investors were buying circulated Trade Dollars as bullion investments, not realizing that they were paying more than a slight premium over melt values. If they wanted silver, they could have gotten it for less with circulated Morgan or Peace Dollars. This still holds true — even more so today. You do not buy Trade Dollars to sell as bullion.

Price increases in the half decade between 1965 and 1970 made more investors aware of Trade Dollars, though some were still hesitant about these coins. The increases during the next five years, from 1970 to 1975, were greater than those in the late sixties, bringing a clear investment profit on all the Common Dates. Some of them scored very large gains, going from $95 to between $350 and $400. The results from 1975 to 1980 were not as favorable, most of the Common Dates falling somewhat short of a third consecutive period of investment profit. Some observers blamed their sluggishness on the high prices attained in 1975, claiming they were fully priced at those levels and unable to move much beyond them. Virtually the same situation repeated itself in the years from 1980 to 1985, with only one of the Common Dates (the 1873-CC) registering a gain sufficient for clear investment return. All moved forward, but the rate of advance was slow from an investment viewpoint. The speculation that they reached their full price levels in 1975 is probably mistaken. They do not appear to have reached that point even yet, with the increases that have followed in the succeeding ten years. Rather, their failure to mount a strong cumulative gain in the late seventies and early eighties was more likely caused by shifts in investor buying patterns. The mid to late seventies was the era when Morgans began to be very heavily promoted for investment by analysts and publishers of investment newsletters. Some of the investment capital going into Morgans at that time, and even today, was undoubtedly channeled away from the Trade series. Possibly some of it was acquired by investors as a result of cashing in Trade Dollars they had bought in the late sixties or early seventies, and on which they had made handsome profits. Our own feeling is that the Trade series still has ample potential. It is a difficult one to analyze, because of all the melting, but its general prognosis is definitely favorable. Because so much of the buying and selling has been done by investors over the past 10-15 years, values have drifted somewhat away from the parities they maintained when collectors had control. This in itself presents an opportunity to select favorable dates. We do not believe it will be very long before all the Common Dates are over $1000, with the better ones selling at $2000 and more. Already the proofs are well over $2000 and on their way to higher ground. In terms of surviving quantities, the proofs may be just as plentiful — perhaps more so — than uncirculated specimens of the business strikes. For example, 865 proofs were struck of the 1873 Philadelphia Trade Dollar. It would not be unreasonable to suspect that the bulk of these are still in existence. Out of 397,500 business strikes, the surviving total of "uncs" could well be in that range.

Let's look at this group of 14 coins according to date:

1873 First in the series. It has arrived at a $1000 price on the current market after languishing for ages (before our chart begins) as one of the lower valued Trade Dollars. It was selling for only $12.50 in 1955. The increase from 1980 to 1985 was fairly strong, having started from $600. We do not see it as being fully priced yet, as the mintage is low at 397,500 and the attrition rate certainly diminished that total. As a long termer this coin is probably more favorable than for the short pull, but it could turn out to be profitable in both directions. We are going to forecast a price of $1750 by 1990 and $3250 to $3750 by 1995. We see this one as the second best of the Common Date Philadelphia Trade Dollars, surpassed in its investment potential only by the 1876.

1873-CC The first Carson City Trade Dollar. Its mintage is very low compared to the output at Carson City in the following year, 397,500 against more than one and a quarter million. This is the lowest mintage of any Common Date Trade Dollar and it is — as it should be — carrying the highest price at $1450. For as far back as our records reach, it was always the highest priced Common Date. In spite of this, it does not appear to be fully priced at the present sum and has good prospects of making strong gains between now and 1990 or 1995. Generally speaking we would be more confident of this as a long term coin, as it may need more of a breathing spell before making another sizeable climb. It went from $700 to $1450 in the years from 1980 to 1985, more than doubling in price. Another doubling by 1990 might be too much to expect, though this coin certainly has the capability for such a performance. We tend to see it getting to around $2500 by 1990, then going close to $5000 or possibly even surpassing that figure by the mid nineties. Will a large cache of these Carson Cities come out of hiding? That seems remote at the present time.

1873-S The Frisco mint fell just a bit shy of striking three quarters of a million Trade Dollars in that initial year. There is good reason to believe that the attrition (or destruction) ratio on the 1873-S somewhat surpassed that of later San Francisco strikings, especially so far as uncirculated condition is concerned. As one of the first Trade Dollars it was subject to a great deal of handling by the curious. You cannot compare mintages and prices of San Francisco strikings with those of Philadelphia. If this were done the 1873-S would seem overpriced at its current $1175, as its mintage was considerably greater than that of the 1873 Philadelphia (which sells for $1000). We know beyond all doubt that the San Francisco strikings were subjected to much more wear and tear, and that the survival rate of uncirculated specimens was much lower. It is impossible to give an exact percentage figure but they were sharply lower. This coin almost doubled in market value from 1980 to 1985, starting at $600 and falling just $25 short of a 100% increase. With a slightly smaller increase in that half decade we would not hesitate to recommend the 1873-S for investment. Having gotten to $1175, it may very likely fall into the category of a brighter long term than short term investment coin. Our projection is for a price close to $2000 by 1995, then rising to around $4000 by 1995.

1874 In the second year of striking at Philadelphia, output was a shade below one million. While the current price of $700 cannot be considered high, we are not advising investment on this coin. For the same price of $700 you could purchase the 1876 Philadelphia, which had a mintage of less than half as much and has proven to be the better investment buy on the current market. While the 1874 should be advancing, it will probably not advance fast enough. We're looking for a price of about $1000 by 1990 and $1500 by 1995, ruling it out both as a short and long term investment.

1874-CC This was a high mintage date. Obviously the number of specimens available on the market is a bare fraction of that total of 1,373,200. Yet, with all facts taken into consideration, it would not appear that the price of $975 leaves sufficient room for growth within the next five or ten years. The 1874-CC would be doing well to get to $1500 in 1990, falling short of the profitable range, with prospects for a gain to around $2500 by 1995.

1874-S This two-and-a-half-million mintage coin was the highest-output Trade Dollar up to its time (thereafter surpassed several times over). Even if the ratio of surviving specimens is identical to the 1873-S, its current price of $700 would not seem to merit purchase for investment. The price gained from $500 in 1980 and most likely another increase within this general range is all that could be anticipated between now and 1990, bringing it up to $900 or possibly $1000. Thereafter we project a price in the neighborhood of $1500 by 1995, leaving it short of an investment profit. It is a scarcer coin than it looks from the mintage but you can find better investment dates within this Common Date Trade Dollar group.

1875-CC Though this has to be ranked as a borderline item, it does have good prospects and could be the "sleeper" of this group. The price of $900 seems a bit thin and should be higher at the moment. What the next few years will bring is difficult to say. It has the potential to get close to $2000 by 1990, though we will not go so far as to make that prediction. Its long term prospects are slightly better, as the Common Date Trade Dollars should be pulling a larger overall cumulative gain in 1990-1995 than in 1985-1990. If you want a coin that could ultimately surprise half of the investment community, the 1875-CC is a possibility. Sooner or later it will make money for you, if you hold it for a prolonged period.

1875-S The giant mintage of 4½ million is in no way indicative of the availability of this coin, but it is (unfortunately) enough to put to rest any real expectations of an investment profit. Now registering $700, it would be very optimistic to gauge this one for an increase to more than $1000 in 1990, with a projection for 1995 of about $1500. It is one of several dates in this lineup that will prove profitable if held sufficiently long, as the rising prices of the scarcer Trade Dollars should take care of that.

1876 This is the most appealing of the Common Date Trade Dollars for investment. With a mintage of less than half a million, it can be purchased for $700 — the very same price at which dates with considerably higher mintage totals are now selling. We like the 1876 enough to forecast a price of $1500 by 1990, though we are less confident to predict its performance thereafter. Often with an underpriced coin, one has to anticipate a leveling-off period following a readjustment. The 1876 is due for a readjustment in the near future, and that could mean a slowdown in its pace of advance thereafter. Consequently this ranks as a coin which should be bought early if you intend adding it to your Silver Dollar investment portfolio.

1876-CC Another coin that could prove a real sleeper. We are not going to the extent of calling the 1876-CC a BEST BET, as we do not see any Common Dates falling into that category. But it does look appealing with that mintage barely exceeding half a million, and a current price of $900 (only $200 higher than the lowest priced Common Dates). If you want to think in terms of mintage figures and prices vs. the other Carson Cities, you could hardly ask for better numbers. It has one-third the mintage of the 1875-CC and is selling for exactly the same price; at that rate it should be $2700 right now. Of course, the mintage totals cannot be taken that literally in an attempt to gauge the extent to which a coin is underpriced, but with a difference this sharp it is obvious that the 1876-CC is thinly priced. We look for it to reach the $1750 to $2000 category by 1990 and approach $3500 in 1995. We see it as a brighter prospect for short term, rather than long term investment, so you may want to begin shopping around for a good uncirculated specimen before the price starts its inevitable readjustment.

1876-S A very large mintage, as the output was increasing year by year at the San Francisco facility. There was very good reason for this: Trade Dollars were not coming back into the country in the quantities they were expected to. For every hundred sent out, about ten would return, and of course most of them went out again. Though you can get the 1876-S for $700 — a reasonable price if you're collecting Trade Dollars — it does not shape up as a worthwhile coin for investment.

There is little chance of it rising in price beyond $1000 in 1990, unless the entire market on Trade Dollars comes in for very heavy buying pressure. Even if that occurs, you would do better on some of the other Common Dates, which are underpriced at the present time.

1877 This coin had the largest output of any Philadelphia-struck Trade Dollar, going over three million. That total is dwarfed by some of the totals recorded at San Francisco. At $700 it is fully priced with really no place to go in the near future, and lucky if it can climb as high as $1000 by 1990. We do not see this as either a short or long term winner, as our projection on its value level by 1995 is only $1500.

1877-S San Francisco struck close to ten million Trade Dollars this year, in a valiant effort to keep them in foreign circulation. The government vastly underestimated the pace at which Japanese smelters could absorb Trade Dollars. Even if the output had been a hundred million per year, they probably would have disappeared just as rapidly. Say "no" to the 1877-S at $700 and watch for it to do absolutely nothing in the next five years. Our projection for its 1990 price: $700.

1878-S In the final year of striking circulating Trade Dollars, the output fell to somewhat over four million in San Francisco. Under more normal circumstances you would be able to call this coin about twice as scarce as the 1877-S, but where Trade Dollars are concerned the mathematics do not always hold up soundly. In reality it is probably not twice as scarce as the 1877-S, but it must be somewhat scarcer. At that rate it could be moving up in price from its present figure of $700, but inching up would probably be a more appropriate term. Our prediction for 1990 is that this coin will attain around $1000, far short of the profitable range.

Obviously you can't buy Trade Dollars "across-the-board" any longer, the way some investors were doing a decade ago. It was feasible then because some of them were underpriced and due for readjustment. Today you will need to proceed with caution and pick and choose. Much of the profit has already been milked from this group, but it is not exactly finished as an investment series.

Beware of fakes with Trade Dollars! We cannot stress that point too vehemently. Trade Dollar fakes are more numerous (considering the relatively small number of dates involved) than fakes of ANY OTHER Silver Dollars. They They were made from the inception of this series, and there is every indication they are still being made, though the techniques and motives have changed. All of the early specimens were circulation counterfeits, made with the intention of passing them as money. They usually had lead cores (lead is heavy and approximates the weight of silver) covered with a thin silver plating or a simple silver "wash." The molds were made from genuine specimens and the fakes produced by the casting process. These are crude fakes. They seldom fool collectors but they could, and often did, fool the persons on whom they were palmed off in the 1870s. If the fake reasonably resembled a real coin and had approximately the correct weight, it stood an excellent chance of being accepted. Later, fakes aimed at collectors were made from fake dies or impact dies, using real silver of the correct weight and fineness. Some collector fakes were also made by the casting technique. Usually when a fair quality fake is offered for sale, the seller in all innocence and good faith describes it as a "weak strike." That is precisely what most of the fakes look like, if you do not realize they are fakes. They give the appearance of being weakly struck specimens of genuine coins. Once you accept them as weak strikes, it is unlikely that you will investigate further, as they are very convincing in other respects. Weak strikes should always be suspect. There ARE genuine weak strikes, but the fakes are weaker than a genuine weak strike — whole areas of detailing are lacking, and the figure of Liberty is hardly raised from the field. Sometimes it gives the impression of having been struck through a layer of cloth, as if something got in the way of the die and prevented a full impression. The design may be weaker on one side than on the other.

TRADE DOLLARS — SEMI-KEY DATES

Year	Mintage	1955	1960	1965	1970	1975	1980	1985
1875	218,900	$20.00	40.00	60.00	175.00	450.00	800.00	1425.00
1877-CC	534,000	65.00	100.00	150.00	250.00	550.00	675.00	2000.00

TRADE DOLLARS — SEMI-KEY DATES

% of increase:		
	1955-60	65%
	1960-65	50%
	1965-70	102%
	1970-75	208%
	1975-80	48%
	1980-85	81%
overall % of increase:	1955-85	3118%

Only three of the Trade Dollars struck for general circulation fall outside the Common Date category. Two of them are now classified as Semi-Keys while the third is a Key Date. As the mintage was kept high throughout the duration of this series it is not surprising that so little resulted in the way of scarce dates. As stated in our comments relative to the Common Dates, mintage figures in themselves can be misleading with reference to Trade Dollars. The 1877-CC, ranked as a Semi-Key, has a higher mintage total than several of the Common Dates. It is unquestionably scarcer on the market, however, than any Common Date and fully merits its Semi-Key status.

The price histories of these two Semi-Keys closely parallels those of the Common Dates, with the exception of the 1980-1985 period in which the Semi-Keys enjoyed a greater value advance. They both profited in the years from 1970 to 1975, then both failed to profit from 1975 to 1980, and was more or less the situation among the Common Dates. Having started from $675 in 1980, the 1877-CC shot to $1100 in 1982, which is not shown on our chart because of lack of space (in most cases it would be unproductive to show year by year changes, as values do not reflect a noticeable change in one year). From that plateau it certainly seemed capable of coming home a winner in 1985, but in the next three years it managed a cumulative advance of only $100, bringing it up to its current level of $1200. This gain was not sufficient to turn an investment profit for those who had purchased in 1980. We would not advise giving up on it at this juncture, however. Having come this far it needs only a relatively minor advance to slip into the profitable range, and that should occur shortly. If it gets to $1400 in 1986 it should be salable at a profit for those who purchased at $675 in 1980. Our projection on the price for 1990 is $2000 — fine if you already own the coin and bought it when it was under a thousand dollars, not too encouraging if you're contemplating purchasing it at the present time.

The 1875 Philadelphia has an attractive low mintage, though the figure (under a quarter of a million) would be absolutely miniscule if this were a San Francisco or Carson City striking. The Philadelphias did not find their way overseas in as large a percentage as the specimens struck out West, and hence their ratio of preservation was quite a bit higher, maybe by as much as 3-to-1. The current price of $1425 does not look high, despite the healthy jump from the $800 at which this coin stood in the 1980 market. It has some distance to travel before becoming fully priced, but not enough distance (in our estimation) to qualify it as a favorable coin for investment. Our projection for its 1990 price is $2250, and we think it will be getting to between $3000 and $3500 by 1995. Progress, but not enough progress to place it into the profitable category.

TRADE DOLLARS — KEY DATES

Year	Mintage	1955	1960	1965	1970	1975	1980	1985
1878-CC	97,000	$110.00	190.00	325.00	550.00	1400.00	2500.00	2500.00

TRADE DOLLARS — KEY DATES

% of increase:		
	1955-60	72%
	1960-65	71%
	1965-70	69%
	1970-75	154%
	1975-80	79%
	1980-85	0%
overall % of increase:	1955-85	2173%

The one Key Date among the Trade Dollars is the famous mystery coin, the 1878-CC. It is the only Trade Dollar struck for ordinary circulation with a mintage of less than 100,000. This in itself is a low total, but the actual quantity released for circulation may have been considerably less. The Mint report for 1878 mentions a melting of 44,000 Trade Dollars in July of that year, without further explanation. They could not have been Philadelphia coins, as the Philadelphia mint was striking only 900 proofs that year. They COULD have been San Franciscos, but considering the rate at which Frisco Trade Dollars were being consumed in the Orient, it is not too likely that the mint would have wanted to destroy any. The other alternative is that the 44,000 melted specimens were not dated 1878 but represented a stored supply from some previous year or a combination of years. We do not know and we never will. The general feeling among most experts is that the destroyed coins were Carson City strikings of 1878, which would have brought down the actual total released into circulation to 53,000. In any case the coin is a scarce one, and it would be very easy to believe that only 53,000 were released.

In our view the 1878-CC is the one and only BEST BET among the business strikes of Trade Dollars. It has the highest price at $2500, and generally one would not consider the most expensive coin in a series to be a BEST BET. In this case there are extenuating circumstances. At that price it is not really running too far ahead of dates which are considerably easier to find on the market. In terms of its scarcity it should be three times the price of any other Trade Dollar, but it is not even double the price of its nearest rival. Furthermore the price stalled between 1980 and 1985, giving every indication that this coin is ready for a strong surge within the next couple of years. Actually it had reached $3000 in 1982, which is not indicated on our chart. After hitting that level it slipped back again to $2500, its starting point in 1980. In light of the desirability and scarcity of this coin, it should have continued climbing after attaining

$3000 and reached at least $4000 in the 1985 market. Why it failed to do this cannot be easily explained, but was possibly the result of profit taking on the part of those who had purchased it in 1975 when the price was $1400. Our feeling is that the year 1990 will find the 1878-CC right about at $5000. In other words we think it will gain the amount it should have already gained (between 1980 and 1985), with an additional $1000 added. This will bring it squarely within profitable territory. This coin has not doubled in price in any five year period since 1970-1975. It is overdue for a substantial increase and we see one on the horizon.

TRADE DOLLARS — PROOF DATES

Year	Mintage	1955	1960	1965	1970	1975	1980	1985
1873	865	$ 37.50	95.00	160.00	450.00	650.00	5500.00	7250.00
1874	700	30.00	75.00	125.00	340.00	650.00	5500.00	7250.00
1875	700	37.50	80.00	130.00	340.00	625.00	5500.00	7250.00
1876	1,150	27.50	57.50	100.00	340.00	600.00	5500.00	7250.00
1877	510	37.50	95.00	160.00	500.00	650.00	5500.00	7250.00
1878	900	30.00	75.00	140.00	460.00	650.00	5500.00	8275.00
1879	1,541	27.50	57.50	125.00	375.00	625.00	5500.00	8500.00
1880	1,987	27.50	52.50	125.00	350.00	625.00	5500.00	8500.00
1881	960	32.50	62.50	125.00	400.00	625.00	5500.00	8500.00
1882	1,097	28.50	57.50	125.00	375.00	625.00	5500.00	8500.00
1883	979	35.00	62.50	125.00	420.00	675.00	5500.00	8500.00
1884	10	800.00	2000.00	8750.00	8750.00	30000.00	52500.00	52500.00
1885	5	1500.00	4000.00	9000.00	9000.00	—	—	

TRADE DOLLARS — PROOF DATES

% of increase:	1955-60	119%
	1960-65	87%
	1965-70	202%
	1970-75	61%
	1975-80	205%
	1980-85	23%
overall % of increase:	1955-85	4851%

The Trade Dollar proofs became the focus of widespread investor activity in the years from 1975 to 1980. With investment interest in Trade Dollars on the increase in those years, the proofs became the favorites of many investment buyers. They had been undervalued previously and the heavy buying of the mid to late seventies resulted in price increases that sent them from the $600/$650 range to $5500, one of the largest overall increases ever registered by a group of Silver Dollars (proofs OR business strikes). One of the great attractions of these coins is that mintage figures are known for every one. By the era of Trade Dollars the mint was finally keeping records of the number of proofs it was striking year by year. Thus the uncertainty and confusion that prevails among Liberty Seated proofs is avoided with proofs of the Trade Dollar. Also, they have a certain investment advantage over business strikes of these same coins. Because of the extensive melting of business strikes, which hit this series very heavily, it is difficult to determine the ratio of quantities in existence for one date vs. another date. This problem does not exist with the proofs, which were not melted. The only loss to occur on these proofs was normal attrition suffered by all proof coins through accident, fire, flood and the like. In cases where the recorded mintages are reasonably far apart, it can be safely presumed that the date struck in the smaller quantity survives today in the smaller quantity. Using this approach it will quickly be evident that the current prices, as shown on the above chart, do not reflect the actual fair value. This is unquestionably a series for investment speculation, for those who can afford coins in this range of price.

The mint was already in the practice of striking proof Dollars when the Trade Dollar series began in 1873. It had done this for years with the Liberty Seated Dollars, gradually increasing the output of proofs to satisfy public demand. By 1873 it was a foregone conclusion that coin collectors and dealers would want proofs of any new coins introduced by the mint, especially large showy coins such as Silver Dollars. Additionally the mint officials were trying to popularize the Trade Dollar in every possible way, as its passage through Congress had not been without heated debate and press criticism. Editorials led the public to believe that (A) such a coin was unnecessary, and (B) it would destroy the confidence in Silver Dollars that were already in circulation, since it contained more silver at the same face value. Many efforts were made to combat these views. The government knew that one of its chief allies would be the coin hobbyists, who could be found in all walks of life including influential positions in banking and trade. If the coin was well received by collectors it stood a far better chance of winning general approval. Thus in the first year of striking, it was considered important to make a large number of proofs available so that they could be widely dispersed, talked about, and — hopefully — admired. The total in that first year was 865, dropping to 700 the next and remaining at that figure the following year. In four of the years in which Trade Dollars were struck, the issued quantity of proofs exceeded one thousand, but in three of those four years (1879, 1880, and 1882), it was no longer being produced as a circulating coin. All of the Trade Dollar proofs, during its span as a circulating coin and afterward, came from the main Philadelphia mint. Philadelphia was deemed the ideal place to strike proofs because it was located in the heart of collector territory.

The final year of striking for the Trade Dollar as a circulating coin was 1878. Yet it continued on until 1885 in the form of proofs, making a total of seven years in which the coin was struck exclusively as a proof. This circumstance, though not unique in mint history, has proven beneficial for investors and will continue to do so in the future. It creates an extra demand for these later proofs on the part of coin collectors. If a collector is attempting to build a collection of Trade Dollars, proofs are the only specimens available for these dates — so he must have proofs or nothing. This makes proof buyers out of some collectors who would, if given the choice, settle for these dates in regular business strikes. This factor must be taken into account in gauging fair value levels and future price potential: there is slightly more demand for the proofs dated 1879 and later, than for those dated between 1873 and 1878. As you will see, this circumstance is already well reflected in the 1985 price standings, as the later dates are running ahead of the earlier dates. This in itself does not mean, however, that the price spreads or levels are necessarily fair.

The obvious question to be asked is: why did the mint continue striking proofs after 1878? If the Trade Dollar was terminated as a circulating coin, why did it carry on in proof form? Although various theories have been advanced, most of them implausible, this was simply a case of collector influence coming to the fore. A market had been established for Trade Dollar proofs, not only among collectors but coin dealers, who would buy them in quantity. While it was far from being extremely lucrative, the mint saw no reason to deprive collectors of these coins nor deprive itself of the money that accrued from striking them. By the late 1870s the mint was very much attuned to proofs; it was trying to make them as widely available as possible, and it saw nothing peculiar in striking proof specimens of coins that were not actually in production. It could mount a good case, too. As far as the mint knew (because it was Congress that made the ultimate decisions), the decision which terminated the Trade Dollar could be reversed at any time. There were some people who wanted it back.

According to the annual Mint reports, the final year of striking Trade Dollar proofs was 1883, but we now know this to be incorrect. In the early 1900s, proof specimens dated 1884 and 1885 were discovered. Both of these had very low mintages and are the great rarities among the entire Trade Dollar lineup. For all practical purposes they are outside the realm of investment. With such infrequent sales it is difficult, if not impossible, to make valid projections of future price performances. We show these two dates on the chart, but we are unable to enter into any discussion of their investment prospects. All of the other dates, from 1873 to 1883 inclusive, are available to investors. While these are expensive coins they are far from impossible to get. They are regularly supplied by the leading dealers. You will notice ads for them appearing in the weekly coin collecting periodicals, and additional specimens can be found at auction sales.

As we have stated in this book, the actual availability of *proof* coins cannot be calculated in the same way as availability of *circulating* coins. Proofs are always available in greater quantity, in terms of the original mintages. In this instance, we have mintages ranging from slightly over five hundred to slightly under two thousand specimens, covering a period of eleven years. Business strikes having mintages this low would be on the verge of extinction. Yet for proofs, five hundred or a thousand specimens are not considered particularly low mintages. Proofs did not go into circulation, were not worn down by handling (except for an occasional specimen that slipped into circulation), and above all they were not melted to obtain the metal content. Even in the 1870s and 1880s, no one was melting proofs. This would have been foolish because they could have — even then — been sold to a coin dealer for a premium over the melt value. In addition to the other factors, one must also consider that the proof strikings of these Trade Dollars stayed at home, in the U.S., while most of the business strikes went to the Orient. They had every advantage for a much longer lifespan. This is not to say that all specimens were preserved, nor even that all preserved specimens are still in the original condition. But a high percentage of them are. They traveled from collection to collection, seldom coming into the possession of persons who would mishandle them. Of the proof specimens that were not mishandled, the only harm that came to any of them — and it was certainly a minority — was "cabinet wear." You will encounter this expression often in the lists of coin dealers, not only with reference to proofs but other coins as well. In the earlier days of collecting, some hobbyists had wooden cabinets in which they stored their coins. The cabinets had slots in their trays, and each coin rested in the slot without further protection. Thus the coin directly contacted the wood or other material with which the tray might be covered, such as velvet or sateen. In pulling out the trays, to inspect the coins, each coin would shift as they did not fit tightly in the slots. Over a long period of years this caused slight wear on the side facing down (or on both sides if the collector turned his coins occasionally). It can be distinguished from ordinary circulation wear by an expert, and is known as "cabinet wear." Mostly it is found on rare coins of very high value, as cabinets were used by collectors who could afford the best. When proof coins show cabinet wear their value is somewhat reduced. We would not recommend investment in such specimens.

Prices commanded by the Trade Dollar proofs were meager in 1960, with none of them (except for the two giant rarities) reaching $100. In 1955, not a single one was as high as $50. They did reasonably well in the years between 1960 and 1965, but this was more the result of overall interest in silver coins than in Trade Dollar proofs specifically. Still the rate of increase in that period was not sufficient to yield an investment profit for those who bought the dates randomly. One could have profited at that time only by selective purchasing of the most attractive dates. It was quite a different story in the late sixties. With prices still far below fair levels, there was a sharp overall increase bringing all the dates within the profitable range. The percentage gain in that half decade was 202%, which meant that many investment owners could have sold at wholesale after buying at full retail and still gained a profit. A lull in the subsequent five years, from 1970 to 1975, was followed by the gigantic price leaps of 1975-1980 to which we have already referred. These resulted in all the proofs (again with the exception of the two rarities) standing almost ten times higher in price in the 1980 market than they had in 1975. Though the prices for individual years between 1980 and 1985 are not indicated on our chart, our files contain these prices, and they tell quite a chaotic story. After coming together at a common price of $5500 in the 1980 market, all the proofs tumbled to values between $2000 and $2250 in 1982. In two years they had lost more than half their market values. To many observers at the time this seemed remarkable, insofar as coin prices on the whole were advancing. Actually it was a predictable turn of events in light of the circumstances. These coins were not overvalued at $5500 and if all things had been equal, they could have easily continued to gain in price or at least hold their own between 1980 and 1982. They were brought crashing down solely because the series was, at that point, over-held by investors (in other words, the vast majority of specimens were in the hands of investors as opposed to dealers and collectors). Every investment owner had paper profits of huge proportions on them. Feeling the time to be right for cashing in, they began to sell in the years between 1980 and 1982. The volume of selling so far exceeded the volume of buying that it forced prices down. For every specimen sold by a dealer, three or four investors were knocking on the door with specimens to sell. The dealers had to reduce their buying and selling prices, and this made for lower prices in the auction rooms as well. Even the investors who had no intention of selling in 1980 decided to sell soon thereafter, when they saw the prices beginning to slip down: "It's now or never," they concluded. And MORE Trade Dollar proofs swarmed on the market.

What happened thereafter was yet another drastic turn of events! Instead of losing confidence in the Trade Dollar proofs because of their setback, new investors coming into the market recognized that this was a golden opportunity. The $2000 to $2250 figures represented the bargains of the age — these had been $5500 coins just two years before. Shortly thereafter, things turned completely around. The buying pace became just as heavy as the selling pace had been a year earlier. That is a most unusual situation, for coins in the four-figure price range. It was certainly possible that some of the buyers were the very persons who had sold these very coins earlier — they were anxious to make a second profit on them. And they did! In the three years between 1982 and 1985, prices rose from a minimum of $2000 to a minimum of $7250. Some of the $2000 coins went up to $8500. Quadrupling in price within three years, for coins already at $2000, is not something you will witness often. Even in the most booming markets this is a rarity. Interesting enough, the rare 1884 date scored a much, much smaller gain. It slacked off down to $30,000 in 1982, from the $52,500 at which it stood in 1980. By 1985 it was back to $52,500, while the others had well surpassed their 1980 price levels.

There is not too much doubt but that history will repeat itself on these coins. You can make good profits on them if you time your purchases, which means keeping track of the prices. Many specimens are now in the possession of investors who bought them in the deflated 1982 market. Having the opportunity, once again, to realize very substantial profits on these coins, one would have to assume that this is precisely what will be happening. The next year, or possibly next two years, will likely find the prices falling as the quantities returning to the market increase. All you need to do is catch these coins the next time they're down. They are not overpriced at the current levels. They fully deserve to be commanding those sums, and they would remain solid in price but for the prevailing situation. These are investor coins and the investment owners are clearly in control. They own at least 80% of the available specimens, and whatever they choose to do — hold or sell — dictates the price patterns. If another heavy selling wave comes, as we feel very confident it will, the prices will drop below the 1980 levels. You could conceivably have a chance to buy any of these dates for $3000 to $4000 within the next couple of years. At that point they would rank as superb investments, as little doubt exists about the prices going up again. If the prices are averaging $3500 by 1987, they could well be in the $9000 or $10,000 territory by 1990. This would be fast movement, but the Trade Dollar proofs have more than demonstrated their speed of price movement on the market. They have been volatile coins ever since the late seventies. They are not going to stop, especially now that so many investors have found them to be immensely profitable.

To further improve your prospects you can, of course, concentrate on certain dates. The 1985 price spread, while not exactly immense, is sharper than any price spread that has existed on these coins in quite some time. It suggests that the future movement will be more and more in the direction of individual coin-by-coin price levels. This would be only equitable as the Trade Dollar proofs are not equally scarce in equal across-the-board demand. The three best dates in this group are the 1877, 1881, and 1883. The 1877 is good because of its low mintage. The 1881 and 1883 are favorable because they have the lowest mintages of any of the later dates. As we pointed out earlier, the late dates come in for somewhat greater buying demand. Do NOT buy them at the current prices. Wait until the prices get down to around $5000, then see (by watching weekly movement in the coin market) whether they pick up any sizable buyer support at that level. Chances are they will continue going down until they've reached the $4000 zone or slightly lower. This will be your cue to buy. It should not be necessary to hold these coins for more than five years, after purchasing them, to realize a good profit. You may have the chance to turn them over profitably in a much shorter time.

A recently discovered variety, the 1876-S Trade Dollar with repunched 6 over a high 6, worth a 15% premium.

NOTE: Less well known, but important to the investor, are two hubbing varieties which result in strong doubling of the reverse on the 1877-S and 1878-S dollars. The latter is the stronger of the two and will bring a 50 to 100% premium over the normal coin for the date. These can often be found in stocks of unobservant dealers for the normal price. If you can find either one at the normal price, you will automatically make a profit, and by 1990, these varieties will be as high or higher than the 1875-S/CC.

THE MORGAN DOLLARS

OBVERSE

REVERSE

Two factors brought about the Morgan Dollars. One was the fact that the western silver mines were yielding ore faster than it could be consumed and increasingly large amounts of silver were being exported. The other was the major effort by Washington to resolve these problems with different levels of value in gold, silver and paper money.

By 1877, the three were just about equal, with an unexpected result. Silver coins, which had been exported to Central and South America in 1861 and 1862 suddenly returned and the country was literally swamped with subsidiary silver coins. The cry went up from the silver states for a silver dollar. Some plans had already been underway for just such a coin for several years. By the end of 1876, English engraver George Morgan had been hired and had already started work on the necessary designs.

Rivalry between Morgan and Chief Engraver William Barber was soon apparent and Barber apparently did everything possible to hinder and delay the acceptance of Morgan's designs. Friction is apparent in a number of technical problems and delays that are recorded, including the fact that there are several hundred die varieties of the 1878 dates resulting from both major and minor changes, perhaps the most notable being the 8 and 7 tail feather variations and the hubbing variety which resulted in the 7 over 8 tail feather version.

The Morgan series is the longest and largest dollar series, struck from 1878 to 1921 at five mints — Philadelphia, Carson City, New Orleans, San Francisco and finally, in its last year of production, at Denver. Astronomical quantities were minted. The Morgan was struck in a total of 96 dates and mints, and 79 of those mintages were a million or more, capped by the 44 million struck at Philadelphia in 1921.

It would seem from these statistics as if almost all of the Morgans are common dates, but this is far from the case. As you will note, several of the million plus mintages qualify as semi-key dates. This may be the first surprise, but certainly not the last, when you begin studying the Morgans. The series is one of the most complex in our coinage.

The Morgans, perhaps more than any other series, have been the victims of the mass melts that have occurred periodically. In 1918, the Pittman Act resulted in the melting of more than 270 million silver dollars, although the figures do include some of the earlier dollars as well as the Morgans. Hundreds of thousands have gone into foreign melting pots as a prime source of silver. India absorbed huge quantities that remain either as jewelry made from melted coins, or as buried bullion, hiding from the world and the tax collector. These factors alone have been enough to cause many perplexed students of this coin to toss their mintage charts aside and use blind guesswork.

For a number of years now, the hobby has been recuperating from the impact of the announcement of the Redfield hoard of dollars. Until then, many dates and mints were thought to be scarce, rare, even very rare, only to have date after date, mint after mint turn up by the bagful in Redfield's vaults. Many of the coins have been damaged by time and the elements, but there are still more that are as beautiful and unmarred as the moment they left the dies. These coins will be having an impact on the hobby for many years to come, if for no other reason than that the horde has provided the hobby with an unexpected source of large quantities of dollars to meet the collector and investor demand for them.

We have watched dealer after dealer during the recent silver bullion boom, as they frantically tried to buy silver dollars — any dollars — any grade, to fill the demands from the customers. It was not at all unusual in many shops around the country to display signs saying "Sorry — NO Dollars!"

The statistics in this chapter should surprise you if you have any knowledge of silver dollars at all. The Morgan dollars have been the most overworked, overpromoted, oversold, overexamined, and overdone series in anyone's coinage. There are countless books touting this dollar or that dollar and, in almost all cases, the books are about Morgans. Some experts would have you believe that they can tell within a fraction of one percent just how many Morgan dollars for a particular date or mint still exist. Some go even further and tell you they know exactly how many of that exact number of survivors are MS-60, exactly how many are MS-55, and so on down the line; which, of course, casts doubts on their qualifications to make investment recommendations. No one has access to such information, or any reliable means of calculating it. Charts and tables of this nature are published solely to lend sales appeal to the books or bulletins in which they appear.

The truth of the matter is that they are guessing because there are too many variables. We could write a book on some things that can happen to coins that take them out of the hands of an investor or collector and put them in the junk pile to be melted down. The best of experts cannot tell exactly how many of a given coin exists unless they were present when the coins were struck and have had it in their possession ever since. They can make some very educated guesses and be surprisingly accurate, but don't be fooled by anybody who tries to tell you EXACTLY how many coins are still in existence. The guessers are well protected, as nobody can disprove their claims. They can invent logic to support their statistics. But an intelligent investor will not look for easy answers, or accept them without question when offered.

Despite all of the books, magazines, and other laudatory writings about Morgan dollars, they represent a good way to bankrupt oneself if you aren't exceptionally careful.

For example, let's look at the Common Date Morgans. Here's the chart:

MORGAN DOLLARS — COMMON DATES

Year	Mintage	1955	1960	1965	1970	1975	1980	1985
1878-8	750,0000	$ 5.00	10.00	23.00	15.00	20.00	50.00	75.00
1878-7	9,759,950	3.00	3.00	2.50	5.50	12.00	50.00	65.00
1878-CC	2,212,950	4.00	5.00	10.00	16.00	30.00	85.00	135.00
1878-S	9,744,000	2.50	2.75	2.25	4.75	10.00	40.00	65.00
1879	14,807,100	3.00	3.00	2.25	4.25	10.00	36.00	55.00
1879-0	2,887,000	22.50	4.50	9.00	7.50	17.00	50.00	60.00
1879-S	9,110,000	2.75	2.75	2.50	4.00	22.00	34.00	56.00
1880	12,601,335	3.00	2.75	2.00	5.00	10.00	36.00	54.00
1880-0	5,305,000	15.00	5.00	6.00	6.00	12.00	75.00	85.00
1880-S	8,900,000	2.75	2.75	2.00	3.75	10.00	35.00	65.00
1881	9,163,975	3.00	2.75	2.00	5.00	10.00	33.00	60.00
1881-0	5,708,000	10.00	3.50	5.00	4.50	10.00	30.00	55.00
1881-S	12,760,000	3.50	3.75	2.00	4.00	10.00	35.00	60.00
1882	11,101,100	3.00	2.75	2.00	4.00	10.00	35.00	60.00
1882-CC	1,133,000	12.50	4.00	30.00	32.50	35.00	75.00	110.00
1882-0	6,090,000	12.00	3.50	5.00	4.00	10.00	30.00	55.00

Year	Mintage	1955	1960	1965	1970	1975	1980	1985
1882-S	9,250,000	2.75	3.00	3.50	15.00	10.00	30.00	60.00
1883	12,291,039	3.00	2.75	2.50	4.00	10.00	30.00	55.00
1883-CC	1,204,000	15.00	4.00	30.00	40.00	35.00	50.00	112.00
1883-O	8,725,000	6.00	3.00	2.00	4.00	10.00	25.00	55.00
1884	14,070,875	3.50	2.50	3.00	4.00	10.00	50.00	60.00
1884-CC	1,136,000	10.00	4.00	40.00	40.00	35.00	50.00	112.00
1884-O	9,730,000	6.00	3.00	2.00	4.00	10.00	25.00	50.00
1885	17,787,767	5.00	3.00	2.00	4.00	10.00	25.00	50.00
1885-O	9,185,000	6.00	3.00	2.00	4.00	10.00	25.00	50.00
1886	19,963,886	6.50	3.50	2.00	4.00	10.00	25.00	50.00
1887	20,290,710	6.50	3.00	2.00	4.00	10.00	25.00	50.00
1887-O	11,550,000	11.00	4.00	10.00	7.00	15.00	40.00	57.00
1888	19,183,833	6.00	4.00	2.00	4.00	10.00	28.00	50.00
1888-O	12,150,000	15.00	4.00	5.00	5.00	10.00	35.00	50.00
1889	21,726,811	6.00	2.50	2.00	4.00	10.00	30.00	50.00
1890	16,802,590	6.50	3.00	2.00	5.00	12.00	35.00	60.00
1890-O	10,701,000	5.50	6.50	4.50	8.50	21.00	60.00	65.00
1890-S	8,230,373	2.75	2.75	7.00	10.00	20.00	70.00	65.00
1891-S	5,296,000	2.75	2.50	12.00	14.00	27.00	80.00	65.00
1896	9,967,762	10.00	3.50	4.00	4.00	10.00	35.00	50.00
1897	2,822,731	10.00	3.00	12.00	7.50	11.00	30.00	60.00
1897-S	5,825,000	3.00	2.50	10.00	13.50	28.00	100.00	65.00
1898	5,884,735	10.00	3.50	4.50	5.00	10.00	25.00	52.00
1898-O	4,440,000	12.50	375.00	5.00	5.00	10.00	28.00	52.00
1899-O	12,290,000	11.00	6.50	2.00	4.00	10.00	25.00	55.00
1900	8,880,938	10.00	3.50	2.25	4.00	10.00	27.00	50.00
1900-O	12,590,000	5.00	5.00	2.00	4.00	10.00	25.00	55.00
1900-S	3,540,000	4.50	3.50	22.50	30.00	110.00	125.00	145.00
1901-O	13,320,000	10.00	6.50	2.50	4.00	10.00	25.00	55.00
1902	7,994,777	10.00	10.00	6.50	9.00	35.00	60.00	65.00
1902-O	8,636,000	15.00	85.00	2.50	4.75	10.00	25.00	50.00
1903	4,652,755	17.50	3.00	7.50	8.75	20.00	70.00	60.00
1904-O	3,720,000	55.00	150.00	3.75	5.50	10.00	25.00	50.00
1921	44,690,000	2.00	2.00	2.00	4.00	10.00	25.00	38.00
1921-D	20,345,000	2.50	2.00	4.00	6.50	12.00	35.00	40.00
1921-S	21,695,000	2.00	2.00	5.00	6.50	11.00	56.00	45.00

MORGAN DOLLARS — COMMON DATES

% of increase:	1955-60	87%
	1960-65	-57%
	1965-70	28%
	1970-75	95%
	1975-80	160%
	1980-85	48%
overall % of increase:	1955-85	673%

The Morgan Dollar, bar none, is the favorite of all investment coins. Not just among Silver Dollars, but among all U.S. coins. It is the favorite of numismatic investors looking for inexpensive, moderately expensive, and VERY expensive collector coins. It is the favorite of roll investors (those who buy their coins by the roll). It is the favorite of Carson City investors (those who specialize in Carson City strikings). It is the favorite of proof coin investors. It is also the favorite of bullion investors, as the tubs of worn and battered Morgan Dollars in coin shops indicate. Even when thought of strictly in terms of its three-quarters of an ounce of silver bullion content, the Morgan Dollar seems to have a magical attraction. The silver content is precisely the same as that of Peace Dollars. Yet, when given a choice, most bullion investors will instinctively take Morgans.

It is a class coin, a coin rich with history, drama, romance. Its design is claimed by many to be the finest ever appearing on a U.S. coin — some say the best on any coin, anywhere, though that seems to be carrying things to excess (the ancient Greeks made some extremely attractive coins). George T. Morgan, the designer, won everlasting fame — which he almost surely would not have possessed otherwise — for his work on this coin. As an artist he did not have Gobrecht's reputation nor, probably, his skills. This was his only Silver Dollar and the design is not particularly original: a Liberty head on one side and an eagle on the other (both the old Flowing Hair and Draped Bust Dollars had that combination). It was devastatingly popular in its time; it became more so afterward. Almost as soon as the first Morgan Dollar was issued, in 1878, it started to be made into watch fobs, pendants, and miscellaneous jewelry. Jewelers did everything conceivable with Morgan Dollars, as well as turning them into "love tokens." This was done by grinding down the design on one side (usually the back) until it was perfectly smooth, then engraving a heart, a few small flowers, a couple of ribbons, and an affectionate message. They were personalized for each customer by adding the name or initials of the giver and recipient. A hole was punched through the top, so they could be worn on a chain, or they were set in wire jewelry mounts. Merchants and manufacturers also saw the potential in Morgan Dollars. They scraped off the back and added their own advertising messages. These "advertising coins" were still legal tender, and continued to be passed around in circulation — where the ad was sure to be noticed. Some went even further, inserting brass or copper collars around Morgan Dollars and displaying advertising on the collars. Competitions appeared in newspapers and magazines, in which amateur artists could win "art scholarships" by sketching the portrait of Liberty as it appeared on the Morgan Dollar.

As part of its colorful history, the Morgan Dollar was the first Silver Dollar used in the gambling halls of the West. Thanks to it, there were at least a few saloons in almost every territory called "The Silver Dollar." It was the coin Old West marksmen tossed in the air, and tried to shoot a hole through. It was the coin of card games and banking transactions, and for stuffing into the Christmas stocking of children whose parents could afford it. It was the coin used by stage magicians who billed themselves as "King of Coins." It was the coin which traveled — by the multi thousands — in the Wells Fargo strongboxes across the western plains. It was the coin that people like Jesse James and Cole Younger killed for. Eventually — though not in 1878 or for a long while thereafter — it was the coin that came to symbolize the gaudiness of American capitalism. It was a symbol of wealth and power among other things. It even became an issue in one of the most bitter political campaigns, when Bryan and McKinley battled over whether America should be on a gold standard or silver standard. This led to the private striking of the "Bryan Dollar," supposedly the alternative to the Silver Dollar.

The Morgan Dollar had an impact on coin collecting like nothing before or since. Due to the huge quantities struck year by year, it was available at every bank. Anyone could build at least a date collection — if not a mint mark collection — just by searching through Morgans received from the bank. In most cases there would be uncirculated specimens, too. By the time the Morgan Dollar had gotten to be 20 or 25 years old, anyone inclined towards numismatics could have a bonanza with rolls from the bank. Anything was liable to turn up, including dates which by then had acquired a premium over face value. Whenever a "find" was made, it sent others scurrying to the bank. Many bank tellers were kept busy dispensing rolls of Morgans. Dealers got them from banks, too, and spent no small amount of time processing them. There was nothing to be lost except time. Most coin shop customers were happy to get the dealer's unwanted Silver Dollars in change when they made a purchase.

Much of the greatness of the Morgan Dollar resulted from the public's reaction to it — collectors and non-collectors alike. In the days of the Liberty Seated Dollar, few hobbyists took a real interest in it. They could have built up date collections from specimens in circulation, but hardly anybody cared to do this. It was just a "modern" Silver Dollar, and serious collectors concentrated on the Flowing Hairs and Draped Busts. The feeling was entirely different with Morgans. They were well received. Nobody seemed to think of them as "modern" and unworthy to be collected.

Not only was it the first Silver Dollar to be heavily collected while it was current, it was also the first to be hoarded by non-collectors. This had nothing to do with a change in public attitude. It was strictly because of the widespread availability of this coin. The Liberty Seated Dollar was struck in far less quantity, and not nearly as widely circulated; there were areas of the country into which it did not penetrate. Morgan Dollars could be found everywhere, Indian Territory included. Being distrustful of banks, many of our ancestors preferred to keep their savings in the form of gold or silver coins. This was not as unreasonable in the nineteenth century as it seems today. There was no F.D.I.C. to insure bank accounts, and coins in those days (unlike today) had intrinsic value. If you had a hundred dollars in Silver Dollars, you truly had a hundred dollars — not just tokens that could be SPENT for a hundred dollars, which is the case with our modern coins. So the Morgan Dollar went into cookie jars, closets, attics, and was even buried in many a backyard in the late 1800s. This was to have a long-range impact on collecting, though no one realized it at the time. Some of the stashed hoards consisted of huge quantities of the same date and mint mark. When they came to light, the date became a bit less scarce than had been supposed. Then there were the collector hoards, and those built by persons who seem to have been primarily money savers but who took a more than ordinary interest in Silver Dollars. Some of these were of gigantic proportions, to the point where tens of thousands of specimens of the identical date were included in the same accumulation. The most famous was the Redfield hoard, the largest stockpile of Silver Dollars ever gathered by a private individual. When this began to be released into the coin market, it did some very bizarre things to prices. No other coins have EVER had their market values so drastically influenced by large quantities going on sale simultaneously. You may very well think some of the prices shown on our chart for these Common Dates are misprints, such as the 1898-O falling from $375 in 1960 to a mere $5 in 1965. They are not misprints.

This was the result of hoard coins hitting the market in appalling quantities, far beyond the pace at which they could be absorbed in the normal course of buying and selling. This could not happen with other coins, as no other coin was hoarded in the same manner as the Morgan Dollars.

One factor in the immediate popularity of the Morgan Dollar is that it marked a return of the standard Silver Dollar. In 1873 the mint had ceased striking the traditional Silver Dollar, which at that point carried the Liberty Seated design. The new Dollar was the Trade Dollar, slightly heavier in weight, which became the target of considerable criticism. At the time of introduction of the Trade Dollar, there were no plans to ever reintroduce the regular Silver Dollar. It was felt (by the government, at any rate) that America needed a heavier Silver Dollar to compete in foreign trade against the heavy dollar-size silver coins of other countries. Supposedly the gold Dollar was intended to take the place of the old Silver Dollar in ordinary day to day commerce. When it finally became clear that this was not a workable arrangement, the Bland-Allison Act of 1878 brought back the standard Silver Dollar. The mint responded by working overtime, producing the new Morgan Dollar in quantities that would ensure widespread circulation.

As a collector's coin it has few equals. Production came from five different mints, to the great delight of mint mark collectors. It was struck in Philadelphia, New Orleans, San Francisco, Carson City, and Denver. There are numerous varieties, some of them reminiscent of the type that occurred on our early Silver Dollars: some 1878 Morgans struck at Philadelphia show the eagle on the reverse side with eight tail feathers, when on other specimens he has seven. There are overdates and even — very unusual — overstampings on mint marks. A portion of the 1882 New Orleans output has the "O" mint mark superimposed over an "S" for San Francisco. This happened again in 1900, once again at New Orleans, when the "O" was placed over a "CC" for Carson City. These are die varieties. The new mint mark was not impressed after the coins were struck, even though it may give this impression. Coin dies are originally prepared without mint marks, which are then punched in afterward. In these cases, a second punching was done to alter the mark as it appeared in the die. Apparently this was the result of a change in plans, at the last moment, about the allotment of dies for the subsidiary mints. As the San Francisco mint struck close to ten million Morgan Dollars in 1882, it obviously had an ample supply of dies. One or more of the dies intended for San Francisco was diverted to New Orleans, with the addition of an "O" to blot out the "S." In 1900 the explanation was even more readily apparent. Dies were prepared carrying a "CC" mint mark, in the belief that Silver Dollars were to be struck that year at the Nevada facility. It had not struck Silver Dollars since 1893 and, as things turned out, it would strike no more. There was no production of Morgan Dollars at Carson City in 1900, so the CC dies would have been useless. They were merely overstamped with an "O" and sent on to New Orleans, which reached a production of twelve and a half million Morgans in that year. Of course there were proofs, too, of the Morgan Dollars, and the proofs have likewise proven favorites of collectors and investors. The mint was wise enough not to strike in overly excessive quantities and thereby dilute their exclusivity. The struck quantities were similar to those of the Trade Dollar, and they were released into a world which had more coin collectors and dealers.

Investors and investment analysts have studied the Morgan Dollar series far more intently than any other Silver Dollars. Investing in Morgans has become a science unto itself, and some analysts confine themselves strictly to this series, having worked out myriad theories, calculations, predictions and the like. In a sense, various strategies used in coin investment have filtered down from those devised for use on the Morgan Dollar. One may want to debate whether the Morgan Dollar is the supreme investment series among coins. What cannot be debated is that the series has proved a lucrative livelihood for those who sell investment advice, newsletters, and coin investment manuals. To this end it has been, unquestionably, over publicized. Excessive publicity has been damaging in various respects. Worst, it has led many beginners to believe that Morgan Dollars are a completely risk-proof investment, and that they will always be sounder as an investment than any other Silver Dollars. Additionally, the vast media attention given to Morgan Dollars has resulted in publication of numerous trick or gadget theories for investment, which further confuse the beginner. Some analysts profess to know the surviving totals of specimens, date by date, from each of the mints. They not only tell you the overall totals, but the totals existing in uncirculated condition; and they go further, with breakdowns on quantities owned by investors, collectors and dealers. All of this makes fascinating reading, until you stop to realize that such statistics are merely estimates (though presented as hard facts). The actual tangible information available to investors in Morgans is no greater than that available to investors in Liberty Seated or Trade Dollars. Thus, one of the first steps for the beginning investor is to sort out the *useful* from the *useless* information: what he can believe and make use of in planning his investment purchases, and what he cannot. He must also rid himself of the notion — widely promoted by some analysts — that the price performances of Morgan Dollars are more predictable than those of other Silver Dollars. This is simply not the case. Our chart covers 30 years of investment activity on Morgans. In that period of time there were just as many surprises among Morgans as any other Dollars, and there are bound to be surprises in the future. No one has the Morgan harnessed. Despite thousands of words of supposed logic, they still move at their own pace on the market. You CAN profit from them, but only by taking a rational approach.

One thing that can be said in favor of Morgan Dollars as investments is that the very heavy pace of buying and selling usually makes for quicker price readjustments. When a price gets out of line — either too high or too low in relation to other dates in the series — it does not remain out of line too long. Their current prices at any time are easy to establish, as they are so widely advertised. This is true not just of the Common Dates but all the way down the line. Moreover this very extensive advertising often presents the opportunity to buy from a seller who is offering slightly more favorable prices. You can do marvelous comparison shopping on 95% of the Morgans.

Before entering into specific investment advice, several items should be discussed bearing upon references often made in conjunction with Morgan Dollars.

Quantities in Existence. It is true that mintage totals on the Morgan series do not always faithfully reflect quantities in existence, but the discrepancies have been exaggerated. One can easily see why this has happened. Mintage figures are available to everyone. If an investment analyst merely presents mintage figures, he is not offering any exclusive information. So the analysts have developed a habit of playing with "quantities in existence," referring to some dates as much scarcer than the mintage figure indicates and to others as much more plentiful. This is the core of most of their investment theories — that the mintage figures are almost totally useless in gauging quantities in existence. The smart investor should take the opposite position and pay good respect to the mintage figures, as they at least represent solid information without conjecture or speculation. Of course we know that very large numbers of Morgan Dollars have been destroyed over the years, and that this destruction could not have been perfectly uniform among all the dates. Still there is no solid evidence that it affected some dates more than others. There were two principal sources of destruction: that carried out by the government, and that by commercial industry (i.e., silver refineries). In 1918 the mint melted 270 million Morgan Dollars, after the coin had been out of production for 14 years. These were stockpiled specimens that had never been released into circulation, but were held as the Treasury Department's backing for Silver Certificates. In those days, Silver Certificates could be exchanged for Silver Dollars and the government kept a large supply of Silver Dollars on hand for that purpose. Nothing even approaching 270 million Morgan Dollars had ever been struck in a single year, so it is obvious that this wholesale melting comprised specimens of various dates. Melting by refineries has been of long standing and continues today. The quantity of Morgan Dollars melted by refineries cannot even be estimated with any degree of accuracy. It is probably quite a bit less than the 270 million melted by the mint. In any case, there is an important distinction to be drawn between government melting and the melting done by silver refineries. All the coins melted by the government were uncirculated. Of those melted by refineries, only a minor portion have been uncirculated, and the ratio of "uncs" being melted has declined to practically zero in recent years. Almost everyone now knows that uncirculated Morgan Dollars have a premium value as collector's items, regardless of their date. Perhaps in early years there was a fair percentage of "uncs" being thrown into refinery melting furnaces, but no longer. Since the government is no longer melting Morgan Dollars, and the refineries rarely melt any "uncs," the quantities of uncirculated specimens in existence have not changed very much over the past ten to twenty years. Nor will they be changing greatly in the future. Despite this undeniable fact, one constantly reads of certain dates "becoming increasingly difficult to obtain in uncirculated grade." How can that be? The answer is that it cannot! The frequency with which any particular date is offered for sale can vary from time to time. This does not signify any change in the scarcity of the date.

Intermediate Grading. On no other Silver Dollars will you find so-called intermediate grading used so commonly, as on Morgans. Intermediate grading is the use of condition grades that fall between the standard accepted A.N.A. guidelines for coin grading. On uncirculated coins, the A.N.A. recognizes three specific grades: MS-70, MS-65, and MS-60. The MS-70 grade is for a perfect or very nearly perfect specimen. The MS-65 grade is for a specimen with some bag marks, but fewer than would be found on the normal MS-60. The lowest uncirculated grade, MS-60, is for a coin with no circulation wear but with the usual amount of bag marks and scratches (which, on Morgan Dollars, means plenty of them). In the view of the A.N.A., these three grading levels are sufficient to grade all uncirculated Morgan Dollars. In other words, every specimen should fall into one of the three grades. Dealers and auctioneers, however, are not content to use just three grading levels on Morgan Dollars. For example, they will grade a Morgan as MS-63, meaning (in their opinion) it is better than an MS-60 but not as good as an MS-65. They utilize every number on the scale between 60 and 70. Of course their selling prices are fixed accordingly. They charge more for an MS-63 than for an MS-60. Intermediate grading is a problem for investors. Any coin bought at an intermediate grade is a question mark in terms of resale. The dealers do not always agree on the standard grades, and their agreement on intermediate grades is nil. This is hardly surprising, even if we assume that each dealer is wholly objective in grading. It is not too difficult to determine whether a Morgan belongs at MS-60 as opposed to MS-65. But if you have a choice of putting it into MS-60, MS-61, MS-62, MS-63, MS-64, or MS-65, that is quite another matter. The fact of the matter is that dealers nearly always buy these intermediate grade specimens at the price they pay for the next lowest standard grade. An MS-63 will be bought as an MS-60. An MS-67 will be bought as an MS-65. You pay a premium when you buy but you do not receive a premium when you sell. Hence it is very unwise to invest in intermediate grade Morgan Dollars unless you can, by some stroke of uncanny luck, get them very inexpensively. An investment portfolio of Morgan Dollars should be concentrated upon straight MS-60 specimens for which no premium has been paid. Even though these coins may be "baggy" and not the most desirable specimens available, you have the advantage that they can be resold in the same condition grade as purchased. So long as they are uncirculated, there is no argument about their grading. They cannot be uncirculated and grade any lower than MS-60.

Proof-like Specimens. Many uncirculated Morgans are described as "proof-like." This indicates a coin which is not a proof but gives the appearance of one. Usually it is an early strike from a fresh die, made before the die had an opportunity to wear down on its fine points. This term has been overworked, to the point where it is sometimes applied to any attractive uncirculated specimen. In most cases a premium is charged for proof-like Morgans. This does the investor very little good. Just as with specimens in intermediate grades, he pays a premium buying but does not receive one selling. What is proof-like is, in large measure, in the eye of the beholder. It is generally in a seller's eye much more frequently than a buyer's. Once again we suggest that you stay with ordinary MS-60 specimens.

Toned Specimens. More toned specimens of Morgan Dollars are in existence than of any other Silver Dollars — and the sellers never let you forget this. In any offering of 50 or 60 Morgans, you will invariably find at least a dozen referred to as "beautifully toned," "rare toning," "exquisite toning," "mirror-like toning," and a whole array of similar expressions. The colors include purple, blue, pink, yellow, gold, steel gray and various others. Toning is the result of the 10% copper content with which the silver is alloyed. Copper can take almost any color of the rainbow as it ages, as collectors of early copper Cents are aware. The color toning it achieves depends on the specific atmospheric conditions to which it is exposed over the years, and the acidity of substances with which it comes into contact. While some colors are rarer than others on Morgan Dollars, and some toned specimens are very handsome, the beginning investor should be aware that toning can be easily induced with chemicals and heat treatment. Many toned specimens on the market are not naturally toned, and it is virtually impossible to tell the difference. If collectors are willing to pay premiums for toned specimens (and some of them are), you can bet that more and more such specimens will appear on the market, the majority of them being fakes. Investors should either avoid toned Morgan Dollars or, at least, not pay any premiums for them. The presence of toning could always be used by a prospective buyer as a reason for REDUCING the valuation. It is a common practice for toned specimens to be bought at reduced prices and then sold at premiums.

If it sounds as though we are advocating the building of a basically dull, unglamorous portfolio of Morgans — we are! An investor should not try to emulate collectors. What matters to collectors is outside an investor's realm. He has to watch the prices he pays. He has to obtain salable coins that he can liquidate without any potential problems. They should be ordinary, standard uncirculated specimens without any special features that could get in the way of an appraisal or quick sale.

This is precisely how some investors outsmart themselves on Morgan Dollars. They try too hard to build a dazzling portfolio that measures up to a fine private collection. You expect to find these special specimens in a private collection, but they are out of place in an investment portfolio. They give a collection character and of course the collector may take some pride in owning specimens that are truly beautiful or out of the ordinary. For the investor it is strictly a dollars and cents proposition. He will not have a more salable property if his portfolio looks like a collector-made collection. It may be no more salable at all, and in terms of gross profits it may do considerably worse than one consisting wholly of standard MS-60 Morgans.

Roll Buying. All of the Common Date Morgans are available in rolls: 20 specimens of the same date with the same mint mark. The price is usually a bit less than 20 times the price of individual specimens, so that in itself offers an inducement. There is nothing wrong with buying Common Date Morgans by the roll, so long as you know the coins are all uncirculated. It is simply a matter of selecting the right coins for investment purchase. If you have a coin with excellent profit potential, it will have excellent potential singly or in rolls. The only advice we would give is this. A portfolio of Morgans is usually stronger when it is somewhat diversified. If you can afford to buy all the best dates, do so. If you have a choice between buying a roll of one attractive date, or single specimens of various attractive dates, we would lean toward getting different dates. In a group of well-chosen dates, you will almost certainly have more winners than losers. With a single roll you are pinning all your chances on one date, and if that date hits a snag you have a bad investment.

The percentage of increase statistics don't even tell the real story here, as there is considerable evidence of price rigging back in the 50s and early 60s. Remember, the mintages weren't generally available until 1965. It is very obvious, in studying the prices we quote in the above chart, that many prices were arbitrarily adjusted upward or downward in the 1960-1965 era as the mintage figures became better known. This should account for at least some of the fluctuation.

As you will note on all of our charts for the Common Dates, Semi-

Keys and Keys, there are coins on each chart which have distinctly "freak" pricing patterns. In the Common Dates, we would draw your attention to the 1898-O and 1904-O. The 1904-O was classed as a Key coin in 1955, despite a 3.7 million mintage, jumped to $150 in 1960 and was down to $3.75 by 1965.

There are at least two factors in these freak prices. One is that accurate mintage figures were not generally available to the hobby, and the other is that many New Orleans Mint dollars turned up in the bags of coins sold across the counter by the Treasury in 1964. This sharply deflated the market on post-1900 New Orleans strikes especially and our two "freaks" met much the same fate.

They are by no means the exceptions. A line by line check of the Common Date chart will show a substantial number of dates and mints that either remained the same or declined. These price fluctuations have resulted in the first major half decade that we have recorded for a group of Dollars, the Common Dates between 1960 and 1965.

Our flat recommendation for the Common Date group is to ignore them as an investment target, tempered with the suggestion that very careful study probably can find you some winners. Their track record is generally so poor that we cannot go along with all of the self-appointed experts who see them as the road to riches. Most of this advice is coming from dealers anxious to sell slow-moving coins rather than from a neutral corner. If you add up the original mintages for this common date group, then subtract at least three-quarters of the figure, you still have a stupendous number of coins for the market to soak up.

If we absolutely had to recommend a coin or two from this group, we would suggest going after every one of the coins — except the 1921-P. Don't accept anything but the absolute best grade you can get. The 1990 pricing is going to show these coins up to the same levels as most of the others in this group, meaning a better than average gain for them. One other late starter would be the 1878 8-tail-feather variety which is the only listing in the Common Dates with a mintage of less than a million.

The above should not be regarded as a slander against a noble race of coins. Morgan dollars rank high as collectors' items, and as relics of art and history. As investment pieces they are far less irresistible.

MORGAN DOLLARS — SEMI-KEY DATES

Year	Mintage	1955	1960	1965	1970	1975	1980	1985
1879-CC	756,000	$ 15.00	22.50	150.00	205.00	500.00	900.00	890.00
1880-CC	591,000	45.00	7.50	50.00	60.00	75.00	140.00	210.00
1881-CC	296,000	65.00	6.50	50.00	80.00	85.00	450.00	220.00
1883-S	6,250,000	5.00	5.00	16.00	55.00	310.00	450.00	575.00
1885-CC	228,000	35.00	7.50	60.00	65.00	72.00	150.00	240.00
1885-S	1,497,000	6.50	5.00	11.00	17.00	34.00	90.00	130.00
1886-O	10,710,000	20.00	12.50	20.00	18.50	95.00	250.00	380.00
1886-S	750,000	5.00	4.00	30.00	37.50	95.00	155.00	130.00
1887-S	1,771,000	2.50	2.50	20.00	17.50	36.00	110.00	75.00
1888-S	657,000	3.75	3.50	30.00	40.00	100.00	250.00	130.00
1889-O	11,875,000	11.00	9.00	5.00	15.00	32.00	120.00	100.00
1889-S	700,000	4.00	4.00	40.00	37.50	75.00	140.00	75.00
1890-CC	2,309,401	3.00	4.50	18.50	30.00	70.00	150.00	250.00
1891	8,694,206	6.50	3.00	5.00	13.00	28.00	175.00	95.00
1891-CC	1,618,000	3.75	4.50	18.50	30.00	60.00	130.00	215.00

MORGAN DOLLARS — SEMI-KEY DATES

Year	Mintage	1955	1960	1965	1970	1975	1980	1985
1891-O	7,954,529	12.50	10.00	5.00	14.00	31.00	150.00	95.00
1892	1,037,245	10.00	5.00	20.00	22.50	55.00	100.00	170.00
1892-CC	1,352,000	8.00	6.00	47.50	65.00	225.00	300.00	375.00
1892-O	2,744,000	12.50	12.50	12.00	25.00	45.00	150.00	150.00
1893	378,792	11.00	6.00	50.00	60.00	275.00	300.00	380.00
1894-O	1,723,000	10.00	10.00	17.50	62.50	215.00	500.00	550.00
1894-S	1,260,000	6.00	6.50	35.00	55.00	200.00	350.00	450.00
1896-O	4,900,000	17.50	15.00	12.00	50.00	150.00	400.00	850.00
1896-S	5,000,000	17.50	25.00	75.00	225.00	410.00	800.00	480.00
1897-O	4,004,000	11.00	10.00	11.00	40.00	125.00	300.00	460.00
1898-S	4,102,000	4.00	4.50	30.00	32.50	115.00	300.00	165.00
1899	330,846	10.00	9.00	35.00	27.50	52.00	100.00	120.00
1899-S	2,562,000	4.00	4.50	40.00	40.00	170.00	350.00	170.00
1901	6,962,813	10.00	15.00	30.00	85.00	350.00	700.00	1050.00
1901-S	2,284,000	5.00	4.50	30.00	40.00	120.00	315.00	325.00
1902-S	1,530,000	5.00	5.00	35.00	100.00	165.00	200.00	250.00
1903-O	4,450,000	275.00	500.00	40.00	40.00	47.00	200.00	260.00
1904	2,788,650	5.00	6.00	10.00	20.00	35.00	125.00	115.00
1904-S	2,304,000	8.50	12.50	92.50	95.00	465.00	800.00	950.00

MORGAN DATE — SEMI-KEY DATES

% of increase:	1955-60	14%
	1960-65	50%
	1965-70	66%
	1970-75	156%
	1975-80	99%
	1980-85	13%
overall % of increase:	1955-85	1546%

The Semi-Keys have made big gains in the last 25 years. Just as with the Common Dates, a significant number of Semi-Keys dropped between 1955 and 1960. The loss was made up by a small group of coins which rose sharply, leading to serious thinking about the possibility that the market was being deliberately manipulated. An average 3% gain for the period shows that they too were not immune to the unnerving price jockeying that was going on. While the base period gain is back in the four digit figures, it is not that significantly higher than in the old chaotic days.

Again, we have two coins with freak price histories in this chart — the 1881-CC and the 1903-O. The latter, as we explained earlier, was one of the coins that turned up in the Treasury Department's "over the counter" sales. The 5-year figures do not tell the whole story either as the coin at one time in 1963 reached $1100. The price for the 1881-CC, as well as most of the other Carson City dates, has been diluted by massive stocks of the coins that the General Services Administration sold to the public.

There are definitely some second stage bargains in the Semi-Keys, and our recommendations center on the nine low mintage listings with less than a million struck. From this group we would exempt the CC listings, leaving us five attractive prospects. The 1886-S is underpriced although it is currently in better shape than some of the others. The 1888-S is approaching parity, but still well below what it should be, and due for a 50% annual appreciation. The 1889-S turned up in the Redfield horde, but should wipe itself clean of the Redfield stain. We'd project it as a $500 coin by 1990.

It's unusual to find low Philadelphia mintages, so we have automatic affection for the 1893 and the 1899, the former at a good current price but due to move into the Key classification in the next five to ten years with a matching price rise. The 1899 is so badly underpriced that it cries for attention. The date has been manipulated, but holds all kinds of promise.

MORGAN DOLLARS — KEY DATES

Year	Mintage	1955	1960	1965	1970	1975	1980	1985
1884-S	3,200,000	$ 15.00	20.00	22.50	55.00	650.00	900.00	1075.00
1889-CC	350,000	40.00	95.00	400.00	950.00	2000.00	4000.00	4825.00
1892-S	1,200,000	45.00	125.00	250.00	1500.00	9250.00	6000.00	4425.00
1893-CC	677,000	11.00	32.50	110.00	215.00	600.00	900.00	925.00
1893-O	300,000	20.00	17.50	95.00	210.00	575.00	900.00	1150.00
1893-S	100,000	250.00	500.00	1775.00	5250.00	16000.00	20000.00	20000.00
1894	110,972	10.00	35.00	275.00	210.00	550.00	700.00	1075.00
1895	12,880	—	350.00	—	—	—	—	—
1895-O	450,000	22.00	42.50	100.00	250.00	1675.00	2000.00	2150.00
1895-S	400,000	22.00	52.50	300.00	525.00	1675.00	1800.00	975.00
1903-S	1,241,000	75.00	45.00	140.00	350.00	1775.00	1500.00	1675.00

MORGAN DOLLARS — KEY DATES

1795 % of increase:	1955-60	89%
	1960-65	270%
	1965-70	174%
	1970-75	265%
	1975-80	11%
	1980-85	-1%
overall % of increase:	1955-85	5444%

The 1892-S and 1903-S both have done quite well despite similar high mintages. The 1895 is a paradox, as mint records show that 12,000 were struck. The only specimens available are the 880 proofs. Quite possibly they were never issued, were a "bookkeeping" coin of the previous or following year or were shipped to a single buyer who recycled them into watchfobs.

We look for the 1903-S to recuperate from the drop recorded in the 1975-81 period, and are suggesting this as a top level investment. It should record a substantial gain and by 1990 be well on its way past $7500. Next best choices are the 1895-O and S, which should be doing far better than they have.

MORGAN DOLLARS — PROOF DATES

Year	Mintage	1955	1960	1965	1970	1975	1980	1985
1878-8	500	35.00	95.00	135.00	300.00	525.00	4000.00	5775.00
1878-7	500	50.00	55.00	115.00	380.00	875.00	5000.00	8350.00
1879	1,100	16.00	55.00	90.00	220.00	360.00	4500.00	6000.00
1880	1,335	13.50	50.00	85.00	220.00	360.00	4500.00	5500.00
1881	975	14.00	55.00	85.00	220.00	370.00	4500.00	5500.00
1882	1,100	13.00	50.00	75.00	220.00	345.00	4500.00	5500.00
1883	1,039	15.00	50.00	75.00	220.00	360.00	4500.00	5500.00
1884	875	16.00	60.00	80.00	230.00	360.00	4500.00	5500.00
1885	930	16.00	52.50	85.00	220.00	360.00	4500.00	5500.00

Year	Mintage	1955	1960	1965	1970	1975	1980	1985
1886	886	17.50	57.50	85.00	230.00	360.00	4500.00	5500.00
1887	710	18.50	67.50	90.00	230.00	360.00	4500.00	5500.00
1888	832	16.00	60.00	90.00	230.00	360.00	4500.00	5500.00
1889	811	16.00	60.00	90.00	230.00	360.00	4500.00	5500.00
1890	590	27.50	80.00	130.00	285.00	375.00	4500.00	5500.00
1891	650	22.50	70.00	100.00	260.00	375.00	4500.00	5500.00
1892	1,245	15.00	50.00	85.00	230.00	360.00	4500.00	5500.00
1893	792	17.50	65.00	90.00	275.00	400.00	4500.00	5675.00
1894	972	16.00	52.50	300.00	700.00	750.00	4500.00	5600.00
1895	880	225.00	625.00	3250.00	4750.00	6750.00	30000.00	32500.00
1896	762	25.00	62.50	95.00	240.00	360.00	5000.00	5500.00
1897	731	22.50	62.50	90.00	240.00	360.00	5000.00	5500.00
1898	735	22.50	62.50	90.00	240.00	360.00	5000.00	5500.00
1899	846	20.00	60.00	90.00	275.00	370.00	5150.00	5500.00
1900	912	17.50	55.00	90.00	225.00	360.00	5200.00	5500.00
1901	813	17.50	60.00	90.00	225.00	435.00	5600.00	6325.00
1902	777	17.50	62.50	90.00	240.00	360.00	5000.00	5970.00
1903	755	30.00	65.00	90.00	240.00	360.00	5000.00	5500.00
1904	650	35.00	72.50	90.00	275.00	360.00	5000.00	5500.00
1921	(36)	60.00	150.00	100.00	—	—	—	

MORGAN DOLLAR — PROOF DATES

% of increase:	1955-60	188%
	1960-65	162%
	1965-70	99%
	1970-75	49%
	1975-80	844%
	1980-85	19%
overall % of increase:	1955-85	22469%

The 1895 proof is the darling of the collector and the investor, leading the proof prices with a strong percentage of increase. We have a sleeper hiding among the statistics however that you might like to meet.

This happens to be the fact that there are actually two varieties of the 1878 7-tail-feather proofs. 200 of them have parallel arrow feathers, while the other 300 have slanting feathers. The parallel, or straight feather version is known as the Second Reverse and the slanting feather is the Third Reverse. Although both are listed on the current pricing charts at the same price, the Second Reverse proof is by far the better buy, with only two-fifths of the mintage. The Third Reverse is underpriced at that figure as well, so we'd say buy either one but prefer the Second Reverse.

These two are the second and third smallest mintages for the series, behind the estimated 36 of the 1921 proofs that were struck. The 8-tail-feather proofs rank third and are also well below their real value, so we look for all three of the 1878 proof varieties to charge hard and fast in the coming decade.

VARIETIES

The Morgan Series probably has one of the heaviest concentrations of minting varieties for any of the Dollars. Van Allen and Mallis list in their comprehensive book more than 1200 Morgan dollar varieties. Hundreds of them are being bought and sold by knowledgeable collectors and investors every day. Thanks to the Van Allen-Mallis book and supplements, a tremendous amount has been learned both about the minting process and background of some of the important — and very valuable — varieties to be found.

Some of these have gained enough recognition to be commonly listed in the major pricing guides and coin magazines. Unfortunately, with the exception of the 7 and 8 tail feather varieties, this began too recently for us to give you a price history as with the regular coins, but we will note as many of the important ones as we can.

1878: The 7 over 8 tail feather variety is commonly listed often as "7/8TF," so when you see that listing you'll know what it is. Usually the coin is not considered a good example of the variety unless it shows at least four of the 8 under-feathers.

1879: The 1879-S is listed with the Second and Third Reverses, as described earlier. The Second gets a slight nod on value.

1880: All four mints have overdates, showing all or parts of the 79 under the 80. There are a number of dies so be sure of what you are doing as prices vary markedly. The 1880-CC is found with the Second and Third Reverse at the same price.

1882: The 1882-O is found with the O punched over an S mint mark, currently cheaper than the normal mint mark. Buy, as this coin should sell for a minimum of 150% of the normal coin. There are six dies with O/S, and a number of repunched mint marks as well, that will bring a premium.

1888: The 1888-O has a hubbing variety that strongly doubles Liberty's lips. This variety demands a 15 to 25% premium.

1890: The 1890-CC has a heavy die gouge from the tail to the wreath, known as the "Tail Bar." Listed at the same price as the normal date, but worth a few dollars extra.

1900: The 1900-O has six dies with the O mint mark over a CC. These are currently listed with a $10 premium, but as with the 1882-O, they are worth about 150% of the normal coin, so buy the over mint mark at any opportunity.

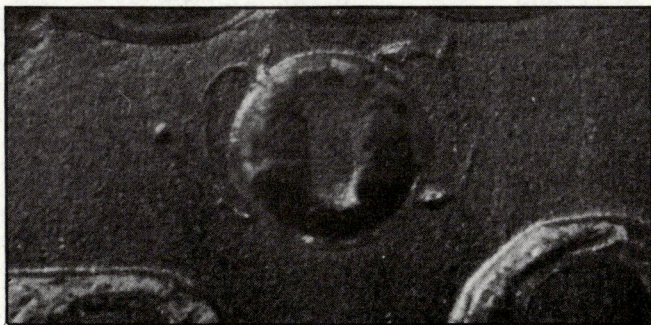

A 1900-O Morgan with O punched over CC, over mint mark.

1901: Look for the 1901-P with a strongly doubled eagle on the reverse, worth at least 50% over normal price.

There are numerous other varieties that will add 10% or more to the value of your Morgan dollars, making it well worthwhile to learn about them as they can make significant investments.

THE PEACE DOLLARS

| **OBVERSE** | **REVERSE** |

In 1921 the Peace Dollar came upon the scene, with just over a million struck at Philadelphia in December of that year and released to the public in January 1922. Production was based on replacing the 270 million silver dollars melted in 1918, and the minters went at it with vigor, registering new production records as Philadelphia struck 51 million in 1922 alone.

The 1921 strikes were a high relief design which was found to be difficult to strike properly, so the design was modified for the 1922 coins. Only a handful of proofs were made for 1921 and 1922 and none for the later years. Proof dollar production would not resume until the first Ike dollars of 1971.

The Peace Dollars were struck until 1928 when production stopped because the provisions of the Pittman Act of 1918 had been fulfilled, and the 270 million dollars that had been melted down had been restruck. The Pittman Act provided for melting a total of 350 million coins. If it had been carried through, it would have been necessary to continue striking the Peace Dollars or strike larger quantities of them. Production was resumed in 1934 when new legislation authorizing the striking of silver dollars was passed. The Peace Dollar design was continued into 1935 when a lack of need and the Great Depression spelled the silver dollar's doom. The coin was no longer needed as the Silver Act of 1934 said that paper Silver Certificates should be backed by a dollar's worth of silver, not necessarily in the form of coinage.

Production was set to resume again in 1964. Authorization resulted in the striking of 30 trial pieces at Philadelphia. All but two were immediately melted, the others held in the Mint's Office of Technology and melted at some later date. The Denver Mint was geared up for production, and struck 316,076. When Congress balked, the Mint deftly changed the status of the coins to "trial strikes," a paper change to get around the law and later ordered them melted down when President Johnson directed that production be stopped.

The coins were melted by weight. It is believed that a number of the 1964-D coins escaped from the Denver Mint by various routes, although nobody has yet come forward with any of the coins, despite increasing offers for one. The Treasury Department has taken the stand that the coins were "illegally issued," and thus remain the property of the Government subject to confiscation. However, this same classification applies to the 1913 "V" nickel and several other coins. So far there has been no active effort to confiscate them — although the coins certainly would never be returned if they were ever sent to the Mint for authentication.

If the owner is willing to risk a confrontation with Uncle Sam, a 64-D dollar is going to be a big ticket item. On today's market we would estimate that the first one to surface would likely draw a $100,000 bid, and since there are a number of dealers, collectors and investors who want the coin, the bidding is likely to go much higher.

For the investor, the Peace Dollar series is another one fraught with pitfalls. Let's look first at the Common Dates.

PEACE DOLLARS — COMMON DATES

Year	Mintage	1955	1960	1965	1970	1975	1980	1985
1922	51,737,000	$2.00	2.50	2.50	4.00	10.00	18.00	40.00
1922-D	15,063,000	2.50	4.00	5.00	6.00	11.00	30.00	45.00
1922-S	17,475,000	2.25	2.50	5.00	7.00	11.00	55.00	45.00
1923	30,800,000	2.25	2.50	2.00	4.00	10.00	18.00	40.00
1923-D	6,811,000	3.75	4.50	8.50	13.00	12.00	50.00	45.00
1924	11,811,000	2.50	2.50	3.00	5.50	10.00	20.00	42.00
1925	10,198,000	8.50	2.50	2.00	5.50	10.00	20.00	45.00
1926	1,939,000	2.25	3.50	12.50	10.00	19.00	35.00	65.00
1926-S	6,980,000	2.50	3.50	7.50	9.00	20.00	40.00	65.00

PEACE DOLLARS — COMMON DATES

% of increase:		
	1955-60	2%
	1960-65	71%
	1965-70	33%
	1970-75	75%
	1975-80	153%
	1980-85	51%

overall % of increase:	1955-80	1443%

Their overall record is nearly as bad as the Peace Dollar Common Dates, and for much the same reasons, except that for the most part the mintages for Peace Dollars average much higher than for Morgans.

The gain rate until the last ten years simply has not kept up with inflation and the interest rate, and the investor who purchased any of these dates in 1960 had to wait agonizingly long for a profit. We do not look for that situation to change radically unless the bullion price goes back up into the $30-$50 range, but there are certainly no immediate prospects of that happening any time soon.

Peace Dollars have not been affected by the melting situation except that undoubtedly a quantity of the lower grades of these common dates went to the smelters in 1980. This means that there will be a trend toward slightly scarcer low grade coins and possibly higher prices. But we have to remember that we are dealing with millions of coins, not just thousands. There is no single coin that I would pick from this group as an investment buy, but the small investor can make a relatively safe profit by buying the top grade coins and salting them away for a decade. The series is almost guaranteed to climb to a certain extent, and there is always the possibility that bullion prices may go through the roof again. If you want to gamble, and can afford it, these could be your coins.

PEACE DOLLARS — SEMI-KEY DATES

Year	Mintage	1955	1960	1965	1970	1975	1980	1985
1921	1,006,473	$6.00	11.00	30.00	35.00	115.00	245.00	255.00
1923-S	19,020,000	2.50	2.75	5.00	7.00	11.00	80.00	45.00
1924-S	1,728,000	5.00	5.50	32.50	40.00	70.00	135.00	235.00
1925-S	1,610,000	4.00	5.50	17.50	20.50	47.50	180.00	150.00
1926-D	2,348,700	5.50	8.00	15.00	12.50	18.00	120.00	70.00
1927	848,000	5.00	6.50	40.00	30.00	40.00	75.00	150.00
1927-D	1,268,900	4.00	12.00	25.00	37.50	80.00	250.00	215.00
1927-S	866,000	3.50	7.00	32.50	47.50	125.00	250.00	240.00
1928	360,649	6.00	15.00	100.00	110.00	160.00	275.00	300.00
1928-S	1,632,000	4.00	6.00	25.00	30.00	70.00	175.00	215.00
1934	954,057	4.00	6.50	35.00	25.00	42.00	75.00	130.00
1934-D	1,569,500	5.00	7.50	25.00	35.00	70.00	100.00	190.00
1935	1,576,000	4.00	7.00	25.00	18.00	110.00	60.00	85.00
1935-S	1,964,000	4.00	14.00	28.00	45.00	110.00	125.00	250.00

PEACE DOLLARS — SEMI-KEY DATES

% of increase:		
	1955-60	80%
	1960-65	281%
	1965-70	13%
	1970-75	117%
	1975-80	101%
	1980-85	18%
overall % of increase:	1955-85	3981%

I'm sure that somebody is going to ask, "A Semi-Key with a mintage of 19 Million?" It's a bit hard to believe that the 23-S would be up in this class, but considering the current prices, it has to be a jump ahead of the Common Dates. Most coins of this date are poorly struck, but a substantial quantity turned up in the Redfield hoard, two opposing factors playing on the price. The crux of the matter is that top quality strikes are rare.

We'd pick the 1928 as being underpriced for the mintage, and look for this coin to be past the $1000 mark by 1990.

It's almost as hard listing a fistful of coins with 1 million plus mintages as Semi-Keys, but they fit. This is a group with a serious up and down pricing problem although, on the average, they've done satisfactorily in the last quarter century.

PEACE DOLLARS — KEY DATES

Year	Mintage	1955	1960	1965	1970	1975	1980	1985
1934-S	1,011,000	$30.00	50.00	175.00	240.00	600.00	1350.00	1350.00
1964	30	Trial Pieces — All Melted						
1964-D	316,076	Rumored to exist, but never legally issued.						

PEACE DOLLAR — KEY DATES

% of increase:	1955-60	67%
	1960-65	250%
	1965-70	37%
	1970-75	150%
	1975-80	220%
	1980-85	0%
overall % of increase:	1955-85	4400%

Our lonesome Key has done fairly well for itself, despite a roller-coaster price situation much like the Semi-Keys. This coin, purchased in 1955, would have done better than almost any other Peace Dollar. It probably will continue to climb, although I see some challengers back in the pack (especially the 1928-P) which are likely to match or exceed the profits from this coin by 1990. This is probably going to be the first Peace Dollar to reach the five figure level.

PEACE DOLLARS — PROOF

Year	Mintages
1921	7
1922	6

Because of World War I, the Mint decided to halt production of proof dollars. When production was resumed in 1921, none were officially made, but a quantity of Morgans were struck as Proofs. Breen says a number of different figures have been alleged, ranging from 20 up to 200, with the exact quantity not known. One source lists an estimated mintage of 36, which may be an update of Breen's 1977 figures. The same work gives a total of 7 proofs for the 1921 Peace Dollar, two of them being satin finish and the other five a matte finish. One of the latter sold for $9000 in 1971 according to Breen, and we feel that today it would probably bring $50,000 to $75,000.

Six proofs were estimated for the 1922 mintage, five of them being the matte finish type of 1921 and the sixth a unique satin finish type of 1922 but markedly different than the circulation strikes for that year. Breen noted a standing offer of $15,000 for one of the known type of 1921 proofs prior to 1977 so, again these look like moderately high five figure items when one does come on the market.

VARIETIES:

Other than the high and low relief marking the first two years of issue, there were few significant varieties.

1921: The 21-P is found with abnormal reeding ("infrequent reeding") on the edge, due to the use of a collar with a smaller than normal number of grooves. Value is 10 to 15% above the normal coin.

1934: The 1934-D is found with fairly strong hub doubling on the rays above the head. Premium for this variety runs from 50 to 100% above normal value.

1935: The 1935-S has two varieties of the reverse, one with three rays below ONE, and the other with four rays. Current prices are the same, as no determination has been made of the relative rarity. Try to add at least one of each to your holdings, just to be on the safe side. They should not be difficult to find.

The 1922 Peace Dollar with Design Hub doubling of TRUST. Note that all of the Peace Dollars have the TRVST spelling. It is not a mistake, but merely an artistic use of the Greek letter, common on public buildings.

THE EISENHOWER DOLLARS

OBVERSE

REVERSE

The Eisenhower or "Ike" dollars were placed in production largely to satisfy casino operators in Nevada who needed a dollar coin to use in their slot machines. The public as a whole still had no particular interest in a dollar coin, but the Treasury Department's long range plans, which later resulted in the economy-sized Anthony dollar, were to gradually replace the expensive to print dollar bill with a more economical coin. The Ike dollar also served to satisfy public clamor for a coin to honor Eisenhower after his death. He almost replaced Washington on the quarter but tradition won out.

The coin also almost became a new 90% silver dollar to continue the traditional bullion content, but with increasing upward pressure on the price of silver, this was impractical. The silver interests were reluctantly satisfied with a silver clad coin which contained two outside layers of .800 silver bonded to an inner core of .210 silver, the remaining metal in the cladding layers and the core being copper.

THESE 40% SILVER IKE DOLLARS WERE ISSUED ONLY FROM SAN FRANCISCO AS PROOFS OR AS SPECIAL UNCIRCULATED COINS, AND NONE — REPEAT — NONE OF THE CIRCULATION STRIKES CONTAIN ANY SILVER AT ALL.

The coins issued for circulation were a copper nickel alloy clad layer on each side of a pure copper core and contained NO SILVER. We stress and repeat this point, because a good majority of the public is still convinced that all of the Ike and Anthony dollars contain silver. In our charts we have noted either AR for the 40% silver issues, or Cu-Ni for the copper-nickel issues. The Ike series is a very complex one since so many different finishes and metal combinations were struck at the three mints. You will note too, that all of the proofs (and special uncirculated coins) carry an "S" mint mark, the first regular proofs to be struck anywhere but at Philadelphia. Proof production was moved to San Francisco in 1968 when manufacture of proof sets was resumed.

Another important note is that the Special Uncirculated Ikes struck at San Francisco in 40% silver were sold in blue boxes while the 40% silver proofs were sold in brown boxes. However, do not depend on the color of the box when buying, especially the 1973-S 40% proof, as switches have been made for the much cheaper copper-nickel proof-coin.

The 40% silver coins usually have a faint coppery tinge to the edge, while the copper-nickel clad coins have a distinct copper core showing (beware of plated coins).

Several specific changes were made in the Ike dies. There were also several other unannounced changes which we will discuss later. For example, the 1971-S 40% Uncirculated coins are low relief and the 1972-S 40% Uncirculated coins are high relief. All of the copper-nickel issues from 1971 are low relief, as are the 1972-D Denver issues, but the 1972 coins struck at Philadelphia have a high relief as well as a low relief version.

EISENHOWER DOLLARS — COMMON DATES

Year	Mintage	1975	1980	1985
1971	47,799,000	$1.50	1.50	2.15
1971-D	68,587,424	1.50	1.50	2.15
1972	75,890,000	1.50	1.50	2.15
1972-D	92,548,511	1.50	1.50	1.75
1974	27,366,000	8.00	1.50	1.85
1974-D	35,466,000	8.00	1.50	1.85
1976 I	4,019,000	—	2.75	3.00
1976 II	113,318,000	—	2.00	2.50
1976-D I	21,048,710	—	2.00	2.85
1976-D II	82,179,564	—	2.00	2.50
1977-	12,596,000	—	2.00	2.25
1977-D	32,983,006	—	2.00	2.00
1978	25,702,000	—	1.80	1.50
1978-D	33,012,890	—	1.80	1.50

We have not attempted to give you statistics on percentage of increase for this series as the coins are of such recent origin. The mintages obviously are substantially higher than those for the earlier *silver* dollars, and, being a base metal, do not have the bullion incentive to force prices up. As an example of the this, the $8 figure in the 1975 listings for the 1974 coins merely reflects the premium placed on issues as they first appeared, fueled somewhat by the fact that mintages dropped significantly although, at the time of compiling, the 1975 figures the total mintages for 1974 would not have been known.

The only coin we would recommend in the Common Dates as a

potential investment would be the low mintage 1976 Type I coins. The Type I may be identified by the fact that all the letters "O" on both sides of the coin are thick and round, while all of the letters "O" on the Type II are tall and thin, with a much larger center hole. The change was made because the Type I design was not striking up well and you will find it extremely difficult to locate top grade, well struck coins. Accordingly, any that you do find will ultimately be demanding a really worthwhile premium and are well worth buying now. By 1990, we would expect such a coin to bring $45 to $55.

SEMI-KEYS

Year	Mintage	1975	1980	1985
1971-S AR	11,133,764	$4.75	3.50	6.50
1972-S AR	4.004,687	5.00	3.50	10.00
1973	1,769,258(a)	12.00	8.50	10.25
1973-D	1,769,258(a)	12.00	8.50	10.25
1973-S AR	1,883,140	8.50	4.50	10.25
1974-S AR	1,900,000	13.00	3.50	8.00
1976-S AR I	11,000,000(b)	—	4.75	8.50

(a) More minted, but released only in sets, the remainder destroyed.
(b) Total minted, but not all released.

Here we are looking once more at price more than mintage in determining which coins to put in the Semi-Key class. As you will note, we have all of the 40% silver issues plus the two coins with artificially low mintages because none were produced for circulation. The Ike dollar was not a well liked coin, particularly because the circulation strikes contained no silver. There was almost no incentive to use them and despite repeated efforts of the Treasury Department, they could not be popularized. Again we have not attempted to quote percentages.

The most interesting coin in the Semi-Keys for the investor is the 1974-S 40% Special Uncirculated which shows a 50 cent drop because of a less than 17,000 increase in the number minted over the 73-S. For the small investor, this may not seem significant, but it could add up for the person who picks up a hundred of them, undoubtedly doing so at a discount to begin with.

The 72-S has shown the most spectacular gain in the past six years, but primarily because of the leveling apparent here. In 1990, the prices on this chart will be even closer than they are now. The 72-S has climbed because of the sharp drop from the 1971 mintage, not because it is any rarer than the other mintages below the two million mark. Part of the cause, too is that prices for Special Uncirculated dollars were raised by the Mint in the later years of production.

PROOFS

Year	Mintage	1975	1980	1985
1971-S AR	4,265,234	11.00	7.00	8.00
1972-S AR	1,811,631	12.00	20.00	13.50
1973-S Cu-Ni	2,760,339	12.00	4.00	7.00
1973-S AR	1,013,646	20.00	73.00	87.50
1974-S Cu-Ni	2,612,568	10.00	4.00	5.00
1974-S AR	1,306,579	13.00	28.00	25.00
1976-S Cu-Ni I	2,845,450	—	12.00	6.50
1976-S Cu-Ni II	4,149,730	—	3.50	4.25

Year	Mintage	1975	1980	1985
1976-S AR I	4,000,000*	—	7.50	10.00
1977-S Cu-Ni	3,251,152	—	4.00	4.00
1978-S Cu-Ni	3,127,781	—	11.00	9.50

*Total minted, but not all issued.

Here for the first time we have proof mintages exceeding the million mark, unfortunately with a corresponding lack of quality. The early proof Ikes especially would rate only "proof-like" when compared with some of the low mintage European proofs. This is not a new criticism, but one we have made a number of times in our writings, based on visits to all three of the U.S. Mints and a dozen of the European Mints.

The one "key" coin of the Ike series is the 1973-S 40% silver proof, which had been up around the $120 mark during the height of the bullion boom, and is still quoted by some sources at the $115 level. This is the one on which we advised earlier about careful checking, to make sure it isn't a doctored Cu-Ni proof.

All of the proofs are high relief, which makes them handy to compare with the similar high relief and low relief coins mentioned earlier.

VARIETIES:

1971: The 1971-S and 1972-S 40% silver proofs have a peculiar variety in that a number of dies were made with the serifs missing from the base of the left leg of the R in LIBERTY. These were nicknamed the "Peg-leg" Ike. The variety was originally explained by the Mint as resulting from the serifs being polished off the die but, for the first time in print, we can say flatly that this was *not* the case. Most likely, they are the result of changes in the Master Die or later tools made by the then Chief Engraver, Frank Gasparro. Substantial numbers of dies were produced in 1971 and a lesser number in 1972; so that the variety is not scarce but as an intentional die change. It should demand at least a 25% premium.

1972: See explanation above.

Example of a special uncirculated 40% Silver Ike Dollar.

1974: Several Ike 40% proofs and 40% uncirculated coins are known with repunched mint marks, the first reported for the entire Ike series. Values are high, so check the mint mark closely. Proofs have a mintage per die of about 3000, severely limiting the number of coins struck with a variety die.

THE ANTHONY DOLLARS

| OBVERSE | REVERSE |

Although NONE of the Anthony Dollars contain any silver, we are including them in this book on silver dollars, as they *are* direct descendants of the Silver Dollar. The last U.S. Dollar coins with any silver are the 1976 issues from San Francisco, as noted earlier.

The Anthony Dollar, with the portrait of Susan B. Anthony, a champion of womens' rights, was controversial from its inception. It was intended by the Treasury as a circulating coin, carrying out the intent of long range plans to replace the multitudes of paper dollars with coins, which are both cheaper to produce and have a much longer service life. The coins have a projected life of 15 years, while a paper dollar usually lasts less than eight months.

Unfortunately, a number of judgmental blunders were made in designing and producing the Anthony Dollar. From the inception of the plan to replace the normal size Ike Dollars with a "mini" dollar, the coin has drawn criticism from all areas. Some of the supporters of the womens' rights movement claimed the coin was rejected by the public because it pictured a female, but it had other, more serious, strikes against it. More damaging was the fact that the coin was nearly identical in size to the long established quarter and smaller than the half dollar. This created a psychological barrier to its use as well as causing great confusion in commerce, where the two coins were often confused in making change.

The Anthony Dollar shared with the Ike Dollar the taint of bad likeness of the individuals pictured, lacking the artistic verve of some of our earlier coins. Both rank high on our list of visually unsatisfactory coins. Frank Gasparro had proposed a design using a Miss Liberty based on the original 1794 Flowing Hair Dollar, but was overruled by a Congress intent on honoring a celebrated female.

Production in 1979 exceeded 760 million, and when the first coins were released, there was a minor flurry among collectors rushing to get examples of them. The public exhibited a wholly disinterested reaction and the vast majority of the 1979 dated coins have never left the vaults of the Federal Reserve Banks where they are stored. A minimum of 25 million were struck at each of the three mints in 1980, and only enough coins to fill the mint sets and proof sets were struck in 1981, making this a three year coin.

Before the demise of the Anthony Dollar in 1981, efforts were underway to both change the alloy to one containing silicon — which would give the coin a browner color — and to replace the traditional eagle on the reverse with a large numeral "1," but these efforts failed.

There is only one significant coin in the series, and that is the 1979-S proof with what has become known as a Type II mint mark. In the summer of 1979, the single letter punch which was used to impress the letter into all "S" Mint dies broke, and Chief Engraver Gasparro was ordered to make a new one (along with a "D" punch to replace the damaged punch then in use.)

The old punch, which had been in use since some time prior to 1955 when the San Francisco Assay Office closed, and which was returned to service in 1968 when it reopened, had worn badly. Proof coins of 1977, 1978 and 1979 show the distinct deterioration of the punch, to the point where the mint mark was little more than a shapeless "blob" with a faint trace of an S on top of it. This, with the introduction of the new punch, automatically became the Type I mint mark. We had complained several times in our writings about this, urging the Mint to replace the punch, and Gasparro is quoted as responding by saying that he was "not about to change the mint mark and provide collectors with a new variety." Fate, in the form of a broken punch, was kinder to collectors.

The new punch has a very clear, distinct and markedly different "S." Depending on the force used to drive the punch into the die, it shows an unmistakable indentation in both the upper and lower loops, with a light punch actually showing the field extending into the center of the loops, such as we have not seen on any proof coins since the mid or early 70s.

There is a key point of identification that distinguishes the Type I and II mint marks. The Type I has straight edges at the front and back of the letter, at the point where it meets the coin field. The Type II has clear notches at the opening of both the upper and lower loops, breaking the straight line, so that a glance with a magnifying lens will easily identify it.

Determining the difference is important, because the Anthony Dollar with the Type II mint mark is the "key" coin of this series. The Mint acknowledged officially that about 500,000 were struck. However, not all of them were delivered to collectors, and we believe that some were destroyed. We are estimating that the delivered mintage was around 350,000, making this the lowest mintage proof coin of ANY denomination since 1955. This places the coin on a par with the 1909-S VDB cent which had a mintage of 484,000 and other low mintage coins.

ANTHONY DOLLARS

Year	Mintage
1979-P	360,222,000
1979-D	288,015,744
1979-S Pr	3,677,175
1979-S	109,576,000
1980-P	27,610,000
1980-D	41,628,708
1980-S Pr	3,547,030
1980-S	20,482,000

ANTHONY DOLLARS

Year	Mintage
1981-P	*
1981-D	*
1981-S Pr	4,000,000 (Estimate)
1981-S	*

*Minted only for inclusion in Mint Packaged Sets.

VARIETIES:

1979: Type I and Type II Mint Marks, as noted above. Mintage for the Type I appears to be about 3,177,000, which will probably be the second lowest mintage proof dollar for the Anthony series and make it a worthwhile buy as well.

1980: A proof 1980-S die has been discovered which shows either a repunched S over S, or possibly S over D. Value is estimated at $1,000.

And so ends the saga of the U.S. Dollar, which began in 1794 with a crude design, and ended in 1981 with a design which some have labeled equally as crude. We would certainly not say that this is the end of the U.S. Dollar coin, since, as we have shown in this brief history, the Dollar has seen worse times and always succeeded in rallying itself for a comeback.

WHAT DO YOU WANT IN YOUR INVESTMENT DOLLARS?

We will presume you have decided to make your silver dollar investments in collector coins rather than bullion coins. The next step is then to select the specific dollars in which you want to invest. Selection is the vital key to investment success, as some silver dollars are certain to score greater value gains in the coming years than others. That much we know for a fact; the rate of price increase always varies from coin to coin. Careful selection will give you the silver dollars with the best potential for substantial price increases. Random selection vastly diminishes your opportunity for gaining a worthwhile profit. Even if you have the financial resources to buy one uncirculated specimen of EVERY silver dollar ever struck, this would not be as strong a portfolio as one consisting entirely of the strong potential gainers. Some silver dollars, like some coins in all groups from half cents onward, simply do not have inviting growth prospects at the present time. They are either overpriced or fully priced, in relation to their availability. They will eventually increase in value, perhaps very significantly, but these increases are not apt to occur until far into the future — too far for smart investing.

There is no mystery about the qualities to look for, in any silver dollar, in arriving at a decision on whether it should be bought for investment. Certainly, some intangibles are involved, which nobody can predict. If the coin market enters one of its periodic eras of enormous prosperity during the next several years, it is entirely possible that ANY silver dollars will bring an investment return. However, investment strategy must be founded upon events that are most likely to take place. A sound investment strategy means profits even if the overall coin trade is not riding high.

In a sense, every dollar from the 1790s to 1930s is a candidate for your investment capital. They should all be examined, or at least those which fall into your budget range. The investor should not begin with preconceived notions. One of these, which has been widely promoted by some coin investment analysts, is that silver dollar investment centers wholly upon the Morgan and Peace dollars. Such is simply not the case. The investment quality of other silver dollars, especially the Trade and Seated Liberty designs, should be obvious from their price histories. The Morgan and Peace dollars are more in evidence, because they are more common on the whole. This can easily lead one into ignoring their predecessors. Every series of silver dollars contains dates with investment potential.

Another preconceived notion, which should likewise be dismissed, is that the current value range of a silver dollar has some bearing on its investment potential. There are persons (new to investing in silver dollars, obviously) who believe that $1,000 coins are automatically better investments than $75 ones, or vice-versa. There is no "right" price range for investment coins. The attractive investment dollars include some of very high current price, medium price, and many of modest price. In investing, the only important factor is rate of growth. If a dollar bought for $75 climbs to $150 after five years, it has been a better investment than a $1,000 specimen which gains to $1,500. The fact that the latter gained $500, while the former gained only $75, is immaterial. The less-costly coin doubled in price, while the other did not. It was the better investment. Ten specimens of that coin, at an investment of $750, would have climbed to the same value — $1,500 — as the one expensive coin. This example is given solely for the purpose of making a point: examine the coin and its growth potential, rather than attaching any importance to its current price range.

The following is a summary of some things to look for — and not look for — in silver dollars under consideration for investment. Above all, do not be unduly influenced by one single factor without taking all factors into account. There may be offsetting factors in any given coin, for example a very attractive low mintage figure, but a current market price which classifies the coin as "fully priced" or perhaps even "overpriced." In that event, the low mintage is no longer so appealing.

Also: read this entire book before buying any silver dollars for investment. The present chapter will be informative for you, but the information it contains must be supplemented with other advice and suggestions elsewhere in the book.

LOW MINTAGE. One of the more obvious considerations, in making an investment selection, is the coin's mintage total. This is the official figure recorded by the U.S. mint, or one of the branch mints (as the case may be), stating the total number of specimens produced with that date and mint mark. Mintage figures are available for nearly all silver dollars, and are given in this book. Mintage figures are a tool for the investor, really his most useful tool next to value performance. While they are not absolutely foolproof for use in making investment selections, they do at least represent concrete information rather than hunches, guesses, predictions, or theories.

How good are mintage figures?

In terms of showing quantities manufactured, they are probably close to 100% accurate. Some margin for error always exists with statistics of any kind, but it is unreasonable for an investor to doubt the mintage figures. Some parties claim that certain mintage figures must be grossly inaccurate, as they bear no resemblance to the value of the coin. In these instances, the disparity is undoubtedly caused by events transpiring after the coin was manufactured, and is not indicative of inaccuracy in the mintage figures. If the government held a large portion of the minted quantity in storage, for example, this would explain a high market price on a silver dollar with relatively high mintage. The mintage figures are production totals only. They do not take into account the number of specimens placed in reserve as opposed to those channeled into circulation. Large quantities of the Carson City, Nevada, silver dollars were withheld by the government in the 1870s and 1880s for the purpose of backing the Silver Certificate paper notes. Such notes could be turned in to Federal Reserve Banks in exchange for their face values in silver dollars. It was therefore necessary to maintain a large supply of silver dollars in readiness, in the event that some economic condition might spark a wholesale "cashing in" of Silver Certificates.

Many potential investors are misled by the term "low mintage," which frequently appears in items of investment literature on silver dollars and other collector coins. Low mintage is relative; it is a coin to coin situation. There is no way of placing a numerical definition on low mintage, at least not for the investor. If a hobbyist owns a silver dollar struck in only 10,000 specimens, he can take great satisfaction in having a coin which is undeniably scarce or even rare. That same coin may not be suitable for investment at the moment, and hence its low mintage is meaningless to the investor. On the other hand — odd though this will surely seem to the beginner — some silver dollars struck in the millions of specimens are attractive for investment because of their "low mintage." From a collector's standpoint, these are not low mintage coins. From an investor's, they are — for special reasons. A silver dollar is referred to by investors as a "low mintage date" (or "low mintage mint mark") if its mintage figure is lower than that of silver dollars selling for as much or more. It is low mintage under the circumstances; it is low mintage from a mintage vs. price perspective. It is not necessarily low mintage from a numismatic viewpoint, and it might not belong in the collection of someone collecting low mintage silver dollars. The investor looks at mintage figures in terms of the information they can provide on future value growth. That is all he wants to learn from mintage figures. But he must learn HOW to learn it, and that means comparing mintage figures against current selling prices and looking for inconsistencies.

Ideally, all silver dollars — all coins of all types — should carry market values that relate directly to their availability. A coin which is 10% scarcer than another should be worth 10% more. This is particularly true of silver dollars from the same groups, such as Seated Liberties of the 1850s, Morgans of the 1880s, Peace Dollars of the 1920s. The demand for all dates (and mint marks) should be reasonably equal, from coin to coin; therefore the prices should be a mirror-like reflection of availability. We know, however, that in actual practice this does not turn out to be the case. Values are not a true indication of availability. Availability remains more or less constant, on the great majority of silver dollars, but relationships in value from one coin to another do not. There are various causes for this, including the publicity of a gala auction sale, or reports speculating that a certain date or mint mark is really scarcer than anyone believes. Whatever the specific causes may be, in any given case, the fact is that some dollars become underpriced in relation to their mintage figures; others become fully priced (that is, worth just about what they should be); others reach the point of being overpriced. These fluctuations form the basis for investment. The investor selects the silver dollars which are underpriced at the time he buys, restricting himself entirely to such specimens. This strategy works, nine times out of ten, because few silver dollars remain underpriced very long. Buyers notice that these coins are underpriced and a flurry of activity surrounds them, sending them upward. Within five years, most underpriced silver dollars advance sufficiently in value to return a worthwhile investment profit. By then, of course, other dollars have become underpriced, so the investor can make fresh choices and continue indefinitely. The market never reaches a point of evening up with all silver dollars worth the prices they should be worth, due to the many positive and negative forces that are constantly at work.

Thus, as you can see, investment choices depend very much on the question of availability. If a coin is priced low because of easy availability, you do not want to consider it for investment. If it is priced low as a result of being truly underpriced, it is an investment coin. Naturally the mintage figures reveal nothing about quantities melted or otherwise lost over the years. These subsequent events, which occurred after the coin was released into circulation, could have contributed to one date or mint mark being scarcer than another.

What about these "unknown factors?"

On the whole, they have been overrated.

Some investment analysts have seized upon the unknown factors and used them to develop original or unique investment theories. Since an investment analyst cannot create anything original out of mintage figures or current selling prices, the unknown factors provide the only sphere for speculation. Unfortunately, most of what has been written constitutes nothing beyond personal opinion or guesswork, and is of no real value to an investor. One investment analyst tips off a certain silver dollar because he BELIEVES it to be much scarcer than the mintage figure indicates; another analyst tips a different dollar. There are even those who go to the extreme of estimating quantities in existence, and making breakdowns on quantities held by collectors as opposed to those owned by dealers. It is understandable that an investment analyst should feel compelled to offer something to the public that other investment analysts are not. He should appear to have useful information that is not generally available elsewhere, something beyond mintage figures and prices which anyone can obtain. He should appear to have conducted some personal research and investigation — in other words, he should give the appearance of having worked for his money, whether that money comes by way of being an investment broker or publisher of a "hot tips" circular. That would all be well and good, but for one problem. The most dedicated, hard laboring individual in the world cannot gather such information, because it is just not obtainable. There are records of totals minted; there are not records of totals in existence. Any speculation along that line is just that: speculation. It is not fact, as it cannot be supported by evidence. With silver dollars scattered through millions of hands, not only in this country but throughout the entire world, no one will even come reasonably close in their estimates of specific quantities in existence for a given date. My guess is as good as yours. You stand about as much chance of being accurate as do any of the investment analysts.

There is only one possible approach, and far from a satisfactory one, to making judgments on quantities in existence. This is called "market watching." There is no way of knowing who owns what — or how much of it — but when a coin is sold it may receive some publicity. Publicity comes in the form of advertisements in coin collector publications as well as listings in dealers' and auctioneers' catalogues. These are called "recorded sales," and the recorded sales of any given dollar forms the basis of its current market price. Keeping track of the frequency with which a particular dollar is sold gives some indication of its availability on the market. There are vast shortcomings to this approach, however. It is far more useful in establishing values, than in estimating quantities in existence. If we have records of 300 sales for the same coin within a six month period, we can average out these prices and arrive at a very reliable figure. As far as availability is concerned, we do not know how many specimens were sold across the counter in coin shops without publicity, or how many were sold at coin shows. Most collector-to-dealer sales leave no trace, as no kind of advertising is involved. Thus the number of specimens actually circulating throughout the market, in that six month period, might have been two, three, or ten times the "recorded" total. Furthermore, it would be a task of monstrous proportions, to actually keep abreast of every single recorded sale. Silver dollars are sold by dealers and auctioneers, too, in other parts of the world. Then, added to the problem, there is the fact that many coins are sold twice within a short period of time. If we recorded 300 sales of a given coin within six months, we would not know what percentage of that total represented DIFFERENT SPECIMENS and which are DUPLICATES or even TRIPLICATES. As you can see, this kind of information is virtually meaningless to use as a basis for estimating quantities in existence. It is not even reliable in indicating quantities sold.

It would be a great help to know the quantities in existence, even roughly. But we do not and it is pointless for anybody to pretend otherwise. Speculation on the subject does more harm than good, as it leads one astray from the mintage figures. Use the mintage figures as your primary investment tool. Do not take them lightly. The fact that they are available to anyone, not just a select group, is no reason to downgrade their usefulness. Quite the opposite! History has clearly shown us (as in 1979/80) that investments based on speculation, unfounded theories, etc., lead to wildly unrealistic prices that require years to readjust to sane levels. There is no messiah in coin investment. Nobody has a plan or approach that works better than anyone else's. The logic presented in this book is the simple, sound logic that sensible investors have been using for many years. We have not developed it; thousands of investors developed it from trial and error. It is the only logic that consistently works. It is the only logic that reduces risk while still providing for good growth potential. It is not "gambler's logic." It is not, moreover, the sort of logic that analysts or tipsters like to furnish, because it is not original enough to make them appear brilliant.

RAPIDLY RISING PRICES. Anyone who begins investing in silver dollars without first learning the correct techniques is likely to be over-influenced by rapidly rising prices. Certainly there are fields of financial investment in which a quickly rising price would be a deciding factor. This would indicate strength, popularity, and a bright future. Coin investment is different in this respect than most types of investing. The best silver dollars for investment are not necessarily those currently gaining the most in value. In fact, the opposite is often the case. A silver dollar soaring in market value might be fully priced or overpriced, which would rule it out as an investment for the present time. A sluggish dollar which has not shown appreciable price increases for several years might have some "catching up" to do, in relation to the rest of the field. These are the "sleepers" — sleeper meaning, in this case, a coin that appears to be totally dormant but is due to rise from its slumber. If a fully priced silver dollar is rising rapidly in market price, the investor should assume (and most times will be correct) that it is headed for a leveling off, a period of a year or perhaps several years when it shows no really impressive increase. It would be unreasonable to expect such a coin to continue at the present pace, if it has, in reality, nowhere to go. It could possibly rise to the degree of being somewhat overpriced, but that would not yield an investment profit. You need a coin that has strong potential of doubling in value within five years to produce a worthwhile profit. Any coin which is now fully priced does not have this potential under normal circumstances. The words "normal circumstances" are important. Quite a few dollars that were fully priced in 1975 could have been bought at that time, and would have returned very handsome profits by 1980. This was the result of strong overall advances in coin prices — dollars and everything else — in those five years. It cannot be depended upon to happen again. In an average coin market year, coin values ON THE WHOLE (taking into account all collector coins of all denominations) advance by about 10%. This is due partly to inflation and partly to a greater number of collectors coming into the hobby and competing for the available supply of coins. Obviously the supply cannot be increased, so the higher demand means higher prices. During that same year, some coins will score a 20% increase, and a few will possibly increase by 30% or more. There will also be a certain number of coins which show no price change, and some that decline in price. All this can happen in a normal year. As an investor your goal is to select the silver dollars that will increase in value by 20% or 30% in at least FOUR out of the NEXT FIVE years. You cannot anticipate a steady rate of increase on any coin, over a five year period. Even a great investment coin may have a slow year, but will then rebound. You can, however, tell which silver dollars are the best bets for scoring the largest overall increases at the conclusion of a five year holding period. (Just to clear up one point: some readers of this paragraph will inevitably ask, "How can inflation add to the price of a coin, when it was manufactured many years ago?" It does, and to almost the same extent as any currently manufactured products. This is because all the variables involved in the "overhead" of the coin business increases in price: advertising, shop rent, telephone, labor, supplies, postage. The coin dealer has only one alternative to offset these increases, the same as that of every other retail merchant. He raises his prices.)

So, be cautious about those quick gainers. The people who bought them a few years ago are making money on them. YOU want to select coins that have most of their growth potential ahead of them. There are numerous silver dollars in that class, as we will show in this book.

BUYING TRENDS. These do occur from time to time, and investors who bought the "trendy" coins are obviously in a very favorable position. Two points need to be made about trends:

(1) They are neither as frequent or as influential as you would be led to believe, from reading some of the available coin investment literature.

(2) Many more investors have lost money from guessing wrong on trends, than those who have made money by guessing right.

Trends are hard to predict. Not only their focus but their time duration is a matter of chance. The coin market gives the appearance of having more trends than it in fact does. This is because many trends are merely in the eye of the beholder. A certain coin or group of coins starts showing impressive gains. Those who review the market for coin publications remark on this activity, and suddenly everyone is thinking "trend." By the time news of the trend has circulated, the buying may have waned and there is no trend any longer.

The word "trend" is misused in relation to silver dollar investment. One often reads statements such as, "A real trend seems to be developing for the 1889 Philadelphia dollars in MS-60." While probably given with well-meaning intent, such observations indicate a lack of understanding of the coin market. When a given coin continues to advance in value, this does not constitute a buying trend or shift in collector emphasis. It is a normal, predictable readjustment of value that in nearly all cases is occurring because the coin was underpriced to begin with. There is no sudden extra popularity for the coin. The situation is not comparable to — for example — commemorative half dollars selling brisker than they did a few years ago. With groups of coins, there can be recognizable trends. With individual coins within a group, there is seldom any logical explanation (with one exception, which we'll get to) for calling a rising price a "trend." Nobody is going to build an entire collection of 1889 Philadelphia dollars. At best, this coin will be purchased by the date-set collectors who want as many different date and mint mark combinations as they can get for Morgan Dollars. It will also be bought, more or less randomly, by some collectors of type coins — who just want a Morgan Dollar and are unconcerned about the date. Beyond that, what special trend could there be? Why would collectors want this particular date more than another one?

There is, however, an exception, and it provides the only clear cut example of what could be called a "trend" within the silver dollar market. This involves the coins of subsidiary mints and is particularly noticeable with Morgan Dollars from Carson City and New Orleans. The Carson City and New Orleans Morgans have a habit of going through phases of strong upward movement, followed by a period of stagnation followed by renewed climbs. Some sort of trendy buying (and selling) has to be the cause as there is no other logical explanation. The price movement of these coins, or at least some of them, is not in line with the Philadelphia Morgans. The great publicity given to Carson City dollars creates extra glamor for them and might appear to be the catalyst for buying trends. In fact, if this is indeed the case, it would be the investors and not hobbyists who are responsible. If any numismatist collects Carson City Morgans to the exclusion of all other Morgans, he is following a lonely road. For the vast majority of silver dollar collectors, Carson City strikings are something to be included in one's collection — not to constitute a collection in themselves. This means that collector demand is really no greater for the Carson City dollars than for any others, leaving one to conclude that periods of upsurging prices are brought about by investors.

The buying trends that occur on Carson City and New Orleans Morgans have reached the point of being reliable enough to be trustworthy for an investor. The fact that they do command attention — no matter where it derives from — gives them added investor appeal, and the buying trends help rather than hinder investment strategy.

Aside from this one instance, the effort to predict trends and profit from them usually proves fruitless. A popular method for investment analysts to predict trends is to select one group of dollars, such as Seated Liberty, as being ripe for strong across-the-board buying increases. Many impressive sounding arguments can be advanced to support such theories. One group of dollars is underpriced on the whole vs. other groups; one is more historical; one has better designing; and so on. Even if these points are entirely valid, the truth is that collectors seldom change their buying habits on this large a scale. All silver dollars are old. None have been struck since 1935. They have existed on the coin market long enough to be exposed to generations of collectors, and the viewpoints toward them are not likely to change very much. The current ratio of collectors for each group (Flowing Hair, Draped Bust, Liberty Seated, Morgan, Peace) is just about the same as it was 10, 20, 30 and 40 years ago. It does not change more than fractionally even over a long period of time. Economics is one of the reasons. Collectors collect what they can afford. There are fewer buyers for Flowing Hair and Draped Bust dollars as these coins are expensive. The majority of new collectors coming into the hobby are not rich, and they gravitate toward the groups that comprise coins they will be able to safely afford.

An excellent case could be made for Seated Liberty dollars being on the verge of widespread price increases. Coin by coin they are scarcer than the Morgan or Peace dollars. They are older and, if that matters, more historical. They were designed by the most famous artist who ever worked on U.S. coins, Christian Gobrecht. Their current prices are low, in relation to mintage figures, if you use the Morgan series as a barometer of silver dollar values. Every sign would seem to point toward an imminent upward climb in the whole Seated Liberty group. Yet we know that the best to be expected is a modest increase. The lofty increase which these coins deserve is nothing but a dream. They deserved it 40 years ago. They deserved it 20 years ago, and it has yet to materialize. They do not sell for the prices at which they would sell, if all things were equal. Why? Because all things are not equal in coin collecting and especially in the demand for silver dollars. The new collectors find arrays of Morgan and Peace dollars in their local coin shops, and that is what they start collecting — unconcerned that any other groups exist. Some Seated Liberty dollars are good investment choices at the present time, but the series as a whole is likely to remain underpriced for a long while to come. The late Kamal Ahwash showed the world that Seated Liberty coins had tremendous research and collecting potential, that the number of die varieties had only begun to be identified. Unfortunately his voluminous writings did much more to stimulate the interest in low denomination Seated Liberty coins than the higher denominations.

DATES AND/OR MINT MARKS TIPPED BY ANALYSTS. As you have probably already surmised from reading the above, our advice on "tipped" coins is to approach with caution. If the coin does not meet the usual qualifications of a sound investment dollar, it does not become any more appealing as the result of receiving an analyst's recommendation. This becomes all the more evident when one stops to consider the motives and causes behind the "tip." For one thing, the analyst is required to find coins for tipping. If he does not find new selections regularly, the public loses interest in him and switches its attentions to someone who keeps tipping coin after coin. Often, the coins recommended for investment purchase are those which the analyst (who also runs a brokerage service) happens to have in stock at the moment. A plausible sounding case can be made for almost any silver dollar, and if the analyst has a dozen BU rolls in his vault you can be certain he will try hard to come up with something. The analyst does not have a direct line to any exclusive information. If he has a telex, he receives his information a little sooner than you do in the weekly coin magazines. But the difference of a few days makes no difference whatsoever in long-range investment planning. Aside from that he has no advantage over you, if you keep informed about silver dollars and the market.

DIE VARITIES. These are fine if the die variety is universally recognized and if the specimen you buy shows it distinctly. As with all series of U.S. coins, there are many minor die varieties to be found among silver dollars. They are perfectly acceptable for a hobbyist who wants a representative collection, but their investment potential is doubtful. If you are paying a premium because of the variety, you run the risk that the coin's value could slide back to that of a normal specimen by the time you sell. This happens repeatedly with varieties. They are an esoteric group of coins with no real firm foundation of support. Only the arch specialists want them. There will be perhaps one buyer who seeks out the die variety, for every hundred buyers who simply want that date — whether they get a die variety or non-variety specimen. Die variety collectors will never even come near challenging the ranks of date collectors.

PEDIGREED COINS WITH ANA (AMERICAN NUMISMATIC ASSOCIATION) PAPERS. Yes, definitely. Coins that are accompanied with ANA papers are an excellent choice for investment in most cases. They bring risks of fakery and misgrading down to the absolute minimum. Generally, however, only coins in the medium to higher ranges of price are sold with ANA papers. On coins costing under $500 the dealer will not supply papers unless he received the coin with papers. He will not submit the coin to the ANA board, as the cost involved would not be offset by the added salability of the coin. Also, there is a considerable delay in receiving the coin back again, and a dealer does not want to tie up large portions of his stock in this manner. You can get your own ANA papers on these coins, but consider that you will be adding to your investment cost by doing this, perhaps as much as 20%. A person to whom you sell in the future will not expect your lower priced coins to have ANA papers, so their absence will hardly be significant. However on expensive coins you should either buy them with the ANA certification, or obtain it thereafter. If the ANA certification does not agree with the dealer's description, you have grounds for returning the coin or at least attempting to. Most dealers will accept such a coin back again, even if the deadline for returns has passed, as it is bad publicity for them to be overruled by the ANA.

AN INVESTOR'S APPROACH TO BUYING DOLLARS

This section deals with the specific steps or considerations involved in buying silver dollars, after you have used the investment strategy presented in this book to decide WHICH silver dollars to buy. Perhaps you will choose to buy some of the dollars we have ranked as "Best Bets." Perhaps your own application of our investment strategy will lead you to conclude that other dollars are more suitable for you, depending on your circumstances, budget, investment expectations, etc. In any event, the actual purchase should be treated with as much care as your overall investment planning. It, too, calls for strategy. Mistakes in buying can be just as costly as mistakes in selection. The wrong specimen of the right coin is not apt to turn an investment profit; neither is a worthy specimen of a dollar which is wrong for investment. Combine good investment judgment with good buying judgment, and you should have the right formula for investment.

To begin with, you should know precisely what you want to buy, before you buy it. There should be no decision-making of this sort in the coin shop or the auction gallery, or when scanning a dealer's advertisement. An investor cannot be a browser. He must come prepared, knowing in advance the dollars he wants to buy, and disregarding any attractive opportunities that might arise to acquire dollars not on his list. For anyone who has been (or still is) a collector or lover of coins, this is not very easy, particularly in a coin shop. Ordering from a list helps one to avoid being sidetracked by dollars he did not intend to purchase. For the beginning investor and non-collector investors in general there should be no difficulties of this sort.

Having decided which dollars you want to buy, you will then want to decide where to buy them, and how much to pay for them.

If the chosen dollars are common dates or semi-keys, there will always be numerous potential sources for them. Even in the case of most key dates, there is no real trouble finding them for sale. More coin dealers have comprehensive stocks of silver dollars than of any other U.S. coins. Even the small dealers who may have little to offer in the way of Large Cents or 3¢ Nickels have a selection of silver dollars, both bullion and numismatic.

This widespread availability of silver dollars in virtually all dates and mint marks works to your advantage. It means there is more competition for the collector's and investor's business, on the part of dealers offering these coins. Each seller knows he is not the only one from whom the buyer can buy. He cannot be unreasonable on his prices and expect to sell. Thus, the prices at any given time, for the same dollar in the same grade of condition (assuming each specimen is correctly graded), are nearly identical from one dealer to another. In buying, however, you should not assume that the price quoted by one dealer is typical of the entire market for that week. There can be individual circumstances among the dealers to cause variations in the prices of certain coins in their stock. By thoroughly checking all the published offerings, as well as coins available in local shops which may not have been advertised, you may discover that one source is particularly favorable for a certain coin. This same source may be unfavorable for another dollar. It is very rarely, if ever, the case that one dealer is consistently higher or lower in his prices than other dealers. The variations that occur are from coin to coin and are wholly attributable to personal factors. A dealer may, for example, have bought several rolls of a certain dollar at the wholesale roll price, with the intention of retailing them as rolls. If they have not sold after several weeks, he might choose to break the rolls and sell individual specimens. In doing this he can expect to begin making sales quickly, however it would be some time before all the coins are sold. To recover his investment more rapidly he may undercut the current Greysheet or teletype "sell" price. Presumably this would still leave him some reasonable margin of profit, as the purchase was made at the wholesale roll price. By reviewing the ads that appear each week in numismatic newspapers, you will find many in which special circumstances have created favorable buying opportunities. In most instances you will not know the reason for variations in price, and before very long you will cease being curious about it. You will simply buy from the dealers who have the best prices. This is not to say that you should take risks, such as buying from unknown dealers or those who do not offer a guarantee of satisfaction. All responsible dealers allow coins to be returned for refund, within a stated limit of time, if the customer is not perfectly pleased with them for any reason. You should certainly exercise this privilege when the situation calls for it.

The 1985 prices given in this book are your best general guide to the current market, insofar as they were prepared from the prices of numerous dealers. Your investment selections should, in most cases, be made on the basis of being successful in obtaining the dollar or dollars at OR BELOW the price stated in this book. This rule cannot be strictly hard and fast, however, as the inevitable time factor is involved. Coin prices change. If they did not change, investment would be impossible. The prices shown were compiled approximately two to three months before this book arrived at bookshops, owing to the various stages through which a book must pass. Even in this brief passage of time, it is possible for some values to change slightly. Then there is the question of time lapse between the book's availability and TODAY — right now. Some of the values will be the same today, as they were at the time of tabulation. Others are likely to have changed, though probably not very much. So before you resolve rigidly against paying more for any particular dollar than the sum indicated in this book, it would be wise to ascertain its current standing in the market. This can be done easily by comparing prices from one offering to another, in the advertisements of dealers (auction sale realizations should not be used for this purpose, as they have a tendency to fluctuate without discernible cause). If a dollar listed here at $300 in MS-60 is now priced above $300 by ten dealers, and not below $300 by a single one that you can readily locate, there is every reason to believe it has made a value advance within the past weeks or months. It may be impossible at that point to purchase the coin for the price quoted in this book. What should you do? One school of thought would protest that the coin is no longer favorable for investment. Their reasoning is this: you have missed the early stages of its price climb, and you would do better buying a dollar (or dollars) which has not yet started to advance. Assuming the coin has been selected with trustworthy strategy, its price advance should be acknowledged as clear evidence that it is, indeed, a good investment dollar, that it is moving as it was anticipated to move, and that it will not remain dormant for months or more following its purchase. We would recommend the purchase of such coins, even if their market prices have risen considerably beyond the levels indicated here. You need think only in terms of the length of time required for that dollar to reach its future projected price plateau. If it was projected to advance by 20% annually in a five year period, and is now doing better, it has the potential to turn a profit sooner than expected.

In all cases, we would strongly recommend that your investment selections be made utilizing the information and suggestions in this book, BEFORE you attempt an in-depth review of current dealer offerings. Otherwise confusion, and possible poor selection choices, are apt to ensue. So far as the dollars recommended for purchase in this book are concerned, these recommendations are based on a study of the market for three decades and all the various factors that can have bearing. The conclusions reached cannot be altered by a few months' worth of market activity following publication. We firmly believe that the dollars recommended will remain the best investment choices for a considerable period of time, possibly even until the next revised edition is published. This level of confidence is inspired by the fact that ALL recommendations contained in this book are based on minimum five year holding programs, and no dollar has been selected which did not appear to have excellent growth potential for the entire five year duration.

SO — read the book, make your selections (use ours or your own), check the current dealer prices, and BUY THE COIN.

How should you buy?

First, you should buy your investment silver dollars in MS-60, which (translated from numismatic jargon) means uncirculated specimens which rank as average in terms of bag marks, hairlines and nicks. They have not endured any circulation wear, but they are not as pristine and without fault as specimens grading MS-65 and MS-70. It will probably be obvious to most beginning investors that MS-60 specimens are more favorable for investment than circulated specimens (assuming one is not making a bullion-oriented investment). But are they more favorable than the better specimens grading MS-65 and MS-70? Of this it is not so easy to convince potential investors. Many beginning investors presume that the absolutely best available specimens are the logical choice.

There are several sound reasons for choosing MS-60 or "sixties."

For one thing, the price histories of MS-60 specimens are well documented. It would be difficult, if not impossible, to compile the sort of price performance charts given in this book, if the prices were based on MS-65 or MS-70. The term "uncirculated" has been used by coin dealers for over 100 years, but it is only since the 1970s that a large number of dealers have graded using MS-65 and MS-70. Prior to that time there may have been differences in selling prices between a superb "unc" and an average "unc," but seldom any difference in terminology. Hence we do not know with certainty how the MS-65 and MS-70 grades have advanced in price from year to year, or era to era. We know that they HAVE advanced, and in some cases astoundingly, but this alone is not too informative for making investment selections.

For another, the MS-60 grade is less open to dispute than MS-65 and MS-70. If the specimen is truly uncirculated — which is not too difficult to determine, even for someone who is far from an expert — it cannot be less than MS-60. Once you have established that an MS-60 dollar is indeed uncirculated, all question of its condition is settled. This is not the case with specimens grading MS-65 and MS-70. They must likewise be established as uncirculated, and then, additionally, there must be agreement between buyer and seller that they merit their grading. Instances are numerous in which a potential buyer — be it a dealer, collector, or other party — takes exception to an MS-65 or MS-70 grading and refuses to buy the coin unless the grading is reduced. When you purchase such a coin for investment, a greater level of expertise is required on your part to determine if it has been correctly graded. And even if you are fully satisfied that this is so, a prospective buyer at some future time may not share your view. This presents a serious obstacle to investing in MS-65 and MS-70 dollars. You have a coin for which you have paid a substantial premium, and the reason for that premium is a very tenuous thing which may not stand up. Buying as a hobbyist is another story. If a collector is satisfied that a coin is an MS-65 or MS-70, then the enjoyment he receives from owning it will be a sufficient return on his money — he need not convince anybody else of its grading.

Don't forget that this is not simply a matter of some prospective buyer downgrading your MS-65 to MS-60, or your MS-70 to MS-65. Today we have the phenomenon (not too welcome, but it exists and refuses to go away) of slider grading in the coin market. You will see dollars graded MS-69, MS-68, MS-67 and so on, down the line. These are "slider" grades, so called because they "slide" past the official grades recognized by the ANA. Though there is a tiny numerical difference between these grades, the difference in price is anything but tiny. An MS-64 is not worth as much as an MS-65. And, certainly, it is an easy matter for a potential buyer to claim that the coin is really MS-64. When hairs get split that fine, it's anyone's opinion. This cannot happen with MS-60 dollars. Nobody can drop them one numerical level (which would technically be AU-59, or Almost Uncirculated), because a coin is either circulated or it isn't. If the coin is definitely uncirculated, it cannot be worse than MS-60. So with MS-60 you have coins that nobody can downgrade, as they have nowhere to go.

So you have selected a certain dollar for investment purchase. You have determined to purchase it in strict MS-60 grade. You have reviewed the current dealer offerings and are purchasing at the most favorable price.

Now for the coin itself.

What do you want to learn from the coin itself? This is the final step in the buying procedure. It is by no means the least significant. Even if the preceding steps have been smoothly executed, the purchase still falls sour if there is anything wrong with the coin itself. There could be. Buying from a dealer of international recognition does not preclude such a possibility. One should never place extreme confidence in a dealer that his merchandise receives less attention than his description of it. Some inexperienced investors buy in this manner, trusting the superior knowledge of the dealer to remove all pitfalls. This can never be the case. The size of a dealer's operations could in fact work against you occasionally. If a dealer is handling thousands of coins per week, buying and selling, it is quite likely that assistants do some of the examination work. Even if he personally does it all, this sort of volume leaves a margin for error; he cannot devote the same attention to each individual coin. This is one reason why the dealers gladly extend their privilege of return with full refund, to give the customer a chance to catch any error they might have committed. Since you are not buying dollars at such a hectic pace, you can give each purchase more attention, and you should have no real difficulty deciding whether any particular coin measures up to investment status. Once again this is somewhat different than buying a coin for hobbyist motives. The hobbyist may have certain personal likes and dislikes, or foibles in his coin taste, which he can indulge to suit his pleasure. He need not think of the necessity of his coins pleasing another buyer in the future. The investor on the other hand must not consider his personal preferences, but what will ensure the coin's sale at full market value when the time arrives for "cashing in." In this respect he must not be attracted by color toning, nor ever, under any circumstances, pay a premium for a coin because of its attractive or unusual coloration. Toning, though highly prized by some collectors, is really just a freak of nature that in no way involves the minting process. In relation to cash value it is not intangible, for which some buyers will pay extra and some will not. Most dealers will not. In fact they will explain, when you wish to sell such a specimen, that most shades of color toning can be artificially induced.

You have the coin in your hand. What do you look for, how do you look?

If the coin has been ordered by mail you have some advantage in this regard, as the examination can be deferred to a perfectly tranquil moment, or can be repeated as desired (so long as one does not overstep the return-period deadline). In a coin shop, or at a show, you must first of all teach yourself to take time and not become distracted by anything. Use the dealer's lamp and, if you have not brought along you own, his magnifying glass as well. There is no breach of etiquette in this. You are not casting suspicions on the dealer or his coins by examining them carefully. He examines just as carefully, when he buys — or at least he should.

You are essentially looking for three things:

1. That the coin is genuine.
2. That it is correctly graded (that is, truly uncirculated).
3. That there are no problems which would cause it to be less desirable than the normal MS-60 specimens.

Additionally, but of somewhat less significance, you will want to take note of whether or not the strike is strong and crisp. This is really a more abstract point than the three listed. To accurately judge the quality of strike you must be familiar with the general grade of strike on that particular dollar. Dates from some mints were just weaker than others and you may not acquire a really good one.

The risk of the coin not being genuine is rather minimal but this possibility should not be ignored. If the coin itself is genuine, then consideration must be given to whether the date or mint mark has been altered in any way. Doctored dates and mint marks are more numerous than coins which are wholly faked, and are somewhat more difficult to detect. The fact that they often escape detection is, however, frequently because the purchaser does not stop to realize that they could be doctored. Once having concluded that the basic coin is genuine, his investigation ceases.

A person of limited experience will not achieve 100% accuracy in determining whether coins are genuine or not. This in itself does not mean that there is any real danger of buying fakes. It means simply that you will, occasionally, encounter a dollar which creates suspicion. At this point you should not attempt to arrive at any conclusive decision, but simply regard the specimen as unsuitable for purchase. In other words you should only buy dollars about which you have no suspicions, and these of course will comprise the great majority of those presented in any coin shop. If a specimen does not look right, even if your reasons for feeling this way cannot be defined, it should not be purchased. You are not alone. Dealers will decline to buy specimens which "don't look right," without being able to pinpoint the cause of their doubts. Some coins just look wrong. Some of them are perfectly genuine, of course; but when a coin has a questionable appearance, it can hardly be a worthwhile investment item.

In addition to the coins which just "look wrong," there are fakes which can fairly easily be recognized as such. The dealer should have spotted them but you cannot rely on this. If a silver dollar has depressions or cavities anywhere on its surface, if the reeding is irregular, if there appears to be a seam running along the rim, if the design is struck up in places but not in others, if the design gives the appearance of being struck through cheesecloth, these are strong indications of a fake. A cast fake will exhibit cavities caused by tiny air bubbles in the cast, as air became trapped between the mold and the liquid metal. Also, the lack of sharpness in cast fakes is easily distinguished from the normal lack of sharpness present in weakly struck genuine coins. It is not just a matter of the clarity of fine details, or the height to which the designs stand up from the background. There is an overall blurriness, even to the strongest points of the design, in a cast fake. Thus the outline of Liberty's profile seems to fade into the coin's field, the eye is dull and unexpressive, the hair totally indistinct, the lettering lacks the characteristic chiseled appearance, the whole coin is lifeless and obviously a reproduction. Once you have seen your first cast fake you will see what we mean. Unfortunately these points do not translate well into photographs.

In most cases it will not be necessary to remove a dollar from its holder, for the purpose of conducting a conclusive examination. If the holder is a 2x2 flip or "flipette," the entire coin can be seen within the holder just as well as if it were removed. Most dealers use these holders. If the coin is enclosed in a cardboard holder with vinyl windows — the old-fashioned type of holder which was used in the 1950s and 1960s — both surfaces can be effectively examined, but the reeding along the edge will be obscured. You are within your rights as a customer to request permission to remove the coin from the holder, and this request will almost always be granted so long as it is not abused (do not randomly open holders on any given visit to the shop). Do not remove two specimens of the same coins from holders simultaneously, as a question could then arise as to which is which.

If you intend to invest on a large scale or to buy particularly costly individual coins, you may want to get a specific gravity testing device for use in the home. Since it cannot be taken along to shops, shows or auctions, it will not solve all the problems related to authenticity.

Determining that the coin is correctly graded will be of greater overall importance than making a determination of authenticity. Without making any examination whatsoever, you might very well succeed in purchasing hundreds of silver dollars in coin shops, or through mail-order dealers, and not receive a single fake. Odds of this sort would not exist on grading. If you bought three dollars randomly without making a CARE-FUL examination of the grading, one of them would likely prove to be misgraded. Some investors (and collectors) maintain that out of every TWO silver dollars, one is inaccurately graded. That may be a little too pessimistic. In any case, a good investor is a good grader. Grading is a necessary art. You cannot depend on anyone else to do it, unless you have the funds to hire your own expert agent. Fortunately there is no great difficulty in it. You will need a small magnifying glass that can be conveniently carried. In examining MS-60 coins you look for evidence of wear — that is, rubbing or scuffing caused by handling — at the highest points of the design. The ANA grading guidelines published in this book will simplify matters by telling you exactly where to look, for dollars of each different design.

If any circulation wear is evident, the coin is misgraded at MS-60 and must be disregarded for investment purchase. This is true whether the wear exists on one or both sides. MS-60 is the easiest of all the condition grades to identify. If a specimen is graded MS-65, you must not only look for circulation wear but the number of scratches, marks or nicks on each surface. A stronger magnifying lens will be needed, probably one with a built-in illuminating device. Still, no matter how adept you become at identifying MS-65 coins, there will be instances where your opinion does not agree with that of the owner. Because with any grade over MS-60, a certain degree of opinion or interpretation enters the picture. This is one reason why we do not advise investment in silver dollars grading over MS-60. Nor do we recommend investment in those grading under MS-60, except for very scarce early specimens that are difficult or impossible to get in MS-60.

Take a critical approach to grading. Take the position that a coin labeled MS-60 is something less until proven otherwise. Many of them are. If the dealer has several MS-60 specimens of a coin that you want to buy for investment, don't stop at the first one that proves to be a real MS-60. Look at all of them. One is almost certainly going to be better than the others. Even if it is not actually better in terms of the numerical grading, it will be handsomer, and this attribute might be a selling point for you in the future. With non-keys in the Morgan and Peace series, you may have the opportunity to examine a dozen purported MS-60 specimens at the same time.

Having established that a specimen is a true MS-60, it is still essential to discover if there might be other detractions, not related to the grading but which would rule it out as an investment purchase. The grading system is solely based on the presence or absence of circulation wear. It does not take into account anything that can happen to a coin as a result of accident or injury, and of course damaged coins are by no means infrequent. You will find silver dollars with bullet holes in them from target practice (in the Old West it was believed that if you could shoot out a silver dollar at a given distance, you should be able to hit a human target through the heart at that same distance). You will find silver dollars that are uncirculated but badly scratched, nicked, bent, and otherwise mauled. These are not investment coins regardless of the price discount that may be offered by the dealer. They will not appreciate in value strongly enough to show an investment return. Verify that both sides of the coin are problem-free, as well as the rim. Anything odd about the coin, even if not really objectionable, should disqualify it from investment consideration. You want a portfolio of coins that can be presented to a future buyer without any danger of objections being raised on any ground — you want MS-60s that will continue to be MS-60s.

FINDING THE "CHOICE" DOLLARS

The art of "Cherry Picking" or choosing the "cream of the crop" has been developed to a science by many collectors, and some dealers are known to indulge at times as well. Simply stated, it is the art of picking out a coin which is a significant variety at the price of a normal coin, such as finding a 1900-0/CC mint mark variety for the price of a normal 1900-0 dollar. A knowledge of varieties, coin values and sharp vision are helpful to the Cherry Picker.

The usual hunting ground for the Cherry Picker is the dealer's bourse table, or even his shop display cases, with valuable finds frequently turning up among the items in a "junk" box, or bargain bin. The supreme satisfaction is using your knowledge and skill in detecting valuable varieties to make a profit on a coin. Finding a single underpriced coin may enrich your investment portfolio by a substantial margin.

Few coin dealers have the time, or knowledge, to keep up with all of the known varieties — or new ones that are constantly being discovered — and for this reason are fair game for the Cherry Picker. Naturally, one does not walk up to a dealer's table and say, "Do you have any underpriced coins?" Coolness counts. You play the part of a potential customer and ask to see various dates that exist with valuable varieties, not mentioning your interest in these varieties. If you have done your homework well, you will recognize a variety and, if you are lucky, it will have been overlooked by the dealer and you can purchase it for a much lower price than you would normally have to pay.

Dealers recognize this and, in most instances, take being "picked" with good grace although, to be on the safe side, it is not wise to start crowing about a find until after the deal is completed. The suave Cherry-Picker keeps mum even afterward. Who knows what other sleepers are in that dealer's stock which might be roused out of their slumber by a careless word? You may want to stage a return assault on that shop.

There is one basic tool that the Cherry Picker — and everyone who has any dealings with coins — should have and that, of course, is the magnifying lens. To detect some varieties, it is absolutely necessary to at least use a lens. In some cases, it may require confirmation with a stereo microscope, but the mere fact that you use a lens gives you an edge over those who don't and may result in detection of varieties that the eyesight of previous customers was unable to.

Knowledge is, and can be, of great value to you. A single piece of knowledge, perhaps even one of the facts you have read here in this book, could equal several weeks or months of work at your regular occupation. Like any skill, Cherry Picking requires practice and constant refreshing and updating of the knowledge. We usually recommend, depending on the scope of your memory and the amount of knowledge you have gained, that you begin by concentrating on a single coin and expanding from there.

For example, several years ago the only known Swiss overdate, a 1925/1924 1 Rappen, was reported. I happened to be at a coin show in Switzerland shortly after I had examined and photographed an example of this coin, so I decided to see if I could Cherry Pick one for my own collection.

I visited every Swiss dealer's table at the show, as well as several other dealers who had Swiss coins displayed. In the course of about two hours, I examined about 50 1925 dated 1 Rappen coins, and in the process discovered two of the overdates, which I purchased for the normal price of the 1925 date. While in this case there is not more than a couple of dollars premium for the overdate at the present time, I consider the coin a prime long term investment. As the market for world overdates continues to climb, my two "cherries" are going to climb even faster because they are perhaps unique in the entire Swiss coinage. I have only a few dollars invested in them, so any significant jump in values will produce four figure gain percentages to match those we have quoted in this book.

A knowledge of varieties, gained through the practice of Cherry Picking, cannot but help the investor, just as it helps the collector. Many varieties demand far higher prices than the normal coin, and tend to increase at much the same ratio as some of the other minting rarieties we have listed here in this book. A single three figure purchase of a variety can propel your investment into four or potential five figure values in a substantially shorter time than the same investment in a regular coin. Varieties most often are limited to a single die, and almost invariably occur on only a fraction of even the lowest mintage regular coins in a series.

Does Cherry-Picking sound inviting? It calls for a bit more work than usual investing but the labor is amply rewarded. Very likely, the investor who is willing to learn and pick off underpriced varieties where possible, will be the person who profits most (and the most quickly) from this book.

THE FUTURE OF DOLLAR INVESTING

Much of the stress in this book has been on the relatively short term investment potential. For the most part, we have looked mainly at what is likely to be happening to your dollar investments in the next five or ten years. We cannot leave the topic without giving some thought to what lies beyond the current decade and the early nineties.

Some of you who are reading this are now in your 20's. Long before you reach retirement age — which is likely to be 75 or 80 by the time you get there — you will have set up a retirement plan, and no doubt will want to hold some of today's investments for that far off date (which, unbelievable though it seems at the present, will arrive). Thus you are looking at a retirement date of around the year 2030 to 2040 if present trends toward advanced retirement age continue.

By that time, many analysts predict that this country and most other countries of the world either will be using total mechanical transfer of funds, with no coins or currency, or will have switched to plastics or ceramics for coins as we suggested earlier. This of course will mean that any coin — of any metal — will have the added attraction of belonging to a vanished race.

The 1981 Anthony Dollar may be the last U.S. dollar ever issued. Attrition over 60 years will have reduced the available coins by a significant percentage, and in the case of our earlier coins by then well over 200 years old, the attrition rate will have approached or exceeded 90%. Already, more than half of the Morgan Dollars have OFFICIALLY been melted down. Many more have gone into commercial melting furnaces, and probably one-fourth of the Peace Dollars have been commercially melted. Of course, the attrition (or loss) of Liberty Seated, Trade and earlier dollars will be slower than of Morgans and Peace Dollars, as these coins are not melted.

Every passing day marks the demise of more and more coins, destroyed by flood, fire, earthquake, melting, vandalism (including that of jewelry and novelty manufacturers), or whatever cause. Every coin lost to the investor or collector means one less accounted for, and an upward pressure on the value of the reduced number remaining. Wear alone is the one great enemy that destroys the value of all but a minute fraction of all of the coins produced. So you have many natural factors helping your investment, if you make it now and plan to keep it for a lengthy period.

Some coins undoubtedly will never show a profit. As an investor you need to learn which coins to avoid, just as much as which ones to seek. As we have attempted to show, high mintage is not necessarily a red stop sign. There are numerous instances of high mintage coins that were ignored by the collectors and became hot investment prospects, merely because nobody bothered to save any top grade specimens. Despite the fact that the 1979 Anthony dollar mintage is more than three-fourths of a billion, a MS-60 roll set of the three mints undoubtedly will be quite valuable by 2040. We'd hesitate to predict that it would be profitable compared to some other investments, but the prospect remains, simply because almost no one has bothered to save any of the high mintage Anthonys.

By 2040, the coins which we have projected as big gainers may well have been eclipsed by other, less well known coins that have not made as spectacular gains up to now. One wishes he could know the future. But, if that were possible, he would alter and destroy the future. If it was known today that a certain coin selling for $30 would become worth $3,000 in 2040, investors would "bandwagon" it. It's value would soar rapidly, then very likely fall just as rapidly when anxious holders — not content to wait 60 years — start cashing in their chips.

One advantage to dollar investing that the gloom predictors play on is that besides having numismatic or investment value, silver coins always will have barter value, and there is always the possibility that a collapse of the world's government structures could put us back to bartering. When, and if, such a calamity happens, you will be in a much better position than most, and while you may lose some of your investment return, you may well find that survival is much more important than a hefty dividend check.

Silver currently is at, or very near, one of the lowest prices it will ever hit. One thing we have not mentioned is the concept of investing in "junk" silver, which fits right in with the barter situation we just mentioned. By "junk" we mean the worn, common date dollars that are sold for a slight premium over their bullion content. These coins on a rising silver market will provide you with juicy short term profits that could well rival the most favorable interest rates currently available. Right now, silver is bargain-priced for the investor. Either for short or long term, bullion coins can be a good money-maker, if you have enough storage space available. Many coin dealers are over-extended, deep into silver they bought when the price was much higher, and the smart investor who shops around often can find junk silver at bargain prices.

One factor to consider is that a great many economists and others who study the market believe that silver is going to reach the $100 mark in the near future. Silver has plenty going for it: its value to industry, the fact that the world is using substantially more silver than it's producing, a general downward trend around the world in new silver production, and increasing uses for silver. All of these supply and demand factors can have but a single effect on the price of silver, to force it upward. Even if all of us are wrong in predicting a short term rise, ultimately silver has to rise. Supply cannot meet demand.

Another interesting fact to consider is that the world is running out of metals, or will be running out in the next few decades. It is already profitable to "mine" dumps for their scrap metal content. Copper has been replaced in the U.S. cent because of increasing costs, so by 2030 or 2040, metal may be obtained exclusively from recycling, without fresh mining. If you plan your investments to take advantage of that likelihood, every coin you own will be worth an additional premium, as it will by then have slipped into the category of a museum relic.

Our best advice is to concentrate now on the next five to ten years as the time to make money, but don't neglect long term investments. If you're young, keep a significant percentage of your investing focused on coins that could boom after the turn of the century. We can't help thinking that some investment historian, coming across a copy of this book a century from now, is probably going to amuse himself by picking our predictions apart. But historians always have clearer vision than those who attempt to see the future. Some of our forecasts will inevitably go awry, but we firmly believe that most of the coins recommended will make money for most of those who buy them.

COUNTERFEIT DOLLARS

The one most serious problem that the Dollar investor must face is the counterfeit and altered coin. As a rule of thumb, any coin which has a three figure price tag is subject to and likely to be counterfeited or altered, so it is important for the investor to use some caution.

Counterfeiting is improving as rapidly as the official minting process, becoming more and more sophisticated every day. As the world mints develop new ways to thwart the faker, fakers devise new ways to improve their technology and produce better — and more dangerous — bad coins.

Most investors and others unfamiliar with coins assume that counterfeiting is still in the era of the lead alloy fake, but a few minutes talking to any expert in the field will be quite a jolt. Modern counterfeiters can often turn out a coin that will defy all but the closest checking by well-trained specialists. Present methods use such tools as the electrical spark technique of producing dies which ape the original like an identical twin. In several countries, such as Lebanon and Taiwan, counterfeiting coins is a "cottage" industry which turns out hundreds of thousands of fakes which are spread all over the world. Several countries actually encourage the export of counterfeits.

The chances of purchasing a fake coin increase with the value of the coin. Naturally, the counterfeiter wants to make as great a profit as possible from his coins, and the more the genuine coin is worth, the greater the profit in faking it. The investor who purchases a valuable silver dollar must demand adequate proof of its authenticity, and obtain the right to return the coin and recover his money if it proves otherwise.

This limits you to working only with a reputable coin dealer, one who has an established business, one who values his standing in the trade and would not risk tarnishing it, and one who freely offers a money back guarantee if the coin sold turns out to be a fake. Even the best, most honest, most reputable dealer can make a mistake. The investor should never take anything for granted about a coin, should always have the deal in writing (receipt) and a written agreement relative to return of the coin. Along those lines, most dealers have specific rules concerning the coins they sell, revolving around the concept that if you remove the coin from the dealer's holder, "the coin is yours". This means that you cannot return it for whatever reason, as there is no way to prove that the coin is the one sold to you. Learn those rules to avoid problems.

The best course with any expensive coin is to demand certification that the coin is genuine. This is usually done by an authentication service, such as the American Numismatic Association Certification Service (ANACS), which can also grade your coin. The simplest and safest method is to agree on a price with the dealer and then, before accepting delivery of the coin, ask the dealer to have the coin certified by ANACS, agreeing, of course, to pay the fee involved, which amounts to a modest percentage of the value of the coin plus postage. The coin is genuine, you can sleep nights, and if it is not, you can refuse to accept delivery.

It is illegal to own, buy, sell, trade or otherwise dispose of a counterfeit U.S. coin, or a coin which could be passed as money in any part of the world. If you find yourself in possession of one, the proper procedure is to send the coin to:

U.S. Secret Service
Counterfeit Division
1800 G St. NW
Washington, DC 20223

This will save you from a potential stiff penalty, including a fine or jail term if you are caught with such a coin in your possession, or while attempting to dispose of it. It is not illegal to own for research and study purposes, counterfeit foreign coins that are no longer valid as money. It is, of course, illegal to *sell* any counterfeit as a genuine one. In actual practice it is very difficult to obtain a conviction on such a charge, however. The burden of proof is on the prosecution to show that the seller KNEW the coin was counterfeit, and it is next to impossible to obtain such proof unless the individual's home contains equipment for making counterfeits.

Beside the counterfeit coin, the investor must be on guard against altered coins. On occasion the date, but more frequently the mint mark, is altered to increase the value of a coin. Hence these are the two key features to check. A false mint mark may be added to a Philadelphia Mint coin by soldering or gluing. Most such additions can be detected fairly readily, but as a rule of thumb, the more valuable the coin, the more likely the work will be skillfully performed and difficult to detect.

Some fakes are created by taking two coins, cutting one down and then hollowing out the other so that they can be fitted together. This leaves a seam in, or along the rim, rather than on the edge of the coin. Expert alteration can be extremely difficult to detect, except under a high power microscope. This method is used to produce thousands of two-headed or two-tailed "novelty" coins as well, these having no collector value but a very high "nuisance" value in the hobby.

One of the common tests for a dollar, or other silver coin, is to "ring" it, by dropping it on a wood surface. We must warn that this is, at best, only a negative test (as we will explain) and can damage a high grade coin if done carelessly.

We do not recommend ringing as a test. A coin which is perfectly genuine may, because of an internal and invisible flaw in the metal, respond with a dull "thud" instead of a ring. It is thus a negative test, in that if you get the proper ring from the coin, it is probably genuine, but the lack of a ring does not prove that it is counterfeit. If you must "ring" a coin, it can be done by placing the coin on a pivot of some sort and then tapping the coin gently with the object softer than the coin metal, such as your fingernail.

The 1893-S Dollar, because of its rarity, is probably the most subject to counterfeiting and alteration of any of the dollars. It is frequently done by adding an S, or by changing the second 8 on an 1898-S to a 3. The 1883-S is also altered by removing the second 8, and substituting a 9, the method likewise used to fake the 1895-S. Best defense against this kind of fake is to learn the different types of letters used for mint marks on different years at San Francisco, as they are easily spotted. Key coins from other mints are faked too, such as by removing the mint mark from an 1895 branch mint coin to mimic the rare 1885 Philadelphia.

Much of the work in detecting and identifying altered or counterfeit coins depends to a great extent on one's knowledge of the variation between strikes, dies and die preparation at the various branch mints. As we have mentioned, the specialist can often identify the mint striking a coin without seeing the reverse or the mint mark, merely by the appearance of the obverse, and in many cases can identify the year by the appearance of the reverse without seeing the date. You will not, of course, reach this level of expertise overnight. But it can be obtained and almost inevitably *will* be obtained, if you handle enough silver dollars and pay close attention to their characteristics.

There are several excellent sources of information about altered and counterfeit dollars that can be relied on, including Van Allen and Mallis' book on the Morgan and Peace Dollars, and Harshe's book on detecting altered and counterfeit coins, listed in the Recommended Reading chapter. Besides depending on the reputation of your coin dealer and ANACS, these books are a must for the serious investor to keep up with modern advances in counterfeiting and counterfeit detection.

We would close by saying that the investor must be concerned about the possibility of unknowingly buying a counterfeit or altered coin, but should not allow himself to become terror-struck by the danger. You have help available, more than those who invest in many other kinds of items. Never buy a coin that you know is priced well below normal retail, as a "fire sale" price is a warning signal that should not go unheeded. If the coin is priced below what you know to be the wholesale price, the coin is either stolen or a fake. You can only lose, so find the nearest exit and use it. Dealers don't run "sales" on coins.

INVESTMENT OPPORTUNITIES

The investor who is interested in Dollars is not limited to his own personal investment plans. As with some other forms of investing, it is possible to join groups of investors with a common interest, in plans sponsored by large scale investment firms. It is also very easy to find coin dealers who specialize in this and other areas of coin investing.

As we have suggested before, your local coin dealer often may be a one-stop source of information, coins, and a specific investment program. By talking to him you may be able to settle on a particular plan of investing, such as putting a specified sum each month, quarter or year into dollars. If your investment is going to be large enough, you would do well to contact any of the numerous major coin firms scattered across the country who will be happy to send you literature on their specialized investment plans for coins.

Before settling on any plan and committing your investments, it would be well to study the plans offered as closely as you will be studying the coins you buy and sell. Certain advantages and disadvantages are to be weighed. For example, some plans deliver the coins to you. Safe storage is your responsibility and expense. Others may offer included storage, or even joint ownership of a group of coins retained by the company. Here you need to ask yourself what your storage costs would be, compared to the cost written in by the company in storing your coins, or as your share of a group cost. What is the risk involved in relinquishing physical possession of the coins? Dealers have been known to go bankrupt, leaving the investor with a serious loss, so you need to know about the history and stability of the coin company you deal with before making that kind of a decision. In general, it is unwise to invest in coins without gaining physical possession of them.

You are also going to need tax advice. An absolute necessity is to retain a record of every purchase and sale of all coins you own. The IRS is firm about demanding such records to prove when and where you bought the coin, what you paid for it, and the resulting taxable profit. You also will want as much current tax advice as possible from your coin dealer, or the coin company you deal with, as it specifically applies to your investments, as well as concurrent advice from your accountant or the person who prepares your tax retruns. In this respect, the larger coin companies who have tax authorities on their staff, can be very useful.

At the same time, you should be deciding on a long range plan for your coin investing, covering both short term buying and selling, and long range retirement plans. This requires keeping informed of day to day and year to year changes in tax laws, keeping an eye open for the necessary tax breaks that will frequently add as much or more than the appreciation of your coins. Retirement looms as a big milestone in any investment plan, since it is usually the point where buying ends and judicious selling begins.

It is certainly not the point where you stop learning, stop gaining knowledge, or stop paying attention to the world around you and its effect on your coin investments. Learning to sell is just as important to your financial success as learning to buy, and the knowledge is not all interchangeable. If your plans revolve around buying for a long term holding action, then obviously you will be obliged to learn selling based on the situation at some point in the future. You will have the experience gained in buying, plus the opportunity to learn even more about the coins you have. Undoubtedly, you will have either learned about or spotted new varieties yourself that will add to the value of your holdings.

Another important factor that must not be neglected is the possibility that you may not be able to handle the sale of your own investments. Coin portfolios do, sometimes, outlive their owners, and your plans should include specific actions and procedures in the event of your death. It is not enough to say in your will, "I leave all my possessions to my beloved wife . . ." since your wife may know little or nothing about your coins, or how to go about selling them. Far better to specify, "In the event of my death, the ABC Coin Company or such other reputable coin dealer as may be picked by the executor of my estate shall appraise, evaluate and subsequently sell my coin holdings." You may not be around to see their gratitude, but your heirs will praise and thank you for your foresight.

For the investor without any specific knowledge of coins, professional advice is a must, and the need for that advice increases with the type and amount of investment that you are planning. By all means consider it in making your investment plans. A buyer of stocks expects professional help from his broker, and the same is true in almost any field. Coins are not an exception. Much of the advice is free for the asking, but paying for the advice you want and need is a legitimate investment expense. The lack of proper advice can be far more costly.

ALL ABOUT COMMISSIONS

In buying and selling Silver Dollars — bullion and numismatic — you will be paying a commission or handling charge when you deal with the "trade." The trade includes all individuals who make a business of dealing in Dollars, such as coin dealers, auctioneers, brokers, scrap merchants and the like. This commission is an "add-on" or a "take-off," and represents the difference between the actual value of the merchandise and the sum of money that changes hands. It meets the dealer's operating expenses and provides him with a margin of profit. Anyone investing in Silver Dollars should educate himself on the subject of trade commissions and the ways in which they vary. Although it is difficult to entirely avoid paying a commission, your goal should be to pay the lowest commission possible on each transaction. By studying the market and the practices of different dealers, a savings of several percentage points in commission is possible. The difference between (say) 10% and 12% may seem insignificant, but in investing every percentage point or even fractions of a percentage point are important. By selling under a low commission charge, a sale could be profitable that might not be otherwise. The same is true of a purchase. In fact, the rate of commission you pay in buying and selling will determine to a large extent whether your investment yields a satisfactory return.

Commission Charges on Bullion Dollars. Handling or commission fees levied on bullion Dollar transactions are more apparent and easier to calculate than those on numismatic Dollars. While the merits of numismatic coins can be debated between buyer and seller, bullion coins are worth what the "spot" indicates on that day — regardless of condition, regardless of whether the dealer is overstocked. Therefore with bullion Dollars you have a firm starting point to work from. You (and the dealer) know what the merchandise is worth, and the price depends on the margin of commission.

When you buy bullion Dollars, you will be paying the full spot price with a commission charge added. The commission charge on Dollars is higher than on other U.S. silver coins. It may be as much as 35% over the spot price, depending on the dealer and the circumstances at that time. Usually it is somewhat less than this. The simple fact of the matter is that Silver Dollars, even mutilated specimens that could not possibly have collector appeal, have greater value than the mere bullion content. They are the only U.S. silver coins that can be depended on to sell for a higher price than the value of the bullion they contain. You have to pay more when buying them, compared to what you would pay if the same quantity of silver was contained in Roosevelt Dimes or Washington Quarters, but you will get more when you sell.

In selling Silver Dollar bullion coins to a dealer, you should get at least 15% over the spot price and possibly as much as 20% — again, depending on the dealer, the competition against which he's working, and conditions in the silver market.

So long as the dealer continues to buy, his prices must be based on the daily spot quote, and he has absolutely no way of controlling that figure. His only method of regulation is by changing his commission rate. Rapidly rising prices are an advantage to him, as he can sell higher. But there is always a danger — as in any commodity dealings — that the price could slip back dramatically, leaving him with substantial unsold stock in which he has a large investment. Say, for example, that on a given day silver is selling for $40 per troy ounce and the dealer is buying Silver Dollars for $48. Suppose he buys 1,000 Dollars that day, which cost him $48,000. His selling price that day is $55. He may sell 500 Dollars, bringing him $27,500. Further suppose that when the next business day begins, the price is $25 per troy ounce. This is not apt to happen, but it's a possibility. He cannot sell for more than $30 against a $25 spot price. He then loses money selling the remaining 500 Dollars, if indeed he does sell them on that day. He could choose to put up a "NO BUSINESS TODAY" sign and hold them for a while. In any event there is some measure of risk involved. So he will raise his commissions on buying and selling when prices soar upward. He attempts to reduce the risk as far as practical, but of course he cannot eliminate it entirely any more than can the private investor. He could end up losing money on those 500 Silver Dollars regardless of how he proceeds. This would, presumably, be offset by the profits obtained earlier, on silver that was bought and sold as the market was rising.

The dealer acts for you as an agent, if you want to think of it that way. You could get a better price selling to a private individual, but you might incur some overhead expense by doing that and it would certainly take more time. Therefore, what the dealer says, in effect, is "I'm paying you less than the full value of your Dollars, but I'm saving you some time and expense." The same is true, though in a slightly different way, in selling numismatic Dollars or just about anything of value that you sell to a dealer. You take a reduction in price for the sake of achieving a quick, convenient sale, and getting "cash on the barrelhead."

Part of the commission goes toward paying the dealer's operating expenses. These include shop rent, employee salaries, utilities, advertising and miscellaneous costs which every business incurs. Obviously the dealer would not be in business and would not be able to buy your coins, if he did not take care of these expenses.

Commission on Numismatic Coin Transactions. Commissions charged on the purchase and sale of collector or numismatic coins are not referred to as commissions. Nevertheless, the dealer's operating costs and margin of profit are figured into these transactions, just the same as when he buys and sells silver bullion coins. The percentage of commission tends to be hidden on numismatic transactions. A price is named and there is really no way of knowing what proportion of that sum represents the dealer's opinion of merchandise value vs. commission. All you know is that when you pay $100 for a coin, the coin did not cost the dealer $100. And you further know that when you sell a coin to a dealer for $100, it will be resold at a price higher than $100.

There are many more variables involved in commissions on numismatic coins. The percentage or rate of commission, and thus the margin of profit, can be very small on some coins and literally tremendous on others, depending on circustances. The dealer has a leeway on numismatic items that is not offered to him when buying and selling bullion material, since he must work off the spot price on bullion transactions and cannot, employ salesmanship or any other business arts. Depending on his expertise as a businessman, the knowledge or lack of knowledge of the customer, and (not to be forgotten) the degree to which the customer succumbs to persuasion, the dealer can make very favorable purchases and sales of numismatic Dollars.

The dealer does not, generally, count on tacking a standard mark-up on numismatic coins bought from the public. He does not buy a coin with the intention of putting it on sale at a flat 20% increase, or 30% or any other particular figure. The mark-up could be 100% or more, if he succeeds in buying the coin low enough. This does not happen very often with Uncirculated Dollars. But every dealer makes occasional fortunate purchases, and when a dealer buys low — well under the market — he does not pass along the savings to customers. He prices such a coin at its full current market value. The big profit garnered on this kind of buy makes up for coins that he must "reach" to buy, paying somewhat more than he would really care to. So long as the *total operation* shows a satisfactory profit, it is not necessary that there be any standard margin on each coin. Obviously there must be some profit on every sale, but there is no objection to some registering low profit if others are made at a healthy margin. Much depends on the kind of trade being done. A dealer who makes a specialty of rare U.S. coins might have in mind a minimum, profit, or commission percentage, that would be acceptable for him on every coin he buys. Therefore, he would refuse to purchase any coin, offered to him by the public, which in his opinion could not return that minimum profit — even if it had the potential of realizing *some* profit.

If a dealer has customers waiting for the particular coin you want to sell, which is often the case with specialist dealers or those during a large volume of business, he can afford to operate on a tighter percentage. When a sale is quaranteed or virtually quaranteed with no waiting, the dealer might pay as much as 90% of the retail price. He can go high in these situations because there is no need to take a "risk discount." The so-called Risk Discount is a percentage (the size of which varies with the dealer, and often with the value of coins being bought) deducted from the purchase price to allow for the possibility of a slow sale. Slow sales are the vipers of the coin business. A dealer never worries as much about not being able to sell a coin as he does about taking time to sell it.

Commissions on Collections or other Large Lots. Commissions are usually figured differently when a dealer is buying a large group of coins. Unless the collection is very choice, it will likely contain some items in the slow-moving category or even material that the dealer does not normally handle. The dealer may calculate a retail value on the collection as a whole, then use a deduction percentage (for his commission) higher than would be applied on buying fine individual coins. Or he will apply his normal commission on the better grade material, and add a bit to the purchase price to cover the lesser items. In cases such as this he really makes very little investment in the questionable or undesirable coins. So long as he sells the better items at their usual retail price, he can virtually give away the remainder and still profit.

Auction Sale Commissions. Unlike retail coin dealers, auction houses openly use the word "commission" in referring to their handling costs and margin of profit on the coins they sell. Most auctioneers do not personally own the coins offered in their sales. The lots are submitted by private parties, and often by dealers. A coin percentage is deducted from the prices realized as the house share of the proceeds. The remaining sum is then paid out to the owner or vendor of the lots.

There are no standard commission rates in the auction field. At one time, 10% was the general rule, but few houses operate on this low a commission any longer. The average in coin sales is from 12½% to 20%. In some cases, the per-lot commission is reduced slightly if lots fetch more than certain specified sums of money. For example, a house might charge 15% commission normally, but only 12½% on lots selling at more than $10,000. This is essentially a European practice but it has been tried in this country. It is naturally much more profitable for the auctioneer to hold a small sale, consisting mostly of valuable coins, than a large sale of mixed-value material. He saves money in bookkeeping and other clerical expenses, catalogue printing, mailing costs and the like. It therefore pays to sell valuable coins at a reduced commission. An increasing practice today is the use of a 20% commission split between the seller (10%) and the buyer (10%). This means that if a lot reaches $1,000, the actual price paid by the buyer is $1,100. The seller (consigner) receives 90% of the "hammer price," in this case $900, NOT 90% of the total price paid by the buyer. This system, developed in Europe, is intended to draw more choice coin collections into the auction rooms.

ELIMINATING THE MIDDLEMAN

When you buy Silver Dollars, as an investor, you naturally attempt to pay the lowest possible price while maintaining high condition standards (M-60 Uncirculated in most instances, as we have recommended throughout this book). You must give more attention to cost than if you were a coin hobbyist, since your purpose is to derive a profit from your coins. A hobbyist can take pride in ownership, or possibly satisfaction in winning an auction battle against other potential buyers — even if he paid more than the coin's current retail value. An investor has to be cold, calculating and objective. He can enjoy owning his coins but he must put cash values first and foremost. If a coin isn't a good buy from an investment viewpoint, he shouldn't buy it. If there's a chance that a specimen could be purchased for less elsewhere, in the same grade of condition, he should try purchasing it elsewhere. he has to learn to say "no" to dealers when necessary, and to himself. He has to drive a hard bargain, because every penny counts. The slimmest margin of percentage in buying and selling could tip the scales between a favorable and unfavorable investment. Pay just a little too much, and you might have a bad buy. Sell for just a shade under what you might be able to achieve, and you could wipe out plenty of profit.

Since the smallest of percentage points count in Silver Dollar investing, you may (especially after reading this book) be asking yourself the following question:

Why can't I avoid the commissions charged on purchases and sales of my investment Dollars by doing my own dealing and avoiding the trade?

Well, you can. There is nothing to prevent you from buying from the public (though in some areas you may need to be licensed to buy silver coins from the public), and selling to the public. You would thereby be able to buy Silver Dollar bullion coins at a substantial discount from sums charged by dealers. You could buy bullion Dollars at "wholesale" prices. You could sell silver bullion Dollars at spot plus 20% or more. You could sell numismatic Dollars at the real retail values, and not have to take the discount imposed by dealers to cover their operating costs and margin of profit. In short, you could gain an awful lot of percentage points in every transaction you make. And that would add up to greater profits — or the opportunity, in some instances, to sell your Dollars sooner.

There is no reason why a private individual cannot successfully buy and sell on his own. However, we have to point out that "eliminating the middleman," as desirable as it might be, is not the ideal course of action for everyone investing in U.S. Silver Dollars. We do not advise all readers of this book to attempt becoming their own dealers. For some individuals it would simply be unwise, since they do not have the time, patience or necessary business skills to make a go of it.

As an investor/dealer, you will be encountering some overhead expenses. These must be kept careful track of and figures in on the overall cost of your investment Dollars. When selling, you have to achieve a satisfactory profit not just on the coins but on your operation as a whole. In this respect, you cannot delude yourself into believing (as some investors apparently do) that by buying from the public and selling to the public they score an enormous savings on trade commissions.

You will save the trade commissions but at the same time you will be spending money — chiefly for advertising — that would not be spent in dealing with the trade. If you go too far overboard and build up a big operation, you will need to do a large volume of buying and selling — at favorable prices — to compensate for your overhead.

Also, you will be advancing capital at the outset without immediately receiving any coins in return for it. You will be gambling somewhat with this capital because there is no absolute assurance of success. But there is much you can do to reduce your risks as low as possible.

If you get into business as an investor/dealer, a great deal of paperwork will need to be done. Plan for this ahead of time and get record books and a good filing system. If someone in the family has secretarial experience, this could be a big help.

Buying from the Public. Before you do any selling to the public, you'll be doing some buying. We'll assume that you do not already own investment coins, and that you want to acquire them from the public.

There are many possible approaches to buying from the public. We would suggest that you do not refer to yourself as a "dealer" in your advertising, nor even as an "investor." Dealers who buy Silver Dollars are undoubtedly already established in your area. You cannot hope to challenge them head-on in "dealer vs. dealer" combat. Chances are they do more advertising than would be wise for you to do (you have to keep operating costs modest), have a reputation in the neighborhood and advantages for customers that you could not offer — such as better parking facilities and regular business hours during the daytime. Do not try to compete against the dealers on their level. It would not be sensible for you to attempt this unless you were opening up a shop and going into the business fulltime. Since you will be dealing only part-time, you are not really in competition with them. They have to do enough steady volume to run a business. All you need do is buy enough Silver Dollars to build up a portfolio. You have one important advantage that a regular dealer lacks, and this should be used to its ultimate. You can refer to yourself as a private party, or even as a collector, if your chief goal is to buy numismatic rather than bullion Dollars. This gives a favorable impression, as it plants the suggestion that you will pay higher prices than a dealer could afford to. If you check the classified section of your newspaper, you will probably find that other individuals in the area are already buying investment Dollars with this approach. They may not be well established in the sense of a shopkeeper, but they undeniably draw some customers who would otherwise go to a dealer. Or who — maybe — would not sell at all.

Of course, you can also purchase through the mail if you wish. The obstacle in your path, in buying by mail, is heavy competition from the numerous other Silver Dollar buyers. The coin newspapers carry hundreds of ads each week from dealers and private parties who buy numismatic and bullion Dollars. It is very difficult to make any dent against this competition unless you pay higher prices (which isn't too smart) or go in for splashy advertising. Both are expensive.

Selling to the Public. Selling to the public may be slightly simpler than buying from the public. This is certainly true if you confine your selling to mail-order. In selling by mail, competition is not quite as strong a factor as in buying by mail. Most of the advertisers in the coin press are dealers, who are naturally selling at the full retail prices. If you could discount from those prices slightly on the coins you wish to sell, by even as little as 5% for top-quality coins, you would probably succeed in making sales. Of course, you will (as mentioned) encounter overhead expenses, especially if you have a list printed.

PLANNING AN INVESTMENT PORTFOLIO

The concept stressed in this book — and agreed upon by nearly every independent analyst — is that ANYONE in ANY FINANCIAL CIRCUMSTANCES can make money by intelligent investment in Silver Dollars. But this does not mean that every well-chosen Silver Dollar portfolio is right for every Silver Dollar investor. In order to receive the maximum possible benefits from an investment, each investor's portfolio should be structured to his own needs and circumstances. You have to determine, for example, how much to spend, and whether you want long-term or short-term coins — or a combination of both.

Just as there are stock brokers who will assemble a portfolio to suit your personal circumstances, there are coin investment brokers who will do this with Silver Dollars. We strongly recommend that you do not avail yourself of their services. Most coin investment brokers are perfectly honest and try to do their best for you. However, you must pay for their consultations and paperwork, either in the form of a flat fee or higher prices for their coins. Also, there is always the very real risk, when dealing with brokers, that your portfolio will end up consisting of coins that they're overstocked in — whether these coins really represent the best investments or not. You can do just as well on your own, without a broker, and save money in the process. One reason why you can do better is because you know your personal situation much more intimately than anyone else. You know your income, obligations, plans, goals and desires. You can give all your investment thought to YOU.

It will be beneficial for you to become fully acquainted with Silver Dollar history, lore, and price performance before thinking about your own portfolio. Unless you know all the details, you cannot even begin to structure a portfolio intelligently. Nor will Silver Dollar investing even seem attractive or worthwhile to you, until you examine its performance record. You *should* be a doubter, if you are not presently informed about Silver Dollar investment. You *should* be skeptical. No rational person would invest money in something just because someone tells him to. We advise you to study Silver Dollar investment from all angles before spending a penny for a Silver Dollar. We have provided sufficient information for you to do just that and we think you will agree with our very positive feelings about the future potential of Silver Dollar investing.

One matter you will need to decide is how much to invest and (a related topic) whether you should invest the decided-upon sum all at once or gradually. For most individuals, the answer to the first part of this question would be: an amount that you can comfortably tie up.

What does "comfortably" mean? Well, you have to understand that any money put into an investment (any investment) is no longer in the form of money. It has become an object or possession. It cannot be drawn upon in time of need in quite the same fashion as banked money. It can only be turned back into money by selling it. With Silver Dollars, this can be accomplished quickly and easily — much more easily than with many other kinds of investments. It requires nothing more than a trip to the coin shop. However, if you sell your coins (or some of them) soon after purchasing them, the odds are that you will lose some of your capital, because you buy them at a retail price and sell them at a wholesale price. Therefore, you should try not to place yourself in a position where the sale of any investment Dollars might be necessary before maturity. It may be very tempting, after reviewing the spectacular growth record of Silver Dollars, to convert all of your cash and other holdings into Dollars. This is not recommended. This adds an *unnecessary risk factor* to your investing. The risk is not in whether your Silver Dollars might fail to be profitable. The risk is that you might need money somewhere along the line and sell some of your investment before you ought to.

We do not advise anyone to wipe out their bank accounts for the purpose of buying Silver Dollars. This would be foolish. Everyone needs some available cash, but ALL of your money doesn't belong in the bank. Some should be invested, and we feel that Silver Dollars are your best bet for investment. Exactly how much you invest is something you'll have to decide for yourself. The wise investor takes a middle road between being overly cautious and going overboard!!!

Should the sum you decide to invest be invested all at once?

Many readers are certain to be asking that question. It *is* an important question and should be given careful consideration.

There are two ways of looking at it. If you start out gradually and stretch your purchasing over a period of time, you will learn more about Silver Dollars and how to buy them along the way. Your later purchases are apt to be more selective than your first efforts. This is a very potent argument in favor of going slowly.

But, on the other hand, prices are likely to be rising. The sooner you invest your capital, the more it will probably buy.

There's no easy answer to this one. Our feeling is that if you carefully read and digest the information in this book, you should (even if you previously knew nothing about Silver Dollars or investment in general) be capable of buying effectively. We would suggest that any *standing capital* (money already on hand) that you intend to put into Silver Dollars should be invested without undue delay — though not, of course, in a mad rush. This will be the foundation of your investment portfolio. It can then be — and should be — supplemented with periodical purchases made from freshly accrued capital. In any event, we suggest that all of your investment Dollars be purchased outright with full physical ownership, and not be bought on credit or through any plan that call for periodic payments. Our opinion is that rising values *will* make it unfavorable for you to delay your investment purchasing. It is not our intention to affect the market, but, obviously, investors will be buying our "Best Bet" dates and mintmarks in heavier number than previously. Within a few months after this book's publication, prices on many of our "Best Bet" selections may have risen dramatically. Time is important in investing. You may not only buy the right coins, but buy them at the right time. We think that most new investors would be well advised to get into the market without unnecessary delay, and get their pick of the still-undervalued coins. (Incidentally, you can follow the price movement of our "Best Bets," or any other Silver Dollars, by comparing the values in this book with those in each new edition of the annually revised *Blackbook Guide of*

Coins. This handy reference volume can be ordered directly from the publishers by sending $3.95 plus $1 for postage and handling to The House of Collectibles, 201 East 50th Street, NY, NY 10022.

Another consideration in planning your Silver Dollar investment portfolio is whether you merely want to keep ahead of inflation or accumulate money for some particular purpose at a definite time in the future (such as sending children to college). While the basic motive is still the same, to get coins that will be saleable at a profit, the strategy changes somewhat depending on your goals. Your age at the time of beginning your investment is a factor too. If you are primarily interested in keeping ahead of inflation — that is, making your money work for you in something more lucrative than a bank savings account — and are fairly young, you would probably want to get Dollars that fall into the long-term investment category. These are dates and mintmarks which cannot be counted upon to turn a substantial profit within the next few years. They do, however, look very favorable for profit making within ten years, and further into the future. The commentary included in the listings section mentions many such coins. Then there are other Dollars, also pointed out in this book, which show excellent potential for returning a satisfactory profit in five years or less. *Five years* is our minimum projected length of holding time for Dollars purchased in the current market. This is not to say that Silver Dollars don't have the potential to register a good return in less time, but much depends on the events in the numismatic market. During 1979, when values soared, some Dollars which were bought at the beginning of the year were saleable at wholesale for a 100% profit by the year's end. This could certainly happen again at any time. It only requires a few sparks in the coin collecting market to get the fire going. Very likely there are many coins among our "Best Bets" that will be sold at a profit in less than our five-year minimum holding period. We are working with a "five-year minimum hold," because these surges in prices, such as occurred in 1979, cannot be predicted or counted upon. When projecting prices, one has to work on the assumption that the market will move at more or less its established pace. If it does better, that's gravy for the Silver Dollar investor. Even if it does worse, which is unlikely, most of our "five-year minimum hold" selections should still be saleable at a good profit when that length of time is up. Slumps in the market are a possibility and they do occur from time to time, but, historically, they have not lasted very long. Even if a slump were to last for a full year, this would be insignificant in a five-year holding period, because there is ample time for the market to adjust itself and for values to resume climbing at their usual pace.

We have used the phrase "short-term investment" for all our Best Bet coins that should be saleable at a satisfactory profit after holding for five years. "Long-term investment," coins are Dollars which the owner should count on holding for more than five years, and in most instances ten years, to achieve the best return. Some of these recommended long-termers will, almost surely, get hot and become profitable within five years — perhaps even sooner. If you're holding any of them in 1990 and discover that the market has risen substantially, it then becomes your option whether to take your profit at that time or continue holding for a more substantial gain in the future. Obviously, some coins could follow different growth patterns than we have projected, since projecting is not an exact science. There have been surprises in the past (mainly favorable ones) and there will be surprises in the future. But *we would still maintain* that our Best Bet "long-termers" would be more profitable to the investor if he continues holding them for ten years or even longer, even if these coins climb to the point of being profitable in five years. Most of these coins have either recorded strong growth in recent years or, for one reason or other, are not currently in the "undervalued" category. Even if they show healthy upward price movement in the next five years, it can reasonably be anticipated that their performance over the *following five years* will be *even better.* It is a different situation with the coins we recommend as short-term investments. Our short-term investment Dollars are dates and mintmarks which are clearly undervalued in the current market. They are due for an imminent price jump. These are coins which, if you delay buying them, you will not be able to obtain at such favorable prices. Many will rise in price from 20% to 30% within a year after the publication of this book, and with any kind of push behind the market they will do even better. They are likely to continue rising at approximately a 20-30% annual rate for the next several years, which, of course, will put them out of the ranks of the underpriced. By 1990, the majority of these Dollars will be fully priced — and, quite likely, a few will have gone over the top of the hill and become overpriced. This is why these coins rank as attractive short-term investments. They will score their best price gains *now,* rather than at some point in the distant future. These are the coins to buy as soon as possible, in Uncirculated condition (MS-*65* or better for Morgans and Peace, when obtainable), if you want to have the opportunity to turn a profit in five years or less.

The simple fact of the matter is this: good short-term investment coins are generally not favorable as long term investments; and good long term investment coins cannot be counted on to do well as short-termers. These are exceptions, naturally, but, on the whole, this reasoning will hold up. In most cases, you are well advised to sell a coin bought as a short-term investment after it has been held for the recommended length of time — unless some very extraordinary things have happened in the market which lead you to different conclusions. It is very tempting to keep holding coins bought as short-term investments, if they have registered the anticipated increases. Someone who is not well informed about the coin market would assume that these coins, having displayed such strength, will go right on doing so for *the next five years.* But, in most instances, they won't. Their rate of growth will slow down, and it may even come to a halt. This is because the cycle will start going in the other direction. After they become fully priced, in line with other Dollars in their group, investment buying of those coins will slacken off — and, at the same time, sales by investors will increase. Investors holding these dates and mintmarks will sell them in order to take their profit or to buy other coins. If they're going to continue investing, they will want to shift their capital into Dollars that are *underpriced at that time,* rather than keeping it in coins which have attained fair price levels.

Will there always be underpriced Silver Dollars? Beginning investors — and even some with a fair degree of experience — question the likelihood of *any* Silver Dollars remaining underpriced by 1990, 1995, or at any time in the future. It is easy to see their line of reasoning. They look at the huge numbers of new investors getting into Silver Dollars, and the continued steady growth on coin collecting as a hobby. With so much more money being spent on Silver Dollars, and so much publicity directed toward them by books and other media, how could it be possible for any dates or mintmarks to be underpriced in the future?

Yet, that is precisely what will happen. No matter how many investors and collectors are buying Silver Dollars, even if the sums of money spent on them triple each year, there will always be underpriced dates and mintmarks.

Sound impossible?

Stop and think for a minute. The underpricing of a Dollar is a condition that exists merely in relation to the prices of other Dollars. A certain Dollar worth $200 today in BU condition could rise to $500 in the future and still be *more underpriced than it is now*. It all depends on the price movement of other dates and mintmarks in that dollar's group. An underpriced coin is simply one which is not fully valued in comparison to the other dates and mintmarks of that design. There will always be undervalued Dollars, because this vast series of coins does not and cannot (given the whims and odd buying patterns of the public) reach a point where every date and mintmarks if fairly valued in relation to each other. It just can't happen. There will always be undervalued Dollars, and there will always be overvalued Dollars. The object in investment is to distinguish between them, and buy the undervalued coins while their prices are still low. Or, if your goal is long-term investment, you should get top-quality, popular Dollars that are fully valued at the moment, but will probably rise significantly within the next *ten* years.

If you want a favorable long-term investment portfolio, we do not recommend that you buy the "Best Bet" Dollars suggested for short-term gain. These are very good coins — much better, obviously, than those which have not been included among our "Best Bets" — but they are not really suitable for long-term gain. If you care to get more involved in the mechanics of investing, you could start out by acquiring these short-termers, then sell them after five years and buy other dates and mintmarks which are underpriced at that time. This will call for a more careful study of the market on your part, and it will require some adeptness at timing both your sales and your purchases. We have the feeling, though, that many of our readers, once they have learned enough about investing to gain confidence in their abilities, will choose to proceed in that fashion. There is a certain flexibility in doing this, which will appeal to many investors. The thought of owning a certain coin or group of coins for ten years or more may seem confining. This is up to you. Quite likely you could do a little better, in terms of eventual overall profit by concentrating on short-termers and cashing in your holdings (or some of them) from time to time. Much depends on movements in the market, and your willingness to keep fully informed about them. If you aren't interested in subscribing to coin publications and buying the other current literature of the hobby, this approach to investing is probably not for you.

HOW TO PROFIT IN AN ERRATIC MARKET

Prices of Silver Dollars do not remain balanced. In fact they are never, at any given time, fairly and justly balanced. A fair and just balance would mean that every Dollar — every date and mintmark — is selling for a price in relation to its availability on the market. The most difficult to obtain coins in BU condition would always be more expensive than the less difficult to obtain. And there would be a degree of difference in price for the degrees in difference of availability. Each series of Dollars would move upward in value at the same pace, and within each series the individual coins would rise in price according to their numismatic appeal. The market would be orderly and predictable.

As we all know, this is not the case. It has never been the case, and it is even less so today. Even with much greater available numismatic knowledge at the present time, prices are more unbalanced than in 1960 or 1950. They are less reliable in reflecting the scarcity or numismatic desirability of dates and mintmarks. This is because of the heavy pressure by investors during the 1970s, who were buying haphazardly and threw the market out of kilter. Some new investors coming on the scene today are likewise buying very unselectively. Another cause of unbalanced prices is investor selling, which often is badly planned as investor buying. The market receives these repeated jolts and it cannot stand firm in the face of them. Values bounce around and often reach very unrealistic levels from one coin to the next. Some coins become temporarily overpriced while others are temporarily underpriced. If you watch the Silver Dollar market for any length of time, you will notice certain coins performing oddly. You will think you've read misprints, because such-and-such coin has no business selling for such-and-such sum of money. But the amount that a Silver Dollar *should be* selling for and the amount that it *is* selling for are often two different things.

As an investor, you can take advantage of these developments, if you learn to recognize and correctly interpret them. In fact, erratic prices are one of the chief blessings for the investor. The profit potential on his coins would not be nearly so great if he had to depend on buying at the full value and watching them advance at an orderly pace. Undervalued coins should be the investor's prime target. We have attempted to point out some currently undervalued coins in this book. But to become a really skilled investor you will need to do your own "spotting," too, because the market changes rapidly and some very attractive buys could be available at any given moment. That is the purpose of this book: to show you how to make it on your own as a Silver Dollar investor, which ought to be the ultimate goal of every investor. The more he relies on books, hot tips, or the opinions of others, the less successful he is likely to be. He should try to build up his own investment talents and not be afraid to use them.

The charts in this book show prices of every Silver Dollar in 1955, 1960, 1965, 1970, 1975, 1980 and 1985. The prices themselves are informative, but unless you know *why price changes occurred* it is very easy to draw mistaken conclusions and possibly invest in the wrong coins. It is AN ABSOLUTE MUST that you read this entire book, cover to cover, before doing any investing (or any further investing, if you already own Silver Dollars). Do not skip the text chapters in the belief that our charts tell it all. Actually, the charts are, in themselves, very inconclusive and require interpretation. They are simply a record of prices at five-year intervals, but they tell nothing about actual market conditions or who was buying and who was selling. During the years covered by these charts, coin investing grew from minute beginnings to a billion-dollar operation. Coin collecting multiplied in size several times over. There have been up periods and down periods. There have been pressures of all kinds from various sides. There have been changes in prices that look, on the surface, to be utterly unexplainable.

When investors first started getting heavily into Silver Dollars, in the early to mid 1960s, they bought "across the board" without great regard for dates or mintmarks. They were not overly careful about condition, either. They were more concerned about Silver Dollars as bullion pieces than as coins with a numismatic premium. This, of course, was prompted by events of the era, which witnessed the change-over from 90% silver to clad composition for our dime and quarter, and the reduction to 40% silver from the half dollar. The single event that undoubtedly started more people as Silver Dollar investors was the Treasury Department's refusal to continue exchanging Silver Certificates for Silver Dollars. When the announcement of this decision was made on March 26, 1964, it immediately gave Silver Dollars an aura of enormous glamor in the public eye. Holders of Silver Certificates chastised themselves for not redeeming them when the opportunity was offered. But they resolved to circumvent Washington and get Silver Dollars anyway, even if it meant paying a slight surcharge at the coin shop. Certainly if the government no longer wished to part with its Silver Dollars, they must be worth the additional premium charged by coin dealers. And who knows what the future would bring?

So throngs of anxious persons, most of them totally uninformed about silver supplies or commodity markets, made their way to the neighborhood coin stores. They asked the proprietor if he had Silver Dollars for sale. The reply was "Yes, we have them. You can buy Average Circulated from that little box on the countertop, at $1.50 per piece. Or I'll show you whatever dates you need in Very Fine or Uncirculated."

As soon as they learned that they could buy three or four "Average Circulated" for the price of a single "Unc," they demolished the contents of those little boxes. And they went away with pockets and bags and briefcases stuffed with Silver Dollars.

This was the first wave of Silver Dollar investing. It lasted at its briskest for no more than six months. It slowed down out because the anticipated rise in raw silver pieces did not materialize. Some of the holders panicked and returned, downtrodden, to the coin shops from whence their Silver Dollars had been purchased. They sold them back, for a very fractional price over the face value, and in many instances they lost money. Some dealers declined to buy Silver Dollars for a while, because the number of sellers so far exceeded the number of buyers. But this was the mid 1960s and things have changed considerably since then.

In fact, they started changing right about at that time. When it seemed that no decent profits could be gleaned from investment in bullion coins, a certain number of investors became attracted to numismatic Silver Dollars. They say that values for "Uncs" were rising faster than the price of silver bullion. So they went back to the coin shops, and, this time, instead of buying scratched and dented coins from the countertop bins, they bought from the dealer's regular stock. This was something of a new phenomenon for the dealer, too, who had been accustomed to selling his coins to collectors — collectors who generally were well informed and had very definite likes and dislikes. He was not selling to a class of customers who could not find the mintmarks on coins and, when located, often did not know the meaning. There are some investors even today (thankfully a far lower number) who believe that O-mint Dollars were struck in Ohio and that Morgan Dollar had something to do with J. Pierpont Morgan.

These early Silver Dollar investors operated about as barbarically as cromagnons, and their immediate successors displayed little improvement. When investors got to the point of buying books and looking at facts and figures, they invariably misinterpreted what they read, drew the wrong conclusions, and bought just as unwisely as if they had done no reading and no thinking. They tried to be selective in their buying, but their lack of investment skills and numismatic knowledge played against them.

This situation prevailed all during the late sixties, and even up into the early seventies. The more seasoned investors were learning from their mistakes, and buying better coins. But new investors coming into the market were buying as senselessly as the new investors of five, six and seven years earlier. Now, however, much larger sums of money were being spent by investors. During the 1960s, investors had not been quite so potent a force in the trade. In the early seventies, the pendulum swung very definitely in the direction of investors and they took control of the Silver Dollar market, as well as the coin market in general (except for some specialized series or groups that were not discovered by investors until a slightly later date, such as silver 3¢ pieces). Investors were overpowering collectors with the volume of their buying and selling. The fact that they did not buy along sound numismatic lines resulted in utter chaos for prices. It put prices on a roller coaster. And it gave skilled investors the chance of a lifetime. There were more "sleepers" on the market than ever before, and more than there are likely to ever be again.

The uninformed investors of this era, who would be better termed speculators, bought in some very strange ways. Their favorite approach was to buy Silver Dollars that had gone up the most sharply in price during the previous year or two. This, to their simple way of reasoning, was the mark of a good investment coin. They bought these high-rising coins with a vengeance, which naturally caused the prices to climb more sharply. But it was a short-lived bliss. The high prices induced almost immediate selling, from holders who did not trust their coins as long term investments. The market reeled and tottered.

Many people who bought Silver Dollars for investment in the early seventies profited, even if they bought blindly and broke all the rules of sound investment. They profited because the level of coin buying increased very dramatically throughout that decade, and resulted in higher prices for nearly all dates and mintmarks. This kind of situation will definitely not occur in the 1980s. There will be profits to be made on Silver Dollar investing in the eighties, but they will be gained by careful, selective, informed investors.

You can make money by buying undervalued Silver Dollars in Uncirculated condition, from any series (Flowing Hair through Peace). Undervaluation occurs from time to time in all the Silver Dollar series. One recommendation we make, by way of being your own investment analyst, is to compare value levels in 1955/60 against those of today. Whenever you discover a certain date or mintmark leading its field in price in 1955/60, then slipping from the lead later on, you can be fairly assured that this now represents an undervalued coin. The 1955/60 prices were set almost exclusively by collector buying and selling activity. They reflected the numismatic desirability and availability of each coin. Values got out of balance when investors started coming in the market. Our firm belief is that the 1980s will witness much greater numismatic education on the part of investors, and that their purchasing will reflect this. Hence, we look for the more numismatically desirable coins to return to the top of the heap. They would never have left it, but for the fact that "hot tips" and other investment pressure drove them off. Coins that did not merit high prices became overblown in the 1970s and to some extent are still overblown today. These inflated coins are getting sluggish in their movement and are headed for a complete halt, which may last for years. A very similar situation occurred in the late sixties, when overbought coins stalled or even declined in value over a period of three to four years. The better coins continued going up, but those with less impressive numismatic credentials felt the punch. The 1970s were a dream period for investors. It made experts out of everybody, and it made coin investment seem a child's game. Now we are into the harsh realities of a new age, when skill and planning are imperative.

USING "CAUTION" IN COIN INVESTING

It would be grossly unfair to write a book such as this and leave the impression that investing in dollars or other coins is a "no risk" way of making a profit. We have pointed out a number of pitfalls that you may run into. There are others that we perhaps need to stress a bit more in order to keep you alert to some of the problems you may face.

The majority of dealers that you will encounter are honest businessmen, anxious to make a living, but also anxious to have satisfied customers who will return to them for buying or selling. So long as you take the time to convince yourself that a dealer is reliable, and monitor your dealings to make sure he continues to be reliable, you should have basically smooth sailing.

One problem that you are likely to run into (even in the best of dealer-customer relations) is the continuing controversy in the hobby about dipping coins, a topic we have referred to before. We must repeat that we do not recommend cleaning coins, or buying coins that have been cleaned, because of their reduced value. Dipping is a method of cleaning and despite protests that you will hear from many sellers of dipped coins, a dip is no more than a chemical, which attacks the surface of a coin in order to clean it. Since ANY degrading of the surface reduces mint luster, it reduces the ultimate value of the coin. If in no other way, you will be able to confirm this by the reaction of a dealer offered a dipped or cleaned coin along with one that has not been treated. Even though he is likely to dip coins himelf, he will offer more for the undipped coin. You will never see a dealer ad offering equal value for a dipped coin, so this alone should be ample testimony.

A dipped coin or one that has been cleaned in some other fashion will display an unnatural surface. The more coins you examine, the quicker you will detect such specimens. There are "toners" on the market to "restore" the natural color, but even the best do not, and cannot, restore mint luster. Mint luster, do not forget, is the key factor in determining the potential value of the coin.

This brings us to another long standing problem that you will very likely encounter. As you begin to read dealer ads, looking for the coins you want to invest in, you will often find some very flowery descriptive phrases centered around "toning." This, by the way, has nothing to do with the "toners" we mentioned in the previous paragraph.

Coins which have been in storage for long periods of time develop discoloration, oxides, "carbon" spots and other indications of contact with chemicals, acids and a multitude of pollutants either in the air or in the paper or plastic or other material in which the coin is stored. We have mentioned the hazards of plastics containing PVC, which can ruin a coin in a matter of weeks or months. Many papers contain sulphur, which will darken silver coins, and in extreme cases turn them black.

This discoloration is usually described as "toning," and over the years an aura of respectability has been attached to toning. Many people in the hobby are convinced that toning, associated with age, is an attraction on a coin, and thus adds to the value of the coin. This is a little hard to believe, especially for someone like a chemical engineer familiar with the oxide that can be created by chemical contact, but this is a major selling point for a coin as far as many dealers and their customers are concerned.

One need only read an ad extolling a coin with "Blazing rainbows of flashing colors, spread in a patina of fiery beauty across the glistening surface of this well preserved coin," to realize that your are being sold a coin which has surface discoloration. By the time you wade through this effort by the dealer to Byronic prose, and find the grade buried discreetly behind some distracting and usually meaningless modifiers — or not even given — you must know that the coin itself is not worth describing, and you will wind up paying strictly for the toning.

This position is admittedly controversial, and many dealers will heatedly deny that they are advancing toning before grade in selling a coin, or deny that toning is valueless. Unfortunately the sad fact, unknown or unadmitted by many dealers, is that anyone with a few cents worth of chemicals and a kitchen stove can duplicate any known color on the surface of a coin in minutes. Natural discoloration, or toning may take decades or centuries to produce, but it is no more and no less than surface discoloration. It can be readily duplicated, with no way of determining when or where it was done, or how many minutes or decades went into it.

We have learned, from close and continuous study of the minting process, what is and what isn't part of the minting process, and which characteristics can or cannot be duplicated once a coin leaves the mint. From this knowledge we can say flatly that "Surface color is not a part of the minting process, has no connection that can be proved with the minting process, and thus has no value to the investor or collector." As an investor, this is something that you must learn and remember so that you never find yourself in the position of paying a premium for toning. Like a fighter, you must learn to duck and slip the jabs, and go for the grade. If a collector is so enamored of toning that he chooses to pay a premium for it, well and fine. But the investor must take a more steadfast approach.

There is much to be learned in reading coin dealer ads. By following them closely, you will pick up the pulse of the market and be able to spot trends and fluctuations that may be of ultimate benefit to you. You will also quickly spot the dealers who are making the market, and those who are following along, the dealers whose prices are consistently higher, the dealer whose prices are abnormal — either too high or too low. We keep a computer file of selected prices over the years, especially for the varieties, including prices asked, catalog and auction sales, etc. Studying those figures can tell you some very interesting things about a dealer. Like snowflakes, no two are precisely alike.

If you do have problems with a coin you purchase, help is available. If the coin is purchased through an ad in one of the hobby publications, a complaint to the Ad Department usually will bring quick action. If you have a legitimate complaint and the dealer refuses to rectify it, he may be barred from further use of ad space. The American Numismatic Association exerts similar control over its members, and unresolved customer complaints are grounds for expelling a member. There are organizations such as the Professional Numismatists Guild which carefully police their members under an established and strict code of ethics.

PROFITING IN A STRONG OR WEAK MARKET

Over the long haul, the values of Silver Dollars go up dramatically. This has been the case since the beginning of collecting in this country, and there is little reason to believe it will not continue to hold true — especially, since the number of Silver Dollar buyers is constantly increasing. Look at any ten-year period during the entire 20th century, and you'll find that the majority of Silver Dollars rose in value during that period at a faster rate than national inflation. When inflation increases drastically, as it has been doing recently, Silver Dollars, historically, turn in their best performances.

But, as with any investment material, their values do not climb at a consistent pace. There will be some years with across-the-board gains of 30% or more, and other years that will show increases of only 10%. There will be occasional stagnations in the market, for a period of a few months or even as long as six months, during which time the values will rise on only a comparatively few Silver Dollars. Some may go down, temporarily, until the market adjusts itself. This is normal and unavoidable. These slumps and the effects have been figured into the forecasts we make in this book. We do not believe for an instant that the next five years, or next ten years, no matter how successful these years may be for Silver Dollar investment on the whole, will not witness some occasional slumps. In the event there are no slumps, our price projections will turn out to be extremely conservative.

This is a very resilient market. It can absorb good times and bad times without getting too far out of balance, even when the good times and bad times trigger waves of buy/sell activity. The worst slump in the Silver Dollar market in the past 20 years occurred in the late 1960s, and the strongest gain was recorded in late 1979. Disaster was predicted both times by those who doubted the overall strength of the Silver Dollar market. They claimed it could not effectively recover from the tailspin of the 1960s, and that the dizzying heights reached in 1979 would be followed by a thundering crash in which the bottom would fall out of the market. These dire forecasts proved to be incorrect. Despite the extreme pressures put on the Silver Dollar market both times — both positive and negative — and a lot of adverse publicity by critics, nothing catastrophic happened. The market, at this moment, is healthy. Prices on Gem BU Dollars are at their highest ever, even though the market value of silver bullion is considerably below the peaks reached a few years ago. No matter what happens, no matter what rumors circulate about, the simple fact is that each passing year brings more and more people into the Silver Dollar market as collectors and investors. Nothing alters that fact and other factors, comparatively, are of little significance. Yes, there will be ups and downs. But the strength of Silver Dollars as investments is clearly established, beyond all doubt.

In our own personal opinion, shared by many analysts, a slump of similar proportions to the one in the late sixties, is very unlikely to occur again. Even if it does occur, we do not see it destroying the market, or even having as much impact as it did then; but the odds for another slump of those proportions reoccurring are very minute, because conditions have changed in the Silver Dollar market. Circumstances which contributed to the late 1960s slump are no longer present, and a return to those circumstances is most improbable. The slump of the 1960s was generated mainly by the lack of confidence in the value of *silver bullion.* Many people had bought silver bullion on speculation in the early and middle sixties, when it was highly touted. It did not rise in value as quickly as anticipated, and this temporarily upset the Silver Dollar market. Hoards of Silver Dollars bought as investments a few years earlier were returned to the market by discouraged owners. This is not going to happen again because Silver Dollar investment is far more sophisticated now. It is a branch of numismatic investment and is independent from the silver bullion market. If silver bullion loses glamor as an investment (something else we consider very unlikely), it will have no affect on Gem BU Dollars. Investment buying of Silver Dollars is now approached from a numismatic viewpoint, which, you will have to agree, makes considerable more sense. Why gamble on bullion, when rare coins have such a better growth record?

A beginning investor is apt to be confused about how he should proceed, depending on the current state of the market. The old adage in investing is to buy when the market is low, and sell when the market is high. That's well and good for some types of investment, but a Silver Dollar investor does not wait for slumps before buying. In fact, he waits for nothing in particular at all. He takes the position that NOW is the right time to buy, no matter what the market happens to be doing at the moment — and this is how you should proceed. You can profit in a weak market. You can, likewise, profit by buying when the market is strong, as unlikely as that sounds. In any event, you will profit more by buying as soon as possible, rather than waiting and watching. The "waiter and watcher" accomplishes very little. He stands by, hoping (we suppose) to see prices decline on certain Dollars. Instead, the coins he intends to buy, generally, rise in value, and the longer he waits the further they rise. If he finally admits that his philosophy was wrong, and goes out to buy them, he is then in a position of having to pay more AND WAIT LONGER BEFORE SELLING.

This is likely to be the case especially with persons who have invested in stocks or other traditional investments and are accustomed to using certain tactics. These tactics don't work when buying Silver Dollars for investment. When you buy Silver Dollars for investment, your chief concern should be with picking the most attractive dates and mintmarks at the time your purchase is made. The overall condition of the market at the time you buy is of very little significance. You can count on well selected Gem BU coins to rise in value much more confidently than you can count on the market as a whole to perform as projected. The truth of the matter is that overall movement in the market — up, down or sideways — is NEVER AS GREAT as the individual movement of each particular coin of a certain date. Some dates and mintmarks go up sharply while the market as a whole is dull. The reverse is sometimes the case, too (as you will note from examining the charts in this book): the market may be soaring, but some Dollars are not benefitting as much from it as others. This is why you should concentrate on the coin and not on the market. We are not saying to ignore the market, but do not put off your buying in the belief that "some times are better to buy Dollars than others." This just isn't so. If you select the right coins to buy at the time of purchase, ANY TIME IS THE RIGHT TIME TO BUY. By the same token, if you select unattractive dates or mintmarks, the purchase is likely to be unfavorable whether it's made in a strong or weak market. At any given moment, in a slump or a surge or just an average market year, there are undervalued Dollars to be bought — hundreds of them, usually. These are coins selling for less than what they deserve to be in relation to the prices of comparatively scarce dates and mintmarks of their group. These coins have excellent potential to register substantial gains, regardless of what the market as a whole may be doing in the coming years. This is not a matter of opinion, but a matter of fact. This can easily be demonstrated by reviewing the price performance records in this book. Even in the worst of times (the late sixties slump), carefully selected Silver Dollars made money for their owners. During the mid 1980s, you will do even better with carefully selected Dollars. But you cannot start profiting, even on paper, until the coin is purchased. This is why we discourage anyone from trying to measure the market before buying. It's pointless and it only delays matters. Direct your investment thinking towards the selection of which coins to buy, and put equally as much thought into making sure that the specimens you acquire are correctly graded and fairly priced in relation to the current retail value. This is what will make or break your investment. The market is going to go its own way and do its odd and unpredictable things, no matter what. Regardless, your coins will still be good investments if properly chosen and judiciously bought.

By all means, you must always judge the value of a Silver Dollar against the current values of other dates and mintmarks in that group. The price movement of any coin by itself is really meaningless. Its attractiveness for investment can be calculated only by comparing that price movement to other dates and mintmarks of comparable scarcity. When you buy in a strong market, for example, it is possible that all, or most, coins in a group have registered strong recent gains. Nevertheless, some will still be underpriced in relation to the values of other coins. This is where your investment skill and judgment come into play. Your purpose is to buy the coins that are currently undervalued, at the time of purchase, regardless of whether they were undervalued last year or two years ago. The only thing that counts is *now,* because the current conditions tell you which coins are the most apt to record substantial future gains. A coin that was underpriced last year but is now fully priced (or apparently so) is not a favorable investment, unless you care to buy it on a long-term basis and hold it for ten years or more. If you want short-term gainers, you must go after the Silver Dollars that are undervalued right at the moment, as these are the coins that should show the most dramatic price increases within the next couple of years.

INHERITED SILVER DOLLARS

The following advice is for those who have inherited silver dollars. Often such individuals have no knowledge of coins, the silver market, or of investment techniques, and are at a total loss to determine how their silver dollars can be employed to the best advantage. In general the advice will depend on the size and nature of the collection, and the individual's personal circumstances and future goals. In some cases it may be wise to proceed with a sale, and in others to hold for investment; or to sell some of the silver dollars and hold others.

If the inherited silver dollars are part of a general coin collection containing other types of coins, the remainder of the collection should not be overlooked. To a person unfamiliar with old coins, a miscellaneous general collection is apt to seem insignificant, when in fact it could contain important rarities. This is particularly true of coins struck in base metals such as early half cents, cents, three cent nickels, and early 5¢ pieces. All of these groups have their rarities. By the same token it frequently happens that the value of an inherited collection is underestimated, because it is known that the owner was not a person of means. This was perhaps a childhood collection of a grandfather or great-grandfather, assembled on a very tight budget or possibly by taking interesting coins from everyday pocket change. One must realize that coin values have advanced enormously over the years; also, that rare coins did turn up in pocket change in the days of our ancestors. Any inherited collection, regardless of its size or appearance, is worthy of investigation. It will certainly have some value, and the value may greatly surprise you.

The first step, with an inherited collection, is to determine its value. This can be done only by evaluating each coin individually and adding the individual values. There are no shortcut approaches. Information provided in this book will enable you to determine the exact condition grade of all silver dollars in your possession, and to fix prices on those in uncirculated condition. For details on grading coins other than silver dollars, and for current market prices of silver dollars in circulated condition (as well as of other coins), consult the *Official Blackbook Price Guide to U.S. Coins.* Be sure to use the current edition, which can be ordered directly from the publishers by using the order form at the back of this book.

Assuming that you have incorrectly graded some of the coins, which is likely, the value arrived at will not be precise. It will, however, serve to give a good indication of the collection's value, on which you can then base a decision as to your next move.

You may be wondering whether the silver dollars should be held for investment growth. If they are common dates in circulated condition, their future potential as an investment would be for bullion only. Unless a large number of coins were involved it would probably not be to your advantage to hold them, but if there are dozens or hundreds of bullion dollars then you have the basis of an attractive bullion investment.

If the collection contains semi-key dates in circulated condition, these are not generally regarded as investment coins either as bullion or collector investments. They are not bullion pieces as they sell at a premium over bullion value; and they are not collector investments, as they rise too slowly in value in most cases. You would probably be best advised to sell them, and, if desired, use the proceeds to buy investment dollars such as those recommended in this book.

If there are key date dollars and/or uncirculated dollars among your inherited coins, they may include some favorable investment pieces which should be retained. In the case of uncirculated dollars, we would suggest that you review the charts and investment advice given in this book, to learn if your coins fall within the favorable investment category. As for key date dollars in circulated condition, these are very often "borderline" for investment purposes. It has not been possible to review their investment potential, coin by coin, in this book because of space limitations. Nevertheless, you can gain valuable insight into their investment qualities by checking the investment advice given for MS-60 specimens. If any of your coins have been favorably reviewed in MS-60, then quite likely circulated specimens would be expected to show satisfactory — though smaller — value gains in the coming years. If this is not the case, you may still have dollars which would be salable at substantial prices at the present time on the rare coin market. Specific information on their current values will be found in the *Official Blackbook Price Guide to U.S. Coins.*

If you are interested in using your silver dollar inheritance as the nucleus of an investment, we would strongly advise that it be "weeded out," retaining the pieces with strong investment quality and disposing of the others (using the proceeds to replace them with dollars recommended in this book). In doing this you will undoubtedly reduce the number of silver dollars in your possession, as you may be selling ten coins to buy one, depending on the differences in value. Nevertheless you will have a much better long-range investment. Also, the pieces retained should be transferred from their present holders into mylar holders for best protection, and an identification slip should be prepared for each. This will keep your investment orderly.

COULD DISASTER STRIKE?

When contemplating any form of investment, especially one of which the investor has no great personal knowledge, a question uppermost in one's mind is: Could disaster hit this field of investment? Could my investment be wiped out or seriously eroded by some kind of unforeseen development? How can I be assured this will not happen?

We have all heard of stock investments which, despite glowing claims of brokers, eventually came to be worth no more than waste paper. Does such a danger exist with Silver Dollars?

The simple answer to that question is NO. But a simple answer should not be satisfactory to the cautious, thinking investor. Therefore, we will get into some detail about the risks in Silver Dollar investing.

There is, of course, a certain degree of risk in Silver Dollar investing as in all types of financial speculation. The future is unknown to all of us; hence, things which should happen or might happen tomorrow are uncertain. But the degree of risk in Silver Dollar investing is considerably less than in most other kinds of investing. And it is not (as in some investments) a risk of catastrophic consequences. You will not awake one morning to discover that your Dollars are valueless. You will never walk the streets in search of a buyer, only to be rebuffed. They will always have some value and purchasers will always be prepared to take them from you. The risk is in whether they will appreciate rapidly enough in value to turn a satisfactory profit. This risk can be considerably minimized by careful planning and judicious buying. The more skilled you are at buying Dollars, the less risk you take. Expert investors reduce their risk to nearly zero. Of course, factors play upon values that you cannot control. The market can experience slumps. This is why the risk can never be totally eliminated. But the risk is related in some degree to the length of time you are willing or able to continue holding your Dollars. There is a possibility (slim, but a possibility) that even a carefully assembled Dollar portfolio, bought with the intention of turning a profit in three or four years, will not have arrived at a profitable price level in that time. However, if held for a period of time, it is virtually certain that your coins would achieve the necessary price rise. Therefore when you figure risk factor, you must consider whether you could (or would be willing to) hold your Dollar portfolio for a somewhat longer time than the planned maturity, if it becomes desirable to do so. If the answer to that question is Yes, you have cleaved the already small risk into a minute particle.

As for the possibility of the bottom dropping out from the numismatic or silver bullion markets, such thoughts cannot be seriously entertained. This has not occurred in the nearly 200 years since establishment of the U.S. Mint. Coin values have occasionally wavered under extreme pressure, such as the Depression of 1929-40, but there has never been any total collapse. Quite the reverse; numismatic coins have weathered economic storms much better than many other objects of value. Prophets of doom predicted that coin prices would tumble drastically during the Great Depression. Surely, it was stated, a jobless nation, beset with challenges of daily existence, would abandon hobbies. People would rush to sell their coins, stamps and everything else expendable that they owned to buy the necessities of life. This sounded entirely logical but it didn't work that way. Many coin collections were, of course, sold during the Great Depression, but the volume of selling was hardly any greater than during good times. Collectors in general took the position that it was unwise to sell in a weak market, and they kept holding. Prices declined on many coins, because the level of buying had dropped off. But these declines were not nearly so sharp as had been feared. Not everyone became penniless in the Great Depression. Collectors who still had money to spend — and there were plenty of them despite what you have probably heard about the deprivations of the 1930s — took advantage of the bargains. They went out and bought coins they needed but were previously unable to afford. Thus, buying did not completely cease. These bargain-takers, whom you will always have in troubled times, helped to keep a foundation under prices. Values slipped from their 1920s highs, but did not slide to rock bottom. Coin dealers did enormous business during the Depression and, on the whole, it was a profitable time for many of them. They had the opportunity to buy cheaply and they bought whatever they could, knowing that the national economy would turn around and that coin values would readjust themselves. This took, perhaps, somewhat longer to occur than was anticipated. The Great Depression dragged on during the whole decade of the thirties, and was not finally eradicated until World War II began. But even then, with one calamity added atop another, the numismatic hobby flourished and coin values performed very admirably. At the very same time, many Wall Street stocks were unsaleable at 10¢ on the dollar. These included numerous "blue chips" that their holders believed were solid as stone. In fact, the value of most paper investments — in land, rail lines, oil, manufacturing and other holdings — were cut in half in just two weeks following the notorious "Black Friday" market crash. Banks failed. Millionaires were wiped out. But coins, on the whole, did no worse than losing 30% or at most 40% of their previous values. This was indeed a remarkable show of strength. And, what may be more noteworthy, coin values began improving again *long before* the Depression came to its end.

In the event of another Great Depression, which in itself is unlikely, coins would probably do even better vs. other investments than they did in the 1930s. Investors and the public at large have more confidence in coins today than in the thirties. They have good reason to, because in the intervening years coin values have attained heights that were undreamed of 50 years ago. The coin market has weathered other assaults since the Great Depression, and proven its durability. There would likely be fewer coin owners going out to sell, if another Depression occurred, than sold in the thirties. There would almost certainly be more buyers. If prices were to fall 30% or 40% on choice Silver Dollars during the eighties, numerous investors would find this temptation irresistible. They would purchase in quantity, and they would be followed in their descent upon coin shops by investment groups and (very likely) commercial organizations buying Silver Dollars on speculation. Prices would go down but they would not bottom out. They would stabilize in a short period of time, and undoubtedly start rising fairly quickly. Money would be made on Silver Dollars during another Great Depression.

What about other calamities or disasters? What effect would a World War have on Silver Dollar prices?

Talking of the effects of a World War is difficult. There is no way of knowing what the international circumstances would be: which nations, and how many nations, would be involved; and, more significantly, what kind of weapons would be used and whether civilian life in the engaged countries would continue undisturbed. World War II did not damage the coin trade. Because of circumstances, it actually led to increased coin buying activity. This occurred because the nation was rocked out of its Financial Depression by the war. The war siphoned millions of men from the domestic job market, and at the same time created millions of war-production jobs for those who remained. The country had prosperity during World War II to a level unknown since the 1920s. Prices on just about everything climbed, to the point where government controls had to be placed on many commodities. The coin market did very well during World War II. The charts in this book do not reach back as far as the 1940s. If they did, they would show values on Silver Dollars rising significantly between 1940 and 1945, the year that marked the war's end. Nor did World War II's conclusion trigger a reversal of the coin market's health. In fact, it boomed fabulously after the war. Prosperity continued and many returning veterans took up coin collecting as a hobby.

It is highly unlikely that any panic selling of silver investment Dollars would occur in the event of another major war. Most holders of Dollars and other numismatic coins would consider their capital safer in coins than in money. This would be true not only in the U.S. but foreign countries in general. During any World War, there is fear of demonetization of currency. The currencies of numerous governments (not ours) were demonetized during or following World War II. It is much more logical for citizens of countries engaged in major wars to hold material of intrinsic or saleable value, rather than currency. In fact, it would not be surprising if the reverse of panic selling occurred. There might well be a rush, on the part of many persons, to convert their excess currency into "hard" investments. This could cause a sharp rise in Silver Dollar values which, presumably, would be maintained during the War, and very likely not be seriously diminished thereafter. Of course, the length of the War and other factors, fruitless to speculate upon, would have some influence.

The important point to realize is that the coin market has sufficient strength of its own to get through bad times. It has demonstrated its ability to do this, in the past, and it has now developed and strengthened to the point where it ought to be even less affected by national upheaval. This is not really a matter of interest in coin collecting continuing to thrive during troubled eras. Interest in coin collecting does go on, in good times and bad. But a much more important consideration is the fact that financial calamities, or calamities that spill over into the economy, can encourage coin buying *by people who would not otherwise have put their money into coins.* Numismatic coins and especially Silver Dollars have not arrived at the stage of being an accepted, recognized defense against economic chaos. Rather than turning away from Silver Dollars in bad times, a majority of the public will turn toward them, and be extremely glad that something so trustworthy is available to the average citizen.

Well, then, would a slump in coin prices prompt wholesale selling on the part of investors, and drive prices down?

This is certainly a key question and well worth asking. The investor who fears such an occurrence has some basis for his apprehensions. But he should be careful not to jump to conclusions.

Two nagging circumstances may haunt the potential investor, after he has thoroughly explored the background of Silver Dollar investment. These are:

1. The slump experienced by the coin market in the late 1960s.

2. The fact that a very large number of existing Silver Dollars are in the hands of investors, and that these investors could, by following the same course of action at the same time, virtually destroy the market.

As to the repeat of the late sixties numismatic market slump, there would seem to be extremely little chance of this happening in the 1980s. The sixties slump occurred because of circumstances that do not exist today and cannot logically exist again. Fearing a replay of the 1960s slump is really like being afraid of getting trampled by a runaway horse in a modern city, just because such things once occurred. The coin market was suffering in the 1960s from an overdose of badly planned, haphazard, illogical investment buying. Rare coin investment in those naive times was looked upon, by many, as a "get rich quick" program. People invested huge sums of money in coins, and especially Dollars, without knowing about coins. Not only were they uninformed about coins, they knew very little about the principles of investment. They spend wildly and lavishly, without knowing what they are buying, or what it was really worth, or how long they could expect to hold it before selling. Like the Grecian misers of old, they simply piled coin atop coin. The coin market, even when healthy, had a difficult time coping with this kind of nonsense. Values fluctuated because of unselective purchasing, and the collecting community fumed at the investment community for playing havoc with prices. During those hectic years of the sixties, nobody really knew for sure what a coin was worth from week to week or month to month. Coins that ought to have risen in value declined, and weak coins with no credentials to speak of sprouted halos and became objects of worship. All of this was bad enough, but things got even worse. Beginning around 1966, but more noticeably in 1967, many of these investors started selling their coins. Some of them, thanks to the kind of pure luck that sometimes throws drowning men up on a beach, were profiting from their holdings. They were profiting not because they had made intelligent selections, but in spite of having bought the wrong coins at the wrong prices. They were profiting because thousands of other investors also badly informed, were buying the same coins. Realizing they were in no position to ignore the knock of opportunity, they went out and sold, and took their profits — which many of them turned directly around and put into just as badly selected coins. This vast, unexpected wholesale selling went to the heart of the market. It drove home like a poisoned arrow, and the numismatic trade was down, but not completely out. As prices on certain coins stagnated, other holders panicked. They sold, even if they could not obtain a profit, fearing that to wait might mean a greater loss. Investment coins by the carload were returned to the market in 1967, 1968 and 1969. The troops of sellers who stormed coin shops could not be equaled, in numbers, by the mightiest armies of the world. They staged onslaught after onslaught, and they drove prices further and further into the ground.

The battlefield was bloody. But a faint sun arose over it. Collectors started buying in increased quantity. They snapped up bargains. Gradually, some investors did the same. In time, the market roused itself. Within two years it returned to full health. But the late sixties had been an era it would choose to quickly forget.

The events of the 1960s could not replay themselves, because circumstances leading up to those events are not the same today. Investors are better informed. They make far more intelligent selections, and do not look for overnight windfall profits. The average Silver Dollar investor of the 1980s is prepared to wait patiently for 5 years, or even longer, before disposing of his portfolio. Nor is the current investor as faint hearted as his predecessor. He has more confidence in the stability of his investment. He has learned to ignore tipsters and quick-buck artists and prophets of doom. He has gotten the knack of deafening his ear to rumors. The 1960s slump was a chain reaction brought on by senseless buying and senseless selling. It was not the fault of the coins, or the coin market, or the people who bought wisely. It was attributable to mob violence. That kind of thing is not going to happen again.

As for the second of our two questions, the fact that so many Silver Dollars are currently in possession of investors — is this not, you may ask, some cause for concern?

It is true enough, and we would not dispute the matter for an instant, that the quanities of Silver Dollars owned by investors has become disproportionate to those owned by collectors. Investors now, without question, own the majority of Silver Dollars in existence. They own the vast majority of average circulated "bullion" Dollars, and certainly more than 50% of all numismatic Dollars. The value of investor holdings in Silver

Dollars is probably twice that of collector holdings, if not more (we wouldn't be surprised if it were three or four times as much). Even if you include dealer stocks along with collector holdings, investors still own the majority of Silver Dollars. This might seem frightening. *Should* it be?

It would probably be better for the investment community if a larger share of Dollars were owned by collectors. This would not cause the prices to rise any faster, but it would provide a better guarantee against mass selling. Coins in the possession of collectors tend to remain off the market longer than coins owned by investors. The more specimens of any given coin that are owned by collectors, the more likelihood that the coin will grow steadily harder to get on the market with each passing year. When investors own 90% of the specimens of a certain coin, and collectors 10%, one cannot say with confidence that the coin will be as scarce next year as this year. However, this should not be a matter for undue concern. The investor of today is, as we have pointed out, more skilled in buying and selling. He can be counted upon to hold his coins longer than investors of the sixties or even the seventies. The chances of large groups of investors dumping their Silver Dollars on the market to take advantage of an upsurge in values is extremely remote. Investors will have to learn to trust other investors. This may be asking a lot, based on events of the past. But the eighties has ushered in a new ballgame, with different players and much more attention to rules of the game. Investors are serious these days and there is not much likelihood of them doing anything to hurt themselves or the investment community at large.

THE ENEMY IS INFLATION

Investing used to be a consideration of the already wealthy. Turn the clock back as recently as 20 years and you'll see what we mean. The Average Working Person took care of himself and his family, paid his taxes, and if there was any money left over, he banked it. The Wealthy Individual did not bank his left-over money. He invested it, in things which would (hopefully) pay a better rate of return than bank interest.

The Average Working Person did not think about investment. He simply wanted his money in a safe place. He was content to believe that the bank offered him the best future for his hard-earned money. By just leaving his money in the bank, and not touching it, IT INCREASED! A hundred dollars grew (in those days) to about $103 after a year. If you had $1,000 on deposit, you earned A WHOLE THIRTY DOLLARS in a year — for doing absolutely nothing! Wasn't this much smarter than taking risks with your money, and possibly losing it?

The Average Working Person felt that his future was secure, because he lived in a country with such a fine banking system.

There was just one little problem.

The rate of National Inflation increased faster than bank interest rates.

The Average Working Person who still banks his left-over money continues to draw interest. He gets a better rate of interest than in the 1960s and 1970s. But at the same time, he gets poorer and poorer. His money grows, but the purchasing power to his money declines. He has more money, but it will buy less and less. And the value of money can, obviously, only be figured in terms of what it will buy. Money has no intrinsic value any longer.

This is where investing comes in. Investing is the only viable weapon against inflation. You may be able to *get more money* by getting a raise or taking a second job, but the only way to *keep your money from declining in buying power is through investment.*

The general public was slow to realize this. Billions of dollars of their money was chewed away by inflation before a substantial number of them got tired enough to do something about it. They saw that, no matter what happened in Washington or in the world, their money was going in only one direction: down. They could alter its course only by investing.

Today, many Average Working People are investing. Others are joining the investment ranks every day. The comparatively few who aren't investing have either just given up, or don't know about inflation, or are frightened of the word INVESTMENT.

It is, to some individuals, a scary word. "Investment" conjures up thoughts of Black Friday and stock brokers selling apples on the street-corner in the Depression. To these people, "investing" is just another word for "gambling." We hope this book will make you feel differently about investing. Certainly, there *are* risky investments, and if you don't have a lot of risk capital to play with you should avoid them. There are investments which could turn $10,000 into a million within a year — such as backing a Broadway show that proves a smash hit. Silver Dollar investing is not in this category. It does not promise huge immediate returns. It offers excellent potential for good, steady returns, with a very low risk factor. It is the ideal investment for persons of average means, who would normally bank most of their money. Silver Dollar investing is the prime inflation fighter for the 1980s and beyond. Inflation is easily conquered if you own something that goes up in value faster than inflation. Silver Dollars have consistently done this during the past two decades. They show every likelihood of continuing to do so, right up to the century's end. Nothing else that you can buy as easily, and *in such small quantities if desired,* has that kind of growth record and future potential.

You needn't be an economist to understand inflation. Every time you pay more for something than the last time you bought it — that's inflation. Inflation hits every facet of daily life. The cost of everything goes up: fuel oil, hospitalization, travel, the daily newspaper. This upward movement in prices is known as inflation, and it results in more inflation. Inflation is an octopus with tentacles reaching out in all directions.

Why does inflation happen? It happens because everything involved in the economy is interlocked. The price of one item or service cannot rise without causing rises elsewhere. Milk will cost more if the farmers have higher operating costs, or if the cost of processing increases, or the cost of trucking . . . or dozens of other incidental expenses along the line. Then, in turn, the rising price of milk results in higher prices on everything made from or with milk. All these expenses are, naturally, passed along to the ultimate consumer: YOU. The public pays the bill for inflation. In the past an attempt was made to curb inflation with Wage and Price Controls. These controls proved unworkable, not to mention unpopular. Everyone thought they were getting the worst end of the Wage and Price controls. Other measures have been contemplated and tried in an attempt to combat inflation. Nothing has worked effectively.

Inflation may be with us for the rest of time. If the government is powerless against inflation, the private individual is not powerless in his own personal battle with inflation. Everyone *can* halt the decline in purchasing power of their money, and in fact increase it . . . even in times of very high inflation. This nation had the worst inflation rate in its history in the Carter Administration, yet in those very years Silver Dollar investors were turning handsome profits on their capital. An inflation rate of 17% per year is not very alarming when you own an investment that is rising at 50% per year! These were the statistics for 1979. People who were holding money say it eroded at a record pace. Holders of Silver Dollars had *more* purchasing power at the end of 1979 than when the year began.

Inflation has claimed millions of victims and it could claim millions more. You needn't be among them. No matter what your financial situation is at present, even if you can afford to buy only a few "average circulated" Silver Dollars, you have the power to fight inflation. And you will win! Don't worry about not having much capital to invest. IT DOESN'T MATTER! Money that you *must* spend now, for living expenses, doesn't enter into the picture. You can't bank this money, either, or do anything else with it except spend it — so forget about it. Think only in terms of cash that you *would normally bank,* or any excess monies that go for unnecessary purposes. These are the sums to be invested in Silver Dollars, then your money will work for you, instead of inflation working against you.

INFLATION CHART

We all know that inflation is eating away at the buying power of our money. But we may not be aware of how fast or how dramatically until the facts and figures are put on paper. The following chart shows the decline in buying power of $100 over the coming years, at various percentage levels in the rate of inflation. It is naturally impossible to predict how high inflation will become, or if there will be any success on the part of Washington to reduce it substantially. You can be sure of only one thing: that inflation will always be with us and that as long as it is, any money that you keep in cash (as opposed to a good sound investment such as Silver Dollars) is going to decline in purchasing power.

$100 CASH ON JANUARY 1, 1986

Rate of Inflation	Buying Power by Year					
	1989	1990	1991	1992	1993	1994
7%	93.00	86.49	80.44	74.81	69.57	64.70
8%	92.00	84.64	77.87	71.64	65.91	60.64
9%	91.00	82.81	75.36	68.58	62.41	56.79
10%	90.00	81.00	72.90	65.61	59.05	53.15
12%	88.00	77.44	68.15	59.97	52.77	46.44
15%	85.00	72.25	61.41	52.20	44.37	37.71
17%	83.00	68.89	57.18	47.46	39.39	32.69
20%	80.00	64.00	51.20	40.96	32.77	26.22
22%	78.00	60.84	47.46	37.02	28.88	22.53
25%	75.00	56.25	42.19	31.64	23.73	17.80

If 25% (the highest percentage on our chart) seems ridiculous, we need only remind you that a number of leading industrialized nations of the world have had, or are currently experiencing, a worse rate of inflation.

UNCIRCULATED, BY ALL MEANS

We have threaded this piece of advice through the book, but it is so important that is deserves special attention. Not only special attention, but trumpet blasts, and drum rolls, and bonfires; for if this single phase of your investment approach is overlooked, your investment could be destroyed.

When buying numismatic Silver Dollars for investment (as opposed to bullion coins), BUY IN UNCIRCULATED CONDITION ONLY. Or, "UNC" for short.

Uncirculated specimens of any coins — copper, silver, gold — invariably prove better money-makers than those in lesser condition grades. When investing in Silver Dollars, "Unc" is absolutely imperative, more so than for coins of other types or denominations.

Why? Because the situation with Silver Dollars bears little relation to that of Dimes, Quarters and other investor coins. A very high proportion of existing Morgan and Peace Dollars are in Uncirculated condition. With some of the dates, there are actually more "Uncs" in existence and on the market than circulated specimens. This is not the case with old coins in general. With most old coins, only 5% or less of existing specimens are Uncirculated. Therefore, Morgan and Peace Dollars have very little collector or numismatic appeal in circulated grade. They are not rarities in Unc, except for a few dates and mintmarks, so the collecting community will not settle for them in any less condition. A collector will pay good money for a "Fine" Large Cent, because he may despair of ever finding or being able to afford the coin in Unc. He will not give a second glance to a Morgan or Peace Dollar in comparable state of preservation. A circulated Morgan or Peace is a "filler." It is undesirable for collecting purposes and hence it is not investment material, unless you happen to be investing from a bullion point of view.

Coin dealers sell Silver Dollars in circulated condition, as well as Uncirculated. You will find so-called "high grades" of circulated Dollars at the coin shop, selling for more than the price of "average circulated." They may carry a price tag of $20 or $25, while bullion specimens are bringing $15. At the same time, an Unc may be retailing for $100 or even $150. It is very easy to be misled by this situation — and by a lot of other things that could confront you in a coin shop. This is why we advise you not to do any investment purchasing without reading the entire contents of this book and taking a good hard look at the market. In other words, prepare yourself for what you may find in a coin shop, and have your defenses ready so that bad investment coins do not succeed in seducing you. If you start buying too soon, before learning the ropes of investment and of the coin market in general, you are very likely to acquire some unworthy coins. Remember, always and forever, that your local coin shop is not established exclusively for investors. It is in the business of selling coins, of all kinds and all grades, to whoever is interested in them. It naturally carries some coins that are of interest to collectors and not to investors. It likewise has coins that are not very appealing to either group, but occasionally these coins are sold, too (some people like to mount coins in jewelry). So do not assume that everything you see in a coin shop — whether the shop is small and dusty or big and glittering — deserves investment attention. The fact of the matter is that the majority of merchandise does not. As an investor you must extract the plums from the pie. You must be certain they *are* plums, and that you are not paying full prices for sodden fruit. And if you are firmly convinced that the condition is exactly as represented, you then must convince yourself that the dealer's price is not beyond the market. This, of course, can be established by investigating the prices of his competitors.

If you have not previously invested in Silver Dollars, or collected them, you are probably not aware of the idiosyncracies of their values. It is worthwhile to learn them, and to pay heed to them. Average circulated Morgan and Peace Dollars are worth the value of their silver bullion content (¾ths of an ounce of .999 fine), plus a surcharge for the fact that these coins are Dollars and are therefore more attractive to bullion investors. But this surcharge is really insignificant. The important fact is that the value of average circulated bullion Dollars rises as silver rises, and declines as silver declines, in direct ratio to silver's daily "spot" prices. Therefore you do not profit on Silver Dollar bullion coins unless the value of silver rises rather substantially. What may happen in the meantime, in the numismatic market, will have no influence on the value of a Silver Dollar bullion coin investment. Silver prices and silver prices alone will dictate its fate. Even if the number of collectors for Silver Dollars greatly increases, this will not have an effect on values of average circulated bullion specimens. The prices of Uncs will rise but prices of average circulated bullion Dollars will remain at the spot level plus a slight premium.

Silver Dollars in better grade circulated condition, such as EF, can and frequently do rise in value independent of the silver bullion market. The majority of their value is, generally, in their silver content, but they carry an additional collector value which "average circulated" specimens do not. Usually, better grade circulated Dollars score gains in price from year to year. However, these advances are much smaller, percentage-wise, than those of Uncirculated. During a year in which Uncs of a given date rise by 50%, the increase for EF may be 15% or 20%. If Uncs rise 20%, EF will probably show a 5% climb or none at all. Therefore, there is no question (if anyone could possibly have doubts in his mind) the Uncirculated Silver Dollars are the best investment buy. They have, historically, increased in price at a faster pace than all the Circulated condition grades. In the past few years, this rate of increase has become sharper, and the difference in value between Uncs and Circulated Dollars has grown wider and wider. You will have to pay more when buying Uncs, but you will have a much sounder investment. Do not let yourself be swayed by the fact that you can buy three or four Silver Dollars in better grade circulated condition for the price of a single Unc. You would be getting more silver by taking that approach, but if you're investing in numismatic Dollars this is not the route to follow.

Be sure that your Dollars are indeed Uncs. Uncirculated means that the coin shows no evidence of wear. It is difficult to determine this when a coin is beneath the glass of a display counter, under the glare of light. A first glance impression is not reliable. Many circulated Dollars give the appearance of being Uncirculated at first glance. They look bright and shiny and there is no apparent sign of wear. They seem never to have been handled in circulation, the way the coins in your pocket do. But a closer examination may tell a very different story. Brightness and shininess mean nothing. If the coin has any indication of rubbing, even if very minute and occurring only at the highest points of its design, it cannot be classified as Uncirculated — and its value is considerably lower than an Unc, even if the coin is very, very pretty looking. Some Silver Dollars acquire handsome surface coloration, to the point where a high-grade circulated specimen can really be more attractive than an Unc. You will encounter such examples frequently in coin shops. Attractiveness may add to the value, but it does not make the specimen as valuable as an Unc, nor desirable from an investment point of view. A specimen which is not spectacular looking, but genuinely qualifies as Uncirculated, will always be the better investment choice. Study the gradings as given on the coin holders, and study the coins as well. You should use a magnifying lens, which the dealer will have handy. Do not automatically trust the dealer's grading. He could have made a mistake on some of his coins. Possibly some of them are Borderline Uncs, which he has chosen to call Unc rather than Au (About Uncirculated). Even if you can pick these coins up for less than the full retail price of an Unc, it would be smarter to avoid them, as you will incur a stiff discount from the buyer when you go to sell them. As a collector they might be excellent acquisitions for you, but you must think in terms of their investment potential.

Once you have acquired properly graded Uncirculated Dollars, it is important that they be maintained in the best of condition. This can be accomplished by referring to the suggestions in the "Storing and Protecting Your Silver Dollars" section at the back of this book.

TIMING YOUR PURCHASES AND SALES

In investing, timing is vital. One of the most important lessons to be learned is proper timing. A great coin could be unprofitable if bought at the wrong time, or sold at the wrong time. You will need to become adept at timing to be as successful as possible in your Silver Dollar investing. This is not difficult. It requires only some thought, possibly a little patience, and an up-to-date knowledge of events in the numismatic market.

Timing in purchasing means buying good coins — coins of solidly established collector reputation — which are at the moment selling for less than they should be. You do not, and should not, wait for overall sluggishness in the market to do your buying. There is no reason to hesitate to buy in a thriving, booming market. But even when the Silver Dollar market is at its healthiest, some dates and mintmarks in certain series will be undervalued. This inevitably happens because the level of buying and selling from one coin to the next is not uniform. Some coins are overlooked, often in favor of dates or mintmarks that really do not merit the attention given them. At any particular moment, regardless of the general state of the market, there are underpriced Silver Dollars to be had. We have explained to you in this book how to recognize them. You should focus your attention on these coins, and get them in Uncirculated condition while the price is down. Buying an undervalued coin is just the same as getting a big discount from the dealer on a fully valued coin — which no investor would think of passing up. Yet these undervalued coins are often missed, simply because there are no signs or red flashing lights to call attention to them. You cannot depend on the dealer to recommend them for you. Investment recommendations by a coin dealer, while sometimes helpful, should not be the basis for your purchasing decision. The dealer has a personal interest in the coins in his shop and cannot be expected to be an impartial source of advice. It is up to you to know when a coin is undervalued.

You must, of course, keep up to date with the coin market. This might seem like a colossal, fulltime task. It is actually much easier keeping tabs on coin values than on stock prices. Stock prices officially change every business day. To keep informed of changes in coin values, you need only subscribe to one of the weekly coin newspapers (Coin World of Sydney, Ohio, or Numismatic News of Iola, Wisconsin). Each week these publications carry tables showing the current retail prices being paid, that week, for coins in all classes. This information is further supplemented by the numerous buying and selling advertisements run by dealers. By taking just a few minutes each week to read one of these papers, you will have a good working knowledge of the current state of prices. Since you are concentrating on just one class of coins — Silver Dollars — your task in keeping abreast of the market is much simpler than investors who spread themselves out over the whole field of rare U.S. coins. These few minutes, and the money you spend for a subscription (tax deductible if you qualify for investor status) will repay itself many times over. You will be buying with much greater confidence, and you will know which coins to buy without having to guess or rely on someone's "hot tips."

So far as investment newsletters are concerned, some are useful and others are of very doubtful value. As a general rule, we would advise against structuring your purchasing along the lines of coins touted in these publications. Much of what appears in these newsletters seems to be written simply for the sake of filling space. The publication must be issued on a certain schedule, and even if nothing noteworthy is happening in the coin market it is necessary that comments are made, just for the purpose of putting text in the paper. The coins recommended are, very often, ones that an intelligent investor would not select on his own. Compilers of these publications have the habit of picking coins that are showing current price increases. They tend to overlook underpriced dates and mintmarks in favor of coins that, because of their recent price increases, are on the verge of becoming overpriced or possibly have already gotten overpriced. We believe that on the whole you would do better taking the money required for subscribing to these newsletters (which are expensive) and putting it into subscriptions for auction sale catalogues. The sale catalogues, with their lists of prices realized (which you will receive automatically following each sale), are a far better guide to the current market. The newsletters try to analyze auction sale results, which is all well and good, but an intelligent investor can do this for himself and very likely reach conclusions that are more applicable to his own investment situation. For example, the newsletter "auction summaries" will often overlook the type of coins that you have an investment interest in.

Timing your sales is just as important. Coin investors of the 1960s and throughout much of the '70s were not skilled in this area. They ran out and sold when the market dropped, in fear of further declines. They made "dump sale" after "dump sale," often suffering huge losses. These losses were entirely unnecessary and could have been avoided with better strategy. Timing is, after all, just another word for strategy. Your goal is to achieve the best possible price for your investment Dollars. Your strategy must be orchestrated toward that end, and you must not allow anything to get in the way of it.

For your investment Dollars to show a profit, they must be able to pay off the dealer's (or auctioneer's) commission charge and still return more purchasing power than the money used to buy them. For example, say you bought a Silver Dollar today for $500. While holding it, the inflation rate would be eating away at the buying power of money. Therefore, your $500 capital is not really worth $500 any longer. If you held the coin for three years and sold it for $500, you would not be breaking even. You would be suffering a loss, the exact size of which would depend on the percentage of inflation between now and then. If inflation goes up 10% in a year, you technically have $550 tied up in that coin, not the original $500. You must get back $550 to break even. And so on. This is the way to calculate investment profits. By learning to think in this fashion it will be easier for you to correctly time your sales. You must sell your coins when the market is substantially higher *on the coins you own* than it was at the time of purchase. The definition of "substantially higher" is open to interpretation. It is mostly a matter of how much time has passed since the investment was made. If you can sell an investment Dollar for 20% more than you paid, within a year after making the purchase, this would in most instances rate as a satisfactory sale (with selling commissions deducted, of course; which means the coin would need to climb in value 40-50% in that year). A 20%-over-cost sale after holding for two years is not satisfactory. It would be satisfactory only if the rate of national inflation drops considerably lower than its present level. By the same token, a 75%-over-cost sale after holding for five years is not satisfactory. You would have a large paper profit but, in fact, you would be suffering a loss in terms of the purchasing power of your money. The money that you spent in buying the coin or coins had more purchasing power than the money obtained when selling them. This is obviously not a very pretty picture for the investor. It *can* be avoided. There are *dozens* of Silver Dollars that should, almost without question, rise in value at least 100% in the next five years. We have pointed them out to you in this book. But it is impossible to predict the precise year-by-year rate of their rise. They may stall in value for a year and go nowhere. Then the following year they could gain 50% or more, as happened in 1979 with many Silver Dollars. This is why we recommend coins that look favorable over a five-year period, rather than overnight hot-shots. These five year coins may not climb in value at a steady pace, but at the end of five years they ought to have at least doubled in price over the current levels. We do not recommend selling them in less than five years. However, if the market should become extremely strong and excellent profit opportunities are offered, the investor may want to consider selling earlier. We do not, however, advocate selling during a rapidly rising market, until some signs of leveling off occur. You could very well miss out on a substantial additional profit by selling your coins too soon. When the retail prices of Silver

Dollars in Uncirculated condition are bounding upward by 5-10% per month, which can happen in a strong market, there is very little likelihood that an immediate downswing will develop. You are not running any risk, or at any rate an infinitesimal one, by holding a little longer in these circumstances.

Keep informed of the market, and have your strategy mapped in advance. Have counterplans in mind for any movements the market might make. But, above all, do not panic. Do not be quick to sell your coins if prices go down, or are slow to rise. If you are holding five-year investment coins, you should not make any judgment on their performance until the full five years have elapsed. This will give them ample time to rebound from any sluggishness they might encounter. Silver Dollars in Uncirculated condition are sound investments and you should never place yourself in a position where a forced sale is necessary. This should be considered only if you urgently need the money for some purpose.

HISTORY OF THE 1804 DOLLAR

Although we have mentioned the 1804 dollar in the chapter on the Draped Bust-Heraldic Eagle dollars, we cannot cover the silver dollars completely without examining this particular piece in greater detail. The coin has been controversial from its first discovery, and is without question the single most talked about coin in the entire history of the denomination.

Obviously, it is not a great rarity. 15 pieces are known, and at least some others have been deliberately destroyed. This doesn't begin to compare with some of the famous rarities, some of the unique, meaning that only a single coin was produced or is known. We have often pondered what it might be like to be present at the time and place when, with some certain amount of ceremony, a coin press is prepared, adjusted, the dies placed in exact juxtoposition, a single prepared planchet is carefully placed by hand between the dies, and the press operator moves the lever or presses the button that causes the full force of the press to be exerted on the dies, striking the coin. Just one. Then the dies are removed, carried to the machine shop and the design is defaced or completely ground off, destroying forever the opportunity to strike a second or third coin.

We can picture the careful, even delicate way the single piece is handled, a mint official hand carrying it to his superior, secretly breathing a sigh of relief once he is off the press room floor and safely back in the administrative area of the Mint, where the chance of stumbling, or slipping on an oily spot on the floor might cause him to drop his precious burden.

Now, picture that same formal striking as being done in "the dark of night," the clandestine striking of a coin like the 1804 dollar, which is one of the better known examples of private work done with public tools, but by no means the only such example. But, we are perhaps getting ahead of our story.

The striking of coins at the U.S. Mint is based on an Act of Congress. Over the years, there have been a number of Coinage Acts, many of them mentioned in other chapters. However, President Jefferson, acting on his own, without any authorization from Congress, issued an Executive

Order, stopping the coining of the Heraldic Eagle silver dollars in 1804, before the switch was made to the 1804 date. As we explained previously, the quantity of dollars minted in early 1804 have been determined to have been dated 1803, a common practice, then and for some time in the Mint.

In 1834, the Director of the Mint was ordered to produce two sets of "duplicate specimens of each kind (denomination of coin) now in use." This order, without even the support of an Executive Order, based solely on a request from a bureaucrat, John Forsyth, was to result in the "official" striking of at least two examples of the 1804 dollar. Mint Director, Dr. Samuel Moore, decided the request meant what it said — each coin that was authorized by the Mint Act of 1792, and proceeded to issue orders to have a quantity of 1804 dollars struck.

The two coins were intended for the special sets of coins which were presented two years later by the State Department to the King of Siam, and to the Sultan of Muscat. The set presented to the King of Siam turned up in 1962, discovered by David Spink, and in part confirmed suspicions about the 1804 dollar, and about other coins made specially for the sets, including the 1804 dated proof Eagles ($10 gold).

These two 1804 Dollars, and at least six others, were struck in 1834 and possibly in early 1835. One of the other six went to the Emperor of Cochin-China. The remaining five reached the public eye in various manners, some of them no doubt officially presented, but at least some of the duplicates probably struck to trade with collectors for pieces needed for the Mint Cabinet (coin collection), and some others perhaps leaving the mint by the "back door."

The technical term for these coins is "Antedated Fantasy," meaning that they were struck in a year subsequent to the date that appears on the coin, and they therefore were not a legally executed coin, Dr. Moore undoubtedly would have argued the point at that time, feeling he had full authority to go ahead and prepare dies and strike the coins, under the provisions of the 1792 Mint Act, since there was ample precedent for striking coins with whatever date happened to be handy on a die. One has to be familiar with the immense tangle of red tape that stifles such "creativity" in today's Mint to realize the totally different world in which the 1834 Mint Director operated.

For example, in 1834, the State Department still wielded a significant "hold" over the Mint to be able to order up these special sets directly, without bothering to go through channels, or obtaining official approval, the relationship dating back to before the turn of that century, as we have described earlier. There is considerable evidence, the 1834 special sets being but one example, that the State Department had few qualms about requisitioning special coins for presentation purposes. We spent several months researching a similar proof set presented in 1856 to the Senate of the City of Bremen, Germany, a set which appears to have become the spoils of war in World War II, and now probably is in the Hermitage Museum in Russia.

Remember, these are proof coins, and not just well struck circulation pieces, in a period when proof coins were made only for presentation purposes, or to trade or as "favor" coins to a very select few "friends of the Mint." All of the proof coins produced from 1794 to the 1840s probably could have been hauled out of the Mint in a single small satchel, with very little strain.

Sometime in 1858, the coin was restruck, with a different reverse die. A reported five were discovered in private hands in 1859, and four of them were recovered by Mint Director J. R. Snowden, who destroyed three of them, and placed the single remaining specimen in the Mint Cabinet, later and now in the Smithsonian. Unlike the 1834 pieces, this coin has a plain, rather than a lettered edge, and in 1951, Walter Breen, while examining the coin, discovered that it had been struck on a cut down Swiss Shooting Festival Thaler of Bern, dated 1857.

Interesting enough, part of the fascinating history of this coin is the documented coverup by a mint employee, William E. Dubois, Assayer and Curator of the Mint Cabinet, who wrote on September 17, 1878 that: "This dollar (referring to yet a third version) is one of the original issue and not a restrike."

This particular statement bears some explanation, which Breen details in his book on U.S. and Colonial proof coins in which he divides the restrikes into three, rather than the usual two classes.

For one thing, Dubois was present as a witness when Snowden destroyed the three examples of the unlettered edge coins in 1858. For another, the Mint Cabinet examples of the 1834 Class I restrike and the 1858 Class II restrike were (deliberately?) reversed for some time in their display, because the 1858 was a better example of the proof process, allowing Dubois and others to use them as a basis for claims that the Class III coins were actually the originals.

The Class III coins were essentially identical to Class II described above, without lettered edge, and Breen believes that they may well be leftover coins from the 1858 restrikes that were altered by adding the edge lettering at some later date. The edge dies were not to be found in 1858, but apparently turned up in some obscure corner of the Mint shortly thereafter, and were used in an attempt to "separate" the coins from those confiscated in 1858. Breen also notes that some of the Class III coins were apparently carried as pocket pieces for a time to blur the proof surfaces.

The Class I can be identified by a die crack (thin raised line of coin metal) through the top of NITED in UNITED on the reverse die. The second T in STATES is to the right of center of the cloud below. The Class II and III were struck with the same obverse, but with a new reverse die, without the die crack and with the second T to the left of center of the cloud below.

The known specimens include:

Class I
1. Smithsonian Institution
2. Louis Eliasberg Collection (Sold at Public Auction)
3. David Spink (This is in the Siam set, with a price tag for the set of $1,000,000.)
4. C. F. Childs Collection
5. Harold Bareford Collection
6. Omaha City Library
7. Unknown owner purchased from Mass. Historical Society
8. Willis DuPont — Stolen in 1967

Class II
1. Smithsonian Institution

Class III
1. Unknown buyer for Larry Hanks who purchased it for $400,000 from Garrett Collection on March 26, 1980.
2. Unknown buyer from the Amon Carter, Jr. and Sr. Collection.
3. Unknown buyer from Louis Wolfson — The coin cited is Dubois's 1879 letter above.
4. Willis DuPont — Stolen in 1967
5. American Numismatic Association, donated by Chase Manhattan Bank.
6. Jerry Buss Collection. Sold to Bowers and Ruddy in 1974 for $225,000, through several hands to Buss for a reported $200,000.

Two of the coins are thus unaccounted for. One of the six Class III coins may be the fifth specimen that Snowden was unsuccessful in confiscating along with the other four coins in 1859. The two stolen coins can, of course, be identified on sight, and thus do not have a ready market. They will undoubtedly turn up some day. Obviously, there may be more of the 1804 Dollars that could turn up in some obscure estate collection but the chances are slim that such a rarity would have been hidden or overlooked for this long. One of them turned up allegedly in a bank deposit in Philadelphia, where it was recovered by an alert teller in about 1850, and another reputedly came from a freed slave, but both stories could have been arranged by the mixture of mint employees and private collectors involved in the restrike scandals of that period.

We must close this chapter with a warning that some very excellent counterfeits of this coin exist along with a multitude of copies and imitations, so don't automatically assume that the 1804 date should be enough to whip out your checkbook. As you can see if you read the books written about this coin, every known specimen is very well documented and most if not all have been photographed, so that — with the two noted exceptions — the location of each coin is well known. We will repeat, don't buy this or any big ticket coin until you know the pedigree, or have authentication papers for the coin.

STORING AND PROTECTING YOUR SILVER DOLLARS

Special thanks to George Klabin, noted coin investment counselor and author, for supplying much of the material in this chapter.

To realize a satisfactory profit on the resale of your silver dollars, they must be saleable in the same condition as purchased. In addition to making certain that coins are correctly graded when purchased, they must be stored in a safe manner to prevent deterioration. A silver dollar, like most coins, can easily fall from one condition grade to the next. As you have learned from this book, very fine lines separate the higher condition grades. Slight deterioration will drop a coin into a lower grade, and thereby reduce its value by 20%, 30% or much more depending on the coin. This obviously destroys it as an investment. Hence, storage and protection of your investment silver dollars is of primary importance.

Investors, on the whole, have been lax on this subject. They have not given sufficient consideration to protecting the quality of their coins. Undoubtedly this is because many investors are unfamiliar with numismatics, and are unaware that coins can very easily deteriorate. Some investors store their coins in unsafe holders, or commit other storage errors, and leave them untouched and unexamined for years. By then the deterioration, usually in the form of silver corrosion, is so well advanced that the coin cannot be returned to its purchased condition.

Fortunately, some very significant progress has been made in identifying chemicals that are hazardous to coins. Coin storage is not nearly as risky as it once was, if you know the facts and proceed accordingly. The coin world has spent countless hours and sums of money researching and studying this problem. The fruits of these efforts are available to the investor as well as the collector.

For generations, collectors believed that coins, being made of metal, were strong and durable and required little special care. It was thought they could be damaged only by scratching or nicking, or by wear from excessive handling. When comfortably housed and carefully handled, it was presumed that no harm could befall them. This logic led, in part, to the extreme scarcity of most early coins in MS-60, MS-65 and MS-70 grades. Numerous coins now in the AU (About Uncirculated) category were in fact uncirculated when they reached the hands of collectors, but dropped into the AU grade because of improper storage. This may even be the case with the *majority* of AU Silver Dollars dating before 1900 that are currently on the market.

Yes, it is true that coins are invulnerable to many dangers of other collectors' items. They do not shatter when dropped; they do not tear, or become warped, or fall prey to insects. But they can be — and are — damaged in many ways, some of them extremely subtle. The fact that this damage is not usually readily noticeable is beside the point. Even if the coin holds its damage well, compared to a porcelain statuette or glass tumbler, it is glaringly apparent in the value reduction.

Confidence in the ruggedness of coins led collectors, through the years, to innocently and well-meaningly employ many harmful storage devices — and to let their guard down against very real dangers to the preservation of their coins. The earliest numismatic equipment was, of course, the most barbaric. As the hobby became more refined, improvements were made. But even after collectors became extremely condition conscious, harmful storage devices remained on the market and were unwittingly used.

Typical of old traditional approaches was the coin *cabinet.* You can often still hear of coin collections referred to as "cabinets." This is a throwback to the time when most collections were actually kept in cabinets, before albums came into use. The practice prevailed for more than 300 years, first in Europe and then America. Coin cabinets continue to be manufactured in Europe and are occasionally imported for sale to this country, but serious collectors and investors avoid them.

Coin cabinets were wooden boxes with sliding drawers, each drawer having recessed compartments in which the coins rested. Owners in the 18th and 19th centuries believed their coins were not only elegantly displayed but supremely protected in cabinets, like jewels set in a crown. They did not realize, for one thing, that shifting around of coins whenever the drawers were opened or shut caused rubbing — a condition easily spotted by experts and referred to as "cabinet wear." And they were certainly unaware of hazards such as airborne pollutants or environmental coin enemies, including humidity and tobacco smoke. Handsome as they are, coin cabinets were, and are, about the most unsafe means of keeping coins. Ironically, they were generally used to store the owner's finest treasures. Proofs and Uncs went automatically into cabinets, whereas lesser coins often ended up in envelopes — where they received much safer storage!

At first, storage equipment used as substitutes for cabinets was not designed or intended for increased safety. As the coin hobby grew in the late 1800s, it was no longer a pasttime of the rich. Average collectors could not afford cabinets, or did not own enough coins to warrant a cabinet. Thus they began adopting other means of housing and storage. Paper envelopes were a natural as they could carry the coin's description or other information. These were filed in boxes by country, emperor, or other arrangement. Some collections and dealers' stocks are still kept this way, especially in foreign countries. In the 20th century, further growth of numismatics brought about manufacture of many accessories for collectors. The objection to paper envelopes was that the coin had to be removed and handled to be inspected. Among the improvements was the folder-type album with openings for coins and the familiar 2x2 cardboard holders with cellophane windows. An important advance was (or at least thought to be, at the time) vinyl sheets made to fit standard ring binders, with pockets into which loose coins or 2x2 holders could be inserted.

These accessories, and others reaching the market during the great post World War II numismatic boom, seemed to provide the ultimate solution to safe coin storage in a convenient, inexpensive way. Collectors who bought and used accessories of this kind had no doubts that they were taking the best possible care of their coins. Presumably, a coin housed in a sealed holder ran no risk of wear or injury. If it could not be touched, it could not be damaged — or so the belief was. No thought was ever given to the possible harm these accessories themselves might cause. As products of the coin trade, made for the use of collectors and dealers, it was naturally presumed they were perfectly safe.

Even as recently as 10 years ago, the coin trade labored under a blissful ignorance with regard to storage. Breakthroughs began only when condition became a vital subject of discussion in the 1970s. The high premiums paid by investors for BU specimens was, in part, responsible. The '70s witnessed adoption of strict ANA grading guidelines, microscopic inspection of coins, and development of wide gulfs in price between higher condition grades. As most investors in numismatic Silver Dollars sought coins in the finest obtainable condition, Uncirculated specimens frequently rose in value twice or three times faster than the same coin in lesser grades. Attention paid to condition naturally encouraged a more critical examination of storage methods and devices. Scientific inquiry was made, and continues to be made. Not all the answers are yet known. But the past 5-10 years has seen greater accomplishment toward safe coin storage than the previous 2,000 years of numismatics.

The simple, startling fact of the matter is that traditional, universally used, industry-acknowledged coin storage accessories are not always safe. Not only can they fail to protect coins from external hazards, they can in some cases cause damage themselves. As unbelievable as it may seem, some of these modern "tools of the hobby" are actually more potentially harmful to coins than the old cabinets of yesteryear.

It is not unusual for investment coins to lay untouched and uninspected for five years or longer. Many investors have received rude shocks when removing their coins from storage and discovering ugly black spots, streaks, tarnish, pitting, green crust or other evidence of deterioration. The coins were untouched and had presumably not come into contact with any harmful substance. Yet they came out of storage in an unmistakably lower grade of condition than when put in.

There is no question but that millions of dollars are lost by investors each year through storage damage. While it may be impossible to ever entirely guarantee the safety of a coin, much of this loss could be prevented.

The Silver Dollar investor (and collector) must be aware that not all dollars are subject to the same kind of damage or to the same degree. If you own BU or Proof Morgan and/or Peace Dollars, you should realize that such coins are more delicate and require greater attention than circulated dollars. As their surfaces have not been exposed to much handling, the metal is more vulnerable to corrosion and even to scratching than the metal of circulated coins. The more heavily circulated a coin is, the lower it will deteriorate. This is another reason why "Uncs" are so highly valued. They are definitely an endangered species and could become extinct without care.

Patina May be Pretty on Ancient Coins, But . . . Storage damage, or effects suffered by coins through contact with chemical or other agents, is really another name for patina. If you have ever collected ancient or medieval coins you know the extent to which they carry patina. It is, of course, most prevalent on the copper and other basemetal coins of these early ages, but may be found on silver as well. These coins are expected to bear patina, or heavy corrosion. They were not stored in cabinets or albums but buried underground for a thousand or more years. The more fortunate were encased in clay jars, sunk into the earth by misers of ancient times. Others were haphazardly buried without protection of any sort, and came into direct contact with sand, soil, and the various acids and salts of earth-moisture. Even in relatively dry climates such as North Africa, coins excavated after long burial invariably show corrosion. The weight of such coins may be considerably different than when struck, if corrosion is severe.

Ancient and medieval coins represent the most extreme example of patination or chemical alteration of coin surfaces. Their patina is obvious and unmistakable, even to an untrained eye. But all coins, including modern, are candidates for patina and *most* will acquire it to some extent unless ideally stored. Any slight change in the coin's surface can be ascribed to early stages of patination, even if observable only under powerful magnification. Ancient coins, you can be sure, did not acquire their patina in the space of a few years or even a few decades. It began gradually, microscopically, insidiously. Though they were not buried, modern coins improperly stored would acquire nearly as strong patina in a comparable length of time.

Patina on ancient and medieval coins is not regarded as objectionable, unless built up in accumulated layers to the point of obscuring the design and making identification difficult. Otherwise it is expected and, often, admired. Many collectors of ancient and medieval coins believe that a specimen with even, handsomely toned patina is more attractive than in the original state. Premium prices are sometimes attached to such coins. For one thing, patina on a very old coin is looked upon as proof of authenticity — though it can, these days, be pretty convincingly faked. Even those who do not admire patina on ancient coins accept it as a fact of life. Such coins are archaeological objects and nearly all ancient relics made of metal carry patina. With U.S. coins it is quite another matter. Patina is neither attractive nor desirable on a Silver Dollar. And it *is* preventable, with thought and care.

Toning. The word "toning" occurs repeatedly in the definitions of condition grades for Silver Dollars, as laid down by the American Numismatic Association. Toning is really a delicate word for atmospheric corrosion. Chemicals in the air (indoor as well as outdoor air) can cause changes in a coin's surface appearance, long before anything resembling damage appears. Its color can become lighter or darker, generally darker, or a "film" of a different color can appear to form. This film gives the impression of an extremely thin, wispy, transparent layer of color, through which the coin's true color can be seen. In time it grows more intense. Sometimes it is not uniform but has rainbow-like properties that react to light. It is difficult to understand the causes of toning unless one is familiar with the relationship of coins and atmospheric conditions.

Metals as they exist in the earth do not corrode. The corrosion process begins only with refining, in which the natural chemical balance of the metal is upset. Reaction with atmospheric oxygen forms "oxides," or chemical compounds. This oxidation process is a normal function of nature, but we see it as an evil and label it corrosion or destruction of the metal. In its early stages, when a coin is newly minted, the oxide layer is present but so thin (in millionths of a millimeter) as to be invisible. At this stage, it has no effect on the coin's appearance, and anyone who is not scientifically informed is unaware of its presence. Yet, technically, the damage has already begun. As time passes, this oxidation layer thickens, helped along by manmade and natural pollutants: combustion gases from fires, tobacco smoke, auto exhaust, incinerators, industrial furnaces, and other contributors. These are always present, to one degree or another, in the atmosphere. Sulfur is one of the most common elements of these combustion agents. It reacts readily with silver by electro-chemical means and can cause problems on Silver Dollars. We have all seen how sterling silver turns brown, then black, in a matter of weeks in normal household atmosphere. The coloration acquired is "silver sulfide," as well as other chemical agents.

Pure silver coins, such as those occasionally manufactured in ancient times, are faily resistant to corrosion. Though Silver Dollars contain nine parts of silver to just one part copper, that 10% of copper is sufficient to encourage chemical reaction. Because copper corrodes easily, any metal mixed with copper acquires some of its corrosive tendencies. A very striking example of this is offered by silver jewelry which, if the grade is low, turns green on the finger or wrist as if it contained no silver at all.

The most common forms of corrosion damage to Silver Dollars are:

a) Black Tarnish. The corrosion process progresses sufficiently to produce black, thick patches of silver sulfide and oxides which are often impossible to remove without leaving "pitting."

b) Pitting. Actual holes may be eaten into a coin's surface by severe or prolonged corrosion. Pitting is often hidden beneath tarnish or toning and may be impossible to detect without strong magnification. Pitting is evidence of gross corrosion and causes sharp reduction of value.

c) Spotting. Black spots, sometimes called flyspecks, are also a form of corrosion damage. They appear most often on basemetal coins but also occasionally on silver. Spotting is caused by minute particles of dust and lint resting on a coin and preventing sufficient oxygen from reaching the covered area (coins, too, must breathe!). This results in imbalances in the oxide layers and invites concentrations of oxides to form beneath the particles. The oxidation then continues to radiate outward until, in time, it encompasses an area much larger than the offending particle. This happens because the surrounding metal is affected by this build-up of oxides, even though normal oxygen reaches surrounding areas. The corrosion spreads out, wider and wider, like ripples caused by throwing pebbles in a lake. Of course, it tends to be lighter in color as it gets further away from the center. It is important to take all possible precautions in keeping foreign matter of any kind from contacting a coin's surface. Though a tiny dust speck may seem harmless to a substance as strong as metal, this is definitely a "David and Goliath" situation.

d) Verdigris. A tactile crust, normally green on modern coins but often black, brown or reddish on ancient coins, formed by atmospheric corrosion. Verdigris is actually a combination of copper carbonate and copper acetate. It occurs mainly on copper, nickel, lead, tin, zinc and other basemetal coins, and in coins alloyed with a high proportion of basemetal. High humidity is a contributing factor. For years, hobbyists living in damp climates were advised to collect coins rather than stamps, and thereby avoid dangers to the gum of postage stamps. They were not told about dangers of verdigris on coins. Fortunately, this is not a serious problem for the investor in Silver Dollars whose low copper content renders them unlikely, under normal conditions, to acquire this condition. Nevertheless, if coins are to be stored in rooms where humidity becomes excessive, it might be advisable to purchase a dehumidifier (which, if you meet I.R.S. requirements for investor status, is tax deductible).

Vertigris can generally be removed, or considerably reduced, by "whizzing" the coin or buffing with an electric polisher. However, when verdigris has reached the stage of being visible to the unaided eye, it has usually eaten into the surface and pockmarks or pitting will be left upon removal.

Other Enemies of Silver Dollars. Scratching is among the prime enemies of all coins, and is a greater problem with silver than copper coins because of their softer surface. Silver Dollar owners must take special care that their coins do not contact any objects which could possibly cause scratches. Not only metal objects but virtually anything pointed or bladed, including the human fingernail, could be dangerous to a Silver Dollar's surface. Staples, such as those used in 2x2 holders or sometimes by dealers in vinyl "flips," are among the worst offenders.

Scratch-free Uncirculated Silver Dollars are scarcer than scratch-free "Uncs" of lower denomination coins. Because of their weight, they received more battering from each other while traveling in Mint bags. Very few specimens totally escaped scratching.

Excessive heat, even if not accompanied by high humidity, can injure coins and is more troublesome with silver than basemetal. Intense heat of a fire will melt silver coins faster than copper or bronze. While melting to a liquid state is unlikely unless coins make direct and pro-longed contact with flames, heat generated by a fire can rather quickly distort a coin's design and/or shape. Vault storage provides some measure of protection, but there is no way of absolutely eliminating the danger. Coins kept in a safe at home will bake during a fire, just as in the oven. While the safe itself and possibly its other contents may not be visibly harmed, Silver Dollars are almost sure to show damage.

Though its effects are not as dramatic as intense heat, *grease* qual-ifies as an enemy of coins. Grease may be harmful in a number of ways, first in interfering with mint luster, secondly in preventing oxygen from reaching the coin's surface. But undoubtedly the chief problem with grease is that it attracts dust particles, which, as explained above, could prove the catalyst for corrosion. Grease is acquired by coins in numerous ways. Nearly everything touched by a coin is a potential transmitter of grease, but the worst offender is unquestionably the human fingers. Even recently scrubbed hands carry some natural grease, which is sure to be transferred to coins in handling unless strict precautions are taken to touch only the edges. Simple fingermarking is enough to drop an otherwise unblemished Morgan or Peace Dollar from MS-70 to MS-65.

Investors who have not collected coins, and are unfamiliar with the hobby, are probably rapidly forming the conclusion that coins must be handled as gingerly as nitroglycerine. While this is not really the case, coins face more dangers in the everyday environment and from handling than one might think. These should be a concern to the collector. They MUST be a concern to the investor, to whom a slight difference in condi-tion could result in financial loss rather than profit. Even common *dan-druff* has been cited as an injurious substance to coins. Thanks to its greasiness, dandruff can adhere easily to a coin's surface and encourage corrosion.

Tobacco smoke rates high on the list of coin enemies. Since the smoke of cigarettes, cigars and other tobacco products is heavily laden with contaminants, it deposits a film on virtually any surface it contacts. If contact is repeated, the film builds up and darkens, attaining a deep brown color. Removal is impossible without "whizzing" the coin, and this automatically drops it into a lower condition grade. So long as coins remain relatively unprotected in a room where tobacco is frequently smoked, they will suffer this kind of damage. The owner may receive a most unpleasant surprise when examining such coins after a long period of seclusion.

Fireplaces are another possible source of problems. They dry out and overheat the air directly adjacent to them. It would be advisable not to keep coins too near fireplaces.

Handling Coins. A "touchy" matter, to say the least. Over the years, numismatists have become progressively more sophisticated toward coin handling. Investors must follow their lead. Early generations of col-lectors handled their coins haphazardly. The average collection of a per-son of modest means in the 1800s, who could not afford a cabinet, con-sisted of coins tossed into a jar or tin. Even much later, handling was considered harmless if not overdone. It was believed that harm could occur from handling only by wear of wearing down the coin's design. Other possible dangers were ignored.

Owners of Mint State Silver Dollars must realize that any touching of the surface, even if gentle and occasional, risks injury to the mint luster. By and large, coins are best kept in protective holders and examined without removal. Clarity offered by these holders is sufficient to make a thorough examination. Non-glare holders permit inspection under a microscope with no interference. The only possible difficulty that might be encountered in examining coins in holders is with their edges. However, it is necessary, even in spite of this, to sometimes remove a coin from its housing and physically handle it. Usually this situation arises with newly acquired coins. Many coins bought from dealers and through auction sales arrive in undesireable containers of one kind or another. This will happen with rare and expensive items, just as with cheap coins. Most dealers, even today, will automatically place valuable coins in holders containing unsafe chemical agents, or which are otherwise objectionable. There is no alternative but to transfer the coin into better housing. Dealers apparently use these now-discredited holders because of cheapness, and also because they often change a coin from one holder to another while in their possession (usually to reprice it).

Before removing any dollar from a dealer's container, be sure you want to keep it. Dealers will usually not give a refund or credit on coins no longer in their original holders. While this might seem a harsh practice, it is really the only protection against coins being switched. Of course, the dealer is obliged to deliver the coin in a holder that, even if not suitable for longterm storage, permits thorough inspection.

As we have stated, coins should be picked up by the edges only, without allowing fingers to touch the obverse or reverse. The danger of surface wear being caused by touching the design is far less than that of leaving fingermarks. Fingermarks on lustrous mint Dollars may not become visible until long after contact occurred. The fact that they do not always show immediately could fool a beginner into thinking that such coins resist fingermarking. This is certainly not the case. Any coin with full mint luster will pick up fingermarks even if touched lightly.

Fingernails should be inspected and trimmed if necessary before handling coins. Long fingernails are an enemy of coins.

When coins are being handled, they should be held over a cushioning material as a safeguard, in the event of being dropped. A velvet cloth, such as you will often see on the countertops of coin shops, is suitable. This will also provide help in picking up a dropped coin, which can be taken from a soft pliable surface much more easily than from a hard.

For those who would rather not touch coins with their bare hands, inexpensive "numistatic gloves" made of polyethylene are available. Some practice should be gained in picking up coins with them, before using them with numismatic coins. They may seem slightly awkward at first.

At all times, extra care must be taken in handling proof Dollars. The mirror surfaces are delicate.

Removing Contaminants from Silver Dollars. Opinions on coin cleaning differ, even among the experts. Some feel coins should never be cleaned in any way. Others approve nearly all cleaning techniques, in the theory that a cleaner coin is a better coin. The bulk of modern opinion leans toward the belief that surface contaminants which could be harmful to the coin should be removed, but that coins should not be "whizzed" or polished. Even if one has objections to all types of coin cleaning, it should be realized that removal of surface contaminants is not intended for deception. It is done for sake of the coin's health. In time, it is likely that contaminant removal will become standard throughout the hobby and trade.

Use of a safe chemical formula to remove pollutants without affecting existing oxide layers on the coin's surface, or leaving residue, is essential. A kit has been developed and is now available to safely test for and remove contaminants on coins. With this kit, contaminants become visible and can be watched as they wash free. "TEST-N-SAFE"™ is a liquid blend of solvents safe for coins. It dissolves all dirt and grime without leaving solvent residue. The formula is not a "bath." It contains no acids or reducing agents to interact directly with coin metal or oxide layers. The "TEST-N-SAFE" kit also contains disposable plastic gloves, cotton-tipped applicators and full instructions.

Use of Coin "Dips" or "Baths." Many different brands of "dips," or metal washes, are available in the coin and jewelry industries. All consist of a chemical called thiourea and a small amount of sulfuric or nitric acid. Though this solution effectively removes contaminants from coins, it likewise removes protective oxide layers. If allowed to remain on a coin for more than a few seconds it begins reacting directly with the metal surface. A coin subjected to this treatment eventually loses its luster, brilliance, and evenness of surface. Dull whitish or "flat" spots develop, similar to those resulting from wiping plastic surfaces with alcohol. Needless to say, "dips" should be regarded as a last resort in coin conservation, with a skilled professional in charge.

Coin Containers. Nearly every collector or investor relies on commercially made containers. Unfortunately many of these products, made and sold with the best intentions, contribute to coin deterioration rather than resist it. It is only in the 20th century that coins have been sealed in holders. When plastic holders were developed there was little technical knowledge of chemical effects on coins. Even the plastics industry could not say whether its products were entirely safe for use with coins. It was premused they were, but without any real knowledge.

Investors should choose costly coin products. Use of inferior products could result in permanent and very costly damage.

Coin Albums. Commercially made albums for coin collectors generally consist of still card pages, covered with paper and cut with openings for coins to be inserted. Many leave the coins uncovered on their obverse, while the reverse rests against cardboard or similar material. Albums of this sort have been around for more than 50 years, originating in the days when collectors gave little thought to storage hazards. Each sheet is imprinted with dates and mintmarks under the openings, the object being (as in a stamp album) to work toward filling the sheets and thus complete a set or series. The openings or holes are cut to the exact size of the coins to be inserted, so that by pressing them into place they hold fast. Other albums, similar to these, are supplied with sliding plastic strips that fit over each row of coins on a sheet. The latest types are all-plastic, often made from PVC. This is the highly controversial plastic compound which, in the view of most authorities, is harmful to coins if subjected to prolonged contact.

Cardboard albums present a number of drawbacks to proper storage and are not recommended for investment quality material, certainly not for Uncirculated Silver Dollars. Porousness of the cardboard admits air and, along with it, humidity. Though coins appear to be held securely in the pages, they sometimes work free and fall out. When plastic slips are used, the plastic may not be inert. Chemicals from the plastic ooze out on the coin, and this can be troublesome. Also, repeated sliding of the plastic "protectors" back and forth across the coin will, in time, create a condition similar to cabinet wear.

Coin albums of this type are acceptable for inexpensive circulated coins. Circulated coins are provided with more self-protection, having acquired layers of oxides and grime. Nor do they risk loss of mint luster as it has already been lost.

2x2 Holders. The most universally used and familiar of all coin accessories is the 2x2 holder. This little item came into popularity in the 1950s and multi-millions are now manufactured and sold annually. Most coins bought from dealers come in 2x2 holders. They consist of two reasonably thin sheets of cardboard, joined at the top, identical to each other. The outer surface is white and glossy while the inner is grey and dull. Into each half is punched a hole, usually circular (the earlier versions had square holes), covered from the inside by a thin cellophane type of plastic known as Mylar. Though all such holders have the same exterior dimensions, the "windows" differ in size to accommodate the various different coin denominations. To use the 2x2, the coin is placed face-up on the lower half, directly over the window. The upper half is folded over it, which sandwiches the coin between the two plastic windows and allows both sides to be viewed. The cardboard edges are then stapled together, to prevent the coin from falling out.

It was originally thought that the 2x2 was ideal for coin storage, for its cheapness, ease of use, and the fact that it allows coins to be examined without being touched. Recent investigation has showed quite the opposite to be the case. Numerous objections have been found with the 2x2. The staples can rust with prolonged exposure to humidity, and rust particles can find their way to the coins — where they cause staining and a very difficult removal task. Since these holders are not airtight, heat and humidity build up within them. The plastic is likewise a cause of concern. Mylar is chemically inert (so far, so good), but such thin stock is used that it punctures easily. This allows air to attack the coins unevenly, being concentrated at the point of puncture, causing ugly spotting. When such holders are lined up in rows in coin storage boxes, staples from one will scratch or tear the Mylar of its neighbor. Worst of all, perhaps, is the paper dust carried by these holders. When mechanically cut apart at the factory, the knife leaves behind an accumulation of fine, gritty paper particles. These migrate by static electricity to the Mylar windows, which serve as a magnet for them, and come into contact with the coin. This sets off the chain of events described earlier, resulting in "flyspeck" spotting.

Plexiglas and Styrene. After 2x2 holders had achieved acceptance and popularity, efforts were made to develop an alternative for displaying coins of special interest or value. Thus was born the plexiglas case, a little box usually (but not always) square with a circular recess at the center. The box is made in two separate pieces, which are not joined like the halves of 2x2's. The lid is removed, the coin placed in the lower section and the lid replaced, snapping into place. Walls of plexiglas holders are thick and provide much sturdier protection against accident or abrasion than Mylar. But it is essential that it be made of *pure styrene,* or else harmful acids may form over a period of years. One negative aspect is styrene's brittleness. It can crack and allow air to enter the holder. Also, openings are not designed to precisely fit coins without any possibility of movement. Coin diameters, especially of 18th and early 19th century Silver Dollars, can vary somewhat, and shifting around of specimens within such holders is inevitable. Or the reverse could be the case (as it generally is with Flowing Hair and Bust Dollars): the holder fits too snugly, the coin must be jammed in, and the edge could be injured. The biggest disadvantage of plexiglas containers is their high cost and bulkiness, which makes them expensive and unduly space-consuming for large quantities of coins.

Styrene is generally regarded to be pure, inert, and safe for contact with coin metals. Many roll tubes and proof set holders of the snap-lock type are made of styrene. They provide reasonably good protection but are not "air tight," as is sometimes claimed by retailers.

Flipettes or "Flips." About 15 years ago this type of coin container appeared and was hailed at first as an improvement upon all existing holders. The flipette or flip seemed to eliminate some objections to 2x2's and other containers. It offered maximum visibility, used no staples, and — as it contained no paper — was free of paper dust. Flipettes are still widely used in the trade and by many collectors. But scientific inquiry into their effects on coin metals has brought them bad publicity and might eventually spell their doom. These are 2-inch-square plastic pockets joined at the top. The coin is inserted into one half, and a slip of paper carrying details about it into the other half. The halves are then folded against each other but not, like 2x2 holders, secured by stapling or in any other way. Because of their lightness and pliability, they hold the contents safely without need of stapling. A big plus of flipettes is that very detailed information can be recorded about the coin, which would not fit on a 2x2 holder. Another is that they can easily be reused without damaging them, interchanging coins from one to another as desired. Also, one size flipettes takes all sizes of coins — it is not necessary to purchase them by size. Obviously, these are major advantages. But the very serious drawback of flipettes is that they're made of Poly-Vinyl Chloride, or "PVS" for short.

A furor was created in the coin industry by recent disclosures that PVC is likely to be harmful to coins, especially those in proof or mint state, with prolonged contact. In fact, the contact need not be extremely prolonged. Several years after introduction of PVC flips, some users noticed greenish or bluish colored sticky flecks and stains on their coins. In some cases these blemishes are large enough to be easily seen with the unaided eye. Even when PVC-stored coins do not appear to have suffered damage of this kind, it is often noticeable under magnification.

Analysis has revealed that three components in PVC are responsible for these problems:

1. Plasticizers. These are chemical mixed with the basic formula to give the product flexibility and softness. Pure PVC, without softening agents, is too brittle to make an acceptable coin container. Not only would it crack and split, but surface hardness would abrade coins housed in such holders. The plasticizers serve an important purpose but, at the same time, present certain dangers. Under the influence of heat and humidity they can actually escape from the plastic sheeting and attack the coin metal. Normally this occurs at points where the coin directly touches the plastic. Gradually the plasticizers attach themselves to the coin, partly due to pressure exerted by the coin's weight or possibly a sympathetic action between the coin metal and plasticizer chemicals. Thus, PVC damage is most likely to be found at the highest points of a coin's design. Mint state and proof coins are most vulnerable to PVC attack, as they have less natural protective coating. Once on the coin, plasticizer chemicals can travel easily, since they were originally liquid and now are in a semi-liquid state. This "soup" reacts much more to copper than other metals, but silver coins are not entirely invulnerable to its assaults. In the initial stages, protective surface oxide layers are stripped away from the coin. Then, when the chemicals reach the raw coin surface, they may begin eating into it. The result is greenish or bluish stains and flecks of plasticizer and copper ions, and damage to the coin metal. In severe cases, where humidity is very high or the coins are stored under pressure (such as tightly cramped in a box), coins may actually stick to the holder and prove as difficult to remove as if glued. When this occurs, corrosion spots are certain to be very noticeable, and the coin may be damaged beyond restoration.

Extent of damage seems to depend on the PVC's quality. Not all PVC is alike. Length of time the coin is encased and general atmospheric conditions play a role, too. Nevertheless, the problem is widespread and likely to be encountered, to some degree, wherever PVC holders are used. It does not occur overnight but is a slow gradual process. The distinctive blue or green coloration does not always become visible until great quantities of plasticizer have reached the coin and gotten to the copper alloy.

2. Hydrogen Chloride Gas. A gas released by all PVC products over a period of time, at a quicker rate when temperature and humidity are high. When combined with moisture it forms Hydrochloride Acid, which, even in the minute quanities deposited in this manner, can destroy the luster of mint and proof state coins.

3. Stabilizers. Chemical stabilizers are used in PVC plastic to discourage the release of hydrogen chloride gas, by maintaining molecular balance. For many years it was confidently believed that they performed this task successfully. It has now been demonstrated that stabilizers deteriorate with age and allow the gas to be released. Depending on the quality of PVC formula and atmospheric conditions, deterioration may occur within a year, or not for a number of years. But it is inevitable.

Even if one is left confused or unimpressed by scientific jargon, the important fact is that PVC holders can and do damage coins. Therefore it is not advisable to use such holders. At the present time (fall 1981) all PVC coin containers on the market contain various levels of plasticizers, stabilizers, and the potential to release harmful (to coins) gas. New *co-polymer* PVC formulas, without plasticizers and stabilizers, are in process of development. They may be on sale by the time you read this. However it would be impossible (manufacturers' claims notwithstanding) to declare them fully safe until several years of trial. A possible drawback of such holders will be their stiffness and brittleness, caused by absence of plasticizers. Whether this can be overcome through use of some safe chemical is questionable.

Investors are well advised to examine Silver Dollars currently in their possession for possible PVC damage. Though the shock of discovery may be painful, ignorance is far from bliss. Should damage be found, there is a good chance of eradicating it, if caught in its initial or intermediate stages. The longer that discovery and treatment is delayed, the more difficult removal becomes, and in some instances may be impossible. Check all your coins, even those recently acquired. Even coins not being stored in PVC holders should be inspected, as they could possibly have been kept in such holders by a previous owner. Until recently, examination would have been difficult, as thin layers of plasticizer compound might have escaped visual detection. The "TEST-N-SAFE"™ kit mentioned earlier simplifies this process and at the same time cleans the coins. When applied to the coin surface by the cotton tipped applicator, "TEST-N-SAFE" removes even invisible plasticizer accumulations. Whenever blue or green coloration is noticed on the applicator after treatment, this is PVC residue removed from your coin.

Safe Coin Holders. At present, the most trustworthy longterm coin holders are made of Mylar, or *cast tri-acetate* (marketed under the name *Kointainers*), as well as styrene snap-lock holders. These plastic compounds, when properly manufactured under strict quality controls, yield pure inert containers for coins. They contain nothing, chemically, to injure coins. However, all coin holders permit air to enter, thus failing to eliminate dangers of atmospheric corrosion. It might then be concluded that air itself is, next to unsafe chemicals in storage products, the greatest enemy of coins.

The time is not likely to come when coin owners choose to seal their specimens in airtight containers. Such an approach would be inconvenient and impractical, not to mention very costly. But the coin owner who foregoes hermetic sealing is not necessarily at nature's mercy. Means are available, even at present, to greatly reduce dangers of atmospheric corrosion.

Method of Combating Airborne Corrosion of Coins. Several years ago a product was introduced to the coin market which provides very satisfactory longterm protection against atmospheric oxidation and corrosion. "Metal Safe" is an ice-cube size capsule which, when placed in any coin storage cabinet or other enclosure up to 33 cubic feet volume, permeates the air and renders it far safer for coin metals. It releases nontoxic, odorless vapors which thoroughly saturate the storage area and combat corrosion. Each capsule remains effective for a full year, once activated (prior to activation, they have a 5-year shelf life). "Metal Safe" operates on its own without the need to coat coins or apply it manually in any way. So effective is this product that coins may be left in tubes or other containers (those of safe construction, of course) and still receive full benefit. No alteration will occur on toned coins. Thus, with this simple capsule, a whole investment coin portfolio can be effectively safeguarded against atmospheric corrosion. (NOTE: Neither this or any other product on the market protects against PVC damage, which is chemical rather than atmospheric. Investors must still take care to use recommended containers.)

If this chapter has proved frightening, the investor should take some comfort in the fact that dangers to coin preservation are now identified, and products are available to combat them. Modern science plus the weight of 28 million collectors and untold numbers of investors are on his side.

RECOMMENDED READING

There are a number of excellent books on the market that will be of help to you as you plan your dollar investments. However we should point out that this list is by no means comprehensive. We would urge you to check with your local coin dealer, who usually has a number of books in stock and can recommend others that he can obtain for you.

The Official Price Guide to Mint Errors and Varieties-Fourth Edition. $7.95 The House of Collectibles.

The South Dakota Gold Newsletter (Monthly investment newsletter edited by the author) Sample Copy $2 — Box C, Deadwood, SD 57732.

The Official Blackbook Guide to U.S. Coins-25th Ed. $3.95, The House of Collectibles.

Official ANA Grading Standards for United States Coins.

Comprehensive Catalog and Encyclopedia of U.S. Morgan and Peace Silver Dollars Vol. 2 — Leroy Van Allen and A. George Mallis, 1976 FCI Press.

Encyclopedia of United States and Colonial Proof Coins-1722-1977 — Walter Breen, 1977 FCI Press.

The Encyclopedia of Doubled Dies-Vol. I and Vol. II — John A. Wexler — 1978 and 1981.

The United States Early Silver Dollars-Third Edition — M.H. Bolender, 1980 Krause Publications.

Silver Dollar Encyclopedia — Jim Osbon 1976.

The Official Guide to Detecting Counterfeit Money — The House of Collectibles.

The Official Investors Guide to Buying and Selling Gold, Silver and Diamonds-Second Edition $9.95 The House of Collectibles.

Counterfeit, Misstruck & Unofficial U.S. Coins — D. Taxay.

Colonial Copies, Private Mint Replicas, Modern Counterfeits of United States Coins — Larry Spanbauer 1975.

Standard Catalog of U.S. Altered & Counterfeit Coins.

High Profits From Rare Coin Investment — Q. David Bowers-8th Edition, 1981 Bowers & Ruddy Galleries.

Periodicals:

The following list is of hobby publications which have up to date price listings, dealer ads, articles and news stories of benefit to the investor who wants to keep up with current market conditions.

(W) Weekly, (M) Monthly, (2M) Every 2 Months
*Free sample copies available by writing to publisher.
(W)* *Numismatic News* — Krause Publications, Iola, WI 54990
(W) *Coin World* — Sidney Publishing, Box 150, Sidney, OH 45365
(M)* *COINS Magazine* — Krause Publications.
(M) *COINage* — Behn-Miller Publishers, 17337 Ventura Blvd., Encino, CA 91316.
(M) *Error-Variety News* — Box 455, Quakertown, PA 18951.
(2M)* *Coin Prices* — Krause Publications.

Clubs:
Club membership is frequently helpful to the investor. Among other benefits, you can make contact with other investors with like interests, and keep in touch with trends in investing and collecting. Club membership entitles you to a discount on grading and authentication services in both of the national clubs we recommend.

American Numismatic Association, Box 2366, Colorado Springs, CO 80901.

Collectors of Numismatic Errors, Inc., c/o Alan Herbert, Executive Secretary, Box C, Deadwood, SD 57732.

GLOSSARY

The following terms and definitions are those you are likely to encounter in the course of working with coins, arranged in alphabetical order. Nicknames or slang terms are enclosed in quotation (" ") marks. They are based in part on the ANA Dictionary of Numismatic Terms, and the Official Price Guide To Mint Errors and Varieties.

It should be noted that even some of the experts do not agree on the use of terms or their definitions. Nor do some agree with standard dictionaries or general usage, so the reader should be prepared at times for such differences of opinion.

ABOUT GOOD. A grading term for the lowest acceptable grade. Assigned AG-3 in the ANA Grading Standards.

ABOUT UNCIRCULATED. A grading term between Extremely Fine and Uncirculated for a coin which shows only the slightest traces of wear. Assigned AU-50 in the ANA Grading Standards.

ACCUMULATION. A group of coins which has no particular direction of order.

ADJUSTMENT MARKS. Scratches or cuts on the coin planchet resulting from filing or other removal of metal to correct the planchet weight. Not regarded as a defect.

Ae. Abbreviation for copper, brass or bronze.

ANNEALING. The process of softening a die or coin planchet by heating so that the design may be impressed into the die, or to make the planchet soft enough to yield a sharply struck coin when it is struck by the die pair.

ANVIL DIE. The die placed on the bottom — often on an anvil or a block of wood, upon which hammered coins were struck. Later, usually the lower die in a coin press.

AR. Abbreviation for silver.

ARMS. A coat of arms of a ruler or nation.

ASSAY. A test of the metallic content of an ore, a piece of metal or coin.

ASSAYER'S MARK (MINT MARK). Letters, initials or symbols appearing on coin which identify the mint or the assayer responsible for the striking of the coin.

ASSAY PIECE. A coin or planchet reserved or picked to be tested.

BAG MARKS. Cuts, scratches and other abrasions caused by contact with other coins within a bag or other container. Generally used to describe any such marks, regardless of actual origin.

BASE METAL. A metal other than one classed as a precious metal: copper, tin, nickel, zinc and others.

BILLON. A low grade (less than 50%) alloy of silver.

"BIT." One Eighth of a Spanish Dollar, so named because the coins were sometimes cut into pieces, or "bits."

BLANK. A term for a coin planchet, as in *blanking press,* the punch press used to punch planchets from a strip of coin metal. Also a side of a coin which shows no design.

BLOOM (MINT BLOOM). The appearance of the surface of a freshly struck coin, resulting from the coin metal's contact with the dies as it flows into the design.

"BOGUS." A slang term for a fake or counterfeit.

BOX COIN. A coin which has been hollowed out, or constructed of two coins machined to fit together, in which something can be hidden. Made occasionally as novelties in the 18th and 19th century, especially with big clunky foreign coins such as Britain's two-pence copper of 1797.

BRASS. An alloy of copper and zinc. The ratio may be any percentages of the two metals. The term is often incorrectly used for light colored bronze, and, in general, much abused.

BROKAGE. A coin struck with another struck coin between it and one of the dies, resulting in an enlarged, distorted image, incuse, or into the surface of the planchet.

BRONZE. An alloy of copper and tin. The ratio may be any percentages of the two metals. Lighter colored bronze alloys are mistakenly called brass.

CARBON SPOT. A small circular ring, usually with a black center, made by a piece of dirt or other pollutant on a coin which has caused the coin to corrode or oxidize. So named because the black speck was believed to be carbon. (It isn't.)

"CARTWHEEL." A slang term for a silver dollar, or any coin of large physical size. First used for the copper coins of England struck by George III, by a public which had little fondness for them.

CASE. Usually a glass topped box in which a dealer displays his items for sale, or used to contain an exhibit at a coin show.

CASED SET. A set of coin in a specially designed and fitted case.

CAST. A coin made by pouring molten metal into a die. A once common but not obsolete method of counterfeiting coins.

CATALOG. A list, often with pictures, of coins which are offered for sale, or which are to be offered at an auction.

CATALOGUED. A coin which has been listed in some reference work so that there is a permanent record of it.

CENTENNIAL. 100th Anniversary.

CENTER HOLE. An intentional hole in the center of a coin. Early uses were for stringing coins to wear around the neck. Chinese coins were made with holes. Holes in U.S. coins are a serious defect.

CENTERED. Usually referring to the strike, as "a well centered strike," in which the design is centered on the planchet with even rims.

CIRCULATED. Any coin which shows even the slightest amount of wear. Whether the wear occurred in actual circulation or through mishandling by collectors, counts for nothing.

CIRCULATION STRIKE. A coin struck and intended for public circulation; a business strike.

CLAD. A coin material consisting of a core with two outer layers bonded to it, as the copper core with copper-nickel alloy clad layers used for U.S. dimes, quarters, halves and Ike and Anthony dollars. Other metals such as silver may be used in both the core and clad layers.

CLIP — CLIPPED PLANCHET. A planchet, or the coin struck on such a planchet, which has a missing area resulting from the punch overlapping an already punched area of the coin metal strip. Clips may be curved, straight, or ragged. If the loss occurred after the coin reached circulation, it is worthless.

CLOCK POSITION. A reference system based on the hours of the clock, used to refer to features or damage on a coin, as a heavy scratch at 11 o'clock.

COIN CLUB. A group which was formed to collect or invest in coins.

COLLAR. An appliance of the coin press which surrounds the planchet while being struck by the dies. The hole in the collar is the exact diameter of the desired coins. On reeded coins it carries and imparts the reeding, and in segmented form can be used to apply a design to the edge of the coin.

COMMEMORATIVE. A coin issued to mark an important event, or an anniversary of such an event, or to honor a person.

COMMON DATE. A coin with a high mintage and usually lower value and collector interest than a semi-key or key coin in the same series.

COPY. A reproduction, or imitation.

CULL. A coin that has no numismatic value because of wear or damage.

CUPRO-NICKEL. A copper-nickel alloy. In current U.S. coins usually 75% copper and 25% nickel.

CURRENT. Coins and currency that are presently valid and still in circulation, or that can circulate. All U.S. dollar coins except the Trade Dollar are still legal tender.

DAMAGE. Any injury to a coin occurring after the coin has been minted.

DEBASED. Reduction of the precious metal content of a coin by increasing the percentage of alloy. A common occurrence in foreign coinage for ore than 2,000 years.

DEFACED. A coin which has had the design scratched, cut, ground off, or otherwise damaged.

DEMONETIZED. Coins or currency which have been withdrawn from circulation or which have been declared null and void by the issuing government.

DENOMINATION. The stated value of a coin or note, generally called "face value."

DIE. A piece of tool steel, with the design either incuse or cut into it, or raised in relief, used to strike one side of the coin. The resulting coin is a mirror image of the die in that the coin design is in relief if the die design is incuse, and incuse if the die design is in relief. Dies are used in pairs to strike coins.

DIEBREAK. A raised area of the coin metal, above the normal surface of the coin, resulting from a piece of the die metal breaking off. The coin metal is forced into the hole by the pressure of the dies as the coin is struck, yielding the appearance of a blister or scar.

DIECRACK. A raised line of coin metal, above the normal surface of the coin, resulting from the die cracking. The coin metal is forced into the crack by pressure of the dies as the coin is struck. Diecrack and Diebreak are often misused to mean the wrong thing.

DIE DAMAGE. Any injury to the die which shows on coins struck by that die.

DIE "SHIFT." A meaningless term applied to the very common forms of doubling which occur after the strike, also ejection doubling damage, machine doubline, shelf doubling, etc. Not part of the minting process.

DIE SINKER. An engraver who cuts or punches the design into the face of a die.

DOUBLE STRIKE. A coin which has been struck more than once by the die pair, showing equal doubling on both sides of the coin in all areas affected by the second or subsequent strikes. The term is misused to apply to all forms of doubling.

ELECTROTYPE. A copy or counterfeit made by an electroplating process.

EMISSION. The act of issuing a coin or note.

ENGRAILED. A decoration for coin rims, consisting of an indented design of small concave curve or a circle of raised dots.

ENGRAVING. The art of cutting or punching a design into a die, or of cutting a design into a piece of metal, such as a coin.

ERROR. A minting variety caused by a mistake in the minting process, as a misstrike. The term is usually misused to include all minting varieties, whether accidental or intentional, but most minting varieties are not true "errors."

ESSAY. A trial coin, usually one struck to demonstrate the die design. Sometimes considered and sold as a proof coin.

EXTREMELY FINE. A grading term between Very Fine and About Uncirculated. Assigned as EF-40 in the ANA Grading Standards.

FANTASY. Any object similar in appearance to a coin, but issued privately, or clandestinely by a public mint, which never was issued as a legal coin by the government. Fantasy coins are not as numerous as fantasy postage stamps, but you're apt to get a few in any lot of "mixed foreign."

FAO. Abbreviation for the Food and Agriculture Organization of the United Nations, which has sponsored a number of coin issues in various countries around the world, knows as "FAO Coins."

FDC. Abbreviation for FDC, the French term, "Fleur de Coin," or the mint bloom. When found in a *stamp* catalogue, it means "First Day Cover."

FIAT MONEY. Paper money issued by a government that could not be redeemed in bullion or coin, such as the notes currently used in the U.S.

"FIDO." An outmoded slang term for a minting variety.

FIELD. The flat area of a coin between the rims and the various design elements.

FINE. A grading term falling between Very Good and Very Fine. Assigned F-12 in the ANA Grading Standards.

FINENESS. A term applied to the amount of a precious metal in an alloy, based on an optimum of 1000, as .900 fine silver equals 90% silver in the alloy.

FIXED PRICE. An offer to sell at a certain price, rather than at auction. Fixed prices are not always so firmly fixed that a bit of bargaining would not bring them down — it depends on the coin and the dealer.

FLAN. A coin planchet — an antique term.

FORGERY. An unauthorized copy.

"FREAK." An outmoded slang term for a minting variety. Useful, in a way, because not every variety is either an intentional alteration or an error.

FROSTED (PROOF). A coin, usually a proof, which displays a design with rough surface surrounded by a contrasting mirror-like field, usually bringing a slight premium. Frosted proofs used to be more popular than they are at present.

GALVANO. A copper plated model of a coin die design, used as a pattern to cut either a Master Hub or a Master Die in a reducing lathe.

GEM. A very high quality piece. Not an official grading term.

GERMAN SILVER (NICKEL SILVER). An alloy of copper, zinc and nickel, often used for coins because of its similarity in appearance to silver.

GOOD. A grading term for a coin between About Good and Very Good. Assigned as G-4 in the ANA Grading Standards.

GRADE. A condition value assigned to a coin based on the amount of wear it has sustained. Grading for U.S. coins is based on the Official ANA Grading Standards.

GRAIN. A unit of weight equal to .0648 of a Gram.

GRAM. A unit of weight equal to .0322 of a Troy Ounce. Grains may be converted to Grams by multiplying by 15.432.

HAIRLINES. Scratches found on the surface of a coin resulting from harsh cleaning.

HAMMER DIE. The upper die used in striking hammered coins, placed upon the planchet resting on the anvil die, then struck with a hammer. Later, the upper die in a coin press, or the die activated by a ram or cam to apply the striking force to the planchet.

HUBBING PROCESS. The production of a die by using a hub. Commonly the sequence is from the pattern to a Master Hub, then to a Master Die, then to a Working Hub, then to the Working Dies. The Master Tools are used only to make new tools, never to strike coins.

HUBBING VARIETY. A die variety resulting from some occurrence in the hubbing process of making a die.

HUB DOUBLING (DOUBLED DIE). Doubling caused by a malfunction in the hubbing process (as the rotation of the hub between impressions in the die), or the use of two different hubs with design elements in different locations, or different elements.

INCUSE. Into the surface, opposite of relief, as applied to a design. Intaglio. U.S. Silver Dollars were never struck in this fashion. Some of our gold coins were.

INGOT. A bar of metal or metal alloy, poured in a mold.

INSCRIPTION. The legend on a numismatic item of coin.

INTAGLIO. A printing term applied to a design cut into the surface of a plate used to print currency, etc.

INTRINSIC. The value of a coin's metallic content, as opposed to its face value. The collector value may bear no relation to either.

ISSUE. Coins or notes released in a group of series.

JETON. A game counter or chip, sometimes used in calculating. Made extensively in Europe in the 15th, 16th and 17th centuries.

KEY. A coin which has the lowest mintage or highest collector value or interest in a series.

KLIPPE. A coin struck on a rectangular planchet, so named because the originals were cut or clipped from a sheet of coin metal.

KNIFE EDGE. A wire edge of "flash" of extruded metal along the rim of a coin resulting from excessive striving pressure, caused by the coin metal squeezing between the edge of the die and the collar.

LAMINATION. A thin layer of coin metal which is splitting, or has split away from the rest of the coin.

LAWFUL CURRENCY. Currency which has been specifically named by a governing body to be used in commerce. This is an obsolete term, dating back to the days when banks issued private paper notes.

LEGAL TENDER. Coins or Currency of government sanction, which cannot be refused in transactions in that country. There are not laws on *ille*gal tender, or the opposite of legal tender. Parties to a transaction may use anything they desire as money, if agreeable to those involved.

LEGEND. The inscription upon a coin or other numismatic item.

LETTERED EDGE. A usually incuse lettering on the edge of a coin. May be applied by rolling the planchet through a fixed die, by use of geared edge dies, or a segmented die. Usually used to include designs other than letters on the edge.

MATTE PROOF. A granular proof surface applied to a coin officially after it was struck. A type of proof made between about 1890 and 1940.

MEDAL. Usually of metal, with a design honoring a person, place or event, privately or publically issued, but not intended to be used as money.

MEDALET. A small medal, usually less than one inch (25.4 mm) in diameter.

MEDALLIC COIN (STRIKE). A coin struck with the reverse upside down if the coin is turned over from top to bottom, as opposed to a normal coin strike which has the reverse right side up.

MEDIEVAL COIN. Any coin struck between about 500 and 1500 A.D.

MICRO. A term applied to minute defects, doubling or minting varieties that require magnification to be visible, and rarely add extra value to the coin.

MILLED COIN. A coin struck in a coin press using a collar to retain the planchet, the interior edge of the collar reeded or milled to form the reeded or milled edge on the coin as it is struck. Introduction of milling equipment to the U.S. Mint in the early 19th century brought about coins with uniform diameters.

MINIMUM BID. The lowest figure an auctioneer will accept as a bid on a particular coin. Many "mail sails" are run with minimum bids. Floor sales usually don't have them, but may have unannounced reserves which are minimum bids in disguise.

MINOR (SUBSIDIARY) COIN. Usually any coin of a smaller denomination than the primary denomination of a nation's coinage, as cents, dimes, quarters and half dollars in the U.S. coinage.

MINT "ERRORS." Any coin displaying a mistake or error in the minting process, part of the general group of minting varieties.

MINT MARK (ASSAYER'S MARK). Letters, initials or symbols appearing on a coin which identify the mint or assayer responsible for striking the coin. Not to be confused with designers' initials.

MINT MASTER. Person in charge of a Mint.

MINT SEALED. Usually applied to bags of coins closed and sealed by an official mint, and distributed to the public in that form. It is not a guarantee of top quality condition, as the coins could (and usually do) show bag marks. Furthermore, government agencies do not make refunds or exchanges on coins in disappointing condition.

MINT SET. Usually a set of specially selected circulation strikes. If specified as a Mint Packaged Set, then issued by an official mint, otherwise as set assembled privately. A "Mint Set" is not necessarily a "Proof Set" and proof coins should not be anticipated unless mentioned in the offering.

MISSTRIKE. Any coin which results from a malfunction in the striking process; a striking variety.

"MULE." Any numismatic item resulting from the use of mismatched dies, as in the use of the wrong die or a fantasy die for one face. Hybrid. Term originates because mules are said to have the head of a horse and body of a donkey.

MULTI-STRIKE. A coin or token struck more than twice.

Ni. Abbreviation for nickel.

NUMISMATICS. The science, study or collecting of coins.

NUMISMATIST. A person familiar with or knowledgable in Numismatics.

OBVERSE. The front face of a coin or medal, usually the side with the principal device.

OFF CENTER (STRIKE). A coin struck out of the collar, so that only part of the planchet was between the dies, the remainder remaining blank on both sides of the coin. If only one side is off center, the cause is a misaligned die, and the coin is not an off center strike. Usually, in the case of misaligned dies, the fully struck side shows evidence of unevenness.

"OFF" METAL. An outmoded term for a wrong metal strike, a coin struck on a planchet of the wrong metal or one intended for another denomination of the same metal. For example, a dime struck on a nickel planchet.

ORDER. A group that is officially honored, and the insignia, badge or other decoration that members are awarded, such as the Order of the Garter. Orders do not invariably have government or military connection. In the U.S., many private fraternal organizations award orders.

OVERDATE. A date on a coin or medal which is punched, cut or hubbed over a different date, so that both dates, or parts thereof, are legible. At least one number must appear over a different number. They occur mostly on early coins and represent labor-saving efforts by mint workers.

OVERSTRIKE. A coin or medal struck over a previously struck item.

PATINA. Surface discoloration, usually green, resulting from age, or artificially produced with chemicals on a copper or copper alloy piece. Frequently misapplied to silver, although in some languages (German) the translation applies only to silver and other precious metals.

PIEFORT. A coin struck on a double thickness or thicker planchet.

PITTED. A coin with small holes or indentations in the surface, or similar raised areas, the latter resulting from the coin being struck with a pitted (rusted) die.

PLANCHET. The usually round, metal disc, upon which a coin, is struck by a die pair. Also known as blank, flan, disc, module.

PLANCHET VARIETY. Any minting variety resulting from a malfunction in making the planchet upon which the coin is to be struck. Some are classed as mint "errors."

POR. Abbreviation for Price on Request. Frequently used for coins which fluctuate in value because of their bullion content, or for unusual or rare coins, or where the dealer may be willing to bargain.

POROUS. A coin surface which is irregular or rough, due to the condition of the planchet, or due to cleaning with an acid based cleaner.

PRECIOUS METAL. Gold, Silver, Platinum.

PRESERVATION PIECE. A special coin, often a proof, prepared to be given to an official, visiting dignitary or special guest.

PRIVATE ISSUE. Coins or other medium of exchange issued by private sources without government sanction.

PRIVY MARK. A letter, initials or symbols indicating approval by a special council or group appointed by a government.

PROOF. A special strike using specially prepared and polished dies, striking a specially prepared and polished planchet, the resulting piece having marked sharpness of detail and nearly flawless surface. The coin is struck two or more times to qualify as a proof. Also applied to specimen bank notes. Collecting and investing enthusiasm for proof dollars has greatly increased in the past five years.

PROOF-LIKE. A coin which approaches proof characteristics, but is really a circulation strike.

PROOF SET. A specially cased or packaged set, usually of all of the proof coins issued for a given year.

PUNCH. A tool used to impress a letter, number, star or other part of the design into the face of a die. Archaic: Puncheon.

PUNCH DOUBLING. A double or multiple image caused by two or more blows of a punch, with the punch moving between blows, as in a repunched mint mark.

RAISED. A design in relief.

RARE. A term applied to a numismatic item implying a high degree of scarcity. Frequently modified, as Very Rare, Extremely Rare, etc. Not a grading term.

RED UNCIRCULATED. A descriptive term applied to uncirculated copper coins which still show the mint luster. Not a grading term.

REEDED EDGE. A milled or serrated edge, resulting from the use of a collar which has the reeds broached or cut into the inside circumference.

RE-ENGRAVED. A term applied to a die which has had additional engraving work (cutting) on the existing design. Misused to include repunching and hub doubling.

REGULAR ISSUE. A coin issued for normal commerce — a business or circulation strike, as opposed to a proof coin. Also used to distinguish between standard and commemorative and regular issues.

RESTRIKE. A coin struck after the year of issue, either with the original dies, new dies, or a combination of original, new or fantasy dies, usually officially sanctioned but occasionally made clandestinely by mint employees or officials.

REVERSE. The rear, or "tails" side of a coin, usually the side opposite that carrying the principal device (or "obverse").

RIM. The raised border around the outside of the obverse and reverse of a coin, token or medal, but not the edge of the coin, which is the face at right angles to the field.

ROLL. To reduce the thickness of a strip of coin metal by passing it through a rolling mill.

ROLLER DIE. A die used in a special coining press which strikes the coins on a continuous strip of coin metal, before the planchets are punched from the strip.

ROTATED DIE. A coin struck with one of the dies either loose in the die holder, or with a broken shank, allowing the die face to rotate in relation to the opposing die. Usually as a rotated reverse die.

RUBBING. An impression of a design, transferred by rubbing a soft pencil on a piece of paper, or by impressing aluminum foil down over the design. Not a recommended practice for uncirculated coins.

SAND DOLLAR. A cast Mexican silver One Peso made at Chihuahua during the revolution of 1812-1821, bearing the portrait of Ferdinand VII.

SCARCE. Not common, but found more often than rare. Like all terms relating to availability. There are not clear guidelines for its use.

SECURITY EDGE. A special edge design applied to a coin to deter counterfeiting.

SEIGNIORAGE. The profit made by a government mint, based on the difference between the face value and the actual cost of production of a coin. The U.S. Mint reaps the largest Seigniorage in the world.

SEMI-KEY. A coin which has a lower mintage than a common date in a series, but is not as scarce or valuable as a key coin.

SET. A group of coins which go together, as a set of 1981 dated coins.

"SHIFT." A meaningless term applied to machine doubling.

"SLEEPER." A slang term for a coin which is undervalued or underpriced and likely to suddenly increase in price.

SLUG. A $50 U.S. gold coin, or a worthless piece of metal similar to a coin used in a slot machine, telephone or vending machine.

SPLIT GRADE. A coin which has a different grade for each side of the coin, often listed with a slash, as VF/XF for the obverse and reverse.

SPURIOUS. A fake or counterfeit, false.

STERLING. A silver alloy of .925 silver and .075 copper. Also the British monetary standard. The U.S. has never issued coins with this high a fineness.

STORE CARD. A token advertising a business, often used in lieu of small change.

STRIKE. The act of driving the dies into the planchet, either by hand or in a coin press.

STRIKING VARIETIES. Any minting variety which occurs as part of the striking process, including some mint "errors."

"STRIKING DOUBLING." An outmoded term for worthless machine doubling, no longer used because of confusion with actual mint process doubling which occurs during the strike.

STRUCK UP. A term used to describe the strike on a coin, usually modified, as well struck up.

SUBSIDIARY COIN. A coin of a lower denomination than the standard unit denomination — a minor coin. Generally used of basemetal coins.

TARNISHED. Discolored, covered with vari-colored oxides. Toned.

TOKEN. A piece struck unofficially to serve as temporary money, to bear ads, political slogans, to use in vending machines, pay transit fare, etc.

TOKEN COINAGE. Coins which have a lower intrinsic value than the face value, as do nearly all current world coins.

TOOLING. Alteration of a coin by use of engraving tools, as to enhance the feather outlines on the eagle's breast.

TONING. Discoloration, patina, tarnish on the surface of a coin. Since it is not a part of the minting process and can be easily be faked, it should have no effect on the value of a coin.

TRIAL PIECE. A test piece struck with incomplete dies.

TRIAL STRIKE. A test piece struck to show the completed design of a die to its best advantage.

TROY WEIGHT. A series of units of weights based on a pound of 12 ounces and an ounce of 20 pennyweights or 480 grains. One Avoirdupois ounce equals 437.5 grains.

TYPE COIN. A representative coin from a series. Type coins are collected without regard to date.

TYPE SET. A set of coins containing one of each coin in a given series.

UNCIRCULATED. A coin with absolutely no wear. A grading term, above About Uncirculated, assigned MS-60 in the ANA Grading Standards.

VERY GOOD. A grading term between Good and Fine, assigned VG-8 in the ANA Grading Standards.

VERY FINE. A grading term between Fine and Extremely Fine, assigned VF-20 in the ANA Grading Standards.

WANT LIST. A list of coins that a collector or dealer wishes to buy. A want list sometimes carries price offerings to make it more tempting.

for more information ...

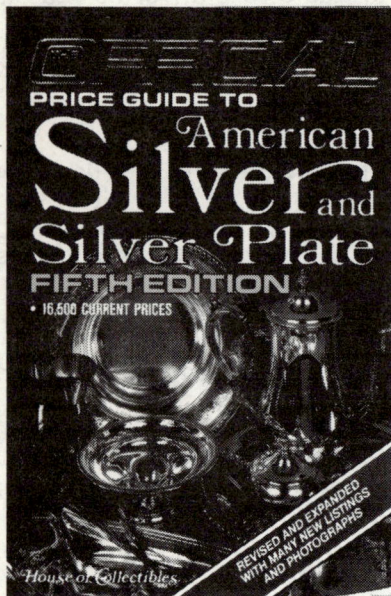

- Over *16,000 detailed listings with current market values* for 19th and 20th century American made sterling silver, coin silver and silver plated items including flatware and holloware.
- **MAJOR MANUFACTURERS** are represented: Wm. Rogers, Gorham, Oneida, Community, Barbour, Kirk, Reed & Barton, American, Holmes & Edwards, Durgin, Tiffany, Alvin, International, Towle, Tudor, Wallace, Lunt, Rodgers & Hamilton and many more.
- **VALUABLE COLLECTOR INFORMATION**—a useful indepth glossary of terminology used by collectors, the care and storage of silver and silver-plated items, safeguards for protecting your collection and a complete Franklin Mint limited editions chapter devoted to their fine line of silver products.
- **FULLY ILLUSTRATED** $11.95

Twenty-fifth Edition contains 281 pages of important collector information.

- over *16,700 current buying and selling prices.*
- Covers *ALL U.S. Coinage-1616 to date-Colonial-Commemorative-Confederate-Gold-U.S. Proof Sets.*
- The history of *The American Numismatic Association.*
- Fully illustrated for *easy* identification.
- *Official A.N.A. Grading System* reveals the method used in the marketplace.
- Detecting altered coins section makes identifying counterfiet coins easy.
- **FULLY ILLUSTRATED** $3.95

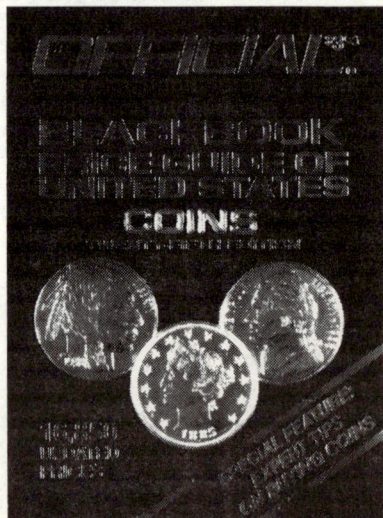

Order direct from —
THE HOUSE OF COLLECTIBLES, see order blank.

THE OFFICIAL PRICE GUIDES TO:

☐ 199-3	**American Silver & Silver Plate** 5th Ed.	11.95
☐ 513-1	**Antique Clocks** 3rd Ed.	10.95
☐ 283-3	**Antique & Modern Dolls** 3rd Ed.	10.95
☐ 287-6	**Antique & Modern Firearms** 6th Ed.	11.95
☐ 517-4	**Antiques & Collectibles** 7th Ed.	9.95
☐ 289-2	**Antique Jewelry** 5th Ed.	11.95
☐ 270-1	**Beer Cans & Collectibles,** 3rd Ed.	7.95
☐ 262-0	**Bottles Old & New** 9th Ed.	10.95
☐ 255-8	**Carnival Glass** 1st Ed.	10.95
☐ 295-7	**Collectible Cameras** 2nd Ed.	10.95
☐ 277-9	**Collectibles of the Third Reich** 2nd Ed.	10.95
☐ 281-7	**Collectible Toys** 3rd Ed.	10.95
☐ 490-9	**Collector Cars** 6th Ed.	11.95
☐ 267-1	**Collector Handguns** 3rd Ed.	11.95
☐ 290-6	**Collector Knives** 8th Ed.	11.95
☐ 266-3	**Collector Plates** 4th Ed.	11.95
☐ 296-5	**Collector Prints** 7th Ed.	12.95
☐ 489-5	**Comic Books & Collectibles** 8th Ed.	9.95
☐ 433-X	**Depression Glass** 1st Ed.	9.95
☐ 472-0	**Glassware** 2nd Ed.	10.95
☐ 243-4	**Hummel Figurines & Plates** 6th Ed.	10.95
☐ 451-8	**Kitchen Collectibles** 2nd Ed.	10.95
☐ 291-4	**Military Collectibles** 5th Ed.	11.95
☐ 268-X	**Music Collectibles** 5th Ed.	11.95
☐ 313-9	**Old Books & Autographs** 7th Ed.	11.95
☐ 298-1	**Oriental Collectibles** 3rd Ed.	11.95
☐ 297-3	**Paper Collectibles** 5th Ed.	10.95
☐ 276-0	**Pottery & Porcelain** 5th Ed.	11.95
☐ 263-9	**Radio, T.V. & Movie Memorabilia** 2nd Ed.	11.95
☐ 288-4	**Records** 7th Ed.	10.95
☐ 247-7	**Royal Doulton** 5th Ed.	11.95
☐ 280-9	**Science Fiction & Fantasy Collectibles** 2nd Ed.	10.95
☐ 299-X	**Star Trek/Star Wars Collectibles** 1st Ed.	7.95
☐ 248-5	**Wicker** 3rd Ed.	10.95

THE OFFICIAL:

☐ 445-3	**Collector's Journal** 1st Ed.	4.95
☐ 365-1	**Encyclopedia of Antiques** 1st Ed.	9.95
☐ 369-4	**Guide to Buying & Selling Antiques** 1st Ed.	9.95
☐ 414-3	**Identification Guide to Early American Furniture** 1st Ed.	9.95
☐ 413-5	**Identification Guide to Glassware** 1st Ed.	9.95
☐ 448-8	**Identification Guide to Gunmarks** 2nd Ed.	9.95
☐ 412-7	**Identification Guide to Pottery & Porcelain** 1st Ed.	9.95
☐ 415-1	**Identification Guide to Victorian Furniture** 1st Ed.	9.95

THE OFFICIAL (SMALL SIZE) PRICE GUIDES TO:

☐ 473-9	**Antiques & Flea Markets** 3rd Ed.	3.95
☐ 269-8	**Antique Jewelry** 3rd Ed.	4.95
☐ 509-3	**Baseball Cards** 6th Ed.	4.95
☐ 488-7	**Bottles** 2nd Ed.	4.95
☐ 468-2	**Cars & Trucks** 2nd Ed.	4.95
☐ 260-4	**Collectible Americana** 1st Ed.	4.95
☐ 294-9	**Collectible Records** 3rd Ed.	4.95
☐ 469-0	**Collector Guns** 2nd Ed.	4.95
☐ 474-7	**Comic Books** 3rd Ed.	3.95
☐ 486-0	**Dolls** 3rd Ed.	4.95
☐ 292-9	**Football Cards** 5th Ed.	4.95
☐ 258-2	**Glassware** 2nd Ed.	4.95
☐ 487-9	**Hummels** 3rd Ed.	4.95
☐ 279-5	**Military Collectibles** 3rd Ed.	4.95
☐ 480-1	**Paperbacks & Magazines** 3rd Ed.	4.95
☐ 278-7	**Pocket Knives** 3rd Ed.	4.95
☐ 479-8	**Scouting Collectibles** 3rd Ed.	4.95
☐ 439-9	**Sports Collectibles** 2nd Ed.	3.95
☐ 494-1	**Star Trek/Star Wars Collectibles** 3rd Ed.	3.95
☐ 307-1	**Toys** 4th Ed.	4.95

THE OFFICIAL BLACKBOOK PRICE GUIDES OF:

☐ 510-7	**U.S. Coins** 25th Ed.	3.95
☐ 511-5	**U.S. Paper Money** 19th Ed.	3.95
☐ 512-3	**U.S. Postage Stamps** 9th Ed.	3.95

THE OFFICIAL INVESTORS GUIDE TO BUYING & SELLING:

☐ 496-8	**Gold, Silver and Diamonds** 2nd Ed.	9.95
☐ 497-6	**Gold Coins** 2nd Ed.	9.95
☐ 498-4	**Silver Coins** 2nd Ed.	9.95
☐ 499-2	**Silver Dollars** 2nd Ed.	9.95

THE OFFICIAL NUMISMATIC GUIDE SERIES:

☐ 481-X	**Coin Collecting** 3rd Ed.	9.95
☐ 254-X	**The Official Guide to Detecting Counterfeit Money** 2nd Ed.	7.95
☐ 257-4	**The Official Guide to Mint Errors** 4th Ed.	7.95
☐ 162-4	**Variety & Oddity Guide of U.S. Coins** 8th Ed.	4.95

SPECIAL INTEREST SERIES:

☐ 506-9	**From Hearth to Cookstove** 3rd Ed.	17.95
☐ 508-5	**Lucky Number Lottery Guide** 1st Ed.	3.50
☐ 504-2	**On Method Acting** 8th Printing	6.95

TOTAL	

SEE REVERSE SIDE FOR ORDERING INSTRUCTIONS

FOR IMMEDIATE DELIVERY

VISA & MASTER CARD CUSTOMERS

ORDER TOLL FREE!
1-800-638-6460

This number is for orders only; it is not tied into the customer service or business office. Customers not using charge cards must use mail for ordering since payment is required with the order — sorry no C.O.D.'s.

OR SEND ORDERS TO ▮ ▮ ▮ ▮ ▮

THE HOUSE OF COLLECTIBLES, *201 East 50th Street New York, New York 10022*

POSTAGE & HANDLING RATES

First Book $1.00
Each Additional Copy or Title $0.50

Total from columns on reverse side. Quantity_____ $ _____

| | Check or money order enclosed $_____ (include postage and handling)

| | Please charge $ _____ to my: | | MASTERCARD | | VISA

Charge Card Customers Not Using Our Toll Free Number Please Fill Out The Information Below

Account No. (All Digits) _____ Expiration Date _____

Signature_____

NAME (please print) _____ PHONE _____

ADDRESS _____ APT. # _____ ⑩

CITY _____ STATE _____ ZIP _____